TEENAGERS
THEMSELVES

TEEN
THEM

AGERS
SELVES

compiled by the Glenbard East <u>Echo</u>

advised by Howard Spanogle

Adama Books New York

Library of Congress Cataloging in Publication Data
Main entry under title: **Teenagers themselves.**

Written and compiled by reporters for the Echo, a student newspaper in Glenbard East
High School, Lombard, Illinois.

Summary: Young people express what they think about family, fun, school, work,
violence, death, sex, drugs, individualism, responsibility, the future, and other aspects of
their lives.

1. Youth—United States—Addresses, essays, lectures. 2. Youth—Illinois—Lombard—
Interviews. [1. Youth—Addresses, essays, lectures. 2. Youth—Interviews. 3. Children's
writings] I. Glenbard East High School

(Lombard, Ill.)
HQ796.T412 1984   305.2'35'0973   83-26568
ISBN 0-915361-04-3

Adama Books, 306 West 38 Street, New York, New York 10018

To previous staffs
whose commitment and high ideals
have made the realization of this book possible,
and to responsive readers
whose encouragement and cooperation
have contributed insight to the Glenbard East *Echo.*

Acknowledgments

Completion of *Teenagers Themselves* (the National Teenage
Research Project) was possible because of the generosity of
the Glenbard East Class of 1983, a major contributor; the
Glenbard East Mothers Club; the Yorktown Merchants
Association; the Lombard Service League; and the Lombard
Sports Core.

Additional help came from a cooperative administration,
understanding colleagues, considerate librarians (who loaned
us their air-conditioned facilities for the summer), helpful
secretaries, and a tireless mail/messenger service to and
within the school.

The assistance of hundreds of publication advisers as well as
scholastic journalism organizations was essential. In
addition, the *Echo* is grateful for the cooperation of its
printer, Downers Grove Reporter, and of the north campus
art department of Lyons Township High School in LaGrange,
Illinois.

Writers of Chapter Introductions:
Erik Landahl, Eric Kammerer, Mike Carr, Abby Rhamey, Holly Hager,
Lisa Holly, Bob Chamberlin, Denise Gajdos, Chia Chen, Joe Judt,
Diana Slyfield, Mike Trippi
Copyeditor:
Christine Zrinsky
Discussion Editors:
Holly Hager, Eric Kammerer, Abby Rhamey
Artists:
Eric Semelroth, John Fenwick
Part Opening Illustrations and Book Design:
Irwin Rosenhouse

Contents

Preface

Out of care and diligence, vision and enthusiasm; from an unexpected but trustworthy source—teenagers themselves—comes this inside story about how teenagers relate to the modern world. Yes, teenagers think. Yes, teenagers feel. Yes, teenagers experience the universal joys and sorrows of being human. Yes, teenagers are individuals. Yes, teenagers are honest. Yes, teenagers are cynical, but only because it is their way of being sincere. Yes, public schools help students analyze information and express insights. Yes, teenagers can commit themselves to quality. Yes, teenagers are capable of tremendous dedication.

That dedication generated the commitment and talent necessary to produce this first-ever effort by teenagers to look at themselves within their community and their nation. That effort began almost two years ago in publisher Esther Cohen's New York office when she suggested, "I think it's time for the *Echo* to help the rest of us understand what teenagers think."

Beginning with that general dictate, *Glenbard East* teenagers took over from start to finish, whether stuffing letters or typing manuscripts, whether selecting quotes or drawing cartoons. The process, like every issue of the school newspaper they publish, involved teenage inquiry, teenage writing, and teenage perspective. First came the brainstorming sessions—suggestions about the what and the how and the who—all the essentials needed to discover the ingredients of good journalism. Hundreds of possible topics merged into chapters; the chapters then merged into three major sections. The book developed as young writers envisioned ways to combine extensive reporting with creative approaches. The project turned into self-investigation with a human interest focus and a literary touch.

Chapter introductions reflect the contributions of 13 writers, whose manuscripts had to pass a critical group consensus test. In-depth interviews reflect the commitment of another 13, who represent the diverse range of a typical middle-class American high school in suburbia. The 13 interviewees attended weekly sessions led by student editors that lasted 75 minutes after school. The interviewees shared honestly, debated openly, and expressed their true feelings about life.

With the help of an adviser and cooperating teachers, the national responses were a year in collecting. Evaluated carefully by students for content, not appearance, they represent the best of nearly 9,000 responses from every state in the nation. The responses to open-end questions varied from pencil-scribbled paragraphs to neatly typed essays.

Now, thousands of hours after the book's initial conception, it's your turn. Enjoy a publication by teenagers who did all this in addition to producing their high quality newspaper, doing their homework, keeping their parents happy, and, for some, working part-time. Step into teenage minds and view life from their perspective. Sit among a circle of serious young people as they share experiences, emotions, and ideas. Move beyond that circle, across the nation, and listen to the concerns of youth—today's teenagers, tomorrow's adults. Find out who they are and what they think.

Howard Spanogle

PART ONE
SELF

Introduction

Teenagers' lives are as complex as their world. Their time is a pie cut into innumerable slices that are hungrily devoured by different entities, new problems, pressing obligations. They are influenced by a wide spectrum of people, from religious leaders selling them salvation to burnouts selling them drugs. Many live in divided families as a result of the 50 percent divorce rate. There is also the greatest teenage mover of them all, the life cycle, a necessary yet often confusing and exhausting device all teenagers must master to attain their ultimate goals of adulthood, maturity, and independence. Teenagers go to school so they can get better jobs when they go to work. They go to work to earn enough money to go to more school or to have fun. They have fun to relax and refresh themselves for the return to school or work.

The trick in mastering this excruciating test, is, of course, to break out of the cycle. How and when is that miracle achieved? That, of course, depends on teenagers' priorities. Teenagers, however, often do not recognize or are confused about their priorities. What then? Well . . . that's life.

Chapter 1.

Time

Ask teenagers how they spend their time, and one of them will probably mumble something like "Well, school takes up most of my time, then there's homework (guilty glance at floor), and I cruise around on weekends."

In all probability, they are suffering from delusions, thinking their physical presence is all that is necessary. While doing homework or cruising, their heads are floating on a stratospheric level. They commune with the clouds. The diagnosis: prep epilepsy, a type of self-hypnosis prevalent among teenagers preparing for life.

Adolescence is a foggy mix of the clear trivialities of childhood and the grinding pressures of adulthood. Active times pass so fast kids feel left behind. Passive times are as insipid and lethargic as a Siberian winter. Understandably, teenagers are paradoxes, having so much and so little time on their hands at once. That kid playing rocket ship with a No. 2 pencil is actually frantic as he feels the impending pressures of the future. Absentminded doodling is an attempt to stop time, a common symptom of prep ep.

Daydreaming, which touches people of all ages, helps them escape daily tedium by injecting a little fantasy into reality. Who hasn't had a hand waved before his eyes and heard a muffled voice cracking, "Earth to space, Earth to space, anybody home?" Prep ep, however, is more severe—a massive overdose of fantasy. Mild sufferers of the sickness are often referred to derogatorily as spaces. Severe cases are called airheads. The airheads are characterized by staring at distant objects, halting speech, and excessive dozing. The symptoms aren't medically curable but, if ignored, can disappear in two or three years.

Essentially prep ep is an allergic reaction to life. Like common allergies caused by pollen and mold, prep ep is caused by the opposite extremes of boredom and stress.

In daily life, the teen years can be stultifyingly boring. Monotonic lectures about animals' intestines at school, menial labor at work, and dull old mom and dad at home conspire to kidnap kids' consciousness. A grand mal seizure of prep ep results, providing a nice warm place to hide. The opposite extreme, stress—both real and imagined—also induces prep ep. Mega-point tests (for 1000 points, draw a hypotenuse in a longitudinal plane), future planning (fill in 30 forms, determine your major, and find a college, quickly), and impending punishment ("No keys for you, longhair—too many D's on that report card") all signify big problems.

The future looks like a problem to many kids. Adults never fail to spew doom and gloom about the economy and the decline of the nation. The immediate future is pressure, pressure, pressure. Choosing a college is harrowing. Entering the job market immediately is terrifying. In the stress state, time is passing too fast, and glassy-eyed contemplation is the result.

Although prep ep isn't contagious, it can be experienced by following a step-by-step exercise:

1. Clear all thoughts from mind.
2. Breathe deeply.
3. Select a simple object, such as a floor tile, to stare at.
4. Look at floor tile.
5. Obliterate sight and sound of everything except tile.
6. Cross eyes.

Pretty scary stuff, huh? Now imagine a teenager who spends ten minutes of every waking hour in that condition. Without even realizing, the teenager slips in and out of prep ep all day.

Adults need to be more sympathetic to airheads. Unfortunately, a telethon probably won't help but a little understanding couldn't hurt. The next time an exasperated adult is talking with a kid who speaks in Cro-Magnon monosyllables and who stares at his tie clip, he shouldn't take it personally. The kid is sick. Time flies while having fun, but who said being a teenager is fun?

First, I hear the annoying and eye-opening sound of my alarm watch telling me that it is seven a.m. and time to get up. Naturally, I ignore it and wait for my mom to come in and get me up. Then is a sleepy state. I fall out of bed (along with my blankets), throw on my average jeans and my average shirt, and go into the bathroom to comb my hair.

After splashing water on my hair to make it stay down, I comb it again and head for the kitchen. "What's for breakfast?" I ask myself. Then I find some Rice Krispies, pour them into a bowl, drown them in milk and sugar, and, still in a sleepy state, put the milk in the pantry.

The national responses were gathered from all fifty states during 1982-83 by the National Teenage Research Project, which was conducted by the Glenbard East Echo, a high school student newspaper in Lombard, Illinois. The opinions represent the diverse ideas expressed by nearly nine thousand teenagers. Though all individuals signed their comments, some names have been withheld because of the sensitive nature of the information. Editing changes have been made only in punctuation and spelling.

After breakfast, I gather my books, say good-bye to dear old mom, and head to the house behind me where my ride lives. On the way the dog bites me, and I drop my books. I finally manage to get to the car, half-eaten. After the short ride to school, I go and talk to my friend "Pete."

The bell rings a few minutes later, and I head for homeroom. On the way I get tripped twice, and my books fall three times. After ten minutes of announcements during homeroom period, I go to trailer one, my beloved Algebra III class. The people in this class are all right, and the teacher is great. But the classroom is the pits. When it rains, I could stay drier by staying outside.

Well, then I go to chemistry. I see "Pete" again, and we talk a lot. Then "Mr. Iverson," the one who looks like a whale with a baby face, tries to teach. After this, I go to third period, French III. "Mrs. Yates," the French teacher, lectures to us that we can't get a job without French. (All teachers think that their subject is the most important.)

Next is "Mrs. Thompson's" class for two periods, English and Journalism. These are my funnest and most interesting classes. During journalism I see "Pete" and another friend, "Eric." We get yelled at every day for talking so one can probably guess what the class is like, noisy.

Lunch and economics are next, and they are both so totally boring that it isn't funny. After that, I go home, listen to my radio, and get bored some more.

My dad comes home, tells me to fix something, and I do it. Then I eat, do homework, watch TV, take a shower, . . . read some, cut off the light, and pray that tomorrow won't be so average, but it doesn't help. Then, quiet.

Next, I hear the annoying and eye-opening sound of my alarm watch telling me that it's seven a.m. and time to get up.

Danny Bolchoz, 16
Charleston, South Carolina

I use my time by going to work with my father after school in a Spanish-American grocery store. After I have done my share of work, my sister takes over. I get to go home and start doing my homework.

Every Sunday I get paid so . . . Monday I go to the bank and deposit my money.

When summer comes, I get a month to rest and take a trip to the Dominican Republic. I stay with my aunt. We go dancing every weekend. On weekdays we go to the museums or visit friends and relatives and go to the beach.

Tammy Defasus, 16
Long Beach, New York

After school I haul wood into the house for the wood stove and do other odd jobs. Then I like to be alone for a while, but I just can't sit. I walk. I walk on an average of 20 miles, excluding school, a week.

I believe that a stereotype has been stamped on us teenagers. We are pictured as having all the time in the world, lazy, anti-exercise, and anti-work. I think it's time that the world stopped looking at us as troublesome. We are human with personal problems that weigh more than they should.

Diane Stremcha, 16
Dakota, Minnesota

On school nights my boyfriend comes over, and we play with our little girl. We go out a lot on weekends to our friend's house or party down at their boathouse.

During the summer we go fishing a lot. We enjoy it because we can be alone. We also go on the river when we are hot and take walks to the Dairy Queen for our favorite sundaes.

Shelley Rudnik, 17
Winona, Minnesota

My typical day at the cabin upriver: The cabin is located near the banks of a branch of the Unalakleet River, North River. It is a small building built as the colonial log cabins were built. It is heated by a small wood burning stove with a lantern as lighting.

Since I'm alone, I can set my own sleeping schedule. So along about noon, I roll out of bed and cook up some breakfast. Afterwards I walk down to the river with a bucket to get some water. Then I clean the cabin and make sure that everything is in order.

When I'm done with that, I go into the woods to see if I can shoot any squirrels or rabbits for supper. Some days are good, and I can bag two or three squirrels an hour. Other days I'm lucky if I get one in four hours. About seven, I head back to the cabin to eat. After I'm finished with my meal, I usually read a book until eleven p.m. or so and then fish until I'm tired enough to go to bed. That might be two a.m. or later since it doesn't get dark.

It's a simple life and a nice escape from the pressure and responsibilities of the real world.

Mark Alan Leafgren, 15
Unalakleet, Alaska

My summer is used to better myself physically, spiritually, and mentally. During the summer I visit many Christian camps. I think summer is great because I don't have school clawing at my back when I want to do something, You know the way one part of you wants to study for school all of the time and then there is the other part saying, "Hey, gimme a break already." During the summer I jump at the chance to get to know myself and my Savior better.

Another thing I do is devote all spare time and effort that I can scrape up into working out in the weight room. I want to be a body builder, you see, and summer is the only time when I can work out

and not have my mind cluttered with thoughts of school and not worry about being pressed for time. My mental attitude can get pretty terrible sometimes so I try to improve it.

Brad Williams, 15
Lubbock, Texas

Usually there's nothing on TV so I get something to eat and start working on a program that I am writing on our computer. Sometimes I spend up to seven hours a day on the computer.

On the average I watch about three hours of TV in a day. If I'm not watching TV, then I am either outside working at a friend's house, or playing ATARI. I love video games.

I'm not the type of teenager (that anti-video gamers talk about) who puts ten dollars a week into video games at the arcade. I play occasionally at the arcade but not on a daily basis. . . . I'm always reading in the paper about people who say that video games are too violent. If I want violence, I will watch the evening news.

At our church service once while the minister was giving his sermon, he really gave video games a bum rap. I'll bet he doesn't even know what a power dot is, let alone a Pac-Man.

Bruce MacMahon, 16
Falmouth, Maine

A typical day in school for me is to go to school, go out in the smoking area, and hope to get high. I usually do. I'll proceed to art, then sociology, then biology, and next to English. After English I go out to the smoking area, smoke a butt, then go either into the bathroom or outside to smoke a bowl.

Occasionally, I may do some speed or other minor drugs. After lunch I go to study hall, next to history, and last to study hall. After school I hop on the bus and head for home. We usually get high on the bus, too.

Then I walk . . . to my house,

EMILY...

CAN'T SHE SEE THAT
I'M BUSY

where I do homework, dishes, or watch TV, make dinner, sleep, or get high.

16-year-old female
Vermont

When I get home from school, I usually sleep for a half hour to an hour. On Monday, Tuesday, Friday, and Saturday I hop into my personal driving machine, a '73 Pinto, and go to International Fitness Center where I lift weights. Most of the time I am too tired, lazy, or busy to go.

I usually watch television till seven. Then I go study. The Key Club meets on Wednesday night, and I usually spend an hour there. I am vice-president and an active member in the club. The club centers around charity and community help work.

On the weekends, I usually go to a movie or a party. But I prefer just to be with friends. Once in a while I will have an AZA meeting. AZA is a Jewish social group, which is also based around community involvement.

During the summer I work as a senior counselor at a camp for the physically and mentally handicapped of the low country. It is one of the most rewarding jobs I ever had and probably ever will have.

It may seem that I am always doing something outside the home, but I would rather sit at home and read a good book.

David Goldmintz, 16
Charleston, South Carolina

I go to school during the school year but on weekends, I rodeo. I am a member of the Professional Rodeo Cowboys Association. During the summer I also travel around the country rodeoing. I am a barrel racer. I feel that my time is used wisely.

I have rodeoed for eleven years, four years professionally. I have seen so many interesting things and learned so much. I have participated at events from Madison Square Garden in New York City to Los Angeles, California to Canada. I find that when I learn about fa-

mous places or happenings in school, I have already gotten a lot of information and a better understanding of them from my travels. . . .

I like what I am doing with my life, and I intend to keep on doing it. It is a very rewarding career to me. Other people might think it's a waste of time, but I love what I am doing.

Kristan Crain, 17
Fort Smith, Arkansas

I have a very major problem with my time. I know what I should do, but I don't do it. . . . I delay everything to the last minute. I do not know why I do this—it just happens.

The most vivid example I can think of is our junior theme, which you must pass to graduate. I did 80 percent of it in the last week of the six weeks. In my class, I would guess 90 percent of the students would admit to wasting and not managing their time well.

All students have a bad realization that looks upon them after school hours . . . homework. . . . We take our books home with us, but we don't even take them out of our car. . . . If we take our books inside, mom will see them. Then she won't let us do anything until she has seen us do our homework. It plagues us all.

Another waste of time is the weekend. Don't get me wrong—I live for the weekends. It is just today's high school student goes out on the weekend. We have a variety of things to do, but it just is not managing our time wisely. When we should be at home doing that ten-page report or helping dad plow a field, we're not. We are out partying. . . .

My parents are like most parents. They have to tell me several times or remind me to do things. Oh, I eventually do it, but I'm like the average high school student—I don't do it when I'm asked.

My parents and I have an average relationship. They tell me. Then they tell me louder. Then they scream it. Then I do it.

Another downfall is my friends. Someone says, "Hey, let's go to the game room." Or, "Meet me at the drive-in." It is usually more fun than sitting at home doing character sketches over every character in *Macbeth*. So I usually go. It is just typical of a senior not to be able to manage his time correctly.

Kelly Curry, 17
Lubbock, Texas

Last year I saw a flyer for an organization called the Guardian Angels on a store window near my house in East Los Angeles. I called the phone number and went through the training, which is mostly exercise and martial arts. Now I spend a lot of my time patrolling with them and working out at my karate studio.

You get an emotional high stronger than any amphetamine when you go out on patrol. It's just you and your division, and you're secure and you know you'll be ready if something goes down and you have to get involved. I'm the smallest, and a girl, so I constantly have to prove myself.

On patrols, you walk through high crime neighborhoods. In my case we patrol not too far from my house and make sure nothing is happening. One time we caught a robber, and another time we got caught in a shoot-out.

Sometimes I get the feeling I should quit and stay home and study. But if I save just one kid or make one little old lady feel a little more secure, it's worth it.

Natalie Johnston, 16
Monterey Park, California

A normal day for me would be getting up at six-thirty to be ready for school by eight. School lasts from eight to two-thirty, then there's track practice from three to five. When I get home from track, I try to squeeze in some time for my horses.

Usually I spend an hour or so riding, but I wish I had more time. I like to stay back in the woods where it's peaceful and away from the smell of exhausts. The woods is a time of relaxation for me so it's important.

When I get back from riding there's always chemistry or algebra to keep me busy a little while longer. I usually crash around ten p.m. I can't wait for the weekend. I can sleep in, forget about homework till Sunday, and the nights are reserved for me and my friends.

Amy Wingate, 17
Hillsdale, Michigan

Usually I get high every day—before, during, or after school. Then I come home and change my clothes and go out and try to find a job. I usually end up at a party with a friend or two, either stoned or drunk out of my head. Then I go home to crash. Mom will be sleeping so I have to sneak in.

17-year-old male
Iowa

I work weekends—Saturday from ten a.m. to six p.m. and Sunday five p.m. to ten-thirty p.m. I work for a service company cleaning a major office. We also party a lot on weekends—smoke dope, drink, and experiment with different drugs. One drug I do (and a lot of my friends do) is mushrooms.

Personally I feel that mushrooms enhance your imagination and psychedelic limitations. I enjoy partying in school, like downers and dope are good drugs for school. I refuse to drink in school, though, because alcohol can really screw up your functions. It's also easier to get caught.

I get B's and C's in school, but I've got spring fever so I keep skipping school. Oh well, school's gonna be out for summer soon so I won't have to worry about it.

16-year-old female,
Vermont

The night was Wednesday and the TP (Toilet Paper) raid was to be at the "Andretti's." They had been TPed both Monday and Tuesday. "Dave," "Brad," and "Nelson" and I had mega toilet paper, shaving cream, and lotion (why I'll never know).

TPing houses late at night is boring for professional TPers as we are. It was eight p.m. as we carefully surveyed the house from behind a large white van. The time was now and we struck hard and fast. Little did the unsuspecting inside know that their yard was being made a shambles, their car being shaving-creamed, and their sidewalk lotioned.

With the yard totally TPed, we decided it was time to knock on the door and run like hell. "Dave," being the quickest, was chosen for the death defying feat of courage.

Bam, bam—and that's our signal to run. But wait—where's "Nelson"? We stop and look back. He's still up in the leafless tree in the yard frozen like a stone. Suddenly

the yard is illuminated with light. Mr. "Andretti" comes out, curses loudly, and slams the door shut. "Nelson" scrambles out of the tree and is safe.

We come back an hour later with hollow grapefruits filled with shaving cream. After all, we are uncatchable. Mr. "Andretti" is cleaning his car off. I yell, "'Andretti', we love you!" And we let the bombs fly and run.

Quickly, "Andretti" is in his car and speeding after us. My friends cut into somebody's yard. I, being smart, think that Mr. "Andretti" will follow the large group. Wrong! He follows me.

If I'm going to get caught, I'm going to get caught with somebody else. So I cut back to the yard with "Andretti," who is now out of the car but on my heels. The large gate in front of me slams shut, and I think I'm doomed.

"All right. You stop right there," yells "Andretti."

I fumble with the gate latch, and I'm in the yard. I hop a couple of fences, and I'm home free. Again the uncatchables remain uncaught.

Jim Hansen, 17
Phoenix, Arizona

Summer is my favorite time. I march in a drum and bugle corps, twirling flags and rifles. I love the exercise and the outdoors for the first week. I hate the regimentation of a 14-hour rehearsal, three days a week outside, rain or shine, corps food, stale sandwiches, and no bathrooms. But every summer I'm right there every day. The music and marching makes me high, and the sun bleaches my hair and darkens my skin. Friendships that were on "hold" all winter soon blossom.

The days that I don't march I work for my dad. He has a shop in the backyard, manufacturing springs, stampings, and wire forms for big companies. He pays

by the amount of work I do, not the hours I work. Sometimes I sweep up and take telephone messages.

Towards the end of the summer, August or so, I start thinking about school and I begin to miss it. My mind wanders to clothes and dances and old friends and teachers. And homework.

Allison Kerns, 17
Kent, Washington

Not being too social, I stay at home most of the time and just be lazy. Unlike a lot of people, I don't feel I have to go out to have fun. I'm kind of a quiet person. I'll just stay in my room and think. When the weather is nice, I really enjoy going for a long bike ride and just thinking, and getting all my stress and frustrations out.

A typical day of mine is to get up at five-thirty and go to school at seven. When I get home from school, I go to my room and sit there and think of how my day went and how I could make it better tomorrow.

On weekends I usually sit home and do nothing. Some people say I'm a boring person. I agree with them sometimes, but I like being a more quiet person rather than a party-hearty person.

Laura Cipcich, 15
St. Charles, Illinois

I think my typical summer day is getting up between six and six-thirty in the morning and feeding the cows and cleaning the barn. Around eight I eat breakfast. Then I go back out to work in the fields, usually to help bring in the hay or to work in our three and one-half acre strawberry field to about twelve-thirty or one.

Then I eat lunch or take a swim in the river for about an hour till my newspapers come—I deliver 75 papers. I get back from delivering newspapers around four-thirty or five, and I feed my animals. Then I usually go swimming until dusk.

Joe Kloiber, 15
Belmont, New York

KITTY ALMY
LYONS TWP. #5

I'm an avid sports fan so I'm often going to games and matches, usually two or three nights a week. I feel I allow enough time to do my studies though sometimes I could use a few extra moments to relax and just sit back and take it easy.

Sports are really my relaxing part of the day. I spend many afternoons staying after school, often till four-thirty or five working on journalism (I'm a sports writer for our paper) or taking pictures (something else I do for journalism and for fun).

I try to leave the weekend days for family. Even if we don't stay home, I still try to do something with them—even work. The time that is left over (not much), I spend with my friends. Either going out or just sitting around watching TV, we have fun. I try to live my life to the fullest and not waste any precious time.

Jenny Gustaf, 15
Midland, Michigan

I utilize my time very inefficiently. A typical day during the school year involves waking up and rushing to get to school on time, followed by attending my classes, seven each day. Often I have study periods which can be used to do most anything you choose.

Very seldom do I utilize these study periods to complete assignments that are due. Instead, I usually talk to my friends and decide not to do my work.

After school I have practice for either basketball or baseball, but these practices often do not start until an hour or more after school ends. Instead of using this time to do homework, I usually sit around or just fool around in the gym with my friends.

After practice I go home, always with good intentions to do the homework I was assigned for the next day. But these good intentions vanish as I sit down in front of the TV, saying to myself, "Well, mom will have dinner ready in an hour so I'll just watch TV till then. After supper I will do my homework." After supper I sit down in front of the TV and simply decide that the homework is not important so I just won't do it.

Mark Carroll, 17
Falmouth, Maine

Patterns in a typical summer day:

I get out of bed about seven-thirty, eat breakfast, and go out to the field to change the irrigation water. I then come back home, get on the three-wheeler, and go out to the cotton fields to spray the weeds with poisons.

I eat lunch at noon and change the irrigation water again. Then I get on the tractor and plow till seven or eight o'clock at night. Then I go back out to the field and change water. After that I go home, eat supper, and go to bed.

Kelly Kitten, 16
Slayton, Texas

I awake to the sound of a blaring clock radio, usually ten minutes fast and set fifteen minutes before I want to get out of bed. After pressing the snooze button six or seven times, I finally realize I had better get up. As I stand up and make my way to the bathroom, I stagger, tripping over the clothes, shoes, and what-not dispersed throughout my bedroom floor.

I get into the shower and blindly reach for the shampoo, my eyes just beginning to open. Once out of the shower, I proceed with my daily ritual of blow-drying and curling my hair. Afterwards I get dressed, eat my breakfast, and listen for the honk of my friend's car that has already been sitting in my driveway for ten minutes.

Once I get to school, that is when the drowsiness sets in. From eight to 12:46, I go to my classes in a haphazard manner, not even thinking about what I'm doing or where I'm going next. By noon my stomach has already begun its grumbling and growling. Finally, 45 minutes later, lunch arrives. I stuff myself, seeing as it will be another six hours and a tough basketball practice until I will eat again.

Seven suicides, countless layup and passing drills, and an hour of treacherous scrimmaging later, I emerge from the gym, nothing more than a limp noodle. A towel over my head, I stumble to the locker room and attempt to open my locker and get dressed.

I arrive home, greeted by a withered dinner that has been in the oven too long and a screaming mother insisting that I clean my room. I ignore it as long as it takes me to pick over and eventually eat my dinner. Once I am finished, I'm really not up to solving algebra problems or reading history. So I check the TV listings and engage in a few hours of television.

Lu Ann Larsen, 16
Bay Village, Ohio

The fourth dimension, time, encompasses a restriction on the lives of all people. Time remains an irreversible law under which people must comply. Time plays no favorites. People are given an equal twenty-four hours a day, seven days a week. However, how people utilize this time can determine the difference between one obtaining their dreams or being a failure. . . .

My typical weekday schedule, consisting of work, school, running, music, homework, and religious activities, allows me to develop discipline by efficiently budgeting my time. My day begins at five-thirty to do my newspaper route. I believe that starting early each day is important. First, it allows for more hours in the day. Second, it develops discipline.

Next, I run a mile and a half to school carrying my books and school clothes. Then I meet with the cross country or track team to run another four miles. I have been involved with distance running for six years and believe that running is the best physical activity for development of body and mind be-

cause of the intense dedication that is necessary.

After showering and eating at school, I begin my school day. This year I am taking seven credits with nine classes and no study halls or lunch periods. Again, a tight schedule like this precipitated knowledge and discipline.

Following the end of school, I will run another seven to twelve miles at track practice, finishing with a one-and-a-half mile run home. By running twice a day, I keep my body in top form and become well trained for advanced competition.

After showering at home, I go to pit orchestra practice from six to seven-thirty. By being involved in music, I contrast the fine arts with athletics, creating liberal knowledge and awareness. From seven-thirty to eight-thirty, I attend a Catholic youth ministry where I am one of the leaders. . . . Once home again I have dinner, do homework, and retire at eleven-thirty.

Paul R. Millradt, 17
Bay Village, Ohio

Chapter 2.

Priorities

Justin Adaise was a sophomore at Chester A. Arthur High School. Typically, some might say, he was an irresponsible teenager. He wore black t-shirts with "Christopher Cross" rock 'n roll logos. He grew his hair long and shaggy. He spent his freshman year attempting to alienate all female faculty members. In his English final exam, he criticized Shakespeare's *The Tempest* because, "It wasn't like the arcade game at all! Where does this Shakespeare get his bullshit from? I don't even think he's played the fuckin' game before. He's never scored over 10,000, that's for sure."

Justin's mailbox was a favorite destination of school progress reports. They all said, "WARNING: FAILING GRADES." Justin's parents were so accustomed to these pink warning slips that they would utter an audible sigh of relief when all they found was the mortgage bill. Somehow Justin passed his first year of high school with a D average. He possessed a good measure of intelligence beneath his shaggy hair. The problem was how to captivate it.

One day Justin Adaise came home and plopped down on his bed. After a few minutes of recuperation from the four-block walk home, he headed for the kitchen. He grabbed some Dutch Apple Pop Tarts, a box of Cheeze-Its, two bottles of 7-Up because he was a health nut (no caffeine—never had it, never will), and, for a change of pace, some Thompson seedless grapes. Being well-provisioned, he plopped in front of the tube. After "Scooby Doo," "Gilligan's Island," and "The Brady Bunch" had flickered across the screen and into Justin's dimmed mind, he shut the TV off. "Christ, Marcia's a fox!" he exclaimed as he put on his headphones. He placed a pile of Led Zeppelin records on the turntable, and drifted into dreamland as he stretched out his torso. Justin was "mellowing out" before going to meet his cohorts for their nightly marathon at the game room.

This night would be different, however. Justin would never meet his pals at the game room. Fate took a turn for the better. When Justin entered unconsciousness to the melodic strains of "Stairway to Heaven," he had a shocking dream—no, it was more of a revelation. Justin Adaise would never be the same. As his snores grew louder, his dreams became reality for a time. . . .

"Private Adaise!" barked the sergeant.

"Yes, Sergeant!" replied Justin Adaise.

"Git yer butt over to Jack Nicklaus' Woods, and do whatever you can to patch them holes in our left flank!"

"Will do, Sarge." Adaise hefted his backpack and slung it in place over his shoulder. He proudly wore his navy blue and gold uniform, the colors of the Alliance for Higher Education. The sounds of battle filled the air as he tramped on toward the left flank at Nicklaus' Woods. This was war, Adaise's first taste of it, and his blood boiled with fear and excitement. He whistled a few short snatches of "Pomp and Circumstance" as he thought about the war—particularly what was at stake. He fought for higher education: for expanding people's minds, for using humankind to its full potential, and for aiming toward a bright future. The enemy was a powerful one. It had already destroyed many teenage futures with its delusions of grandeur, irreversibly twisting their priorities the wrong way. The enemy was divided into three groups: TV and Stereo, which was ripping holes into the left flank where Adaise was headed; Sports, which was being held back on the northern front; and, the most fearsome and powerful enemy Higher Education could ever have, Teenage Employment, which was somehow being held back on the eastern front.

There were many casualties in this war, but little spilled blood. Unfortunately, the victims always lived, doomed to lives of dreaming away the days while watching soap operas and collecting welfare. They were doomed to believe in exaggerated self visions and to pursue impossible careers in the world of sports. Usually the all-conference high school fullback or the all-area forward had his dreams rudely interrupted by the cruel reality of the competitive professional sports world.

Most of the casualties, however, were the result of the most enticing enemy of all, employment. Fooled by the seeming independence and wealth offered by a four dollar an hour or less job, teens neglected their studies to work, work, work. Soon they became trapped in dead-end careers. Grocery clerks, bank tellers, cashiers, and dishwashers everywhere are the lasting mark of Teenage Employment's ironic wrath.

Adaise reached the left flank only to discover that most of the holes had been plugged. Now the tide was turning. The Alliance was on its way to a decisive victory over TV and Stereo. Adaise unslung his rifle and began to blast away at what remained of the enemy forces. Scraps of metal and shattered glass flew everywhere as TVs and Stereos were torn apart by rifle blasts. Adaise gave a brief sigh of thanks to the unknown Alliance officer who had issued the protective goggles. Sadly, the soon-to-be-secured Alliance victory was not won without a price. Here and there, scattered across the battlefield, wandered zombie-like soldiers, victims of the relentless barrage of mind-mushing cartoons, serials, and rock music. They wandered aimlessly, humming Jethro Tull tunes and reciting one-liners from "Scooby Doo" and "The Brady Bunch." Justin Adaise knew that the Alliance kept a crack force of medics and doctors alert at all times and that the zombies would walk and talk like normal humans soon enough. But, as Adaise knew, these people's lives would never be the same. He had seen it before. When returned to the real world, they had almost no chance of making it. They would always be on welfare. They would retain an almost incurable urge to go home from work at one-thirty to catch "General Hospital." Employers wouldn't accept that, and who could blame them? "What a damned shame," Adaise thought.

While he pondered the zombies' fate, Adaise absentmindedly stumbled on a tree stump. It was a nearly fatal mistake. With all the luck of a Republican mayoral candidate in Chicago, Adaise fell face to face with a deadly portable TV mine, fiendishly laid by the enemy. He blankly stared at the TV, mesmerized by its numbing, narcotic glare. "Wow!" he said. "It's

'Gilligan's Island'! And my favorite episode, too. The one where the two Russian cosmonauts crash land on the island, and Ginger tries to seduce them. Ooooh!"

Adaise grew worse by the minute. He began to sing the theme song to "Gilligan's Island." "Just sit right back and you'll hear a tale, a tale of a fateful trip . . ." He was going fast. If he got to the line, "the ship was washed ashore on this uncharted desert isle," he was a goner. Just then, the crisp, staccato sound of a rifle rang out. The portable Sony was smashed into innumerable bits of glass and metal. Adaise felt a great snap in his mind as

his will was freed from the perverting effects of a mindless TV serial. He closed his eyes and breathed deeply. Opening them, he saw the gruff, square-jawed face of his sergeant leaning over him.

"You had a close call, kid. One more minute and you would have been history."

"Yeah, thanks, Sarge. I'm really shaken up. I can't believe it almost happened to me," said Adaise.

Sarge replied, "That's one thing you gotta learn quick if you wanna make it, sonny. Anyone can fall to the temptations of the good life, of watchin' TV and blastin' the goddamn stereo instead of working out wavelengths, angles, and Pythagorean theorems. And you gotta really stick yer nose to the grindstone to read 50 pages of *Hamlet* or *Crime and Punishment* instead of pumpin' an endless supply of quarters into them son-of-a-bitchin' video games. It takes guts, kid, guts. And dedication. And determination. But it's worth it, kid, 'cause that's what we're here fightin' for. We're fightin' for a future—everyone's future. The world don't get any easier to understand as time goes on, kiddo. Every year, every month, every screwin' day, the world becomes a more complex and difficult place to succeed in. You understand me kid? 'Cause if you don't educate yerself, expand that brain of

Priorities   25

yers to its fullest limits, then yer ass is gonna be handed to the enemy on a silver platter. Christ, it's gettin' dark. Can you make it back to camp, kid? Ya look pale."

Justin Adaise was spinning. His head was full of the excitement of learning, of being all that he possibly could be. Yet his enthusiasm was tempered by the stark reality of the battlefield and of his own narrow escape.

"Yeah, Sarge, I'll make it," he replied wearily.

Adaise made it back to camp safely and plopped into his sleeping bag. For the moment, he could not sleep. Though full of wonder, he feared the treasures the world would eventually open for him. The night was cool, the sky was a satin blanket, studded with a thousand million diamonds. The battles had ceased for the night. He thought of the great victory over the inanity of TVs and Stereos. He felt a rush of pride and accomplishment over his part in the victory and over his survival. He thought of the battles with Sports and Teenage Employment that were yet to be won.

"The enemy is still strong and dangerous. There is a lot of fighting ahead. But Higher Education is destined to win. I know it will, I know it will, I know it will, . . ." Adaise murmured as he drifted into sleep. It was a destiny Private Justin Adaise of the Alliance for Higher Education could feel in his heart, in his soul, and, most of all, in his mind.

The last Led Zeppelin album was finished, and the tone arm swung back into place. Its loud snap awoke Justin Adaise of Chester A. Arthur High School. He had been asleep for eight hours. It was now past midnight. Adaise sat up and rubbed his eyes.

"Wow, what a trip," he groaned.

He could recall in vivid detail his entire dream. He flinched and drew back in a moment of fear when he noticed his stereo. "Man, that trip seemed so real. The TVs and stereos attacking me, controlling me. Too much, man."

Adaise ripped off his headphones and tossed them on the floor, staring at them wonderingly. He leaned back, took a deep breath, and closed his eyes. He knew that the visions in his dream were real. He could point to Bill Jones, who was 21 and still bagging groceries at the Jewel. And there was Mike Peterson, an all-conference halfback two years ago. He couldn't handle the pressures of college so now he was collecting unemployment and doing odd jobs around the town. Then Adaise thought of himself and how his path of video games and TV was leading to the same meaningless destination.

"I'm going nowhere, man, nowhere. I've got to get my ass moving, and fast!" Adaise exclaimed.

On the floor was a seldom-used object. Adaise's algebra book. He picked it up and stared at it. Then he carefully opened it and turned the pages as if they were a delicate old parchment. He pulled out some paper. For the first time in over a month, he did his homework. Justin Adaise finally decided where his future was. He wouldn't be taking that eight to midnight job at McDonald's for $3.35 per hour. It wouldn't leave any time for homework. Of course, there would still be video games, TV, and stereo in his life. But he would no longer be their slave. They would be his—to enjoy after his schoolwork was done.

He caressed his algebra book as if it were made of gold. Justin Adaise realized that he held the key to his future, and he intended to unlock every door that he possibly could.

THIS IS MIKE WUFONE YOUR ROVING REPORTER HERE ON THE STREET, TRYING TO FIND OUT ABOUT THE PRIORITIES OF TEENAGERS. HERE COMES A TEENAGER NOW...

Discussions

Thirteen desks are moved into a circle as the teenagers in the discussion group take their places. A tape recorder is set in the middle. Two senior interviewers find seats among the teenagers and look over their notes. The topic is priorities. To understand one another better, the teenagers introduce themselves.

Kelly (*17, senior, twin brothers in college and another in junior high, parents divorced*): I spend most of my time at school. Some of the academic classes—the ones that are difficult—are not as enjoyable as other activities. I spend a lot of time in the drama department. I also

---

All statements in these interviews, including those designated "male" and "female," were made by the 13 members of a student-led discussion group at Glenbard East High School, Lombard, Illinois. Editing changes have been made only to avoid repetition or misrepresentation of an idea.

Religion comes first in my life. I hate to admit it really, but I guess that's where the conflict and struggle part comes in. I'm a Christian, and I am proud of it. I've gone to church and Sunday School, and God really is a part of my life. Without Him I know I'd be lost. When I say "lost," I'm talking about being an alcoholic or a drug addict.

When I say things about church, some of my friends laugh or joke about it. That makes me angry because they are cutting down the same thing that means a lot to me.

I respect my friends, though, and don't ever "push" religion. But sometimes I just want to tell them that they are really missing out on something sweet. Religion is the only thing that is really important because I feel that without it I wouldn't have a family, which comes second.

Pamela Milne, 16
Billings, Montana

PARDON ME MR. TYPICAL TEENAGER, BUT WHAT COMES FIRST IN YOUR LIFE?

THE CHICKEN, NO—THE EGG

I have made the decision that school should come first in my life because I feel that a good education will be necessary as well as beneficial in my adult years. Without an education, I would be competing against millions of people more knowledgeable than I.

Let's face it. The job market is definitely prejudicial between those with a college degree and those without. If I want to be successful in my later years, which I do, a good education will be the first step in my preparation.

Chris Abrahams, 18
Hopland, California

Priorities

My mother and father always wanted me to join the national defense so I joined the Air Force. Although the Air Force is going to play a big part in my life, such as college and employment, my main priority in life right now is to make my parents proud of me.

Some priorities as a student are to graduate, to keep my car . . . and my insurance payments up, and to work as much as possible. . . .

I start basic training in the Air Force on June 27. Then all my priorities as a student will be overruled with the priority of becoming an officer in the military. If and when I accomplish this task, I will have fulfilled my life goal and made my parents proud of me.

Frank Filippone, 17
East Detroit, Michigan

have a job helping people build picture frames—you know, customer service—so it's pretty interesting at times.

John *(17, junior, three sisters, one older):*   It seems I don't get to live life much anymore. I feel old. I used to do a lot more. Now I just work to get money for college. I've got a girlfriend, too. And I'm on the football and track teams.

Melanie *(16, junior, youngest of three children):*   I play the cello, and I think that's one thing I'd like to go into—to study music, maybe as a minor at Northern Illinois or at a Christian college. I'd like to major in child development. I'm really interested in people and helping special ed kids—like people who've been abused or neglected. I

My little sister comes first in my life above everything else. She's mentally-handicapped, and I really think she's special. She always keeps me happy because she's full of spunk. Rhonda can't talk or do many things a normal 11-year-old can do, but she has such a funny personality that it makes everyone around her feel good.

There have been many times when she has been real sick, had operations, and even almost died. She always came out all right and bounced right back. Those serious times made everyone and myself love her even more.

Rhonda seems to look up to me, the big sis and protector in all of her mishaps. She knows that I care for her so she is very well-adjusted around me. I've taught her many things—to say hi, slap me five, hug, play patty-cake.

Sometimes she overgoes her limits, and it turns out funny: one night she got out of bed, turned on her bedroom light, unlocked her bedroom door (we lock it so she doesn't fall downstairs), walked into my room, turned on my stereo, started to play with my stuffed animals, got bored, and came downstairs where the family was watching TV. I teach her things one at a time. That night she put them all together and really was mischievous. . . . That kid is a cute little brat, and I love her! She's so lovable, funny, witty (in her own way), and she always tries. It is so hard not to love her.

Cheryl Klisk, 14
Chicago, Illinois

First, I would like to just graduate from high school because that is the biggest thing I want in life and because I will be the first to graduate in my household. It will be so special for me and my family. . . . That is mainly what I really do want in life.

William Leeper, 18
Camden, New Jersey

In my life the one thing that comes first above everything else is my family....

My mother may be doing work—and I could see that she's working hard—but I would like to go out with my friends.... My mother might say, "Your friends and everyone else always comes first," but that's not really true.

I love and care for my family a lot even if it doesn't show at times. My family will always be there for me, but maybe my friends won't.

Linda Frank, 17
Chicago, Illinois

Success is the most important of my life's objectives. However, it's not a commendable type of success because it focuses on money and power.

Lately I've been told that my ideals and priorities in life aren't things to actually make me happy. They will just keep me reaching higher and higher until I become drained and dissatisfied with myself.

I find it true today because I constantly have my nose in my school work. I'm missing what life is all about because I'm not living. I'm being a machine. People don't relate with machines. They relate with people.

Paula Frazer, 16
Brookfield, Connecticut

like to talk and listen to people with those kinds of problems and see if I can relate and help in any way.

Diane (17, senior, youngest of three children):   I love my job because I work for my dad. I don't do a lot of work, but I get paid a lot of money. I don't have too many hobbies. I take martial arts classes after school, and I raise dogs with my mother. My parents are gone quite a lot. My mother is gone to Florida three-fourths of the year, and my dad's gone a couple months out of the year.

Manish (15, junior, only child):   I am not a native-born American. I was born in India, and I lived there until I was about eight years old. Then we lived in England for a while. I lived in Nottingham, you know, Robin Hood. I enjoy any kind of sports, I guess. I hate school even though I get good grades.

Jeff (16, junior, straight-A student, one younger sister):   I guess I'm not a complicated person. I play soccer for the soccer team. I enjoy school—I work hard at getting good grades. I'm a pretty straight kid, I guess.

Maribeth (16, junior, youngest of four children):   I don't really have any hobbies other than pompons. I'm studying to be a travel agent at Davea (vocational school). Starting next week, I'm going to be at work four days a week at a reservation office in Oakbrook Terrace. I live with my mom, and my father's dead.

Steve (17, senior, older of two children):   I was born in England and moved here about five years ago. I work at a restaurant on the weekends. My major interest is motorcycling. I ride my motorcycle whenever I have time.

Leslie (17, senior, youngest of three sisters, former cheerleader and gymnast):   I don't like school anymore. I find it boring. I went

The thing that comes first in my life above everything else would be learning all I can about superior weaponry and the act of survivalism.... Examples of survivalism would be living when most other people are either vegetables or dead, having enough uncontaminated water and food, and probably the proper clothing would be an important factor in surviving. And if that's not enough, maybe even one or two more people to talk to.

Brian Dary, 18
Greenfield, Wisconsin

I should say God, but I think, in my family, because of my dad's influence, soccer comes first. This brings about conflicts on Sunday morning when my mom wants to go to church and my dad wants to play soccer.

Gary Caous, 16
Greenfield, Wisconsin

First in my life, without a doubt, is my son Anthony Thomas Merritt. Most people will tell you having a son at 16 is not right. I will be the first to admit it was not planned, but I love him very much. Nothing is more important in my life.

Vince Merritt, 16
San Lorenzo, California

I often go out of my way to help somebody when they need it. I'm not meaning to brag or anything. It's just that I enjoy seeing someone's face light up when I do something for them.

I love making other people happy. For example, I work at a camp for disabled kids. One of the greatest things is to see a little boy who's never ridden in anything but a wheelchair, who's never even seen a horse before, suddenly become transformed into a giggling, excited, mini-Roy-Rogers on his very own Trigger.

Becky Elliott, 16
Ferndale, Washington

My family comes first because it's important for me to get my brother and sister back at home. I fight every day to get up for school because they are really depending on me to get them back with mom. Right now they are in foster homes.

I struggle with everything, plus my mom. I try to find a job to help my mom out and also to be at the program so the staff can help me and my family out with things and straighten problems out. Soon my family will be back together, and I will be happy again.

Nanci Elrod, 16
Tucson, Arizona

I put my girlfriend first because that's where I can see results. I can see our relationship growing, and it gives me a good feeling. Logically, I should put school or work first because in the long run, I will gain the most from those. . . .

Many conflicts occur from putting my girlfriend first. My family feels like I don't care about them. It's hard to do my best in school, and I really don't think my girlfriend likes it a lot. It sounds good, but . . . most people don't want to be tied down. . . . I end up

away last summer to college and took a class. I guess that ruined my senior year for me. I'm really looking forward to college.

Matt (*17, senior, youngest of three children*):   Right now I'm playing football. It's almost over, thank God. I don't really have any hobbies. I have good friends, and I like school.

Michelle (*16, junior, older of two girls, parents divorced*):   I like to hang around with greasers, and I like fifties music—Beach Boys, Elvis, Jan and Dean, and stuff like *American Graffitti*. I work a lot. I live with my mom and dad at different times.

Karen (*17, senior, younger of two children*):   I'm sort of a senior. I'm taking classes at the College of DuPage (community junior college). I don't have a job because my parents won't let me work. My hobbies are fencing, horseback riding, and tennis. I don't really like college, but it's better than high school.

Mary (*17, senior, older brother and two younger brothers*):   I went to a regular high school my freshman year. Then I went to another smaller school my sophomore and

expecting more from her than I should because I give her more than she wants.

Bob Knippen, 16
Wheeling, Illinois

In my life I feel that fun activities should come first. I feel this way because if school, homework, or chores come first, there is nothing to look forward to. In later years you don't have anything to look back at and say those were the times when you did not have to work continually.

Annette Noble, 17
McMinnville, Oregon

Money, above everything else, comes first in my life. It's the source and well-being of life. Without money the world would fall apart. With it, we may still fall apart.

Money makes my life happy, and it makes my life easier. . . . Striving to receive the money is the hardest part; however, this is how it should be. After I have the money, I can spend and splurge on my own free will. If, perhaps, I were to run out of money, my parents are a good secondary source.

Money can be a problem too. . . .

Do I have enough? What will I buy? Should I put it in the bank? These are just a few stressful questions that are constantly in my mind.

Mary Kirkland, 15
Omaha, Nebraska

Animals, even ones that don't belong to me, hold a special place in my heart. I feel an unusual closeness to living creatures and try to express it in kind words, a friendly pat, or by cleaning and dressing a wound.

Susan Salzman, 16
Littleton, Colorado

My biggest priority is soccer. I also like rock 'n' roll shows. And I love to tour the kitchen even when I'm not hungry. The kitchen to me is like a shopping center to a valley girl.

Richard Agee, 14
Albuquerque, New Mexico

Something that comes first above everything else happens to be my counselor. . . . I'm the type of person who needs someone to lean on, tell my problems to, and, most of all, to have someone in my life who cares and someone whom I know loves me.

My life thus far has been riddled

junior years. It was a special school for girls—only about 30 people. Then I came back for my senior year. My parents and I don't get along very well. I work, and I love to be with other people.

What comes first in your life?

Kelly: Relationships. The people in my life. My family and friends. I'll do things with them before I'll choose to do things for myself.

Diane: I agree with Kelly, but money is a close second.

Manish: Not exactly dollars, but along those lines. Success. Success, money, respect, etc.

Steve: Mine is the creation of a pleasurable environment.

Jeff: That's mine, too.

John: I could be a snob and say myself. Probably my family or friends.

Melanie: I have priorities I've set for myself. First is Christ—to understand Him. I try to have some reading time. I'm not too disciplined. I put myself right up there, too. Taking care of myself—my body is the Lord's temple so I've got to take care of myself. Loving other people is important, too. If I don't take care of myself, I figure I

with constant letdowns, breakdowns, and fits of depression. A father without a job, a marriage on the rocks, the loss of a home, and the uncertainty of my future constantly lay heavy on my shoulders.

These burdens are made bearable by a very special person in my life. Someone I put above everything. Anyone that would take a young, troubled teenager into their lives, lighten the load of their seemingly endless problems and just genuinely care, definitely deserves the honor of being someone who comes first above everything in a person's life.

I have recently chosen to change the way my life is progressing. It took this very special person to make me realize that I was the master of my own fate and that my life is what I choose to make it. And what I make it is entirely up to me.

Janet Price, 17
Ukiah, California

I love the outdoor life. I love to get up early in the morning and take a walk in the woods and listen to the birds singing away. I love watching a wild animal in its natural habitat. I love to climb to the very top of a mountain and turn around and sit

down and just watch the whole scene, . . . to look down the mountain and say to myself, "I conquered that baby," and feel great.

I love to hop on a horse and just take off into the wild blue yonder, just sitting as the horse guides your way. Then when night comes, you water down your horse and cook your supper. I love the smell of food in the woods because it smells as pure as the air you're breathing.

Then later in the night you sit by the crackling fire, listening to the crickets as they play their moonlight sonata. And as you gaze across the pond, admiring the reflection of the moon, you think of New York City. It is enough to make you sick to your stomach—people conning others who they live with, murderers, rapists, etc.

I feel that the freedom of the outdoors is the only way to really appreciate this grand old country of baseball, hot dogs, apple pie, and Chevrolets.

Donald McGuinness, 17
Brookfield, Connecticut

My home life comes first. This consists of family and chores. . . . I have a conflict because school runs a close second to home life, and I must get my homework done. . . .

Another problem is . . . religious responsibilities. When church services come up in the middle of the week, homework strikes again. My mind is fried with church, chores, and homework.

Terry Howells, 15
Bellaire, Ohio

Money, money, and more money—money can make a bum on a street corner that is laughed at a respected human being. Everyone says money cannot make you happy, but every time I have it, I feel great. I am tired of the middle class. I want to be rich.

Money can get a person in a

can't give unless I've received. Materialistically, what's important to me now is school. I've got one more year of high school, and then I've almost decided where I'm going to college.

Kelly: I think getting to college is a priority. Most of us have been accepted by the school we want, but actually getting there is a priority.

John: Work comes first because I have to pay for college. I can go through school now without studying too much, and I'm getting B's. I've got to decide which is better for me in the long run. If I studied, I could get A's. So I let the grades slide and work. I'm getting 37 to 40 hours a week.

Leslie: I guess my family. Being together and communicating and just being a family. I think that's very important.

Matt: During the school year, school comes first. During the summer, my first priority is work. I have to go to school, and I have to have money to do that. As far as my life during the summer, all my plans with friends revolve around my work schedule. I get called in every other day so I can't make plans ahead of time.

Michelle: My main priorities are having to go to school and then to work every day. I hate it. But as for which comes first—work, definitely.

Leslie: My other priorities are school and my job. And my friends—you have to have friends.

Michelle: My family's not too close. If somebody needs something, we're there. But otherwise, my family isn't a big priority.

Karen: Right now school comes first. I've got nothing else really except athletics. I play tennis. Everything in my life right now is

high-ranking position. Money gives a person a feeling of security and self-satisfaction. Money makes life easy without obstacles.

Hopefully, this is one Johnson that will stay millions ahead of "the Joneses."

Jason Johnson, 17
Lafayette, Oregon

My health always comes first in my life. I work hard to keep my body in good physical condition. . . . I'm not on any sports teams or activities in school . . . but I keep in good physical condition anyway. I figure that I should work out enough to stay in above-average physical shape just for myself until I decide on joining or neglecting to join any sports.

Chris Carpentier, 16
Greenfield, Wisconsin

Up until yesterday, being a member of the varsity pompon squad had been first and foremost in my life. . . . When I tried out for the varsity squad at the end of my freshman year, I wanted it more than anything. I was ready to sacrifice everything in order to get just one position on that 40-member squad. When I was one of the 40 picked out of approximately 300 girls, I was completely stunned. . . .

Since that day, my feelings for my squad have only grown. It hasn't been easy though. Despite the physical pain of jumpsplits and high-kick kicklines, I also endured a lot of emotional pain. But I also found that this pain and heartache and even sometimes anger only make me want to try even harder so I feel that I have grown inside and that the sad times made me feel even more devoted to my squad. . . .

I left practice many times with tears in my eyes. I'd go home feeling as though I was a second-rate member who couldn't do a damn thing.

And yet, I'd still look forward to

the next day's two-hour practice with vigor. The pain and defeat of the day before left me at a point where I could strive for even more perfection, and so I pushed, along with 39 other girls. We'd spend 12 hours on our Saturdays working towards that number one position. We even worked during the school week at night in addition to our two and a half hour practices every day. . . .

There was an electrical current that each one of us had found, and it made us feel, look, and act like one. We were proud—some claimed we were conceited—but we were proud of ourselves and each other. It was a personal feeling inside each one of us, and we

based on school. My future depends on what I learn in school. My parents come right after school, basically because they are paying for it. They provide me with a place to live. They give material but also emotional support.

Mary: My first priority is to go to school and get myself going. I've got to get myself started so I don't have to depend on anyone else.

Michelle: Work comes first for me because I want to be in sales so I want to do well at my job. I'm in sales now—telephone sales. That's what I want to do so I want to get started. I also am going to be 18 soon, and I want to move out of the house. I need money to do that.

were all lucky enough to share it.

I remember each performance. I'd get out on that court or football field and suddenly nothing else in the world had meaning except what I was doing. . . .Those who watched our 40 heads snapping as one and those sparkling eyes could feel the excitement along with us, and that only pushed us on even further. For us, it was a way of life.

For ten months out of the year, we ate, drank, and slept pom-pons. . . .On Saturday, two days ago, we took third place at our state contest. The helplessness and numbness we all felt left us in a state of shock. . . .

I realize that today, the first day

Priorities

in three years, I don't have practice. It leaves me feeling drained and empty as though someone has cut me apart and taken all but a little piece of me away.

Christine Lachman, 18
Oak Park, Illinois

The rank of eagle scout is the highest honor of Boy Scouts. It has been my main goal for over eight years since I started scouting.

Boy Scouting is almost controlling my life with obligations, meetings, counselor appointments, and research work plus my regular duty of quartermaster to the troop. With this consistent working for Boy Scouts, I must remind myself many times that my schooling must not be neglected. I must always try and balance the two sides of the work load evenly.

Don Forsberg, 17
San Lorenzo, California

How have your priorities changed over the last few years?

Diane: My priority now is getting through college. Before it was getting through high school.

Kelly: My first priority used to be the people I lived with. That's changed to my boyfriend as opposed to my family. My family objects to the change, but he doesn't!

Melanie: Your circumstances change. The way you think changes. I've been a Christian for a while, but a couple of years ago all I wanted was to be happy. I wasn't happy, and being happy was my main goal. I changed as I learned more about Christ. I was looking toward materialism—and it just wasn't there for me. Taking care of myself will help make me happy. I have to work at it quite a bit.

Friends are first in my life. You can't just be a hermit all your life, and if you have friends you won't. Who wants to sit by themselves watching television or playing sports? Sure, it's nice to be alone once in a while, but all the time is a little too long.

I hate when all of my friends go out and I don't. It makes me feel dull and alone. So I try to be nice to a lot of people so I won't have to be alone. It works, too.

Laura Jepsen, 16
Oak Park, Illinois

What comes first in my life is quite simple—me. I don't mean this in that I don't care what happens to anyone else. Believe me, I do. I mean this more in the sense that I have to look upon my surroundings, social dealings with my peers, my health, the health of others, my emotions, and most cer-

tainly the emotions of others. In particular, the emotions of a certain young woman. I have to tie these all in together to form an "equation," all variables included, to determine how my life is run and how it is supposed to continue according to plan. . . .

My outlook is that health, happiness, and love far outweigh the more material lifestyles, such as the pursuit of money and fortune. The conflict or struggle I feel is most bothersome to me is the emotional responses I give and receive. If these would only go and come exactly as I want, everything would be great. But they don't, and they probably never will.

Emotions are to be dealt with delicately, but not ignored. Ignoring emotions can be detrimental to my physical health, which is my primary concern. I have had to learn not to suppress my emotions; I now let them be known. I have found that by doing this I am far happier and have more energy and concentration for more important aspects of life.

Brian Sturgess, 17
Utica, Michigan

Jeff: Some people I know talk like school is kiddy time. Sure, work is important, but the job you have now is probably not your future ambition. So, for me, school is it. Getting the grades to get into a college—that's it.

Matt: Now it's work, friends, and family. I think my friends are important now because they'll all be going to different schools next year so I want to be with them now. My priorities will change next year. I'll be playing football at Western so I'll be spending a lot of time doing that.

Leslie: My friends are a lot more important to me now. Dating. I think a social life is real important to me now because I didn't have that before.

Michelle: School should come first, but it doesn't. I'm changing that now. I decided that I want to go to college so I've got to improve my grades. They're not too good right now. I'm going to work hard at school next year.

Leslie: My priorities definitely changed when I was at college last summer. I was there for three

What comes first in my life above everything else? Me. After years of thinking that I was the epitome of worthlessness and uselessness, I finally see I am not worthless. I am not useless. I am worth something, at least to a few people and at least to myself.

For a long time, too long, I expected people to love me when I hated myself. I felt guilty about everything imaginable. My friends and family thought I was happy, confident, ready and able to go places in life. They were wrong.

They were so wrong. They thought I was thinking of my future of brightness and happiness. I was thinking more along the lines of suicide.

I hated myself so much that I put everyone ahead of me. I got walked on, laughed at, used. And I thought I deserved it all. When I couldn't hide it anymore, when I became so engulfed in my hate for myself, I was useless. I dropped out of school.

A few weeks later I committed myself in a psychiatric hospital where I spent three and a half months. Then came months of therapy once a week. I began to realize that no one can love me until I love myself. I cannot function if I feel like a failure. I cannot love anyone else until I accept myself.

I worked to gain some self-respect. I had a tremendous amount of help from friends, family, and professionals. As a result of all this, I can now accept myself. I don't look in the mirror and think I am hideous. I look there now and see an attractive young lady, still with many faults, but she has a good head on her shoulders. I can have pride in myself.

This is why I come first. I worked too hard for my self-respect and pride to let anyone take it away from me. Ever.

17-year-old female
Connecticut

JUDY REWERTS

Right now, I'm going through a lot of changes, and I'm not really positive about anything. I guess if I have to pick the thing that comes first in my life, it would be my parents. By that I don't mean I do everything with them. I mean that because I'm not sure about myself, weeks, and I took one class, which was a psychology course. It helped me develop good study habits. I'd come home from class, I'd study, go to dinner. Then I'd go out and do something, you know, go out on the town or something. Then I'd come home and study.

I do things that would keep my parents happy and proud of the things I do and gain their respect.

I have always been a straight-A student, even in elementary school. Though I know I'm doing myself some good by maintaining these good grades, I have often felt

I haven't done it for myself . . . but because my parents want me to, . . . probably because I feel I'll lose their love if I don't.

I have never felt extremely close to my parents although they've been very good to me. Anytime I ever do anything wrong, I feel they won't understand and will hate me for my mistake. For example, this New Year's Eve I attended a party with some of my friends. Unfortunately, I was foolish enough to drink and overdid it.

I did realize, though, that I was incapable of driving and would not run the risk of getting into an accident and hurting someone else, especially my friends. I then had my brother call my parents to come and get me.

After that was done, I started crying and kept saying that my parents hated me because I did what I did. This, of course, proved to be untrue, but I still cried for three hours that night.

Kirsten Parr, 17
Utica, Michigan

In my life, other people come first because I feel that if nobody cares for them now, then they will be the ones in our society who will end up hurting other people, the way they were hurt. . . . Of course, there are a lot of people who need someone to care for them just as there are more than enough people to care for those that need someone. . . . Unfortunately, the people in our society would rather not get involved with people that seem to have conflict in their lives.

Georzann Chaco, 17
San Leandro, California

My dog comes first in my life. He is my best friend, and he never gets mad.

Stuart Zeller, 15
Redwood Valley, California

The utmost priority in my life is serving Jesus Christ. He comes

Karen: When I was a freshman, I just wanted to have fun and make lots of friends. Now I'm just concerned primarily with my grades. Now getting a good job is a priority. I didn't really care before.

Leslie: My activities changed, too. I realized I wasn't doing them for myself. As a freshman, I got involved in a lot of things. I played the flute because my sister played the flute, and I was a cheerleader— I think because my sister was a cheerleader and she got a lot of attention from it.

Matt: My work is becoming more important all the time. The more I work, the more seniority I get. It's important for me to do that so I can help my parents by earning as much money as possible.

How do your priorities affect your everyday activities?

Manish: What you do every day is try to come closer to your priorities. For example, if you have a test on Friday and this is Monday, you keep studying little by little to fulfill your priority of passing the test. Somehow your major priority affects you every day.

Kelly: Right now I can only see my boyfriend a couple of times a week. That's a priority so I rearrange my whole week to figure out when I can spend time with him.

Maribeth: My job is a priority. I also have chores to do at home. It's my priority to get that done before I go out.

Diane: School's got to be most important from the start, and work will definitely go with it. When you talk about college, you usually talk about classes, but I want to have fun in college. That's a priority for me. I was so concerned with homework while in high school that I didn't have much of a social life.

John: Sometimes I get into

first above everything else. It's not merely because I wish to save myself from going to hell. It's because of everything He has done. Certainly someone who suffered through crucifixion and the persecution as a man deserves some love in return. He died for all the sins that we have ever done or will do.

Serving Jesus is a challenge. There are endless conflicts. Our nature constantly points toward selfishness and pleasure. Many will put you down merely because of what you stand for. . . .

The main struggles I have had are within myself. There are so many highs and lows in the relationship I have with God. Whenever I fall away for a time, I finally come to a point where I see the variety of it all. I see that the only thing I can depend on in this life is His love.

Susie Vincent, 18
Filer, Idaho

Right now in my life, I would say that having "inner peace" is my most important priority. I say this for one reason: Living in the type of competitive and complex world that teenagers do it is very easy for us to be consumed and destroyed by the pressures that exist.

The pressures of academics, athletics, and social interactions often become so great that the teenager almost becomes "mentally disturbed," losing touch with reality and with the more important qualities of life, such as health, friends, and family, that accompany reality. For this reason, I think that my most important priority is to be self-content, therefore enabling me to deal with society and with myself.

Jason Deutsch, 17
Warwick, Rhode Island

situations where if I don't go to my girlfriend's house, she'll get mad. And if I do go, my mom and dad get mad. If I do go, I'll be tired for work the next day. So do I get my mom, dad, and the people I work for mad, or my girlfriend mad? My girlfriend usually wins out.

Michelle: The conflicts usually are between school and work. I work every day from five to nine. My boss just can't understand why I can't finish all my homework before five and have to call in sick.

Karen: Priorities cause conflicts all the time. You'll have a test, but then a concert will come up. So, of course, you'll blow off your studies and go to the concert. I used to do that more, but now I don't do it as much.

Matt: A few days ago I was going to go to a concert. I got called into work, and I didn't get off till nine p.m. So, as far as fun goes, work took first priority as usual. I wasn't able to go.

Leslie: I had no friends—nothing except gymnastics. I went out to the private club every day. It was really hard for me to see all my girlfriends getting boyfriends and doing a lot of fun things I could never do. I was always at the gym. It was really hard—I think that's why I quit.

Mary: Conflicts come with my family and my boyfriend. I want to do what my parents say, like get home on time. But sometimes my boyfriend really needs to talk, and I don't know what to do. I must choose. It's really hard.

Compiled by Abby Rhamey

Chapter 3.

Influences

A dark, warm, peaceful space . . . suddenly she's being pushed out. Bright lights! Noise! Whack! Society slaps her into reality. Baby is born.

Mommy and Daddy look down into Baby's face, smile at her and make funny noises. Baby likes to look up at them. She learns to smile back at them and to laugh at their funny noises. Baby trusts Mommy and Daddy and Older Brother. She knows that they love her. Baby is sad when Mommy and Daddy leave her room. But Baby knows they will always come back—with a blanket, with a bottle, with a touch. Mommy and Daddy teach Baby what is right and what is wrong. Baby wants to be exactly like them.

Baby tries to talk. Her first words are "momma" and "dadda." Mommy and Daddy are proud of her. They teach Baby more words. New ideas come with the new words. One day Baby has a wonderful idea. Baby tries to share it with Mommy and Daddy, but she gets frustrated when she realizes that the words she needs to explain her idea don't exist.

While Daddy is at work, Older Brother is at school, and Mommy is busy, Baby plays with her toys or watches TV. Baby loves the cartoons, especially Road Runner. She learns to laugh when a boulder falls on the coyote or when dynamite blows up in his face. Baby also likes to watch Mister Rogers. Baby learns how she should act with her friends and family. Baby also meets interesting people—King Friday the Thirteenth, Chef Sprocket, and Mr. McFeeley, the delivery man.

Baby is in kindergarten now. First, Baby learns that she's not a baby anymore. Teacher calls her Child. Child likes to go to school because she can play with other kids and discover how to fingerpaint and how to dance. Child likes Teacher. She knows that everything Teacher says must be true so Child eagerly accepts Teacher's answers.

On Sundays, Child goes to church with Mommy and Daddy. Child knows there is a God because Mommy and Daddy tell her there is. Child isn't sure she understands who God is, but she knows that in order to go to heaven she has to believe. Child is afraid that she might need to change the way she acts to please God, but she doesn't worry about it. She looks at the other people who go to church and sees that they don't change—except at church. Child learns to play this game as easily as she learned to play hopscotch.

As the year goes by, Child worries about Older Brother. Child discovers that Mommy and Daddy have conferences with his teacher. When they come home, they're mad. She hears them say that he's "acting up" and that they hope Child will learn from his example. Child does. She sees that Older Brother is unhappy so she decides she will always do her school work. Child doesn't want Mommy and Daddy to be mad at her.

Child is in the seventh grade now. Like her friends, she dislikes being called Child, but grownups only laugh when she complains. Young Teen decides that grownups don't know much anyway. She feels frustrated because Mom and Dad don't understand her. They won't let Young Teen have privileges that her friends have. Young Teen feels embarrassed and out of place when she can't do what her friends do. Young Teen gets especially frustrated when her parents hassle her about her boyfriend. She doesn't understand why Mom keeps dropping hints about what nice girls do and don't do—especially what they don't do. Whenever she asks Mom what sex is like, Mom tells her that she shouldn't be thinking about sex at her age. But Teen thinks the girls in the movies are nice and they think about sex. Young Teen notices that since she started asking about sex Mom and Dad have been limiting her phone time with her boyfriend. Since sex has become a forbidden subject, Young Teen wonders more and more what her first real kiss will be like.

Soon Young Teen enters high school, but she's not afraid. She knows that she doesn't need to worry as long as she's popular. Teen likes to go to school because she can see her friends. Teen finds that staying home is frustrating. Mom and Dad get mad when she plays loud, hard rock on her stereo. Teen attempts to explain how important music is to her. She says that the words help her understand what other people are thinking. Mom and Dad decide that her music is only noise. So Teen buys headphones and listens to her music more and Mom and Dad less.

During her sophomore year, Teen decides she doesn't like school. She gets tired of teachers who are constantly telling her what to do—"Do your homework. Be in your seat when the bell rings. Quit talking to your neighbor." Teen's friends don't do much of their homework. In fact, they sometimes laugh at Teen because she does. She is tempted to forget about her homework so she has more time to have fun with her friends. Teen, however, remembers what happened to Older Brother.

Teen is finally a senior. She wants to get out of high school and get on with life. However, Teen does have a couple of classes that seem to relate to her life. She is writing a paper for her English class about an interesting book. She never realized that a book written so long ago could make such an appropriate comment on her world. Teen is eager to read more books like the last one.

Teen is finally an adult. Adult wonders why she thinks and acts the way she does. Sometimes Adult doesn't like the way she thinks. Adult gets frustrated because she wants to control how she thinks, but she finds control difficult to attain. Adult isn't sure she is the kind of adult she wants to be. She knows that her past experiences helped shape her personality, and she wonders whether she would be a better person if her past had been different. Feeling that she is too success-oriented, Adult wonders whether always working hard in school for good grades was as beneficial as her parents thought it was. Adult also considers trying a different church because her religion seems like a game.

Still, she's not sure which of her past experiences helped her and which hurt her. Adult keeps looking back over her life in an attempt to discover who she is.

Discussions

Julius Erving ... has worked hard ... and ... is considered by a number of top scouts to be the best player in the league. Dr. J plays basketball with great intensity but realizes that this game is not the only aspect of life.

We see this as he treats fans and

Karen: I went with my nursery school class to a sausage factory in Atlanta when I was four. My parents didn't know that I was going there, and it turned out to be a slaughterhouse. I'll never forget that. I haven't eaten meat since. We

reporters just like he would want to be handled. His personality has given him the reputation of being one of the classiest players in the athletic world. Julius is known for his athletic ability but also is possessed with ... intelligence.

I will work as hard as possible to

become the best athlete I can become, just like Julius did. I will try to have fun with basketball and not treat the game like a life-and-death situation. I will study hard for academic success just like Dr. J and hopefully receive a good education in college.

Bill Toole, 17
Bay Village, Ohio

My role model is ... my grandmother Pritch. Although I was three or four years old when she died, the few memories I do have of her and what my mother says about her makes me feel as if she was the grandest lady who lived.

My mother says the older I get, the more I'm like my grandmother. My grandmother always put others' problems first, which I find myself doing often. We both have a love for teaching. She was a second grade teacher for many years before they changed the standards for teaching.

But that didn't stop her. She went back to college and got her degree. Knowing she did that makes me more determined to complete my college education.

Even though my grandmother was busy with school or teaching, she always found time for her family. When we went up for supper on Sundays ... no matter how much work she had to do, she always had time to take us to the park.

Gail Shrock, 17
Elkhart, Indiana

I happen to be obsessed with food. For four years I have had to struggle with anorexia-bulimia, and it has ruined many aspects of my life. All my life, even when I was only five, I always held a great importance on appearance. Then, when I was in fourth grade, I was so upset because I felt chubby and fat compared to my friends.

I would promise to starve myself every night, but instead I would end up overeating. I remember in fifth grade while all my friends

just saw the carcasses hanging and everything. It was really disgusting. There was blood all over the place.

Maribeth: Our family used to go on vacations a lot. It's really shown me that I want to be a travel agent. I first got the idea when we went to the Grand Canyon, when I was in sixth grade. We went on this big tour when we were out there. I thought it was really neat how they could get it all organized. It also seemed really exciting. By the time I went on a cruise with a school group who also want to be travel agents, I was sure what I wanted to be. We got to critique other boats, their cabins, dining halls, their daily routines. It was really fun.

Kelly: A lot of times I'm influenced by an idea that I have found and set up for myself. It consists of my beliefs in my religion—by following the perfect example, which could

were swimming during the week of camp, I just watched—all alone. I was ashamed of my body.

I always saw my body because I took dancing lessons, and I would watch myself in the mirror. For a while, dancing was my top priority. I just loved it so much. But then, I thought to myself, "If I ever wanna become a dancer, I'm gonna have to lose some weight."

One day after eating M&M's, I remembered how my first-aid class teacher told us to stick your finger down your throat to vomit if you are choking on food. So I decided to try it. I was so happy! I saw all the terrible, mean, fattening M&M's out of my body in the toilet.

My dieting became easier. I soon got tired of throwing up. I soon decided not to eat at all. My weight got lower. I would weigh myself every day about three times at least. I was thrilled because my

BILLY BOY, THERE ARE THREE THINGS IN LIFE THAT YOU'RE SURE TO COME ACROSS — DEATH, TAXES, AND OLD FARTS TRYING TO TELL YOU WHAT YOU'RE GOING TO ENCOUNTER IN LIFE

SORT OF SCARY AIN'T IT

birthday was coming soon and I would be able to fit into children's clothes, which are cheaper than teen sizes.

Unfortunately, my father wanted to take me out to dinner. What would I do? I couldn't eat. I would gain weight. Then I read about taking laxatives to flush the food down. "Wow!" I thought. This is too good to be true.

That night I ate a little dinner with my dad. Immediately afterwards, I took about ten laxatives. "What are those?" asked my father. "Just vitamins," I said.

Well, my parents did find out that I was dieting too much. My mother searched my room and found laxatives, old moldy lunches, and cups that I would use to throw up in.

This horrible ordeal has definitely taken over my life. In school, I would worry about my weight or food. If I ate one cookie from a class party, I would have to cut class, walk to the store, and steal laxatives to get rid of "the dirty food."

My parents have aged at least 20 years because of me. They have also lost trust in me because I've had to lie continuously. My sisters now hate me. They think all I want is attention. They think it would be easy for me to stop.

I had to quit dancing because I was too emaciated. I flunked geometry. I lost many friends.

Now, every day I promise that I will "be good," but I keep "messing up." I try to scare myself by telling myself about the hydrochloric acid which burns my esophagus and rots my teeth and gums when I vomit. I try to scare myself by remembering that my intestines may explode, but for some reason I keep slowly killing myself.

Once, I was so disgusted with myself that I ran away and almost killed myself.

How could I have done that? I

be Christ. I always find the right thing to do and the right way to act through the Bible. When my mother doesn't have the answer about how to react to a certain situation, or if someone doesn't understand what I'm saying, I can find a lot of comfort and guidance from the Bible. It probably influences me more than any one person does.

Karen: Another influence is probably my grandfather. He's Mr. Prejudice of the world. He hates everybody. Any ethnic group you can name, he hates. He's got a nickname for every one. And I guess that's rubbed off because I don't really like any ethnic groups either. That's really terrible.

Parents

Karen: My father always wants me to study. He limits my phone calls to five minutes. He's really strict. I don't know if it's an influence or if it's a persuasion.

Melanie: I think it would be an

am a pompon girl. I'm a talented dancer. I love to write and sing. I love life sometimes, but I hate food. I wish I didn't have to eat. Why couldn't God think of another way for humans to get energy?

16-year-old female
California

In my junior year I made the decision to be a teacher, and the best way for me to learn about teachers was to observe them.

There are two teachers at Memorial High School who are excellent role models for me to follow. There are other superior examples walking around the halls too, but one of my math teachers and a club sponsor are the best examples for me to follow. They make extra time to help me and are patient, kind, and loving. Both are constantly smiling.

They are more than teachers to me; they are my friends. We have done many things together outside of school. They often look past my faults and bring out the good in me. They give me confidence in myself.

The friendship between us is mutual. When I'm down, they cheer me up. When their spirits need lifting, I try to make them happy. To often receive a kiss or hug from them is not unusual. The things I have learned from them are of irreplaceable value to me.

Deidre Rink, 17
Elkhart, Indiana

My role model is probably Dan Gable, the Iowa Hawkeyes wrestling coach.... His ability to win, no matter what the odds are against him ... gives me inspiration when I know I'm going up against a tough competitor.

Although he is my idol, I don't necessarily follow him in everything he does because he might also have his bad traits.... I try not to be my idol, only to some day be as good.

David T. Lassiter, 16
Charleston, South Carolina

My role model is Bill Dance, who is a sports fisherman. I imitate the characteristics of Bill Dance by talking like him sometimes. I also try to act like him when I go fishing. I try to use the same equipment he uses, such as Diawa rods and reels, Stren fishing line, and other equipment.

I try to do a lot of fishing where I live, but I have to wait until it gets warmer and the shrimp come in because I live near the ocean. I like to go fresh water fishing like Bill Dance does because it is fun to catch fresh water fish. I hope one day to meet Bill Dance in person because I think he is a good fisherman and a good idol for someone to have.

Johnny Evans, 16
Charleston, South Carolina

Since I am a Christian, Jesus is my role model. I know that I will never be able to be like him because he

influence. My parents are the same way. They don't limit my phone calls or anything like that, but it's real important to them for me to do well in school.

Diane: Well, they give advice to you, and that's what influences you. They don't force you to do things.

Kelly: I think what parents usually do for school is make me stay home and do my homework, or they make sure I have the time to study. They encourage me to do well, or they punish me if I do bad because those are their values. They hope I'll take on those values and pretty soon study for myself because I want good grades.

Diane: I look to my parents for advice. Because my dad is very successful, I would look to my dad to find how he became successful. So I suppose my dad's attitudes in business influence me. But my mom, she never finished high school. My mom and I are very good friends, but we're opposites. I'm very academically-oriented, but my mother never was. But just in general things in life, how you handle situations, I look to my mother. She's got a lot of common sense.

is so perfect, but I try to live up to what he asks me to. For example, not being selfish, being kind to others, loving others, being patient, being joyful, having self-control, and, most important, praying.

Cheryl Croft, 16
Richmond, Vermont

John Lennon has always been my model. He was always writing songs about love, relationships, happiness, and peace. On his last album, "Double Fantasy," there was a song called "Love." The way it was written, I could see that he was a great man. He knew what love was.

Bill Roberson, 18
Oak Park, Illinois

My role model is Art Schlichter, professional quarterback. He advocates no drinking or smoking, which I believe in. It is hard to find professional athletes nowadays who do not drink or do drugs.

I like to idolize sport figures, but there aren't too many like Art Schlichter. He is very personable and polite. I have met and talked with him several times, and I believe he is a great role model for young people.

Tim Agerter, 18
Munster, Indiana

I particularly wish I could . . . have a football game or two with and be good friends with Burt Reynolds, one of the finest actors I have ever seen perform. I like to imitate him by chewing gum, doing crazy things, and making some . . . dirty gestures. He's someone awesome I really want to be like.

Bryan Deyette, 17
Jericho, Vermont

My role model is Jesus Christ. I'm Reorganized of the Latter Day Saints, and we're commanded to be perfect like God so I try.

Zach Zuber, 17
Independence, Missouri

My dad's Mr. Nice Guy. He would just tell me, "Well, let everything slide by, never get mad at anybody." So I can't say he influences me like that. Right now I look to my dad as a successful person. I look to see what he did.

Kelly: I want to live my life differently than my mom, but she pretty much saw what she wanted to do and did it. When she wanted a job, she went out and got one. When she decided she was done working, she stopped working. But I don't want to pattern my life after her other than her approach toward life. I'd like to be successful in both

My father encourages me to succeed. He stresses how valuable a good education is to survive in today's society. I imitate his ability to adapt to difficult situations. I learn to suppress my true feelings like he does.

Karin M. Heinz, 19
Pekin, Illinois

One person who I would like to grow up to be like is Gloria Steinem. She has already done so much for the women's movement, I think it's great. She gives so much of herself just because she cares about others. She believes in equality.

Another person is my grandfather. He is the most generous person I know, and he is also really caring. He always thinks of himself last. Most people complain about their illnesses but not him. Last fall he almost went blind but didn't tell anybody because he didn't want anyone to worry.

Laurel MacLaren, 15
Des Peres, Missouri

G. Gordon Liddy is an idol of mine. . . . I do not admire the fact that he is an ex-convict. I do admire his will. He did not tell on anyone. I believe if he says he is going to do something, he will do it. I try to follow his mind control. Pain is something G. Gordon Liddy seems immune to.

Jonathan Nii, 18
Arlington Heights, Illinois

All my "idols" have common characteristics. Each is famous, creative, and modern. Most are involved with pop-electronic music or are associated with it. An example is Andy Warhol.

Warhol lives for the gimmick in speech, attitude, and dress. He creates for the sake of attention and trendiness. I try to emulate him by dressing and acting apart from the student body, drawing criticism from most and admiration from a few.

Unlike Warhol, my personal life

is not artificial or contrived. I act in two modes, one for the outside world and one for my close friends. My friends are few and are the same in many ways. We try to alienate others or shock them. . . . We are elitists. Within our clique, there is an open, honest atmosphere, and we don't try to impress or alienate each other.

The rest of the school see me and my friends as "weird" or as "fags," but that is precisely the reaction we're striving for. Andy Warhol alienates many except for a cult-type following, but he associates only with his equals, not his admirers. I am egotistical and prejudiced against conformity. I enjoy cynicism and isolation.

Jeff Stafford, 15
St. Charles, Illinois

My role model is Robert E. Lee because Lee was a brilliant soldier. He really helped the U.S. defeat Mexico in the Mexican War. He also had a high degree of loyalty. True, he did fight for the confederacy, but it took a lot of soul-searching to abandon the Union for the Confederate States of America.

When he fought for the U.S., he was fiercely loyal. He demonstrated this in Mexico, against renegade Indians, and at Harpers Ferry. Lee also believed in personal honor. I don't imitate Lee to any great extent, but I, too, am fiercely loyal to friends and the U.S. I also believe in personal honor.

Len Miller, 17
Munster, Indiana

My role model is me. The kids at school call me "Conan," and everybody's afraid of me. I can walk down crowded halls, and everybody gets out of my way. My friends are the Bar-Bearians. We all live in the weight room. It takes long hard workouts to become as great as I am, but it's worth it.

Mike Dobrowski, 16
Morrison, Colorado

family and business, which my mom went back and forth with for a while.

I don't think you can live in a house with someone for 17 years and not have some of their values. My mother thinks I'm extremely off the wall, which means she doesn't see a lot of teenagers. She thinks I have totally radical opinions, but she doesn't realize they are just like hers. The only problem is I refuse to be subservient to her. Blind obedience is nothing I'm familiar with. Because I disagree with her sometimes, she thinks that I don't believe in the same things she does. But actually I do. I say she doesn't know me well enough, but she thinks she does.

Steve: If you did for some reason have values that were different from your parents', how would your parents deal with it?

Kelly: My mother would assume that I'm wrong. She has the opinion that because of her being 20 years older than me she knows more—and she does know more. But she doesn't believe I'm an individual yet. When I go to college, I'll be an individual.

Steve: It's probably a very good thing that you weren't exposed to influences that are very far off and radical from your mother's because you might have developed very differently from her.

Kelly: I was very sheltered in that respect.

Steve: I think another important thing that we neglect is that although you see a great deal of your parents and they have a very big influence on you, they're not the sole influence. What you might see around the world and what happens to you—your environment—is an extremely big influence on what you become. The importance of parents is their taking what you've become and making the best of it.

My role model or "idol" would probably be Bill Murray or John Candy. Both of these actors portrayed characters that added comic relief to the movie "Stripes." The first time I saw this movie was after the death of my father so I was naturally depressed and upset. My brother and I found that the movie was very humorous. For the first time since my father's death I felt very relaxed. Ever since the movie, I try to see comedy as much as I can because I find it to be one of the open ways to let off steam. I think laughter is the key to life and that everyone should at least try to consider this opinion.

Stephanie Schlarman, 14
St. Louis, Missouri

My role model is the actress Jaclyn Smith. To me, she seems very much a lady in the full sense of the word. She also has style and grace. I follow her fashion sense.

Melody Burns, 18
Independence, Missouri

My idol, my hero even, is Pete Townshend, lead guitar and song writer for the Who. That's kind of strange considering he's old enough to be my father. I don't know why I love him, I just . . . relate to him. I really understand what he's trying to say. He doesn't write that mindless pop garbage. Everything he says and does has meaning.

"Love Reign O'er Me" is probably the greatest song ever written. The lyrics don't seem like much at first, but, if you really listen, it all becomes so clear. Whenever I'm depressed or happy or just nothing I can listen to the song and new meanings come to me.

Most of my friends don't understand his lyrics. I guess it's just a gift, or maybe a curse. Either way, I don't think I could live without that understanding.

Laura Beale, 17
Independence, Missouri

My role model and/or idol is the one, the only Eddie Haskell because he's mean and nasty. One trait of his that I imitate is his brown nosing. And why not, brown nosing is the American way. I want to grow up and be a cheating, annoying, mean, nasty, and brown nosing person.

Kurt Van Gilder, 17
Marion, Iowa

I maintain great respect for Robert F. Kennedy—for his independence, character, understanding, and political prowess. I feel that he was the single most appealing politician of recent years because he was able to maintain conservative pragmatism while not being afraid to feel for those less fortunate than himself.

Scott Martin, 17
Munster, Indiana

My role model is Elvis Presley. Even though he had a lot of problems, he was a kind, loving, caring person. He always tried his best to please people. When he took a fall, he always got back up.

I try to be a loving person. I try hard to be good at things and please people. Looking at him, I can understand that no one is perfect. We all make mistakes. I think he was a very down-to-earth guy, and I hope someday I touch someone's life as much as he has mine.

Robin Tompkins, 15
Morrison, Colorado

I like the way Richard Pryor can take all the sadness in his life and turn it around so it is funny. He is a very brave man.

Jim Choi, 16
Wheeling, Illinois

When I get with my friends, I want to be one of the "gang." I'm taught at home about God and the Bible. If someone makes a joke or teases me about it, instead of sticking up for what I believe, I laugh along with everyone else. That's not right.

If I truly believe what I'm taught, I

If you fit in well with your parents, your parents find it easy to accept you. A lot of parents never have to meet the challenge of dealing with a kid who has very different values and ideas from them. The truly great parent is someone who has to deal with that and deals with it successfully. That's tough, but it's going to happen. Kids are going to get involved with friends and situations around them that are going to change their values. Because their parents were not involved in the same situations and were not surrounded by the same environment, there is a conflict.

Diane: My sister had the situation you're describing. She had totally different values than my parents did. It was not a happy house when my sister was home. There was yelling and fighting all the time.

Steve: Possibly you were exposed to and got involved in an environment that made you a lot closer to your parents and created similar values. Therefore it's much easier for your parents to deal with you. Kids these days are getting more and more influx from different kinds of environments because things are speeding up. And because they have a lot more freedom to choose their own environment.

Leslie: My parents told me their rules, and they guided me. I followed their ways, but they let me do my own things too. They know that I'm not going to get in trouble. My parents know that some of my friends do drugs. They don't like it, but they have enough trust in me that I'm not going to do it.

Peers

Mary: I didn't used to idolize her, but I used to look up to my girlfriend a lot because she seemed like she was always happy, always knew how to deal with a situation.

Maribeth: I think I'm influenced

should stand up for it. And if I did stand up to the ones that tease me, it wouldn't be as bad as I think. . . . It's awful hard to take that first step and say what you believe.

Martha MacEwen, 15
Athol, Massachusetts

I have always wanted to be like the mysterious drifter back in the Old West. The guy who no one really knew, who would just kind of drift into a little town in the middle of nowhere and save it from some ruthless outlaws. He is just kind of a mysterious loner, not getting involved with anyone or depending on anyone.

It's the kind of guy that has that steady kind of look that other people can't return. People have heard of him, and he has a reputation for honesty and being a nice guy. But people know better than to cross him. He's good to his friends but ruthless to his enemies. People are in awe of him.

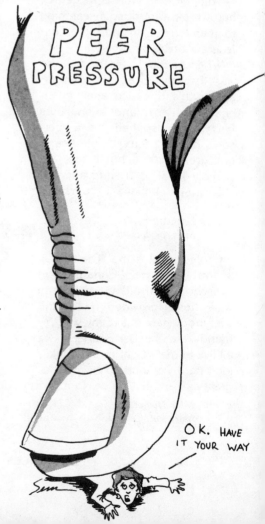

PEER PRESSURE

OK. HAVE IT YOUR WAY

I think it would be great to just drift around without any ties anywhere, just drift in and out of towns, no one really knowing who you are, to be the quiet stranger that everyone is curious about. All the women fall in love with him and the men respect him, but he can't be tied down to anyone.

I realize this is impossible . . . now because of the great size of by everyone I hang around with. I tend to pick up habits of people I hang around, for example, if they use a slang phrase. I think my friends and I have the same tastes. We always seem like we want to do the same things. They haven't changed me, but we always want to do pretty much the same thing anyway.

Matt: My friends have an influence the cities and towns. . . . However, it is still possible to copy some of the characteristics . . . to be a quiet mysterious stranger, with eyes that can send chills down a man's back, or to be soft and caring. In our time, this type of drifter has become the tall, dark stranger that everyone talks about.

Michael Wilson, 17
Falmouth, Maine

Influences   47

over what we do together. If one of them has an idea, I'll just tag along. As long as I'm not too tired or something, I usually go along with them. We're pretty much all the same people, but we do pick up each other's bad habits. We'll pick up a word, and we won't even realize it.

Since I've started hanging around them, I think I've lost a little bit of my class. The way we were brought up was different. Sometimes they act a little too raunchy around girls. I feel I have to watch what I say, but they don't care. Sometimes I've caught myself doing some of those same things too.

Jeff: One of my best friends is probably in the bottom 10 percent of the class. We hang around a lot, but it doesn't really seem to hurt my grades. He understands my situation, and I understand his.

Leslie: My sister was a cheerleader, and she was in the band. She got to be homecoming queen. She was Miss Rah-Rah to me. I was in junior high when she was here. I used to come to the games and go, "Oh, God, she's in the limelight. Look at her." When I'd be sitting around her and all the cheerleaders, I thought that they were really in. I was a little kid, and I thought, "I want to be one of those."

Diane: My sister and my brother were both not too good in school. I kind of felt pressure on myself when I came in freshman year. Was I going to be the only one to go to college? You want to do what your brothers and sisters did, or you want to do the opposite of what they did.

My sister worked as a checkout girl. She went down to San Antonio, and my parents had to bail her out. She hasn't been really on her own. She relies on my parents for everything. And I don't want to do that. I want to be self-

sufficient, and I want to—if my parents need it—be able to support them one day.

Now both my brother and my sister are working for my parents in our business, and they'll inherit the business. I'm the only one who's going to go into a separate field. I want to be self-sufficient.

My parents influenced me to be successful, but that might not have been so magnified if it hadn't been for my brother and sister failing at most of the things they've done.

Money

Karen: I'm influenced a lot by when I went to Montini. It's a Catholic school, and people there are pretty well off, I guess. When I went there, I wasn't really into anything materialistic. When I got out, it was like everything—you've got to be a member of the polo club you've got to have the latest. It was totally materialistic, and that influenced me. People started calling me a pompous snob.

Manish: I'm obsessed with the idea of money, and I think being in the United States influenced me to be like that. It's a capitalistic country. It's always been said, "It's a land of opportunity." You make what you want of it.

I don't know if any of you are familiar with India's social system. Any of you ever heard of the caste system? You have different levels, and actually only 20 or 30 years ago it was illegal to move from your stage to another level of the caste. It's legal now, but the mental anguish is still there. I recall when I was five or six years old, I—you know how you have janitors?—I accidentally touched one, and my grandmother made me take a shower after that because she thought I became impure. Here, it's fine. It doesn't matter what job you take as long as you make money, as long as you live for yourself. You're your own boss. I think that's the way it should be.

Kelly: A lot of people mention materialistic values, but I don't think I'm influenced by material things. I don't have them so they don't affect me.

Music

Mary: I think that some of the lyrics in a lot of the songs are evil or whatever, but nobody really notices them anyway. It's really no big deal. I don't think it does any harm.

Steve: I'm also influenced by music. I'm really into lyrics, and I write poems. I have a lot of friends who are in various groups and who are making first attempts at composing. I'm influenced by Pink Floyd and groups like that. They write a lot of good stuff. If you're prepared to analyze the lyrics, they're like the poets of the twentieth century.

Melanie: My music is a real influence on me. I enjoy it. I like performing cello, but it's no big deal. I perform in church or at concerts in school—little solos. I put a lot of my emotions and thoughts and feelings into my music. I relate it to what the composer was writing about or thinking at the time.

Film

Karen: I guess movies don't really influence me because I go to movies to get grossed out and scared, just to be entertained. As for TV, I don't think anything on TV influences me because I don't watch it.

Kelly: Not many of the entertaining TV shows influence me. A lot of times you'll see an educational program though. When I hear someone speak adamantly about nuclear war or different things like that, it reminds me of how I feel on the subject.

Self-determination

Jeff: I really have to influence myself the most. I'm not a believer in God or anything, and I have to keep myself going. I have to set goals for myself because my parents—though they want me to succeed and do well—are not going to be constantly on my back. I have to set my own standards, and that's what I try to do. As far as influences, physical ones and people, I can't say that I really have any. It's just my own goals that keep me going.

Manish: I don't try to look up to one person or one thing. I try to set my modes because I've basically found out that one person cannot be exactly perfect or cannot have all the qualities you expect him to have. So you take from different people. You know somebody's academic skills you'd like to have so you say, "Oh yeah, that's really good—I'd like to be good in science."

I personally don't think that one person has influenced my life at all. It's been various people and, being an Indian, I feel greatly moved by people such as Gandhi. It's not that I want to be great in politics, or in one area, but I want to be strong all around.

Kelly: I think a lot of times, like some other people have said, that I'm influenced by a variety of people. I try to become what I see in that person, or I try to find that in myself. More often than that, though, I can be influenced by what other people see in me. It doesn't mean if someone thinks I dress funny, I'll change that. It's not the surface things I'd change if people say so.

But if somebody sees me and thinks I'm a good worker, then that influences me to work that much harder. I care what people think about me in respect to how well I work or how well I get along with other people or if I can handle a situation. So those people influence how I behave. For example, I work in the drama department a lot, and there are obviously people in charge of it— the drama director, for one. If he looks at me and says something about how poorly I've been doing or how I have sloughed off on the job, then I don't want this person to think I'm lazy so I work harder.

Compiled by Cathy Zubek

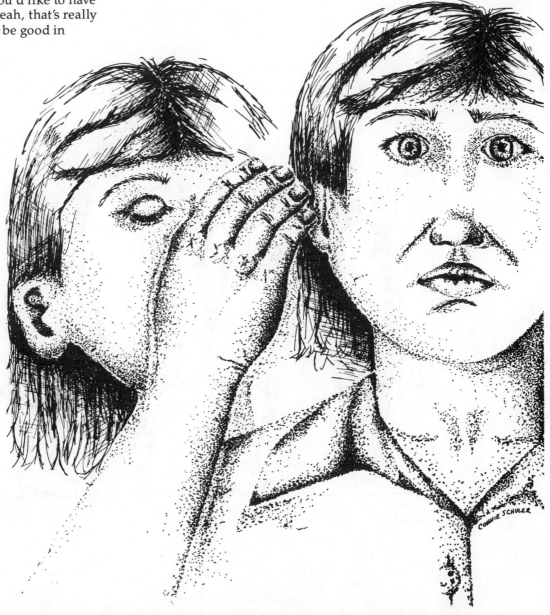

Chapter 4.

Family

A mother, a father, and two sisters—a family, or is it? Mom and Dad married young, and now they hate each other. Sister 1 and Sister 2 fight constantly. Of course, Mom and Dad are still married but not for long. Divorce. Now Sisters 1 and 2 live with Mom, and Dad visits on weekends. Complications: Dad's getting remarried so now Sister 1 and Sister 2 have Mom, Dad, Step-mom and Step-brother. Neat-o!

Whee! Off to Florida! Mom struggles to get a job in order to take care of Sisters 1 and 2. Wow! She finds a dog and a husband. Back to Illinois. Sisters 1 and 2 now have Mom, Dad, Step-mom, Step-dad, Step-brother, Step-sister, and a dog.

Dad transfers to California so Sisters 1 and 2 miss Dad's weekly visits while Mom misses the monthly child-support checks he's supposed to send. Well, at least Sisters 1 and 2 spend summers away from Step-dad and Step-sister. Oops! Step-dad got violent one too many times and now he's leaving. Mom divorced him too. That's okay because his kid made the house crowded anyhow.

Sister 1 is pretty smart—teacher's pet. Sister 2 can't handle the competition so she goes to live with Dad. Mom is heartbroken, and Sister 1 is sad too. The dog dies.

Lord have mercy, let's sort this out! Mom and Sister 1 now live in an apartment, the remnants of Family 1. Sister 2 now lives in California with Dad, Step-mom, Step-brother, and little Half-brother.

Mom hooks up with high school sweetheart. Now Sister 1 has a surrogate dad. Pretty neat, huh? Call him Dad 2. He's "real nice" and takes care of Mom and Sister 1. They like him.

Hurrah! Dad is back in Illinois with Family 2. Now Sister 1 can visit if she can get time off from work, and Sister 2 can visit if she can get some spare time from band, speech team, and other extracurricular activities.

Problem! Family 2 fights all the time, and Sister 1 hates the tension. Who should Sister 1 spend holidays with? Mom and Dad play tug-of-war over Sisters 1 and 2.

What a mess! The outlook appears bleak for the little twosome. No real family left—or is there? Mom and Sister 1 buy a condo—their own little home. Dad 2 moves in since he is so nice and always at the condo anyway. They like Dad 2. They even get a dog! They're on their way to being the all-American family. Though they aren't married, Mom and Dad 2 are Sister 1's parents—she likes that. She can't remember Mom and Dad 1 being together.

Sister 1 tries to explain Families 1 and 2 to Friend. It takes 15 minutes to explain who is related to whom through whom. Friend has Mom, Dad, one brother, and two sisters. They live in a big home on "Happy Street." During spring break they take vacations together to Florida. Friend returns with a tan while Sister 1 acquires a nervous rash. Sister 1 envies

51

Friend's model family. Sister 1 watches "Little House on the Prairie" and cries. Sister 1 wants a model family.

Time for college. No one wants to talk about it. A lot of money for Sister 1. Alas, Dad wants to be cheap. Never fear! Mom and Dad 2 will help. Sister 1 finally has a little family. Dad 2 takes care of her and Mom. They go camping together. Dad 2 promises college—no matter what! Dad 2 and Mom don't fight. They love each other and Sister 1, too.

Soon Sister 1 will be off on her own. Maybe she'll get married. Or will she?

When it comes to family, I feel I am an expert. Having 12 brothers and sisters, you get to know your family very well because of all the sharing and responsibilities you have for one another.

The best thing about a large family is there is never a dull moment. There is always something to do. Another thing is you tend to stick together.

It's incredible how close you can get when something happens to one member. When my brother Steve got cancer, I think that was the most trying for us. I was very young, and it was hard to understand. But everyone stuck together because you never knew if he was going to get better or worse.

Through the whole ordeal, I think our family became closer. His death was a relief, in a way. I didn't want him to die, yet the pain was more agony for him. What I learned the most after he died is that family is so important and there is no substitute.

Esther Hoffman, 18
Tucson, Arizona

At this time in my life I don't spend much time with my family. I'm not at home that much because my family isn't that important to me. I'm becoming independent of them. I'm not relying on them all the time.

Kendra Prodzinski, 16
Winona, Minnesota

I regard my family as people who care about me, and I know that

Discussions

Female: *My mother told me, "I'm not your friend. I guess I never will be." That was the last thing I needed, for her to say, "I'm not your friend"—the very, very last thing I needed.*

If I say, "Dad and Mom, this is how I think," then they'll say, "No, this is how we think." We don't really listen— well, we all listen, but we don't agree with each other about anything.

It's getting to the point where I only care so much. I want to have a good relationship, but it just won't work. After four or five years of trying so hard, both my mother and father gave up on me so I gave up on them. When I was younger, I couldn't even stay in the same room with my dad. My stomach would feel sick. I'd be ready to throw up. It's not that bad anymore.

They want me to want them so bad and to respect them. I want them to respect me for how I am, and they want me to respect them for the way they are. But I don't like the way they are, and they don't like the way I am. They wanted to help me so much. Every little thing that happened to me. They thought, "Oh my God, she's going crazy." If I cut one class, they said, "Oh my God, let's do something with this girl."

So after all the pressure about "that's wrong" and "that's wrong," they put me in a hospital for four months. I didn't think there was anything mentally wrong with me. I knew I was having a hard time, and I didn't really like myself very much. My parents tried. I was kind of mad at them. I don't know what

they love me. Two and a half years ago my parents got a divorce, and just this past February the divorce became final.

I am the youngest of six kids. At the time of the divorce there was just my brother "Hank" and I home. Everyone else is married or out of the house. Now "Hank" is at college. I am home with my dad.

When it first happened, I was very scared and very alone. I guess I was scared that my dad might leave me too, but deep down I knew he wouldn't.

During the separation my brother "Hank" and I became very close. I can remember going into his room and talking to him. He always made me feel better. For "Hank" and I, that was a miracle because we always fight.

I also grew very close to my dad. I guess I consider my dad as my best friend now. I tell him everything (just about).

The rest of my brothers (one) and sisters (three) wrote me letters or called me on the phone. Maybe they don't know how much they helped me. My oldest sister lives about three blocks away from me. She would always let me come over and stay there. I could talk to her, too.

Another sister lives in England. She would call or write and cheer me up. A third sister lives in Oklahoma. She let me spend the first summer my parents split up with her. That helped me talk a lot. . . .

I think my mom and I grew farther apart ... but it's getting better. I can talk to her more about how I feel about the divorce....

Now as I look back on the divorce, I can see how much respect I have for my family.... I know now that I really love my family, and they really love me.

Brenda Fonda, 16
Syracuse, New York

My parents are divorced. They have been since I was six years old. My father remarried.

I grew up with a single, liberated mother who placed an importance on work and comfortable living. Although she tried to show us a lot of attention, she was unsuccessful at making me feel loved. As a result, I grew up somewhat like her: outgoing, optimistic, but emotionally naive.

My mother was also the risk-taking type. After losing a gamble, her own business, she had a breakdown and gave up on life. I finally realized it was impossible to be happy with a mentally-lost mother so my younger brother and I fled to the protection of my father and his wife.

He has provided for his family very well, but there's still a feeling

they ever did wrong, but they just didn't do anything right. They cared about me so much, but it didn't work.

My dad is always demanding things from me—things that I can't possibly give. Even when we were really young, my mom acted like we were older and expected so much from us. They were always concentrating on the negative stuff.

If I ever have kids, I won't spoil them, but I'll make sure they know they are okay, no matter what they do. If they do something wrong, I'm going to tell them it's wrong. But I'm not going to keep throwing it in their faces. I think my upbringing has hurt me. My parents never really made me feel good about myself. So I always felt like shit all the time. It's their fault.

Male: *I don't know if love exists in my family or not, to tell the truth. I've never had those father-son experiences. My dad has never done anything with me like, "Hey, son, let's go play ball." Parents literally saying "I love you" or physically showing love has never happened in my family. My relatives have said to me, "Of course—they're your parents—they love you," but I have seen no sign of it. I assume that it's there. It's not that I feel any great emotion toward them. Maybe it's because they haven't shown a strong liking toward me.*

of division between us and our "step-family." My father is a good man, but he also has a problem showing his feelings. His love, in general, is a home and necessities. Even though there is tension between my father and his wife, they remain together "for the children's sake" and because of financial complications.

In his unhappiness, he stresses a better life for his children, as parents often do, by working hard and getting a good education. He always says, "If you don't try, you'll never get anything or achieve what you want in life."

18-year-old female
Washington

A lot of times my mother's boyfriend and I fought a lot when I lived with her because he was never happy about whatever I did. He yelled at me about any of my boyfriends coming over to the house. I love my mother very much. I just wish we could get along for once in life before it ends.

17-year-old female
Missouri

My family situation was drastically affected by the separation and later the divorce of my parents. My mother gained custody of my three sisters and me and has raised us for the past nine years by working shift hours at a textile plant.

Luckily for us, she never spared love and attention, and we have become a close-knit family as a result.... My grandparents are also very close to the family, and their guidance during troubled situations has made this family a more established, caring unit.

I have the utmost respect for my father, but I cannot feel the same love for him as for my mother. The material gifts he has presented me with have had little impact on my understanding of the relationship we have.

Scott Stanford, 17
Camden, South Carolina

Family

THE MODERN FAMILY

My mother and father got a divorce when I was in third grade, but I don't really remember it that well. People always ask me if I miss not living with my father ... but it really never seemed like I ever had a father so I really don't miss him.

People usually think that when people with kids get a divorce, the kids don't grow up the way that they should. I think that it's just the opposite because you start making decisions at an earlier age.

Paeton Bangart, 17
Bellevue, Washington

I have never been really happy.

I never received as much attention as my sister did when she was young. My parents always took her to Golden Gate Park or the zoo, but they never took me. I still haven't

My mother has not come out and said, "Hey I'm not your friend," but she has said, "I'm not your friend—I'm your mother. You are to respect me." Ever since I was two or three years old, I have been physically beaten to get that respect from me.

Anything I did wrong—crack, hit, smack. She used to throw shoes at me, knives even. This is not a weird story. I don't even know if it's child abuse or not. She used to literally beat me up. When I get her annoyed, she starts scolding, makes that angry face, and opens up her eyes wide. Every time she did that I'd start leaking in my pants. I swear to God I've done that. That woman can command.

When I got to be 11 or 12 and she'd make her eyes large at me, I used to stay there and stare right back into her eyes and enlarge my eyes. But now I get to

even been to Golden Gate Park, and I'm 16.

Every time I'm happy, something always comes around to ruin it. My parents are divorced now, and I live with my dad. I'm always alone, and I hate it. It's not that he neglects me. It's just that he works in San Francisco, and his girlfriend lives there also. . . . We have grown so far apart that he doesn't want to see me. What worries me is that it has affected my grades greatly.

Maybe I'm rebelling. I don't know. I know some day I'll be happy, but I don't think that day will be very soon.

16-year-old female
California

At this time in my life I regard my family as ... well, not as a family anymore. Perhaps I'm indifferent to the situation: my father moved out of the house and into his own apartment two months ago, and I don't think I really care. Last Sunday (I see him once a week when he picks me up to go to Mass) we took a long walk in a park. He told me his problems, and I responded like a psychiatric robot, not caring but doing my duty as his daughter.

My relationships with my mom and 12-year-old sister are equally impersonally agreeable since we rarely catch sight of each other at home. It's like each of us is so full of our own individual lives that other people only get in our way. Of course, we become one on occasional weekend trips to out-of-town shopping malls, but even those are spreading farther and farther apart.

The last time we were as close as a family should be was during a crisis—my sister's spine operation. The seriousness of it all shocked us, yet bound us tightly together in our daily visits to the hospital, where my sister lay in unimaginable pain. Looking back, I cried for three days straight.

But this is no sob story. I rather

enjoy my family situation and support the idea of independence for each one of us.

17-year-old female
California

My parents got a divorce about five years ago. It was real hard trying to live without my dad, but I guess I got used to it. I really hated my dad when they got divorced, but when I got older I understood why they did it.

I don't see my dad as much anymore, but he calls me every day and asks how I'm doing. Sometimes I wish he was still at home, but there is no way he would or could ever come home because he remarried. . . .

At first I thought their divorce was because of me and my two brothers, but I was wrong about that. My dad said that he loves us. He just stopped loving my mother.

My family is now adjusted without him. My mom even has a very great boyfriend, who she loves very much. He is the greatest thing that came into her life after the divorce. I hope someday that my mom will marry him because he respects her and cares a great deal for her.

Jill Jufko, 16
Baldwinsville, New York

My family is different from most because my dad is in the United States Navy. Having one of your parents in the military isn't always the easiest kind of family life. In the past 14 months, I've only seen my dad for two weeks. We move quite a bit because of my dad's job, but you get used to it.

Most people don't understand how our family manages to survive. Even though my dad is gone a lot, there is much love in our household. We're much closer than most families are.

My mother is a big influence on my brother and myself because she spends so much time with us. She tries to make up for the time

the point where if she starts scolding me, I say, "Come on, Mom, why don't you hit me now? Let me see you." I've come out and told her, "I'll break your arm if you hit me."

It's not that I don't like her, I like her—she's my mother. There's no doubt about that. But when she gets angry and the way she resorts to work things out, I think it's totally wrong. Nobody should hit anybody else.

Now when she does that to me, I'm like, "Come on, Mom, let's see you try something." Because I just want her to provoke me enough to hit her back. No, I'd stop her and maybe push her to the floor. I wouldn't hit her back.

Positive Experiences

Matt: Our family is very open. We can talk about nearly anything. I respect my parents very much. I get the same respect and love back from them. Isn't everybody like that? I guess not.

Diane: My relationship with my parents is ultra-perfect. Look, my parents leave me for two months, no problem, and I don't do anything wrong.

Melanie: Don't you get lonely?

Diane: Well, yeah. I start to mind it now. I am totally equal with my mother. We are more like friend and friend than mother and

my dad can't spend with us. . . . My family is a place of love, caring, sharing, and a lot of happiness.

Alicia Loren Clisso, 16
Blue Springs, Missouri

In some sense, having parents divorced is better than having them married. As I see it, I haven't lost anyone in my family. I have lost a lot of trouble and hard times, but with a divorce come new hard times. I guess you could call them better hard times.

I still get along well with my parents, have fun, and do everyday normal things. A divorce does make the holidays a little longer and more aggravating than normal, but nobody ever pays much attention. My families get along as if it never happened. I say families because it's like having two families, one on my mother's side and one on my father's side.

Tony Klick, 15
Blue Springs, Missouri

I believe that communication is the key to any meaningful relationship, especially in the family situation.

The one person in particular that I turn to for security, friendship, and love is my mother. She and I share our true feelings about all kinds of things. Through our

communication, we discover our strengths and weaknesses and learn how to deal with them.

Because of our family divorce, my mother and I have become very close. We can equally depend on each other for comfort, companionship, and a smile to warm our hearts. Through our communication the most important fact is that my mother is my friend. I can tell her things that I can tell no one else. . . .

Although the relationship between my mother and I is the strongest in the family as a whole, all the family members do try to communicate and share with each other.

I feel that because of my fortunate and unique experience with my family, I have become a very strong, openminded, and sensitive person. Communication has been the key to our family success, and it would be great if all families could come to understand and share this same quality.

Shari Rose, 18
Lincoln, Nebraska

Some people can be their own family. I have myself. I'm my own family. People like me have no choice.

When your mother drinks heavily and blames you for all that's ever happened, she's not loving or understanding. She's never sober, just always in a spaced-out daze. She doesn't talk. She babbles on and on about everything and anything.

So who's left to take care of my other younger brothers and sisters? Me. When my mom drank, my older brother got high. Our fathers were all different—all six of us. At the age of eight, I didn't play with dolls. I had real "baby" responsibility.

Then when your mother gets jealous because you do a better job than she does, she sends you to your father—a total stranger.

daughter. We work on an equal basis, and I do with my dad, too. I don't do things to shock my parents. I take responsibility for myself because they let me take that responsibility. I would never fear my parents because I have an equal say in everything we do.

Leslie: I have a very good relationship with my parents, both my mom and my dad. We can talk about anything. We get along well. I can go out with my dad and have a good time with him as I would with my friends. We go on a lot of trips together, and sometimes I prefer to go out with my parents, instead of my friends.

My mom's such a riot. She's a great lady. She's sometimes so spacey, but that just makes her fun. We have a good time when we go out. I mean, even now when we go shopping together, it's not like mother and daughter nagging at each other. I really like my mom as a person, as a friend. We'd be friends if I were her age or she were my age.

Steve: I really care for both my parents very much. I think they've been great parents. They're the kind of parents when I move out—they'll be great friends. I'm looking forward to the time when I can do something with my parents just as friends. I don't like my brother, but I'm confident since he's 16 that he will change.

A good family life is very important. I don't do a heck of a lot with my family. I suppose we're not as close as some families are, but we're pretty close. I can talk to them about most things. The fact that my mother and father are physically my mother and father isn't that important. It's what they are to me as people. That is that much more important. They're my friends, helpers, and advisers. That is very important.

Karen: Me and my mom have a pretty good relationship. It's

She says you're going to live with your "dad" (after ten years of not seeing, hearing, or any contact at all, I go live with him).

So his "family" takes me in. And things were just like a storybook. There was "Mommy," "Daddy," and "Baby." Then came the stranger—me. I was just supposed to blend right in.

Yeah, sure I did. I started playing "Mommy" again. I found out I have a brother who is 12 years younger than me, and soon enough he was my responsibility.

Finally, after two years, I couldn't take anymore so I ran. All the time when most kids were learning how to have fun, I played second mother to kids. I wanted to find out what being a kid was all about.

So the state thought, "Hey, we'll give her a break." So they put me in a foster home. A foster home is where people take in kids who need a family, and they think theirs is best. But they never mention the dollars involved.

A lot of foster parents do it not out of unselfish love but for the greed of money. Here I am 17 years old and not knowing what it's like being a kid. I guess it's too late to go back.

17-year-old female
New York

My brother . . . is the troublemaker. He makes my mom angry. He gets in trouble at school and around the house. Then my mom doesn't know what to do with him.

My mom has a hard time supporting us because my mom and dad are divorced. My dad lives with another lady. My mom hates her for taking my dad away from us, but she tries not to show her anger. She tries to keep us a family. . . .

When my sisters start arguing, I stop them before my mom says something. I try and talk to my brother and sisters. I love my mom so I try and help her. I know these are bad times, and my mom keeps working trying to help us live through these bad times. So am I.

13-year-old female
Arizona

I love my family very much, and I would never let anybody or anything come between us. My parents have raised six children after immigrating into the United States from Ireland, bringing very little with them. They have put five children through college, and I will be entering next year.

I can't remember my parents ever putting their own needs before us kids. We were always the most important people in their lives. My sisters and brother get along very well, and we always support each other in a time of need.

I respect my parents and the rest of my family very much, and I will never stop loving them.

Laura Burke, 18
Fairfax, Virginia

I see hypocrisy in my own family. My dad is the authority in our house, and he makes the rules. He does not always stay by the rules though.

I can remember times when I would get into trouble about something. I would say, "But dad has done that before." The re-

calmed down a lot since I've gotten out of high school. We used to have terrible, terrible arguments. Now we're more like friends. We go to movies and shopping. Since I'm older and plus my brother's gone, my parents are different now with only one kid.

Maribeth: Me and my mom also have a pretty good relationship. I think maybe it's gotten better since my dad's not around. When my dad was around, everyone was home. Now that it's just my mom and me home, there's no one else to talk to. We talk about everything, and sometimes we can share clothes and makeup. Sometimes I'm surprised at what I say to her—like "Yeah Mom. I went to a party, and they had three kegs." She just says, "I hope you didn't drink too much."

Jeff: We have a very open family. I guess we can say anything in our house that comes to mind, and there are no problems. They want to hear our opinions, and that's great. When we're together, we hear each other out. We won't cut each other off and be unfair.

Michelle: My parents are divorced. I live with my mom three weeks out of the month and a week out of the month with my dad who only lives two blocks away from us. My parents still get along really well. They're really close, you know, like good friends.

Mary: Oh, divorce scares me. I don't think I'd be able to handle getting a divorce. Even if I was the one who wanted it. It scares me how so many people can do it so freely.

Modern Parenting

Steve: I don't think a man is any less capable of raising a child than a woman.
Matt: I don't either, but I'd rather have a woman raise my child than a man.
Leslie: Do you think that you could raise a child?

sponse was always, "That is different. He is your father." I have always had trouble understanding why that made it all right for him not to follow the rules.

Selene Curtis, 16
McMinnville, Oregon

My father had to have his leg amputated. I know there are thousands of people in the world who had this horrible thing happen to them. If you are one of them, my sympathy is with you. After seeing what my father went through, I realize how strong he really is. Anyone in the world who has the same handicap is just as powerful.

Elizabeth Farrell, 17
Chicago, Illinois

Being the head of the house when you're still in senior high is a tough trail to follow, but I believe that my wife and I are handling it very well.

Though it's only been four months, those have been the most enjoyable months of my life. We communicate very well, and we are pretty open with each other.

As for our two-year-old daughter, she's the sunshine in both of our lives. We get a lot of enjoyment from her. We are a tight-bonded family with a lot of heart. That's what it's all about.

Chris Sidden, 17
Winston-Salem, North Carolina

I love my family although I feel I don't have much of one. The only time I'm home is to clean, check-in, and sleep. The rest of my time is spent at my best friend's house. Her house is more like my home.

Becky Rademacher, 15
Englewood, Colorado

My family means a lot to me. I have four older sisters that influence me a lot. They tell me how to act toward guys and how to treat them.

When I was in eighth grade, my parents got a divorce. My dad was driving my mom crazy. My sister and I were the only ones in our family that could be in the custody fight.

Both of us wanted to live with our mom, but my mom was unable to handle me. She said I was at a wild stage in my life and that she wasn't mentally capable to take care of both of us. My sister was almost 17, and she would be getting married soon. I was hurt deeply. Neither my sister nor I liked my dad, but I was stuck with him.

15-year-old female
Missouri

My family comes first in my life because I was adopted when I was seven years old and you don't find too many people that will adopt two boys, one deaf, that are older than a year old. . . .

They both went through a lot of trouble to get us and keep us because my natural parents were trying to get us back. Well, they got us, and they had a lot of problems with us stealing and lying because we never learned that it was wrong when we lived with our natural parents. . . . I'm very happy and lucky that I have parents who really care.

17-year-old male
Arizona

Matt: Yeah, I think I could. Maybe I'm a chauvinist, but it seems to me that a woman should do it.

Steve: Well, it's best if both do it equally.

Michelle: When I live with my dad, he never gets mad at me. He'll hold it all in, and then he'll blow up all at once. Like one time, my sisters were fighting in a restaurant. Because I'm the oldest, he hit me first. He hit me with a belt.

Karen: He hit you? Oh my God!

Michelle: There's nothing wrong with spanking your kids or something, but, like, I think if I got arrested or something, my parents would be too lenient on me. That's just how my dad is. I'll come home drunk, and I'll talk to him, and it's funny to sit there and tell him about it because he doesn't get mad. He'll just go on and watch TV or whatever he was doing. I don't even know my parents. I work every night, and it's like I sleep at home, and that's it. I don't even have time to eat there.

Leslie: What about your mom?

Michelle: I don't see my mom a lot

because I leave the house at 7:45 in the morning and don't get home until ten. Then I go to sleep. But my mom's totally religious. She goes to this church that plays rock 'n roll music, and she wants me to go with her. They brought me up Catholic. I still believe in God, but my dad wants me in one church and my mom's going to a different church. So, I can look at both of them and pick what I think is right. Like, I'll have one parent behind me, and the other one saying, "No, no, no. You gotta do this," or "You gotta do that."

Diane: More women are working. There's no one in the home. You find the kids alone all the time—watching TV and stuff like that.

Because more women are working, the kids aren't supervised as much. Then they just go off and do what their friends do.

Matt: I think that's a good reason right there. When I grew up, my mom was always home. She wouldn't let me watch "Ultraman" and "Johnny Socko" because it was violent.

Leslie: My mom went back to work when I was in first grade so I used to come home for lunch in grade school and eat by myself. I'd fix my own lunch and just take care of whatever I had to do. I think that made me a more independent person. It hurt me back then, when I'd come home from school and my mom wasn't there, but—

Matt: How come you didn't stay at school and eat with the rest of your friends?

Leslie: Because I lived so close. I only lived three blocks away. Sometimes I'd go to a friend's house for lunch, or to a friend's house after school to be there, and be with their mother too. Now that I look back on it, I missed not having my mom there. But I know that she did it because she had to do it for herself. She wanted to go

MY MOST IMPORTANT RELATIONSHIP IS WITH MY FAMILY BECAUSE I CAN ALWAYS COME BACK TO THEM WHEN MY BOYFRIEND DUMPS ME OR MY FRIENDS ARE SICK OF ME OR I DON'T HAVE ANYTHING BETTER TO DO

CATHY BARRY

back to work because she was bored. I can respect that now. Though it hurt me a little bit, in the long run I didn't mind it.

Matt: Well, I believe that one parent should work and one should stay home and raise the child. Maybe it doesn't matter whether it's man or woman, just so somebody stays home with the child.

Karen: My aunt and uncle just had a baby, and they hired a governess to take care of it. They have a man help, too. The man does stuff, gets food and all of that, and the governess just takes care of the baby.

Michelle: I think if you have a baby, it should be either you or your husband caring for it, not anyone

else. I have a friend—she's 19, and she's got a kid. She lives at home, but her sisters and her mother take care of the kid. That's not right at all.

Karen: What's wrong with that? If you have a child and you have a working life too, what's wrong?

Steve: All I know is that if I had a kid, I'd hate to miss any chance to be involved in the upbringing of it. That would be the whole thing to me. The actual conception is one thing, but having a kid is a great deal more than that.

Leslie: I want to have a career, get married, work some more, get my marriage stable, and then I want to stay home and have a kid. I want to hear my baby's first words, and I

When I was younger, I couldn't stand being away from my family. I always wanted at least one of my brothers, sisters, or parents with me wherever I was.

Now I constantly try to get away—get away from all the screaming, the fighting, and the noise. I feel lost now. My family used to be my sanctuary. Now I have no place to go, no one to turn to....

I enjoy being with my family sometimes, but the majority of the time, just when I'm starting to realize how much I love my family, I get yelled at and told to do something, or I get punched in the eye by a brother whose coat I'm sitting on....

I can't seem to communicate with my family anymore. My parents have a good strong marriage and love us all, or so they say. I have eight sweet bratty brothers and sisters, who can be sweet little angels one minute and snotty little devils the next....

I know that I love them, though I can hate them at the same time. Yet every day I feel myself floating farther and farther away from my family. I wish they would listen and try to understand—maybe it's just me.

13-year-old female
Arizona

I regard my family with very high respect. Though life can sometimes be uncomfortable with them, I don't think that I could be what I am today. There is a very high moral standard practiced in my home, a discipline that can always be counted on and a firm love that prevails. Even with this high discipline, I have a lot of freedom.

Now that I am to the age of 16, I make my own decisions. My mother has told me that she and dad have taught me what they think is right so now it's my turn to decide what is right. When I make a decision, it's for me that I make it, not for them.

There could be a lot of tension in my home because my dad is the maintenance superintendent for the Palo Verde Nuclear Generating Station. Needless to say, he's under a lot of pressure. Yet somehow we all seem to work together to make home happier. My mother has arthritis, which has left her in a wheelchair. She was once a performer.

The trials that my family have gone through as we've watched her become more crippled have drawn us together for the strength to live on. Yes, my family might seem too good to be true, but we have our faults. My sister and I fight sometimes. And pressures at school, home, and work can ruin a day for everyone, yet we all need each other. My family has the quality needed to survive at home—we love. We love enough to sacrifice for each other.

Gaylene Moyers, 16
Litchfield Park, Arizona

My family is very close. Well, they used to be very close. Many things have torn it apart. My mother, my uncle, and my aunt have all been divorced once and started new families. . . .

Well, when my mother and father got divorced, my mother was . . . cut down and accused of doing mean and awful things to my father. My father was accused of beating on my mother and leaving her for another woman. . . .

Well, three years later both my mother and father have been living with someone else. My father remarried. . . . My mother remarried soon after. Her husband has never been accepted by the family.

When I go to a family get-together, it seems we are all just there to make it look good. . . . It is an awful atmosphere to live in, and I want out.

16-year-old female
California

want to be the first person to see him walk. I want to be the one to experience it.

Steve: Well, at least for the first two years. After two, they could deal with it.

Leslie: But I want to be home with my kids. I want to be home at lunch for my kids. It might sound really stupid, but that thing sticks in my mind. I want a career too, but I'm just going to have to work that out with my husband when the time comes, obviously.

Matt: Maybe he'll stay home with the kid, and you'll go out and have a career.

Leslie: I don't know if I want that.

Steve: Why?

Matt: And you ask me why I want my wife home while I work?

Parental Restrictions

Maribeth: I've been told by my sister, "You're spoiled. You get this, but when I was your age I never got that."

Matt: My parents are a lot more lenient with me than they were with my brother and sister. I could stay out later. I got to use the car more. I don't know if they just got tired of fighting it.

Leslie: I know they're more lenient with me than with my older sisters because I don't have to sneak out to go to parties like I know my older sister did. When she did, she'd get in trouble and fight with my parents. They also have different values toward me for extracurricular activities and for school than with my two older sisters.

Michelle: I have a younger sister who's a freshman. When I was a freshman, my curfew was ten o'clock. A minute later, and that was it—I was grounded. Now she's got the same curfew I do, twelve-thirty to one. You look at somebody 14 years old—what are they going to be doing at one in the morning?

Karen: I can't even stay out that late.

Michelle: Sometimes she comes home later than I do on weekends. I can't see that. I always tell my mom, "I had ten, and she should have ten."

Matt: Most of the town closes up after midnight anyway. There's not much to do unless there's a big party.

Karen: Or unless you're out with your boyfriend. [Laughter]

Leslie: What are you going to do at twelve that you can't do at eight? That's my argument, saying that I won't do anything at one I couldn't have done at eight.

John: They'll say, "Do it at eight." [Laughter]

Matt: I think that if you're a girl, your parents are going to be more protective, especially if you're dating.

Karen: This is a direct quote from my dad: "Boys don't get pregnant."

Michelle: My mom's more worried about me getting VD than getting pregnant.

Karen: Boys can stay out later, and they can get the car later.

Matt: Because girls can get raped and attacked on the street.

Diane: My parents won't let me drive late at night because they're afraid the car might break down.

Matt: And girls can't handle their liquor. [Loud female uproar]

Steve: But it's like Leslie says. Chances are you can get raped at eleven o'clock just the same as you can get raped at one.

Karen: There are more weirdos out on the street at twelve.

Steve: Oh, have you taken a poll? [Laughter]

Karen: My parents regulate who I date. The guy can't sit in the driveway and honk the horn, or else I'm in for the rest of the night. With my dates, my mom has to meet the guy first. If he passes the mommy test, then it's okay. I'm sure that my mother would never meet a guy and then say, "You can't go out with this guy." My mom will say, "Karen, can't you pick some nice friends? Do you have to pick these snobs and stuck-up brats from Glenbard South?" Then I say, "Mom, there's nobody at East. They're all burnouts." I'll tell her that they're all in cliques. You know what I mean, don't you? She also doesn't like me to hang around with much younger or older kids.

My parents also say that I have to do my homework before I can go out on Fridays and Saturdays, or else they don't let me go out. They check my homework to make sure it's done, and no matter what time it is at night, I always hear the familiar "Do you have any homework?" It can be twelve at night, and they'll ask.

Steve: I think my parents have adjusted their standards to mine. I mean, I've violated a number of their standards, and their standards are now different. [Laughter] When I was a sophomore, and early during my junior year, I had a lot of conflicts

with my parents. But I have very few problems now, I guess because we've both compromised somewhat. I have it pretty easy since my parents are lenient. I think their standards have changed because I've pushed hard to develop a compromise.

I got a job when I was a sophomore, and everyone there was much, much older. They used to have parties, and my parents said it was all right to go, but they set curfews like twelve. We wouldn't even get out of work till ten-thirty, so twelve seemed kind of ridiculous. I'd just kind of blow it off totally. For example, I didn't come home until nine in the morning one time. [Laughter]

Michelle: I would get killed for that.

Steve: There was this one party, and it turned out there were a lot of jerks there. I didn't get along very well with the people there. I drove home, and some guys followed me. I parked the car—I had my mom's car. The next morning my mom tries to start the car, but it won't start. The guys who followed me had opened up the car and pulled out all the cables, the spark plugs and everything. It was just a mess.

My parents were pretty upset about that. So now I cannot take the car when I'm going to parties. I have to ride my motorcycle or walk or bum a ride. I used to get upset about that. I'd say, "This is just one incident. I happened to go to this one party, and the guys didn't like me." But I compromised. Now I'm quite happy to walk or to use my motorcycle whenever I can, or to get rides.

Honest Communication

Michelle: If you're at a party or something, a lot of people will come home drunk, throw up in the driveway, come in the back door, go upstairs, and go to sleep so their parents don't know. If I'm more

Family

honest with my parents, I don't get in trouble. I can remember a Saturday night when I came home drunk. I told my dad, and I didn't get in any trouble. He'll ask, "How much did you drink?" I'll have to lie a little bit there, like I won't say I drank twelve beers. I'll say I had three beers. But if you're more honest with them and you tell them the truth, they're going to respect you more and give you more privileges.

Leslie: Sophomore year is when I started to go to parties. My dad was like, "What do you do at parties? Do you sit around and listen to music or what?" I told him there was beer there, and at first he had a fit. But then he knew, when I started coming home and I was okay, that he could trust me. He said that I could have a beer just to fit in with everybody, just so I don't overdrink. Most of the time I don't, but occasionally everybody slips. [Laughter]

I like my mom to wait up for me. We sit up, and we always talk. When I get drunk and she knows it, she gives me a little lecture. It's not being yelled at or anything. She just sits down and talks to me, and she makes me feel guilty. I'll say, "Okay, Mom, okay. I know I did the wrong thing."

Compiled by Diana Slyfield

I love my whole family except daddy. I would do nothing to upset my mom. She doesn't know I party. She thinks I am an angel.

Daddy, on the other hand, is a "bastard." He thinks he knows everything. He calls me all kinds of names, and I just have no respect for him.

*18-year-old female
North Carolina*

Chapter 5.

School

The founders of the United States drew up a Constitution to preserve freedom and establish order. Students find themselves subject to another document: the Constitution of the High School Students of the United States of America.

> **Article I**   The school day shall begin at eight a.m. and continue until three p.m., during which time students shall, through education, expand their minds and explore new dimensions of the world around them.

This article, which establishes the school day, causes grievance among students. The primary problem is eight a.m. A normal 16-year-old brain does not even begin to function until ten. Thus, the first two hours of school are virtually wasted trying to educate students who are barely above a comatose state. By ten, students' stomachs begin to rumble because their rushed breakfast of a blueberry Pop-Tart and a glass of Tang wasn't enough. At two, students begin to anticipate the bell which signals their release. Their minds are occupied with after-school plans, leaving no room for concentration on classwork. Ideally, the school day would begin at eleven a.m. and end at two p.m., with a break from twelve to one for "All My Children."

> **Article II**   The school day shall consist of several classes, in which students will attend lectures, watch films, perform laboratory work, and participate in class discussions.

This article outlines the four basic methods teachers use to encourage learning. The lecture, although fascinating to the teacher, is usually more effective than Sleep-Ease for the students. During a lecture eyes slam shut, minds wander, pens doodle, and occasionally one or two students listen.

In addition to giving lectures, teachers love to show films. Though teachers smile when they announce the "treat," students view films as a chance to sleep.

Laboratory work is a favorite among students. While teachers call it "lab," students call it "fun." Where else but in a high school biology class can a student become head of a neurological team trying to resurrect a dead frog or an amateur chemist living out a Dr. Jeckyl/Mr. Hyde fantasy?

Class discussion, although intended to mean involvement for the students, usually means terror. It instills a great fear of being called on for an answer. The teacher maliciously scans the room for the next victim. To avoid being asked a question, students look at the floor, at each other, or intently at their books. Their attempts are not always successful, however, and every student has a tale of when he was called on for an answer—of course, one which he did not have.

Article III The students will be required to pursue outside study—commonly referred to as homework—as part of their duty to fulfill classroom responsibilities.

Homework—a duty that makes students grimace. Day after day, students stagger home with stacks of books carefully balanced in their arms. They use the books as paperweights and headrests until they hear Johnny Carson say goodnight to his last guest—then it's time for action.

Most homework is not done at home, as the name suggests, but at school. "At school," however, does not mean in study hall or in the class for which it was assigned. It means that students do their English homework in French class, their French homework in physics, their physics during lunch, and their history assignment while walking down the hall to math.

Article IV Students shall be allowed to communicate and socialize with fellow students, provided they do so on their own time.

Students believe that teachers intended this article to protect themselves from class disruptions by keeping their students quiet. In retaliation, students have developed a unique communications system: note writing. Students may seem to be furiously taking notes on a supposedly interesting lecture (see Article II), but if a teacher closely examines the contents of their notebooks, she will discover differently.

Passing notes is no easy task. Students must be able to look as though they are concentrating on the teacher when they don't have the foggiest idea what the teacher is talking about. Students must also have a good defense system, which includes a drill known as "teacher alert." When the teacher approaches a desk, the student must be able to inconspicuously place the note between other papers, inside books, or under the desk.

Above all, students must have a sense of adventure and a love for danger. They know their lives are in the hands of the teacher if they are caught. Students have seen their fellow classmates destroyed as the teacher reads a note aloud to the class. However embarrassed students may be at the recitation of their letter, they will no doubt continue their crusade to preserve a free communication system—in their next class.

Article V Students shall be encouraged to participate in extracurricular activities, provided that these activities do not interfere with their schoolwork.

Whether students choose to play football or to act in the school play, they sense that teachers and administrators place a strong emphasis on extracurricular activities. Students theorize that the creation of classes was to justify the creation of innumerable outside activities.

Students often are frustrated when teachers do not understand why they did not finish their homework. With track practice until six, band rehearsal from seven to nine, and a story due for the paper, something has to go. Homework is the logical choice. If the student misses track practice, he is taken out of the next track meet. If he skips band practice, his solo is given to someone else. And not writing his story means staying at school the next day until midnight. So he decides to risk losing ten points and receiving a lecture from the teacher for not doing his homework.

In students' minds, the choice of activities over schoolwork is a practical one. After all, a letterman's jacket or a cheerleader's skirt attracts more attention from the opposite sex than an A on a term paper. Nor does the satisfaction given by a good test grade equal that given by a fine performance on opening night.

If a straight-A average or a National Honor Society membership were given the same status as an all-conference basketball player or as a lead in a musical, perhaps students would choose to participate in curricular activities more often.

Article VI Students, while in school, shall engage in the fundamental practice of education: learning.

Students will no doubt testify that they do learn in high school, but not in the way referred to by teachers.

Retaining information for long periods of time is a task that students find difficult, if not impossible. A long period of time may be anything from a few minutes (a student cannot remember the homework assignment and must ask the teacher to repeat it), to a few days or weeks (a student remembers that $-b \pm \dfrac{\sqrt{b^2 - 4ac}}{2a}$ long enough to pass a test and then soon forgets it), to months or years (a student remembers the teacher who gave an undeserved D).

In high school students learn new ideas and concepts: chemical reactions, algebraic equations, and historic decisions. These subjects are expounded on as if they were vital for life. The subjects that are truly vital, however, are never tested in high school. By teachers, that is.

Students learn how to communicate and relate to each other in between classes rather than in nerve-wracking oral reports. Students learn responsibility from four years of juggling school, work, sports, and social life. Students learn respect from the memory of a fellow classmate's trip to the principal's office for "mouthing off" to the teacher. Students learn about relationships when they survive their first date. Students learn how to cope with life's problems, not from performing a lab experiment but from selling candy in class during a test.

Most of all, students learn that the Constitution of the High School Students of the United States of America includes the biggest benefit of a high school career: graduation.

The Student Bill of Rights

Although teachers drew up the Constitution for their pupils, students found certain inalienable rights that are not guaranteed in the original document. To protect these rights, students have developed the Student Bill of Rights.

Amendment I. Students shall have the right to escape cruel and unusual punishment, such as pop quizzes and oral reports.

Amendment II. Students shall have the right to sleep during study hall.

Amendment III. Students shall have the right to miss important tests or term paper deadlines by "becoming ill" unexpectedly (five times per semester) or by "attending funerals" of relatives (three times per semester).

Amendment IV. Students shall have the right to seek refuge in the nurse's office to avoid going to gym class when they have forgotten their gym suits.

Amendment V. Students shall have the right to intercept report cards in the mail, thus sparing their parents the risk of cardiac arrest and themselves the risk of losing car privileges.

Amendment VI. Students shall have the right to PDA (public display of affection) in the hallways providing they do not block doorways, stairs, or other passageways.

Amendment VII. Students shall have the right to refuse search and seizure by hall monitors and to refuse to carry "petty passes" when going to the washrooms.

Amendment VIII. Students shall have the right to edible and inexpensive food in the cafeteria.

Amendment IX. Students shall have the right to towels after showering in gym class; these towels must meet size specifications bigger than 3" x 5".

Amendment X. Students shall have the right to procrastinate daily, provided they do one thing on time—graduate.

Discussions

Jeff: This sounds strange, but I do like school. I take school very seriously. I take pride in my work. No one forces me to do it. I take pride in achieving. That's what every teacher's dream is—to have a student like me.

Maribeth: I like school—it's somewhere to go to. There are always people there. When you're home, it's like, "Is this fun?" In summer, when you get bored, people can't wait to go back to school. Just to see people—I like that. I enjoy being with people. I enjoy meeting them.

John: I like to sit around in school just watching people, the way they talk to each other and say different things. Or just the way people dress. I sit and watch them as they walk by in study hall. It's weird, but that's what I do.

Importance of School

Jeff: School is the basis for the rest of my life. Your grades in high school count a lot. I'm going to take high school seriously so I can get into a good college. And after college, maybe I can go out into the real world and get a good job, earn a lot of money, and have a happy life.

Steve: I don't find school pleasurable, but I am not a stupid hedonist. I don't believe in immediate pleasure. I go to school, and I will go to college because I know that in the long run, I will be much happier. It's a matter of paying the price.

Manish: I've noticed from my family members and friends and people I associate with that you have to be a professional—not necessarily a professional athlete, but any kind of professional. Maybe a lawyer, doctor, etc., in order to make money. And I feel from experience and seeing cases of this that the only way you can achieve that goal of being a professional is through education. I'm not saying that I enjoy school or I enjoy doing the homework or I appreciate the company of the teachers and their remarks toward my grades. But I'm saying that it's very important.

Diane: I like to come to school because I like to learn new things. School is kind of my highway to financial success.

Karen: My dad says if I don't get good grades at College of DuPage, then I'm not going to make it in any school. And I'm really worried about that so I'm trying really hard.

Michelle: If I got anything below a C, I was grounded and I couldn't have the car. But now school's for me because I realize that it's you—you have to do it. You have to learn something. You can't be stupid. And that's why I come—to learn. I can't believe I feel that way. I never did before. Some people influenced me—one person influenced me. They just got me to see how I was acting. To see that it was wrong to not care about school.

Motivation for Homework

Manish: I think the biggest thing that makes me do it is my parents— not that they force me, but they can twist my arm. Strong persuasion. That's what is basically doing it to me. I'm not doing it out of self-motivation—no.

Kelly: In junior high and beginning high school, it was always my mom's priority to make me do my homework. She was the one I got the grades for. It was because of her encouragement. She realized eventually that it would be my own priority. I realized it was important to me to get my homework done and to do well in class. So I think I have some motivation that way. Now it's my priority. She doesn't have to encourage me to do it.

Jeff: I do my homework completely

Many teenagers expect to get a job when they get out of school. We were brought up to believe that if you went all the way through school, you would be able to get a job. The society has gotten so bad that it's hard to get one whether you go all the way through school or not. This is discouraging to teenagers because they have nothing to look forward to except unemployment.

Marie Frasier, 16
Southfield, Michigan

When kids start going into junior high, school grades become more important than if you really learned something. . . . Teachers should stress the importance of learning more than the grade you get. Kids are afraid of getting poor grades so they will almost do anything to get an A or B. They don't realize that learning is the reason you are in school, not for grades.

Michael Maly, 15
Winona, Minnesota

I don't always stick by it, but I keep trying. I study hard, maybe stay up late, so that no matter what I do, I do my absolute best at it. . . . Sometimes I get bored or resent having to do all the work—and then sometimes I don't do the work or it doesn't turn out right.

Debbie Giattina, 15
Oak Park, Illinois

I don't know what to expect from our education because we are studying stupid things like poetry. For instance, today I asked the teacher how poetry was going to help us in life. She said there was no way it was going to help us. Instead of reading poetry in English, why don't we write compositions?

David Madden, 14
Lubbock, Texas

I have always viewed education as important. I believe it creates better people and a better society. Yet, as I've become older, I've become more questioning of the time I devote to the purpose of education. . . .

Who hasn't sat through a 50-minute period while a self-proclaimed prophet who is supposed to teach English tells one everything he's learned about life since age two. I have watched teachers totally foul up teaching and I accept this as part of any system.

The thing I find most perturbing is that generally the most incompetent teacher is the most content. The "denser" of my teachers tell me how much they enjoy teaching while the teachers that are very intelligent find it frustrating and a curse. There are, of course, the few teachers who are talented and do enjoy it. . . .

Laura Hill, 16
Iowa City, Iowa

I'd say most teenagers feel they don't need an education. They just want to sit around and do what they want. They're always too tired to get up for school because they stayed out late last night or stayed on the phone till ten-thirty. But if you really think about it, you need school because . . . you wouldn't have half as many friends as you have now.

Michelle St. Romain, 16
Metairie, Louisiana

I think teachers forget they're there for the student and not vice-versa. Teachers don't have the time to be personal anymore. They have too many students, too many classes, and aren't paid enough. The community no longer appreciates teachers as shown by Prop 2½ and similar actions throughout the country.

School regulations make it seem like the administration is paranoid, afraid the students are out to get them. I don't think this is the case. I think many students need to be motivated, but I don't think they're out to get the teachers. Education is important, but I

on self-motivation. My parents never ask me if I've done my homework. If you feel good enough about the work you're doing, you're going to want to get the good grade. You're going to have to do it on your own some day. Your parents aren't going to be twisting your arm when you're in college so you'd better start doing it now.

Leslie: Right now I'm lazy as a student. I don't study as much as I should; I don't do as well as I know I can—like, I don't study enough. I don't have good study habits. I know I studied last year more than I did this year. I think it's because I'm not motivated this year.

Steve: I don't get very good grades. I have a hard time finding the motivation when I get home to do my homework. Often I have a hard time concentrating, and I sort of drift off. However, there is some security in doing homework. Throughout high school, I used to blow off homework constantly. I didn't suffer that much because of it, but there was constantly this irritation. I spent half my entire high school career on the edge, never knowing if I'd put in enough to get what I wanted. I was always worrying that maybe it wouldn't work out or I'd slip up or I'd do something that was too serious to pull out of.

Melanie: I put so much emphasis on school and grades. I get uptight, and I get unhappy. I don't think that's right at all. I think a lot of it is because my parents are really concerned that I do well in school. Sometimes I don't think my parents realize when I've done well. I show them my report card and they say "Oh." I feel that I work so hard to

please them. I do my best. They were not meaning to be cruel because they're not, but that was the way I felt.

I want to be accepted. I ask myself why I'm working so hard for Mom and Dad, but I just want them to accept me. I want to be accepted so bad that I go overboard. I've taken that concern and blown it up to the point where I've got to get all my homework done.

Diane: I used to do everything for my parents. I was so unhappy freshman year, and I couldn't figure out why. My parents weren't putting any pressure on me, but I was trying to be perfect for my parents. I knew I couldn't be. As soon as I changed my way of thinking and I did my homework for me, I was a lot happier.

Kelly: First semester junior year, my grades dropped a lot. I was really upset with myself because I had been getting good grades and my parents were expecting it. I was like, "Oh no, I'm not going to be able to get into college and be able to go to med school." My mother was talking about, "How can you be a doctor with these grades?" So I had to decide for myself what my priorities were. There were always some classes I didn't try very hard in. But in others, because I needed to and wanted to, I did well.

Steve: It seems to me it's not necessary to put your absolute utmost into a class. You could, if you wanted to, spend unreasonably large amounts of time devoting yourself to school and denying yourself any social pleasures. Also, it's irritating if you decide when you enter a class that you're going to put so much effort into it, but you find yourself constantly blowing it off. You feel like you betrayed your earlier cause.

Diane: I knew that was going to happen my last semester in high school. So I just said to myself, "Diane, you're not going to work hard. Why get all worried about it?" I was to a certain degree, but I realized, "Hey, I haven't had much fun in my high school career. I got into the college I wanted. I waited until I was safe." Then I said, "Have a little fun. So what if your grades drop a little bit?"

Steve: I don't think grades always reflect the amount of knowledge you've gained from the class. You may not be getting the good grades because you're blowing off the bullshit homework. Granted, you won't learn as much, but I don't think it accurately reflects the amount of knowledge.

Diane: I think I learned just as much physics my first semester as my second semester. But the grades were very different. I just didn't do all the little stuff. That adds up after a while—all the homework. I got A's and B's on most of my tests, but I got D's and F's on most of my homework. So, I mean, the knowledge was there if I could still get an A or a B on my test. I must have the knowledge. I just didn't feel like doing the little stuff.

Steve: Teachers come up with things that are such an incredible waste of time. It's unbelievable. For example, the labs in science classes. I mean it's so self-evident. You know exactly what's going to happen, but they insist you spend three days doing it anyway. You get a situation where the teacher tells you exactly how to do the lab and what's going to happen when you do the lab. Then you do the lab, and the teacher tells you how you did the lab and what happened when you did the lab.

Diane: How many times would you do your lab and it didn't come out right so you have to say, "Oh, what did I do wrong?"

Steve: How many times do you say, "I don't care what I did wrong?"

Reaction to Teachers

Melanie: I think the worst part can

be the teachers. I can get a bad grade and learn a lot. I think of a science teacher in the seventh grade. I didn't do as well as I could, but I learned so much from him and he was one of my favorite teachers. It was the same with geometry as a freshman. I got the worst grade in geometry that I got all through high school, but I still appreciated that teacher the most because of the respect he had for me. But there are so many teachers throughout high school who are like, "If you don't get the A or the B that I know you can, you are worth nothing!" You respond, "Oh I must be worthless because I got a C plus in your class. I'm sorry."

Kelly: I think the worst thing about school is when it gets boring. A lot of that often has to do with the teacher or the course. Health is one of the most boring classes I've ever had. I was doing the same thing in biology and in chemistry and in medical science. When it's boring, you have no ambition. And when the teacher is boring, it's just as bad.

Melanie: I should reverse what I said before. One of the best things I've found is the teachers. The teachers can also make the best part of school.

Diane: They can be the worst.

Melanie: Both ways.

Diane: A teacher can totally destroy your ambition in a class.

Melanie: You can't let it, though. If that happens, that's your responsibility.

Jeff: That's not a teacher's job—to destroy.

Diane: I only met one teacher in all of my years of going to school that I could not stand. She could not stand me either, and she told me in front of the class. Not only did I not like the class, I did not try simply because she didn't care. She only cared about certain kids. I think one teacher can ruin one class for

think too many people have forgotten that.

Kevin Douville, 18
Auburndale, Massachusetts

Teachers take so much of their time to help people learn. My teachers have always taught me more than English and math. They have taught me responsibilities, loyalty, authority, creativity, and much more. At school this year, my child development teacher takes time to sponsor our Home Economics Related Occupations (HERO) Club along with taking us to hospitals to visit the sick and to zoos with our pre-school children.

My English teacher makes the class more interesting by participation in the writing assignments. When we have to write an essay, he writes one also and then reads it to us. We enjoy hearing views.

I respect teachers a great deal. This is the reason that I will be majoring in education in school. I feel that I owe a great deal to those in authority.

Laura Burke, 18
Fairfax, Virginia

I expect my education to be hard so I can learn. I don't want to be able to pass a class if I don't study. I want the school work to be challenging, to cause me to think. I want an education that will prepare me for college. When I take a class, I want to learn something. If I don't understand the material, I want to be able to go to a teacher and go through it without feeling intimidated.

Beth Wilson, 16
Kent, Washington

What I expect from my education is good grades and know enough so when I have children I want to be able to answer there problems and how to cope with it. I think that every person that go to school should be bless to have a education. Because your school diploma will help you get a more better job

---

and you will be able fill out your application knowing in you mind that you did finish school.

I know this for such that I a pround to have my education. Student that drop out of school sometime. They don't get very much respect all because they didn't finish school. Some in up being bums—drinker—and no telling what else. But I know this for sure that every body should be pround to learn something every day.

17-year-old female
Arkansas

Typical teenagers think being in school and learning is a drag. They mostly expect a school to force them to learn, graduate, and to be something when they get out. . . . I personally probably expect the same as any teenager—to graduate knowing how to earn 400 dollars a week without putting a lot into either school or a job.

Tersa Wightman, 16
Belmont, New York

It's 7:59 a.m., and I am running late as usual. I have exactly six minutes left before I must be obediently seated in homeroom to officially begin another school day. But during the next six minutes I must first sprint from my '75 Malibu station wagon (which allows me to drive it to school on the days when it has decided to be so kind as to start and continue running) through the parking lot, past the gym, around the corner, past the cafeteria, and up the stairs to finally arrive breathlessly (definitely not from anticipation) in front of my locker.

One of these days I really must introduce my lock to my car, for I am positive they would get along just grandly since they have so much in common. The lock also has a temperamental streak and must occasionally be severely beaten and loudly admonished (no doubt in the vernacular) for its unreasonable behavior.

you, but they can't ruin your whole education.

Kelly: Until I got to high school, I didn't know you were allowed to not like a teacher. I was such a puppy in class. I didn't know a teacher could be a bad person. I always respected the teachers and thought they were the best. I started to learn that maybe every teacher wasn't a wonderful person.

Manish: I look at it from a totally different viewpoint. I come from India. Every time the teacher walks in the door for the first time in the morning, everybody gets up at the same time and, in harmony, says, "Good morning teacher." I mean respect, like we have to go up there and kiss their feet. Every time we misbehave it's hands down, and rulers—bam, bam, bam—waste on those knuckles. It was like that. I am totally against hitting your kids or hitting others to teach them right from wrong.

Now that I come to America, I see that the teacher is no better than you are. Just because they're older and they are a teacher, you're supposed to respect them unduly. In India, they treat you like dirt. It's not like that here. The teacher has mutual respect for you, and they talk to you like a person. You don't have to be acting like they are almighty God.

Jeff: When I was a freshman, I was naive. I came in expecting to learn something and thinking that teachers were gods. What they said was law. Now that I've experienced a lot more teachers, I've realized many are BS artists, not gods. I use them for all they're worth. I use what little knowledge some of them have. It's not a very nice way to put it, but you could be good friends with a teacher and yet use them, too.

Melanie: I think it's important that teachers in a math class or history or whatever do not say, "Now these are the dates. Memorize them." You

get all of the trig or whatever, all these rules down, and then that's all there is to it. But I like it when the teacher gets you into it so it's more than memorization; it's experience. And through the experience, you pick up the rules and dates. I don't like it when the teacher is standing in front of you and says, "All right, we're going to study Chapter 3. Chapter 3 is this and this and this"—she just goes on and on.

Then the hour's up, and you're told the assignment and how to do it. And it's like there's no thinking on your own. A class is really interesting when I can add my opinions to it. I like it to be open—not just preaching. I like to express my own opinions and form my own thoughts—and to discuss them so the teacher can discuss back what's wrong or right with them.

Reaction to Administrators

Steve: What really irritates me is the red tape. There seem to be so many petty bureaucrats running around the high school that drive me crazy.

Jeff: Administrators.

Steve: Yeah, that and all the dumb rules and regulations and people's attitudes towards these rules and regulations just get on my nerves.

Kelly: They expect you to act and be like adults, but they treat you like kids. For example, not being able to talk or use materials other than library materials in the library. Not being able to sit and talk with friends even if you can keep it down. Not being able to go to the washroom without a pass.

Manish: Privileges of using the gym or other facilities without a supervisor. They kick you out otherwise.

Kelly: That's mostly for safety reasons. But I know some examples when we were not able to be in school without a supervisor. We had work to do for a play, and the teachers had a meeting. They wouldn't let us work because we didn't have someone standing over our shoulders.

Steve: Idiot things like this big confrontation about smoking across from the school irritate me. I don't smoke, but it's just a ridiculous thing. It's just so stupid. It makes absolutely no sense whatsoever. Just the general attitude.

Okay—admittedly the kids on that street are causing a problem for people who live there. That's not cool. But the administration should say, "Well, we've got a problem here. Let's deal with it." The way to deal with it was not to suspend anyone smoking there or in the general area, not to call the Lombard police and make them cruise every day and night to make sure it didn't happen. They don't have to go through all that bullshit.

Mary: *I'm a senior. I went to Glenbard East freshman year, and then I left for a couple of years. Now I'm back. I went to a school called the Mansion, a boarding school for people who didn't want to go to public school. I left this school sophomore year because I was so confused. My friends were all starting to get high. I never went to school so I failed the whole year. I saw the cheerleaders, and they didn't look like they were having such a good time. They seemed to be faking it. I couldn't handle all of the "you're a jock" or "you're a freak."*

I liked the Mansion a lot better. The people cared about you a lot more. There were only 30 people in the school—you knew everybody. Everybody was really caring and helpful. I have my friends at Glenbard East, but it's not the same kind of place. Everybody talks about people behind their backs and says things they don't like about them.

I made honor roll my senior year. I

Eventually the bell rings. I sigh and sit down, having once again eluded the detention hall that patiently awaits any slight error in timing. Within moments a voice booms down from the speakers, loudly enough to vibrate the entire class from their lethargic state of semi-consciousness.

In a decidedly poor attempt to make up for this cruel and unusual punishment, those sadistic voices carry such earth-shattering messages as "Choir practice is cancelled." As far as I'm concerned, the end of the announcements is enough reason to sing for joy.

Next comes physics, gym, and study hall. Paraphrased these are a study in the conservation of energy, followed by a practical course in which you can apply those principles in order to studiously avoid that disgusting function of the human body called sweating, followed by a class in which energy is conserved by not studying. Then comes lunch—in a "class" by itself (isolated for health reasons). . . .

The designer of the cafeteria obviously learned advanced decor from the ranking official at Sing-Sing. The room has the shape of a large rectangular cell block with strategically placed red brick ceiling supports. At the bases of these posts, and various other places around the room, are monitors whose job it is to appease any visiting VIPs by making everything look under control.

The walls are painted pale yellow, another technique used to dull the senses and pacify the students. Next is the food. Ay, there's the rub, for in that plate of food what nightmares may come when I have shuffled off to my next class must give me pause.

Speaking of my next class (computer math), it is truly an educational experience which teaches patience and perseverance. I sit in front of the terminal typing in

"goto" statements. (Just once I'd like to really tell it where to go!) Suddenly from the maze of complicated circuits comes a message that I'm functioning illegally. (It makes me wonder if Big Brother is such a far-out idea after all.)

After several more arguments which the computer always wins, I am saved by the bell and then "goto" math analysis. . . . Every day, much to my instructor's dismay, I fall asleep. Consequently, that's all I can say about that class.

Finally, my last class arrives, English. By then I'm only interested in the number of minutes left before I am free to do whatever I please until I begin another day in the life. . . .

It is now 1:42 a.m., and the beginning of my typical school day is fast approaching.
Chris Taber, 17
Bay Village, Ohio

I've lived overseas all my school life until ninth grade. . . . I expect the education system not to babysit me and fellow students as most schools do. Once I quit learning, I will have very little to live for. The schools do not prep the student for later life as they are expected to do.

J. Mark Kelly, 18
Longview, Texas

Well, I think most teenagers expect their education to be handed down to them on a silver platter. . . . When entering high school, teenagers are more interested in being a freshman and out of junior high than . . . school and school work. Then comes being a sophomore. Still our minds are on more important things like dating, friends, and everyday zits.

Then comes being a junior. Our minds are still wandering, not in school but in who to take to the prom, dances, and having one more year to go before graduation.

Then as a senior, it hits us and we start wondering, "What have I done to deserve all these years? I

was so happy. In fact, graduation was kind of sad. It didn't really hit me until later when I was walking out. Next year I'm going to College of DuPage. They have a recreation leadership program, and I think that's what I'm going to do.

Jeff: *School is really important. Right now, the most important thing to me is getting good grades. They give me a sense of pride. The pressure's always on me to keep my grades up. I get upset or guilty for a day if I don't get the grade I know I could have, but I'm learning to not get as upset as I used to.*

In junior high, I took regular English and got B's and C's. It was so easy that I didn't bother doing it. Last semester I got a B in business and a B in history— both were regular classes. The classes

were so stupid, repetitive, and boring that you didn't care what you got.

I like my honors classes better than my regular classes. At least the majority of people are on a pretty equal intellectual level. In regular classes you end up talking down to make people understand you. The honors classes are more work, but they are also more challenging. In honors classes it's always something new. You never know what you're going to learn.

I am pretty competitive, and I don't like to lose. I have a standard I try to

graduate in May, and I have no idea what I want in life. And I wish those colleges would stop sending me pamphlets and all that stuff. I have not even finished with high school yet, and they want me to start thinking about more schooling."

We say something like this: "I think I will go to the service and get away from all this education." Then they start sending you things. Then it is graduation day. . . . That day will be like the end of the world until you wake up in the morning, and it all hits you. "I have to get out on my own." You stop for only a second and then you scream out, "Mama!"
Bobby Duncan, 18
Lubbock, Texas

The emphasis is on careers, and skills are taught. Science and math seemed to be propagandized within most high schools to increase future technological advancement. Perhaps it is this emphasis on career success that seems to take away the excitement of knowledge. . . .

It seems as though many of the students take their education for granted. They view school as a job, an obligation, or just a responsibility. But finally there is a good percentage of a class which truly still finds the thrill of learning in their education.

Teachers and administrators for the most part are taken for granted. People like school board representatives and other low or unpaid officers run into many conflicts and few rewards when dealing with students. But good teachers are greatly appreciated. For the most part, students in our school recognize good educators and take advantage of them.

Tracy Kuask, 17
Iowa City, Iowa

I personally hold high priority in education, but I do not believe it is essential to the well-being of all individuals. College, for instance, should not be an experience a person should be expected to have. It should be a supplement for those who have high academic goals.

People should be able to find happiness without college if they so desire. I even believe that those who don't go to college could have low material values and therefore be happiest of all—they live up only to their own, and no one else's, expectations.

Carolyn McKnight, 16
Elmhurst, Illinois

During this day and age it seems many students expect a lot from their education.... A student wants to get a good education but doesn't want to work for it. That is, he wants good grades so he can go to the college of his choice but has very little desire to do anything about it.

Patrick W. Falk, 18
Atchison, Kansas

My teachers' methods vary. When I lived in Albuquerque, I had a science teacher who was very strict in his classroom. If at any time during an assignment he was to drop a straight pin on the floor and didn't hear it bounce, he would keep the whole class in after school for detention.

follow. There's one person I do try to edge out now and then. Even if I don't, I'm pretty happy as long as I edge out the other people. I also try to be "normal." My freshman and sophomore years I was kind of a freak. I was different. I tried so hard to be smart. Homework was first, last, and everything. This year I started blending in more–getting into sports for example. I don't stand out so much anymore.

Sometimes I'd like to be a zombie. I'd like to be stupid for a day. When people ask me something, I'd like to tell them that I don't know the answer. I'd really want to not know.

Karen: *I'm sort of a senior at Glenbard East, but I go to a community college. College has made me a little more serious about my work. When you're a senior you think, "Oh God. I can't wait to get out." You have senioritis. I avoided that by going away. It gave me a chance to start over. A lot of people "laze off" their senior year. I know I would have taken easy things like underwater basketweaving. Instead, I took hard classes that would help me later on in college.*

Leaving my high school friends behind didn't bother me at all because I figured I wouldn't see them anymore

Needless to say, I learned a lot more in his class than I did in a class where the science teacher would not care how much you talked or messed around or bugged others.

Kirk Lunday, 17
Littleton, Colorado

The majority of our students are involved in academics and at least one other activity. I think with this combination everyone will grow and learn to become better human beings. I sincerely believe we could not have a school with just academics....

I like the students talking. I believe we learn so much more from ideas and opinions.... Overall, I believe education in school is the starting place for all human beings to grow....

Tascha Passof, 18
Ukiah, California

Since students do not deal with administrators on a one-to-one basis, they seem rather foreign to us. Everything they do seems like a deliberate attempt to deprive us of our rights toward fun. If we knew them as people, like we do teachers, they wouldn't seem like "administrators." Everyone might understand their motives a little better as they might understand ours.

Lisa Salvia, 17
St. Clair Shores, Michigan

I think what teenagers expect from their education depends on their age. At age 13 in the seventh grade, I had no idea what I wanted to do in life, and I wasn't concerned about what courses I was taking. All I knew at that time was that I wanted easy ones. I had this attitude all through my junior high years.

But when I changed schools and realized that my new school was much harder and that the kids far excelled what I knew, I figured I better hurry up and find out what I wanted for my life. In trying to prepare for what I wanted, I really started looking into what subjects were offered. I found myself expecting more not only out of myself but also out of the courses I would be taking.

Now at age 17, preparing to graduate and continue my education, I find myself expecting the best teachers and the best training out of whatever college I choose.

Melissa Armstrong, 17
Kent, Washington

Education as Mr. Webster defines it: the things a person learns by being taught. That is an accurate definition, but we as students have our own definition: The things a person wants to learn by being taught.

As a student, I should know. Most of the kids I know only want to learn about some of the things teachers have to teach. The subjects they are not interested in they ... just block out. ... When they do that, their grades start to drop. Then they start disliking their teachers because of their poor grades. Hence, they stop learning.

When students take an interest in a subject, they study it. They try to get more information on the subject, and then they remember it. Their grades are good, and they like their teachers. Hence, they learn.

Audrey Clifton, 15
Jackson, Missouri

Education should be thought of as

anyway. The friendships I made since I left Glenbard East have been so much more lasting and meaningful than anything I experienced in high school. I really didn't care what my friends thought. That sounds cold, but I didn't look on high school as that big of a deal. The cheerleaders and the jocks look at high school as the best years of their lives. I didn't like high school at all so I was really anxious to leave it behind me.

I think my attitudes have really changed. I used to hate school. Maybe it's just the age difference, but everyone is more mature and serious in college. Nobody wants to get bad grades anymore. In high school, I didn't care. It was almost funny to have a negative grade point average. Maybe I got older and wiser. Maybe I just got sick of bad grades.

Philosophical Viewpoint
Steve: All these things are coming in and you can share new information and knowledge. That's good because it keeps life interesting. Whether you can get good grades or not, just being around school you're constantly running into new ideas and the opportunity to discuss these ideas with your peers—and that's good. Even when I get out of college, I want to get into something, unlike my restaurant job, where there is going to be constant change and new and interesting things happening so the conversation doesn't become stale.

Compiled by Diana Slyfield

a way to enrich one's mind, to develop oneself as a person and to open one's mind to the people in the world around him. Today the emphasis in school is on grades, not on learning.

There are very few teachers left that work to really teach so that students learn and, more importantly, remember and know how to apply what they learn. More than half of the teachers are too lenient—it's too easy to get good grades today. . . .

However, not all of this is the fault of the teacher. Students today, for the most part, do not value knowledge the way they should, and with all the other activities that exist today (sports, clubs, jobs), there is less and less time left to really study. A person can do enough work to get good grades, but not enough time is spent for him to really learn anything.

In short, if education continues in the direction it is headed, getting more and more lenient and putting less and less emphasis on knowledge, our country will be in serious danger of falling behind the other countries of the world technologically, militarily, and . . . intellectually.

Nancy Spurling, 18
Gresham, Oregon

I don't believe teenagers really start thinking about how their education will help them until they reach tenth or even eleventh grade. A lot

of people, when choosing their courses, only consider, "Will I have too much homework?"

I don't think the importance of your education really hits you until you're close to graduating. Then you start thinking about, "Will I have enough of an education to really get a good job?"

Melissa Row, 16
Fort Smith, Arkansas

School to me isn't fun at all. "It's a drag." No wonder so many kids drop out of school. There should be a law against boring a teenager to death. People practically pray for school to be over.

Rich Prezkop, 16
Bellaire, Ohio

Chapter 6.

Work

To Warren K. Stiff, the opportunity to land a job was the chance of a lifetime. Lured by the prospect of money and independence, he made the big step. As a result, a new lifestyle has emerged for Warren. The minute he steps off the school bus, the footrace begins. Once he arrives at his house, he makes a mad dash upstairs to change into his "Quicki Burger" uniform. While biting into an apple, he heads out the door. Once finished with the apple, he realizes that he has cast aside the only decent grub he'll eat all night. Perhaps he can find time to gulp down some food later at the "Quicki Burger," but he might spend half his earnings if he does.

Finally, Warren arrives at work. As he hastily affixes the "Quicki Burger" sanitary cap to his head with his left hand, he simultaneously punches into the time clock with his right. When he reaches his cash register, Warren is instantly thrown into the rush hour. "May I help you?" are the first words he says. Upon completing the order, he also dares to say, "Have a nice day."

"Hold the pickles, hold the lettuce!"—more words that bring mechanical reactions in his effort to respond to customer demands. For Warren to be understanding about every whim of a customer can, to say the least, be difficult. But being understanding and doing his job are different because he knows customers are about as compromising as a herd of raging bulls.

Now, feeling the cold stare of eyes falling upon him, a quick glance reveals the boss evaluating Warren's job performance. Wondering what he could possibly be doing wrong, Warren checks his name tag to see if it is pinned crookedly to his uniform. More importantly, though, he wonders whether he'll be forced to work on the clean-up crew tonight. When he first applied for the job, his boss said he would work to nine-thirty at the latest, but he soon found out that was rarely the case. Now, working to midnight on a weeknight is common for Warren.

Suddenly he focuses his attention on the restaurant entrance. Lettermen from his school enter. He thinks back to all the great times he had in school athletics. But he had been forced to make a difficult choice. With financial needs pressing, he knew that a job took priority.

Snapping back to reality, Warren fills another order. Time seems to drag tonight. He has a tendency to glance at his watch every ten seconds. Though he thought it would never come, Warren is finally granted a 15-minute break.

Tonight the break has an extra bonus—it's pay day. As he looks down at his paycheck, he can literally see it shrinking when he starts counting his expenses. At first, he thought there would be all the money in the world to spend, but his parents saw otherwise. Before, all his expenses were paid by them. Now, he's expected to be "financially responsible." Clothes, food, and school fees are not expensive, but when added together they are a financial burden. After paying for basic necessities, Warren can forget about depositing money in his savings account. As he remembers, college was the primary reason for getting the job, but somehow he became sidetracked. With all his assets and liabilities sorted, he estimates spending money for the week to be $4.25. Despite all the expenses, Warren has saved a large sum of money over the years. However, because of the time demands of the job, he is unable to find a good college that will accept him because his grades are low.

Tired and dejected, he returns from his break. An unexpected rush developed, which means he'll have to stay for clean-up crew. As the night slowly withers away, much like the french fries he's sweeping up, he notices there's only one hour left in the shift. He despises the last hour, always the hardest.

T minus 10, 9, 8, 7 . . . Not being able to stand it anymore, Warren runs over to the time clock. For him, punching out is the highlight of the day. On his way home he can't quite match the cadence he once had earlier in the day. The only thing on his mind is sleep. But wait, there are still five more chapters of *To Kill a Mockingbird*. Even when doing his homework, he can't escape his boss. A character named Boo Radley reminds him of his boss—both lurk in the corners.

Now, collapsed on his bed, he tries desperately to get up to take a shower. As usual, though, he falls asleep to the odor of rancid french fries.

To Warren K. Stiff, the illusions of money and independence turned out to be hard work and no sleep. No complaining, though. Unemployment has returned the nation to the "sweat shop" era; even minimum wage and job availability are threatened. If Warren doesn't take the job, someone else will.

I think it's great to work. In my case I have to. My mother and father are divorced, and I have to help my mom any way I can. So my brother and I got jobs. He works four nights a week at Woolworths, and I work for the city of Centralia as a sports director.

We both make good money, and we never have to ask for money. Sometimes we even give her money out of our checks. Don't get me wrong—my mom works too. We have made it for two years at our jobs, and we love to work.

Brian Guthrie, 16
Centralia, Illinois

Well, the job that I had was not like I had expected it to be. . . . I couldn't handle it. It was putting too many pressures on me. I mostly worked on the weekends, and that's when

Discussions

Kelly: I used to work as a shampoo girl for my aunt. She wouldn't let me sit down all day. When you're learning how to shampoo people's hair, it's very embarrassing because the hose has a lot of pressure. You're supposed to keep it very close to the person's head, but then it sprays all over the place. I sprayed so many people and my aunt kept going, "It's okay—it's her first day." It's like that cleared everything up and they forgave me. But it's very embarrassing when an older woman comes in wearing a lot of makeup and you get her face all wet, or when you're trying to take the curlers out of women's hair and you get them tangled. I've had people say, "Here, I can do it for you, honey. Let me do it."

everything happens. I couldn't stand to see other people go out. . . .

I am not a lazy person. I just didn't like the job nor the employers. They treated me like I was a nobody. I was trained to work on a cash register, but as time passed they had me taking out trash, emptying a trash can, mopping a large floor, sweeping the floor, cooking, and traying fries. They embarrassed me many times so I decided to just leave it alone.

Charlotte Williams, 16
Madison, Georgia

As a teenage worker, I myself have come in contact with many problems. My father lost his job two and one half years ago, indirectly causing me to get a job. I was 13 at the time. When applying for a waitress job, I put down that I was 17. Believe it or not, the restaurant believed it and hired me.

That was two years ago. Since then, I've constantly had a job with my father still not having a job. Right there it has caused hostile feelings for me.

I ask myself a very important question, one I will never know the answer to: "If my father had kept working, would everything be so difficult for me now?" Working at such a young age made me grow up fast. Where did my childhood go?

School is an issue that has suffered greatly. No one quite understands my problem, and I'm not begging to have people pity me. The fact is no one made me get a job. However, I felt there was nothing else I could do.

The hassles from managers are the worst. How can they sympathize with me when they think I'm going on 18 and not 16. Two years is a big jump—I've learned that. Crabbiness due to lack of sleep is regarded as terrible behavior at work. You are to do what you are told with not so much as a twitch of your eye. . . . I wish they understood.

Maybe for a teenager that gets a job at the ripe old age of 16 things would be different. I feel sorry for those that think jobs are easy to cope with and attempt a job when there really is no need for one.

My advice would be to use your energy toward better things like an education. Work has taken a lot of time away from me that should have been spent on homework and personal time. I sure wouldn't want to relive this job-filled hassle again. Hopefully, the future brings a break for me.

15-year-old female
Illinois

Personally, I work to help support my husband Terry and myself.

Cathy Grubham, 17
Auburn, Washington

A lot of times at the Great Frame Up, where I work now, I say, "This is my first day" if I do something very wrong.

John: My first job was working for my dad. He's a manager of an automobile dealership, and he had to rush delivery on four police cars to get them out. Since I like to work on electronics, he had me come in on Sunday. We had to put on the lights and the sirens and the spotlights. My first job was to drill the holes in the side door to put the spotlight on. I'm drilling with this drill, and I had no idea how to do this. I ended up paying 25 dollars because I went through the side window.

Then he had me put the sirens on. It's a bar across the top. You run all the wiring under the dashboard. I ended up knocking off a few wires in the back of the dashboard. By now you've got the radio not working and the light or something not working. Lucky it was my dad. I finally got the thing working, but I never went back to work for him again.

Diane: I started working when I was 12 at my family's dry cleaning business, and that's hard to remember. But there was one thing that I remember. I got to work and I was so scared, you know, only 12 years old. I can remember the two girls who were training me. We were emptying this dryer, and we use solutions that can make you high. I had my head in the dryer for a long time, and I come out and I'm flying high. And suddenly I see them on the floor laughing. I couldn't figure out what was going on. I didn't know what they were laughing about. I told Carol, the other girl working there, "I'm not waiting on a customer for an hour."

Leslie: My first job, I was a freshman in high school. I don't even know why I got a job, maybe because my best friend got a job. I worked at a local nursery for a total

Among my friends, maintaining a nice car is the primary reason for having a job. Others have jobs so that they can get out of the house and away from mom and dad for a while. Also, having a job provides a form of independence from financial restrictions imposed by parents.

My parents never allowed me to have a job during school. They say that they would rather give me an allowance than for me to be distracted from my studies. So far, it has worked. My grade point average has been 3.8 to 4.0. . . .

In addition, I have been able to participate in forensics, debate, and the school plays. I feel that parents that allow and even encourage their teens to get an after-school job "for the experience" are doing their children a great disservice. One's education and high school experience are much more important and valuable than the little bit of spending money acquired from minimum-wage slave labor.

Jason C. Chaika, 17
McPherson, Kansas

Teenage workers' biggest problem is that their employers don't treat them with enough respect. One of my managers is constantly making plays at me. When I stand up for myself, he threatens me with my job.

Kim Beveridge, 17
Arlington Heights, Illinois

I have a job training and showing horses for different farms. . . . I can't imagine not having to go to the farm after school. Getting there on time, making sure all my horses I work are healthy and doing well is my way of being independent.

It's not necessarily the money. It's more or less the way I try and earn respect for being responsible.

Sunni Kircher, 15
Richmond, Indiana

Personally, money plays only a small part in why I work. I enjoy the challenge of working and going to school. Also, I am getting valuable experience in a field that may be my career (photography). Most teens, myself included, work because it gives them a sense of accomplishment. Therefore, they usually try hard at their jobs and want to succeed.

Ted Anderson, 18
Muncie, Indiana

As a working teenager, I think that most teenagers work because they need the money to pay school tuition and buy personal items from the store. As a teenager, I have been working for four years in mostly the same place and really enjoy it.

I've been working at the North Slope Borough (mayor's office) doing secretarial work like answering the phone, typing memos, filing, making contracts, and running errands for the mayor. The best part of it was that I was privileged to work with the mayor of the North Slope Borough. . . .

The reason I started working as a teen was because I finally real-

Erich Mees

of six weeks. I didn't know if they knew I was underage or not. I just told them I was 16, but they didn't check out anything. I was really scared because I was dealing with people and with money, and that was a big responsibility. But I was really nervous because I was sort of young, and they treated me like I was young.

Michelle: The first day I worked—I worked for a newspaper subscription service—I was really nervous. You're sitting there trying to sound very businesslike, but you don't know the speech so it sounds like you're reading it. I was stumbling over my words. Then all of a sudden it happened. I got my sale, and I got my two dollar commission for it.

Diane: I get to work, and I start in right away. I say hello to everybody, and I start in on my job. On a

ized I have to quit asking for money from my parents, and it helped me start planning what I'm going to do when I get out of high school and try to find a job.

Davida Hopson, 16
Unalakleet, Alaska

Teenage workers encounter many problems—more than most people are aware of. One of the pressures is with school. By the time you get home from work, you may only have one or less hours to do homework, housework, and odds and ends, such as running around or errands.

Then your mom gripes because you didn't do the things that she wanted you to do, and your teacher gripes because you didn't do what she wanted you to. You wake up the next day dreading it because it's going to be the same.

Job hassles are a big problem

too. Guys ... treat you nicely at school. Then at work they treat you like rug mice. Or it can be the other way too. I work in a super-market. The older bag boys think they are hot so they try to hustle you. It's really sort of disgusting sometimes....

Some people actually get mad at you when you tell them you have a job. They look at you like, "You have a job—when so many people with families are unemployed." It makes me sick.

One time in a history class a kid mentioned that he didn't get his homework done because he was working. Our teacher replied, "Well, then quit your job and give it to someone who really needs it." This kid needed it just as bad as everyone else did.

Crystal Dombroski, 16
Hillsdale, Michigan

Teenagers work for many reasons. One may be because the town they are in doesn't offer anything for recreation. After a while we get sick of hanging around on the wall.

Beth Hodge, 16
Surry, New Hampshire

I don't know why other teenagers work, but for me it is mainly parent pressure. I want to make them feel like I'm good for something. Also, I want to relieve them of some financial burden.

I am a very materialistic person and very label conscious. I firmly believe you get what you pay for. Thus, I spend lots of money for the things I want.

Martin Rigby, 18
Reno, Nevada

Many teenagers work because they have to. In my family, my father just had a heart attack, and the hospital bills reached the ceiling. But I've been working before that. My parents raised me to appreciate things better if I had to work for them. It's true ... especially right now when times are so rough and jobs can't be found anywhere....

typical day I get all the other employees to come to me with all of their problems. "Oh, I can't find this. Where are these clothes?" Every day for the last three weeks something's been missing—like a 300 dollar silk blouse—so you move your tail to find it.

I'm kind of a supervisor so all the other employees are coming to me. I have to deal with all the customers who think I'm just a little kid. On a typical day there are three problems in the laundromat, and I've got to go fix the machines. Then I get back to my usual job, which is now piled up, and I'm way behind. When I finally get everything done, I say to the girl who comes after me, "Take over."

Michelle: When school started, I got a job doing phone surveys. I like working there because my boss is really lenient. You wouldn't believe what we get away with. What we're doing is illegal because it's not really a survey. It's just like a business pitch where they try to find the people's ages.

Steve: Though I have had many jobs, the one I enjoyed the most was working as Big Foot for a local toy store during the Christmas season. That was the most fantastic job. I'd just get in the costume and bounce around. I'd have a couple of beers first. I'd see some cute girl so I'd just stroll over. Every single time they'd say, "Oh, how cute." It was great.

Reasons for Working

Kelly: I don't like getting ready for work or going to work, but once I'm there it's fun and I do my job. It's always nice when the paycheck comes in because the bank is between my house and work so I drop off all my money there.

Steve: I've washed dishes since I was 15. I make $4.25 an hour washing dishes. It's not that hard.

Leslie: I'm only working for one thing. I want to go to France this

Many teenagers work because there just isn't any money in the house so they are, so to speak, "the breadwinners." That's hard when you're young....

I appreciate everything I have because I bought it myself. You can still be a grade A student, go through four years of college, belong to a sports or music area, and have a job. It's a matter of determination.

Sherry Myers, 16
Auburn, Washington

A lot of students work because they need the money. Some work because their friends work, and they don't want to be different—a sort of peer pressure. Some teen-agers work because their families push them to work so they can get practical knowledge of what the working world is going to be like.

I like to work because I'm in a situation where I can meet a lot of people.... Too many times students say they hate to work, but inside of themselves they really enjoy the work.

Jerry Wajda, 16
Council Bluffs, Iowa

I've been working in a restaurant (not a fast food place), and you have to take anything from your bosses because they know if you quit, there will be 30 people waiting to take your place. The bosses really don't care if you quit, and they treat you accordingly.

Another thing is what you do to yourself. I've cut my hands more in the last six months that I have in my whole life. I also never have time to study at home so my grades have fallen.

Mark Puksich
Hillsdale, Michigan

We either have to work for that car we've always wanted or for those stylish clothes we say we need. Teenagers also need money for that trip to the beach or those visits to the movies ... or to buy

those drugs they say they desperately need or that case of beer they promised to bring to a party.

Most teenagers can't stand their job and have constant complaints about it. The reason . . . is . . . a job isn't something you want to be doing. A job isn't like a career. It's not something you usually enjoy doing.

Kelly Hayward, 17
Milford, New Hampshire

I have just recently gotten a job, and I really enjoy it. I feel that it's hard to find a job that you enjoy. I couldn't imagine going to work and not liking the job or the people. In that case, money wouldn't be enough.

Teenagers have more expenses nowadays—from the clothes they wear to the school supplies they need. . . . Some teenagers have car expenses—the gas alone isn't any little expense. Another big thing is that teenagers like to have "good times.". . . Movies cost $4.50. That doesn't include popcorn and a soft drink. In order to do just about anything these days, it seems like you have to pay money to do it. . . .

Having a job is great because it gives teenagers something to do with spare time and mainly be-

spring. I dread going to work. I hate it, but when I go to work I do my job because I have the commitment. I have a goal, and that's my incentive.

Kelly: The only reason I'm working is so I can go to college because there's nobody except the government, if I can convince it, who is going to pay for my college.

You start out working for the money. You get a job because you need to save some money. Then you end up knowing you learned something from it, or you know you met a lot of people.

Steve: Work is like my social group. People on the football team and people who do cheerleading, they meet a group of friends through that. Well, I meet a lot of incredibly nice people through working. I enjoy that.

Melanie: I don't have a job now, but I think the reason I want to go out isn't because of the money. You don't get a lot of money being a nurse's aide, or even working at a special ed school. I want to do it because it means a lot to me to be able to help other people. I love working with kids, especially if they have some problem I can help with.

Problems when Working

Steve: I used to work at a 24-hour restaurant. When they had the Ticketron lines and you were working graveyard shifts, all these people were coming in. They're ordering all sorts of stuff and kids were running out without paying. It gets hectic.

John: The worst thing I have is people stealing. I'm working nights, and I've got the most seniority so I'm considered the assistant manager. I have two guys working under me. We catch a lot of people stealing. We've got the peanut bin next to us. I won't yell if somebody takes one peanut, but people take handfuls. Or some

cause it gives me a feeling that I'm doing something and receiving something for my time and effort.

Wendi Wassermen, 17
Schenectady, New York

Teenage workers encounter pressures at school from many teachers who, although they know the student had to work the night before, insist the student should comprehend all of the assignment. Even if the student talks to the teacher and does all the homework eventually, the teacher still gets upset because some days the student doesn't have everything together.

There are pressures at work because most of the employers are in their 20's and 30's. They are married and have children. They think they can boss around the younger employees even if they don't have as much knowledge or experience.

Kris Leonard, 17
Casper, Wyoming

Basically, teenagers have rotten jobs no self-respecting adults would do, such as McDonalds. Management treats you like dirt. They know this is about all you can get so they pay you minimum wage. I don't work for McDonalds anymore.

I work for a carpet cleaning company. My pay is good, and my coworkers are real nice. I'm treated like an adult and a partner or coworker. My only problem is when we clean a restaurant. I don't start until ten-thirty or twelve at night so I usually get home from one-thirty to three in the morning. This is a bit hard since I'll only get three to five hours sleep.

Kevin A. Heggi, 18
Munster, Indiana

I began to work at 15 because I was ready for high school and everyone wore neat expensive clothes. Although my parents would have paid for them, I didn't feel it was fair for them to have to buy my clothes. . . .

Later, as a junior I wanted to buy

a new musical instrument which cost around 1,300 dollars. Again, I didn't feel that it was my parents' responsibility to pay for something I really didn't need. I worked as many hours as I could (up to 40 hours a week) and paid for it myself.

Finally, I decided I wanted to travel before college and planned a trip to Europe, which I also worked for and have paid for myself. . . .

My attitude toward work is great. I love my job and wouldn't quit even if I didn't like the money. Having a job is fun, exciting, and builds good friendships almost to the point of a family.

Tracey Goering, 17
McPherson, Kansas

The prices of gas, food, clothing and many other things affect me greatly. I have a small job at a fast food restaurant at $3.45 an hour, and they want to cut my salary in half. I can't afford everything as it is.

Why does the government want to hurt me even more? And not just me but many other students and adults who won't get hired because students are cheaper to hire. . . .

little kids walk by and stick the Brach's candy down their pockets.

We have our own brand—Roundy's—butter, and then we have Land O' Lakes butter. You know how the butter's wrapped so you can just unfold it and take them out—right? You catch so many people, especially on Saturdays—you'll get a mob there. Somebody will rip open the Roundy's package, dump the butter out, and stick the Land O' Lakes in the Roundy's package. You get the cheaper price for the better butter, and then we get all these Roundy's that we can't sell.

The first time I saw it happen, I was there all by myself. My boss wasn't there, and I didn't know what to do. Should I report the lady? Should I just tell her, "Don't do it again"? I just said not to do it again. But now if I catch somebody, I call the manager.

Diane: I have to call people whose checks have bounced and say, "Oh, excuse me, your check bounced." Not only do you have to tell the people that they have insufficient funds, but you say, "You owe us another five dollars because your check bounced." And boy—can you

My parents can't afford most of the things I need and would like. I have a middle-income family, but things are getting tougher. My boyfriend's mother just got divorced and was forced to go on welfare because she can't afford the bills she now gets. So I help out the little I can.

Most people like to work. I know I do. I wish I could know what it is like to be able to have extra money to spend on whatever I wanted to. I do go out some to movies or to eat, but not near as much as I would like. Teenagers need jobs to help out at home.

Ronda Merfeld, 17
Onalaska, Wisconsin

Recently, I conducted a survey concerning teenagers and working. Approximately 50 percent of the students have a job and are happy with it. Twenty-eight percent admitted that they only wanted money for personal expenses, such as dates, clothes, gas, car payments, and other entertainment.

Some students wanted the experience of working and the chance to learn new skills. Others see their job as an opportunity to meet people and become a responsible, independent person.

I think teenagers should seriously contemplate the advantages of working. The skills they develop and the responsibility they acquire are an important stepping-stone in their struggle to become an independent adult.

Cathy Vicari, 16
Auburn, Washington

Since I started working, I've felt an independence about myself. I don't need my parents to have to buy this and that for me. It's a nice feeling knowing that you're helping your parents. . . . If it wasn't for me working, my parents might have gone bankrupt on my clothes expenses.

Work is fun—at least now it is.

Maybe in ten or twenty years I won't want to work, but now it's a new experience, one that I enjoy. I think it has helped me to grow up a lot and realize what people go through on the job scene.

Pamela Manselle, 16
Independence, Missouri

When you are a teenager just starting out at a job, you get the bad hours and start out at minimum wage. Most of the time if you go to do something for someone, they don't like to let you do it because they think you are not experienced enough.

For example, I work at a gas station. One day this guy calls up and get some good ones, "I do too have sufficient funds." One time I okayed a 50 dollar check. It was over the amount of the purchase, and those people skipped town. We spent a month trying to get that money from them, and I felt really bad. Not only did I okay a check for over the amount, and the check bounced, but they went to Tahiti or someplace.

A lot of times I've had to go out and represent the management and talk to this old guy who thinks, "Who the hell is this kid?" Also, when I work with older people and train older people, I get a feeling that they resent me. I'm training this new woman, she's older, and I get the feeling that she hates my guts. It puts me in a real awkward position because I'm in a higher authority than a lot of other people in the place.

Steve: I think the greatest thing about work is that you are treated like an equal. Most of the people I know are in their 20s or above. We always go out and drink beers and stuff. They treat me just like anybody else. It's great—that's what I like about it.

he needs his car pulled out of his yard. He got it stuck in the middle of the yard. So I got into the wrecker and went to his house. When I got there, he told me that I was too young to pull it out.

He couldn't believe that they would let me out in a wrecker. I told him they wouldn't send me out in the wrecker if I didn't have any experience.

Joe Peterson, 17
Marvon, Iowa

Working has kept me well-occupied. It keeps me out of trouble, especially in the summer when I usually work. Work also lets me meet many nice people.

Teenagers work because they need spending money, need to pay tuition (if going to a private school), or maybe they're saving money for college. I work for all these reasons, but since I'm still in high school and need to pay a tuition for my school, I hardly have money saved up for college.

I like working, but it all depends on what kind of job you have. Once I worked in a fish processing plant, and I had to stand up all the time. . . . There are about 15 workers standing up by a long table. First, the fish has to be headed. Then the stomach is slit, guts taken out, and the fish are cleaned. The fish are then packed.

All these workers have a certain job. What makes it worse is that the water you use is cold. After you work for a couple of hours, you take a 15-minute break and start again. It wasn't very much fun, but after you got your first paycheck it seemed worth it.

Maria Nanouk, 17
Unalakleet, Alaska

Kelly: It's funny at work because I was hired when I was about 15 and everybody else was always older. But instead of raising me up, they all act like children. It's the atmosphere of high school kids running around, when all these people are supposedly adults.

Michelle: Where I work my boss is only 24 or so, and the girls who work there are all in high school. But my boss kind of lowers himself to us. Like when we're working. You'd think with a telephone business it would be nice and quiet in the background, with really mellow music. Well he's got a hard rock station cranking in the background.

Steve: When you first get into the job market, you have no idea what you're worth and you don't know what reasonable pay is. It is a job and you are expected to do certain things, but there are places that will just screw you over. McDonald's is a perfect example. They pay shit wages. They work you ridiculously hard. And if the individual managers don't need you, they will find some trumped-up excuse to fire you. As far as benefits, they'll swindle you out of anything that you'll benefit from. McDonald's attitude is "We'll hire them, push them as hard as we can until they drop, then hire somebody else."

Michelle: With me, I have to keep a really tight schedule because I work Monday through Friday from five till nine. I get home from school, and I have an hour and a half to eat, clean, and get ready for work. Then after being on the phone for four hours, you're too tired to do homework.

John: Just before football season ended, I was going to school and to work six days a week. Right after school I'd go to football, get out of football at a quarter to six, and have to be at work at six o'clock. I'd get out at ten or eleven and then do homework.

Manish: My parents feel that the added pressure from working would cause a slump in my grades, and they want me to benefit from the educational opportunities present at the moment. See, I play soccer and tennis. On a normal day I don't get home until six o'clock. If I would go out and work every night, I'm sure I'd feel lazy and I'd slide in doing my homework. They say if you want to participate in sports, do it. You don't have to work or pay for your own whatever. We'll do that for you right now until you're independent. I'm missing out on an opportunity or the feeling you get from working— independence. Sometimes I feel I'd like to have that. But on the other hand, don't get me wrong. I'm not saying I want to work. I don't have to work. My parents pay for everything.

Compiled by Cathy Zubek

Work   *85*

HOLLY HEEBING

Chapter 7.

Fun

J.D. is the fun-loving envy of his high school. J.D. knows everybody, and everybody knows J.D. Laughing as he downs another beer, he remembers the old days of unpopularity and the years spent refining his character. J.D. endures the school week by thinking about the upcoming weekend. He knows every weekend will be filled with whatever he wants; it's like giving himself a Christmas present two days a week.

J.D. is basically a lazy person, so he relies on others to make his fun. Since he hates monotony, he goes out with various groups of people in hopes of satisfying his appetite for good times.

One of J.D.'s many pleasures is punking out. When he gets in the punk mood, he calls his two fellow punk loyalists, Mike and Frank. They go to see the Plasmatics, the Clash, or Devo if they're in town. "It is important to dress in the proper attire. Torn shirts, leather jackets, chains, and a pierced ear go together well," J.D. explains.

J.D. also likes to drink. When he thinks about drinking, he immediately calls Steve and Greg. They all go out and drown life's misery. Sometimes they try to see how far from reality they can get or what new drinks they can invent to make someone sick.

J.D.'s favorite pastime is girl hunting. When it's girls he is after, he calls up his two favorite gigolos, Marty and Bill. J.D. thinks of himself as an oversexed guy with a bad reputation. He's not pushy with girls, but that glaring look gives away his thoughts every time. He and his friends hit the parties, the game rooms, or the disco. "It may take a lot of beer and wine, but I can usually have the girl I want."

J.D. has become fairly knowledgeable in the art of small talk. When he sees a thirsty-looking female, he makes his way over to her. He pretends to take her side when she tells him about the horrendous treatment she has been receiving from "old what's his name." J.D. promises that he would never cheat on her if she were his girl. "Not such a cute, sweet girl like you, Sharon." Once he has her total confidence, he puts his arms around her, looks into her eyes, and kisses her with all the passion he can muster. J.D. spends the rest of the evening with her and has a lot of fun. But when he drops her off at home, he is through with her forever, he hopes.

Aside from drinking and girl-chasing, J.D. has a bad side that puts him in the mood for mischief, pranks, and practical jokes. J.D. and his pals go around town looking for something in the wrong place. They agree that realty signs in people's yards look better somewhere else. J.D. has put his school, his church, and the mean-old-lady-next-door's house up for sale.

They also think that flashing sawhorses look better in people's back yards. Garbage bags full of leaves look better on people's cars. People's cars are safer on the sidewalk than on the street. One boring night, J.D. and his friends stole a bowling ball from an alley and invented a new sport, street bowling. They painted pictures on the bowling ball and rolled it around the neighborhood at cars, trash cans, mailboxes, and each other.

When they're short of cash, J.D. and his friends party crash. At one party, they noticed that everyone had left their shoes at the door and gone downstairs. When no one appeared to greet them at the door, they took all the shoes and threw them into the snow. Then they turned all the furniture upside down and left the party. At a Halloween party, one of J.D.'s friends won the bobbing-for-apples contest by getting the most apples out of the tub in the shortest time. He sat down in the tub and splashed the apples and the water out of the tub. The girl who had to clean up 20 gallons of water wasn't laughing.

Once in a while and sometimes too often, J.D. must amuse himself alone. Although his free time is usually spent sleeping on his favorite couch, he also enjoys eating junk food, listening to his punk albums, and gossiping on the phone with old girlfriends. When a phone number comes to mind, he calls it and lets his imagination take over. J.D. doesn't care what the girls think about his stories. It's all in fun.

After a long weekend of fun, he composes his wits, sobers up, sleeps a few winks, and trots off to school. He is already planning the next weekend by the time he steps into his first class Monday morning. To him, the endless cycle of a teenager's life means the pursuit of less work, more play, maybe sex, and definitely rock and roll. "What else is there?"

My favorite way to have fun is to play video games. My favorites are Donkey Kong, Donkey Kong Junior, and Centipede. Playing the games makes me forget all my troubles as I put full concentration into the game.

Chet Bush, 16
Baldwinsville, New York

My absolute favorite way to have a good time is by laughing. Whether it be at myself, at others, or maybe I should say with others, or with just one of my good friends, laughing is my way of having a terrific time.

Sometimes, when I'm in a fantastically crazy mood, I go into hysterics. (This also occurs when I am very tired and haven't gotten enough sleep the night before.) When I get started, though, everyone in my way better clear because I can't stop.

When my best friend and I were trying to produce a tape spin-off of the "Twilight Zone" for our photography class, we dressed up in crazy

Discussions

Steve: The thing I like more than anything else is when you have a big convoy of motorcycles. You know, five motorcycles trucking along at ridiculously fast speeds. It's more challenging to ride in a group, keeping up with the guys, moving in and out of cars. And when you stop for lunch, you stop with the group so you're not eating lunch by yourself.

Michelle: I got off work, and I had until two o'clock in the morning. I wanted to go to this bar on Lake Street. It was a nice night, and I didn't want to get there early so I walked. It took me two hours to get to Lake Street. I got there about eleven. The guys there told me to go in. I said, "I can't go in there, I'm not old enough." However, I walked right in and nobody said anything. I was sittin' there drinkin' beers. It was great. I love doing things like that.

Kelly: I was at somebody's house when they played chess out in the

costumes and shot pictures of ourselves in the nearby mall. We made absolute fools of ourselves, but in the process received an A for the project.

Laughing is my way of expressing my best emotions and putting a smile on other people's faces also. Laughing, I believe, is contagious.

Lisa Mangarelli, 16
Scottsdale, Arizona

My favorite way of having a good time varies like my moods. I often like to go with friends into the city to museums, galleries, cafes, and shops. Sometimes I like to sit in a room with a person and just discuss anything, especially debate on things such as "What is truth?" and other such questions (which take hours of answering).

Sitting and talking to a person on an equal status, not having to worry about superficial frivolities, such as what she is thinking about me, is a very rare and unique experience. Surprising my mother and

MY FAVORITE THINGS TO DO
ARE EAT AND SLEEP
I'M HAVING THE TIME OF MY LIFE

taking her out to dinner, bringing flowers to a friend—anything which brightens a person's day—is fun in that I feel as if I have done something worthwhile and meaningful.

Elana Roston, 15
Newport Beach, California

My favorite way to have fun is for me and my sisters to walk to Show-biz and play games like Pac Man, Ms. Pac Man, and Centipede. On Fridays and Saturdays we usually attend dances. Then on Sundays we go skating.

Things that I enjoy on the side are talking on the telephone for three hours, sleeping, watching HBO, or playing football with my two younger brothers. Of all the things that I have fun doing, the one I really enjoy is sitting down and talking to my mother.

Kawana Neal, 15
Macon, Georgia

My favorite ways to have a good time are going to church or Bible study and praising the Lord.

Christopher Barber, 19
Winston-Salem, North Carolina

I like being outside, especially in the spring. Getting together with one or two good friends and doing whatever we can think of is always fun—for example, going on a picnic at the first sign of a thaw or going swimming fully clothed at the end of October. I don't have a favorite thing to do because I always try to be spontaneous and do whatever comes to mind.

Cheryl Snyder, 16
Wyomissing, Pennsylvania

Personally, I am most content playing my guitar, preferably with another musician, and singing. Music is not merely a physical feature in a technological society; music is a feeling and a sensation that very few people can honestly experience. When I strum and pick those delightful harmonious notes

backyard. They used real people as the pawns and kings and queens, and the kings directed the moves. It was fun being a part of it.

Maribeth: I like to be around people that I like. I love to laugh. I love people that make me laugh. I love joking around.

Karen: I used to think a fun weekend was going out and getting drunk and just making a fool out of myself, but now I know that a fun weekend is to go out and get drunk and not make a fool out of myself.

I went out to eat, and we made fun of the waitress because she was new. When the bread came it was so small that my date looked at it and said, "God, we get bigger bread than this in church." He gave it back to the waitress, and she got really mad. After that we drank some booze, and we got in trouble with the police again. We didn't do anything. He was just speeding, and he sped through a red light so we didn't get arrested or anything. I got home a little bit late, and I got yelled at.

Michelle: That movie *The Thing* was on. It's neat to see. You know it has special effects, but it's still scary. If it was real, if I really saw

correctly, there is a certain feeling and understanding of spiritual achievement.

Jim Harrington, 17
Warwick, Rhode Island

My favorite ways to have a good time are being with my boyfriend and going to parties with close friends. I enjoy going to the beach with friends and having a few beers and playing frisbee.

I like to listen to soft rock and roll or just regular music. My favorite groups are Rush, Genesis, Pink Floyd, and Neil Young.

My experiences at parties are drinking too many double shot drinks within two hours and having to leave the party early because I can't drink anymore, then having people ask my boyfriend days later why we left the party so early! I never get sick, but the answer is, "She didn't feel too good." Oh, well.

Then everyone teases me at the parties: "Don't drink so fast, or do single shot drinks instead of double shots."

19-year-old female
New York

My idea of a good time is simply being with friends and laughing.

Fun

The favorite things in life are the simple ones. I like to take long walks with people in natural surroundings. Every couple of months my family and I go to Vermont for a weekend. The woods and lake relax and amuse me. We swim, canoe, and hike while we're there.

The good times are even better when friends, outside of the family, join us. This coming summer I hope to tour parts of Vermont by bike. The countryside, people, and old inns add interest to the fun of biking. I have gone white water rafting a couple of times and love it. . . .

The thrill of being compatible with nature exhilarates me.

Paige Ackelson, 17
Wyomissing, Pennsylvania

After I get paid, go home, shower up, and get dressed, I hop into my Ghetto cruiser and head to town to something like that, I'd be turned off. But you know it's not real, it's just like, "Wow, check this thing out."

Melanie: Some people think that to have a good time you always have to smoke a bowl or get drunk. I'm not looking forward to college for that. I hate alcohol. Not just the taste, because I've had it before. But all I see in alcohol and pot is bad. When I want to talk to someone, I want the person to be normal. It must be impossible to have a good conversation using pot or alcohol.

I like being with a couple of friends in my church. They're older than I am, but they're a young couple. They'll never be old. They're just so much fun to be with. They've got a real sense of humor. I can be serious with them, or I can just joke around. I like to be with people, sometimes in a big group. I like to go to the airport look for some weekend action. In a small town like Eureka, you have to look awful hard. One place to look is Hucks, a 24-hour food and gas store.

Usually some of the gang is gassing up. We take turns driving around every weekend. Now that I've found buddies, we all pile into the designated car and blast to a nearby town, which is just as dead as Eureka, to go get french fries or yell at a rival school and run like mad.

After we've had enough of that, we roll back to Eureka, which has rolled it sidewalks up at seven, and head to the high school parking lot. At the parking lot, there's not much going on, and we sit on our cars and tell stupid jokes or just talk about dates. Pretty soon a wide variety of people will pull in and join in on the massive rap session.

Talking makes us hungry, and we go somewhere to eat. Then we drive around with the stereo at concert hall pitch, which gets constant remarks and deadly looks from elderly people sitting on their front porch swings. I don't know if you would call this fun, but it sure beats the heck out of staying home with the folks watching Lawrence Welk.

Ken Garrison, 16
Eureka, Illinois

My favorite ways to have a good time are to sit and read a good book and to share quiet moments by myself or with friends.

Kim Novak, 16
Denham Springs, Louisiana

My favorite way to have a good time is to go out with some friends and get wasted. My parents hate it when I come home stoned or drunk or when I party at my house. I love getting fucked up, and it's my decision to do so, so I wish they would respect my choice.

16-year-old male
Nebraska

I have two general ways of having a good time—intellectually or purely emotionally. During the school year, I have mostly intellectual fun. Usually I have a terrific time battling a good trigonometry problem or analyzing Shakespeare's plays or (especially) having a good deep discussion with a person or a group.

The best way to have a good time without thinking is to get together with a group of old, old friends—from kindergarten and elementary school—and just mess around. . . . I remember last summer, or maybe the summer before, lying around on rafts in our pool and discussing every possible male (and several impossible males) with a couple of my friends. . . .

I'm moderately conservative, and one of my old friends is what I call a "bleeding heart" liberal. We

and watch the people. At O'Hare you get so many different kinds of people from all over the world.

Kelly: I have a boyfriend who lives out of state so I only see him twice a semester. It's fun just being with a person, going to the Arboretum, or to Cantigny, instead of being concerned about who sees you with whom.

The most fun things of the summer have been being with my friend Scott or my boyfriend Eric. They play off each other in what they say and how they talk so well that it's challenging and fun to be around either or both of them. Driving to the airport with Eric is fun. We have about a half-hour alone to talk, and I enjoy it. I enjoy being with Eric most anywhere.

Diane: I've never been on a date. Girlfriends, yes, but never a guy. We don't go out on weekends cause they live far away. During the day, I work. At nights I watch TV. I just relax.

Jeff: Last Saturday during the day I mowed the lawn and raked the leaves. That night, I went to see a couple of movies. I saw Rocky Horror Show. It was my first time.

Karen: Virgin!

Jeff: And, uh, everyone said you couldn't go in there straight so I didn't. It's also cool to play football when you're drunk.

Steve: Yeah, that's cool. Everybody's like, "We don't care how hard we hit. We're drunk!" I went to this really bizarre thing the other day. It was a mock medieval battle. They had rules for it. Wooden swords and shields. That was pretty cool. It was great.

Michelle: What we do is just, you know, hang around. It sounds kind of dumb, but we have egg fights. While driving—we have 48 dozen eggs—we just drive down the street and throw them at each other. Another time, on a blind date, these guys turned out to be

have the best time making subtle verbal cuts at the other political philosophy. Another one of my friends is not only a left winger but also an idealist. We have excellent arguments, too.

Betsy Perabo, 17
Kirkwood, Missouri

Good times come and go, but the best times I have are with my friends. One of my favorite ways to have fun is by going to Great America Amusement Park. We always do something crazy like harass people and workers at the park but we never get kicked out (thank goodness).

Another thing we do is go to a shopping mall around us and do crazy things like talk to plants and act like we're talking to ourselves just to see the way people look at us.

Mario Galenski, 17
Mt. Prospect, Illinois

To have a good time I do out-of-the-ordinary things with out-of-the-ordinary friends—like walking through a Carl's Jr. drive-in, throwing toilet paper out of a hotel window, munching on ivy leaves at McDonald's, and eating cake with confetti. But I can enjoy life by myself as well. I love to bike ride, especially in the rain through this private country road near my house where cows graze.

Partying is fun—even without alcohol—and the ice cube, water balloon, and shaving cream fights are the best part. Most of the time the good times aren't planned; it's their spontaneity that makes them special. I love to get surprising letters in the mail or last-minute phone calls to go to a movie or friend's house.

Angela Michelle Garcia, 17
Stockton, California

Usually when I want to have a good time, I go out with my friends and we get drunk. I also like to take road trips with my boyfriend on his motorcycle. Sometimes we go over to people's houses while their parents are gone and we party.

It's also real fun to go take a country cruise and find old haunted houses and bust windows out and scare people. But I have one word of advice: if you are gonna get crazy that way, make sure you know what's going on. Both my friend and I were cut bad from broken glass in an old house.

It's also fun to go out of town and go bar hopping and get really wasted. One day my friend and I sat in a bar all day (both minors) having a good time. We left, and we were driving fast. Before we knew it, they were taking me to the hospital and the truck was totalled.

When you go doing things like that, be sure you can handle the situation. Luckily we are both okay now, but it sure can make a person think twice.

17-year-old female
Illinois

I like to get together with some close friends, drink some beer, play some pool, and play some cards, then have them all sleep over at my house. I also like to drive my car fast.

And I like to go in the hot tub with my girlfriend with no suits on. And I like to go camping for weeks

such jerks. They came over with tons of beer and sat around till two a.m. My date was a 33-year-old Mexican who smelled so bad. I just ate and kept eating all night because there was no way I was gonna kiss him.

And on Friday my girlfriend made an 800 dollar phone call to her boyfriend in Japan—800 dollars right out of her pocket to talk to him for three hours. I told her she was nuts.

Manish: I like sports as a means of fun. I like that competitive edge. I like the thrill of winning, the agony of defeat, you know. I can swear or kick sand in their face or kick them in the nuts, whatever it is. I enjoy that.

Jeff: I go water skiing, and fishing. I sometimes take off my shoes and socks and go to the golf course and get all the golf balls I can out of the water hazards.

Steve: Water skiing is great. That's fun. But it's kind of tricky unless you know somebody who's got a boat.

Why is fun important?

Michelle: To get your mind off things that are bothering you, I guess. Not really to relieve pressure, but if something is bothering you at home or with your boyfriend, you'll just want to go out and be with your friends to forget about it. It's boring to sit at home at night. You want to go out and have fun because if you don't you're going to have a boring evening. I've gone out every single night for, like, the last two years.

I work until nine, and I get dropped off at my house. I'll get a car or somebody will pick me up, and I'll go out for a couple of hours, even if it's just driving around or cruisin' up to Dairy Queen to see what's going on. It's not going out and spending money every night. It's just being out of the house.

Diane: Why? Because it lightens the atmosphere. It generally makes

at a time with my girlfriend to fish and hike all over. I also like water skiing at night in the summer and skinny-dipping at midnight with my girlfriend. Basically, I like anything I do that includes her.

16-year-old male
Washington

My favorite way to have fun is to spend time with my grandparents since they are so kind and special and very loving.

Kathy Melvin, 17
Baldwinsville, New York

My favorite way to have a good time is to sit down with my son and play and talk to him. He makes up a good conversation for being only 11 weeks old. He may only "coo" and smile, but watching him and listening to him is better than going out with my friends and drinking or watching television. The time just flies when I am with him.

Theresa Amyotte, 17
Baldwinsville, New York

My favorite way of having a good time is to go cruising with my older friends. We go to the usual hangout and cruise around the parking lot trying to pick up guys. Every once in a while we will go to wild parties or concerts and get drunk. Not many of my friends get stoned or smoke cigarettes.

The best thing to do on a weekend is to go to a weekly rock concert at a local skating rink. At these concerts there is no pressure to drink or smoke. You can just be yourself. It makes you feel good to know you could be accepted by strangers without having to prove something.

I really do have a good time doing these things, but I would have more fun and not feel so guilty if I wouldn't have to sneak around my parents' backs. It would be nice to be able to tell my parents that I drink, date guys, and go to rock concerts, but I'm afraid of what they will think of me. I'm still

their little girl from their point of view. They just won't let go.

15-year-old female
Washington

One of my favorite ways to have a good time is to go out to eat with my fiancé, stop at the store to get a couple of beers, and go back to my house and make sweet, beautiful love when nobody is there.

17-year-old male
Louisiana

My favorite time to have a good time is in the afternoon. I love to be out in the wilderness away from all the modern activity.

My friend and I went on a horseback ride one hot, sunny spring day. We traveled for several hours before we reached our destination. It is our favorite place. It is a canyon that is out between these grassy hills—a place where you never would expect a canyon to be.

things more comfortable, especially if you're dealing with other people, people at work. You can be comfortable with each other, and things will get done much better.

Karen: Escapism. Get away from the real world.

Steve: You have fun because it's more pleasurable, and you actually enjoy existing a great deal more when you're having fun than when you're not having fun. As a hedonist, I could easily say that fun is the ultimate goal in life for me. It's the most pleasurable existence. I go out and do things for fun simply because I enjoy existing when I'm having fun. You have this life to live, and you want to live it in the most pleasant way you can. You find out what you find pleasant, and then you proceed to do things that are pleasant in order to make life better.

We took a couple of Cokes along with some crackers. We sat down under a big tree and ate.

We then go our own way to enjoy the state of freedom that is surrounding us. My favorite thing to do when I am here is to lie down on my back with my arms folded behind my head. A warm sensation wraps around me when I allow the sun to spread its rays upon me.

As I lie here, I let every sound of nature go in my head. To hear all the sounds of several animals makes me feel like I am part of them. It amazes me to hear so many sounds in a quite peaceful area. The sounds make you feel like you are at home.

After lying there for about an hour, I wait for the rejoining of my friend. We then travel back silently and keep our wonderful thoughts of the day to ourselves.

Tammy Wildes, 16
Taylor, Arizona

I enjoy lying in the grass and staring into the sky. Searching for the Milky Way and the Big Dipper is like exploring an unfamiliar area. . . .

The best time to star gaze is after I've had an absolutely rotten day. I talk for hours to the moon (he listens very well), and he always seems to supply a falling star or two to make me wish and reaffirm my goals.

I guess I enjoy solitude, but I also love to share the "star times" with a good friend that likes to dream, too.

Le Anne Drye, 17
Cottonwood, Arizona

I am the type of person that loves to have a good time doing crazy and wild things. I am really involved in theatre, so I'm used to people looking at me. My favorite activity involves people. I like to take the bus with a couple of friends to downtown Denver and ride the elevators.

We love to watch people's reac-

tions so we act like different types of people. A typical conversation in an English accent:

Elizabeth: Oh James! This is so much fun, and I hope my father will let me fly back next weekend.

James (southern accent): Oh Lizzy! I don't understand why you have to live with stuffy old pops anyhow; just come live with me and mom.

Elizabeth: Darling, as much as I love it here, I'm much more comfortable in England with my maids, diamonds, and Rolls

Maribeth: I have fun to make me happy, to always be in a good mood.

Kelly: Fun is something you don't have to do, usually. Nobody's requiring it of you. Most of the time I go out with friends. Everything can't be work. If you have all work and no play, then you've got a very narrow world. You have to do other things just for yourself because you might go nuts if you don't.

Melanie: Fun is an outlet. A release of tension. I like to think that if I'm having a hard day at

Royces. I just don't understand how someone can pick up their own room. How awful.

People give the weirdest looks.

Terri Ducker, 17
Englewood, Colorado

I have many ways of having fun. I talk on the phone (one of my favorites). I listen to music and goof around with friends. I talk on the phone a lot because I'm not old enough to drive. My parents don't like me out much so the phone is the next best thing. It's also good if

94

you have something bad to tell somebody or if you're mad and don't want to see them.

I listen to music because it makes me feel better when I'm down. It sort of takes you away and makes all of your troubles flow away. It also makes your mood intense. You get in such a good mood you just feel like singing along.

Now for my friends—I think I have the best friends in the world! We go to concerts, movies, talk, cry, laugh, and all and all love each other. My best friend and I have about the best time any two people could have.

When she is over at my house, we listen to the stereo, watch TV, and have the normal "pig-out" session. When we're over at her house, we make our own special concoction, a "microwave cheese sandwich," and eat chocolate ice cream and listen to music.

But the best part of our friendship is that we are weird. We make something funny out of anything.

Dena Carney, 15
Bellevue, Washington

One of my favorite ways to have a good time is to go riding on my cycle and race it around the track until I have remembered every part of it.

After that, I go out trail riding. I have always liked riding trails . . . because . . . I could just sit back and let the wind hit me in the face. I have always loved riding cycles ever since I had a mini-bike about eight years ago.

About five years ago I used to race, until I got in an accident and I was in the hospital only a few days. After that, my parents didn't want me to race—and I haven't. But I still get the satisfaction of riding on my Suzuki RM 125 on the trails.

Scott Moyer, 18
Baldwinsville, New York

home, or if I've been working all day, or if my mom and I just had an argument, I can get out and have fun. If I can't get out, I make fun just happen. I'll start teasing my mom, and she'll tease me back. All of a sudden we'll be laughing.

Manish: Fun is what I like. It's what turns me on, man. That's why I have fun—because I like being turned on.

Leslie: Every now and then I need to have fun when I'm under a lot of stress from work or school or something. But you don't always have to have a wild time.

Jeff: Why do I want to have fun? Because it's better than being bored. Everyone wants to have pleasant experiences. Who wants to do something and not have fun? Who's like that except sadists and masochists?

What does fun include?

Kelly: I associate recreation with fun although recreation can just be taking a nap. Between pleasure and fun there is a difference because something can afford you pleasure without being a riot, without being

fun. Just watching TV with my boyfriend Eric is pleasure without being a real rip-roaring time.

Diane: To me, pleasure is just a more sophisticated word for having fun.

Steve: Fun sounds immediate. It doesn't sound long term. If you call fun your immediate pleasure and contentment your long-term pleasure, these are two goals that you're going for. You know you want a bit of both. Fun is part of the ultimate goal in life, to have as much fun as you can without sacrificing contentment.

Recreation tends to be planned while pleasure is a more general term than fun. You can have contentment, which really isn't fun, but it is pleasurable. You can have fun, which really isn't contentment, but it is pleasurable.

Manish: In recreation you find pleasure, which is fun.

Karen: Fun is both spontaneous and planned. Spontaneous fun is a Chinese fire drill or mooning out car windows—which I don't do but other people do that I'm with. It

YOU'VE GOT A LOT OF GROWING UP TO DO. DON'T YOU EVER STOP GOOFING OFF? ALL YOU EVER WANT TO DO IS HAVE FUN. WHAT'S THE MATTER WITH YOU?

OH MY GOD, —I'M A FUNATIC

can also be throwing water balloons out car windows at friends, or throwing snowballs, or going to the beach.

Leslie: Sometimes you search for fun because you're bored, and you look around for something to do with your friends. For the most part, when you're having the most fun, it's spontaneous. That's the best way to have fun. You're with your friends, and on the spur of the moment you say, "Let's go here." You do something different that you wouldn't normally do. Just being weird in regular situations is spontaneous fun. For example, we were at this boring party, and there was a pool. We just started throwing everyone in the pool no matter what their condition was or what clothes they were wearing. The food went too.

Jeff: You don't think about it. Well, sometimes you do—like next week I'm going to go to the beach. That's planning to have fun. But if you feel like doing something, you get up and do it. If I want to play soccer with Manish after this, hey, that sounds like fun. I'll do it.

Matt: Spontaneous fun is more enjoyable than fun you search for. If you have to search for fun, it's not that much fun when you get there.

Kelly: We planned to go to a movie so we went. It was okay, but it wasn't a whole lot of fun. Afterward we went out and had ice cream. We were laughing, having fun just because we were together. Just sitting and talking among the three of us can be a riot.

Steve: You can set yourself up for a potentially spontaneous and fun time. For instance, you know that the chances of having fun are greater if you're surrounded by friends.

Manish: You meet fun on the street. It often pops up when you least expect it.

Compiled by Erik Landahl

96

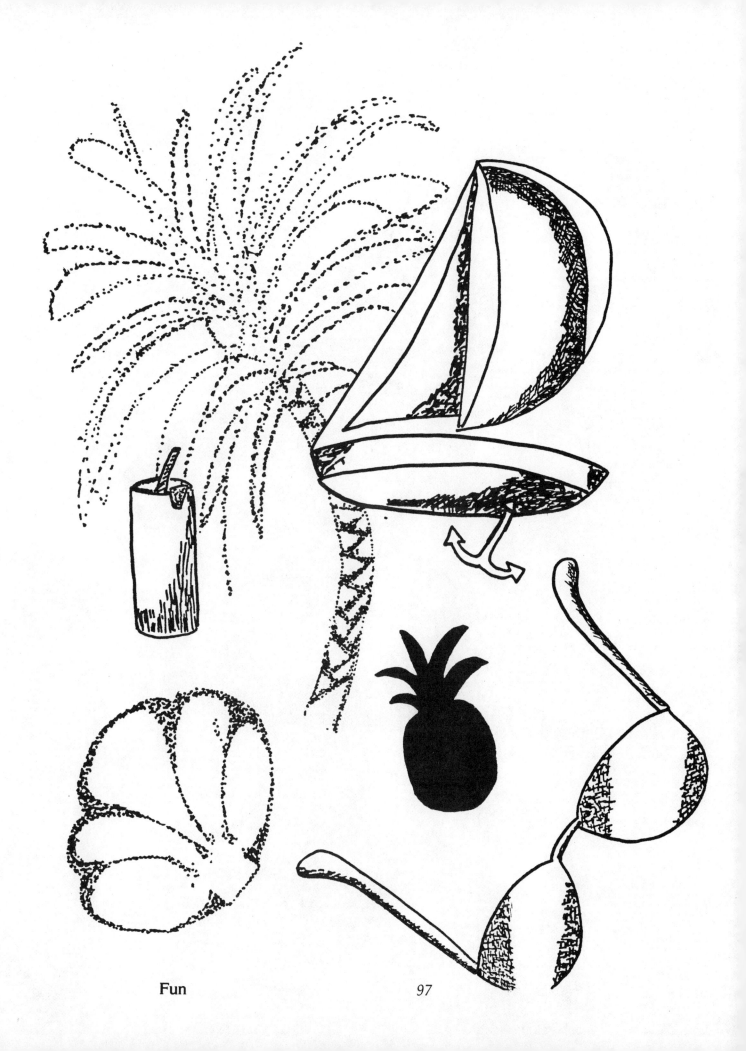

Fun

PART TWO
ISSUES

Introduction

Teenagers must confront and decipher society's dilemmas every day. They face enough major issues during one Saturday night out to keep activists and lobbyists busy for a lifetime.

First, teenagers must decide whether to drink beer or smoke pot or both, and then whether to drive under the influence. After that, teenagers may have to decide whether to go all the way with a girlfriend or boyfriend. Next, teenagers must decide whether to tell their parents the truth and face possibly violent reactions. Teenagers recognize the hypocrisy of today's society: "Honesty is the best policy" belongs with "Tippecanoe and Tyler too." It's catchy but. . . .

Then, in the morning, teenagers must decide whether to ignore the hangover and get up for church. That is, of course, if they believe in God. If not, they can just stay in bed and sleep. Then teenagers can dream about being drafted, or being nuked, or being victimized.

What should teenagers do about issues? Can they do anything? That's an issue in itself.

Chapter 8.

Honesty

First period has begun.

"Cynthia, why have I not received your thesis on molecular kineticism?"

"Umm, I put it off until last night, but then I went out and partied with my friends instead."

General uproar ensues. The teacher gives Cynthia enough failing grades and detentions to merit a dishonorable discharge. Alice, though, could handle the situation with a little more panache:

"Well, uh, my dog has cirrhosis [sniff, sniff], and mom was taking him to the hospital and . . . and [breaks into sobs]."

This explanation is better. It is great. It is a lie. The teacher and class will either buy it hook, line, and sinker or merely laugh goodnaturedly. Alice will probably get off free and clear.

Two casual acquaintances greet each other in the hall:

"Hi, how are you?"

"My dad is sick, our house is being repossessed, and furthermore, I think my goldfish has a mental disease stemming from wartime trauma."

Holy cow, a casual acquaintance doesn't want to hear the whole truth and nothing but the truth in response to a simple question. Casual acquaintances want casual answers.

"Hi, how are you?"

"Fine."

Fine, a compact response to a passing question, not always truthful, but nevertheless appropriate. Honesty may be the best policy, but it can be a big drag, too.

Teacher: Please explain the attitude of Sophocles as pertaining to this book.

Student: I didn't read it.

Grade: F.

Teacher: . . . as pertaining to this book.

Student: Well, as I see it, the feeling that rises to the forefront is one of concern for the condition of society as a whole.

Grade: A.

The second answer is a lie. For all the student knows, Sophocles is a shortstop for the Dodgers. What's important is that the student lied quickly and elaborately. His higher grade reflected that skill. Teachers can't be blamed for rewarding dishonesty. They have no way of knowing who is telling the truth. Students learn quickly that lies can sometimes be substituted for homework.

Fake research sources, cheat sheets, and ambiguous answers to parents' questions are all signs that something is wrong. The most common explanation is that a kid's dishonesty is caused by laziness and bad behavior. Certainly, teenagers can make a full-time occupation out of being slothful and evil, but maybe there is another side. Teachers, out of a sense of duty, are fascinated by overkill. They require five research sources on subjects that need only three and assign ten pages of writing for topics that need only three. Their habits make dishonesty attractive. Then there are parents, whose curiosity is surpassed only by their distrust. In moments of teenage crisis, most parents come across somewhere between a KGB agent and a mental patient. Faces red, windmilling their arms, they repeat the universal, wherehaveyoubeendoyouknowwhattimeitis mantra. These fireworks give their frightened offspring the awkward choice of lying, getting caught, and suffering or telling the truth and suffering.

An upstanding young American is drunk and one hour late for curfew, facing an irate parent. He must choose the best answer to the following question:

1. Where have you been? If you're drunk, I'll kill you.
A. My peers forced alcohol down my throat. Then they made me walk home.
B. My friend's car broke down so I'm late. Of course, I'm not drunk (hiccup).
C. I am extremely intoxicated. Please guide me to the nearest facility so I can vomit.

People who choose A are whiners. Those who choose C are either extremely noble or too drunk to care. Most would choose B, and hope their parents are easygoing or just plain gullible.

Given, lying is deceitful and harmful to character building. Given, lying engenders parental mistrust. But teenagers, though only rarely involved in here and now time frames, are basically short term thinkers. Next weekend is the future; last month is a distant memory. The adolescent mind will readily exchange future character for immediate escape from punishment. The deception doesn't excuse teenagers from lying. It simply explains why they do. Many kids tell the truth and take the consequences. Many don't need to lie, and some lie when they don't need to. The subject of honesty is confusing because it is part of growing up, one of the last great mysteries of life.

At home I am not honest—I can't be. I smoke, I get stoned, and I have a 19-year-old boyfriend that my parents don't know about. I have tried to tell my parents about these things, but they got very upset so I keep it a "secret."

When I am with my friends, they might ask me a question that is personal so I lie. I don't know hardly anybody that is totally honest.

When I'm in class, sometimes I don't bring my books or paper and I'll tell the teacher they were stolen. Who cares whether or not they were stolen? I don't.

Discussions

Matt: Honesty's the truth, and dishonesty's not the truth.

Steve: The truth has been defined as anything that two people agree on. The more people who agree, the more true it is.

John: Honesty is backed up by fact. I'm not saying that socially it's right to do this, but you can prove it. Telling what's right, even if it hurts, that's honesty.

Maribeth: Honesty is when you're not afraid to tell the truth. Dishonesty is when you cover for yourself.

Honesty to me is a lie itself. I mean, nobody is totally honest. The last time I was honest was when I stole something from a store. They caught me and asked me if I had paid for it. I replied, "No, no, I didn't—I stole it."

They called my mom, searched me for more (very roughly), and had me stay on probation for a month. And that was my first time ever stealing.

16-year-old female
Florida

I think dishonesty is a major problem in our society. I don't mean little white lies, such as telling

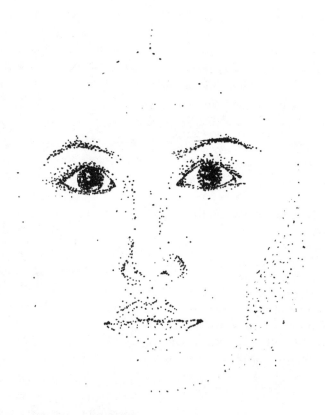

someone you just love their new hair cut, which actually looks ghastly. Rather, I refer to people who build up a wall of security around them and pretend to be what they aren't. . . .

Honesty is crucial with parents. . . . My parents and I trust each other so I don't have stringent rules I must go by. My parents know I wouldn't do anything they consider too wrong because they believe in me.

Jennifer Replogle, 15
Chicago, Illinois

Probably the biggest lie is that the truth will set you free when, in fact, it simply puts you in a different prison.

Scott Shadrick, 18
San Lorenzo, California

So much hypocrisy goes on in school that it's unbelievable. . . . It's illegal to buy cigarettes if you're under 18. Yet this school provides a smoking section with no age limit or even parental permission.

Leslie: Teenagers are dishonest to save their hind ends from their parents. I don't know why parents lie, or if they do. They don't have to lie to anybody.

Kelly: Teens can be more or less honest than adults, but it is usually about less significant things. Very few teenagers can lie about the paternity of a child or about income tax returns.

Steve: Teens are forced to lie on a more frequent basis. An adult doesn't have to lie if he wants to do something. He can generally go do it. But because parents have so much control over their children, teenagers are often put in a situation where it is advantageous to lie.

Matt: You have to build up a trust with them first. Seriously. You tell them the truth for a while, and then you can lie to them.

Kelly: It works the other way too. If you get caught lying to them, it's going to be a while before they believe you again.

You have to stay in the smoking area in order to smoke, but there are teachers here who sit up in their offices in the art building and puff on pipes. . . .

A student is to be in his seat when the bell rings or he has to serve a detention. A teacher in one of my classes has been at least 25 minutes late on three different occasions to our class. But he's the teacher.

Also, they say be to school on time. I get a ride from my father and I'm late a lot. "Ride the bus," my teacher from first period preaches. They send a bus out to Redwood Valley, but . . . to ride it I would have to walk a half mile and catch it at six-thirty in the morning. It's still dark.

How many teachers would walk in the dark at six-thirty to catch a bus instead of riding with someone at seven-thirty?

Robin Huey, 15
Ukiah, California

Coming up the stairs, my parents asked if I had fun the night before. "Yes," I replied.

"What did you do?" asked my mother.

"Went to a movie," I said.

"What was the movie?" she asked.

"Chariots of Fire."

"What was it about?"

"Uuuuh. . . ."

"Well, don't you even know?" mom asked.

"It wasn't too exciting. It was hard to pay attention," I replied shakily, feeling low inside.

I could sense they knew I was lying. The fact remains that I went to a party last night. The question is "Would I be restricted if I told them?" But even if I was restricted, I would feel a lot better about myself.

To ease my conscience, I told them. I explained, and they understood. I was proud of myself.

Kim Davies, 18
Seattle, Washington

Honesty

I see so much hypocrisy in authority, and it makes me sick. It's okay for an older woman to fool around and get pregnant and then get an abortion because she's a "career woman." If a teenage girl becomes pregnant . . . she is immediately shamed.

That doesn't mean it's right, but I think adults should set a good example. There are so many more examples, like drunk driving, smoking, drugs, sex, foul language, and many more. I don't understand why the people who are supposed to be running this country can't set an example for the future leaders.

A lady I know complains about teenagers and how they smoke when they're so young. Then the lady whips out a cigarette. It's really disgusting. Maybe teenagers wouldn't be so screwed up and in so much trouble if adults would set the example and not be so hypocritical.

Jennifer Swanson, 16
Arlington Heights, Illinois

I've run into a great deal of hypocrisy in 17 years, ranging from small business to our government. The

What do teenagers lie about?

John: My girlfriend lives in a different town. It's about two-and-a-half miles, and I go over there after work, about eleven. My mom says, "Okay, you work so you can stay out until two a.m." A lot of times I can't get the car, especially that late, and my mom says, "We're not going to come and get you so she's going to have to drive you home or you don't go."

So I always say that she'll drive me home.

I'm not allowed to walk that late. First of all, I've been spotted by the police, especially after curfew, about seven or eight times. I've never been caught. I always run and then hide behind some bushes or something. But when I get home, I'm sweating like a pig! How would I be sweating if my girlfriend gave me a ride home? I always have to take off my shirt, even if it's wintertime, and walk the length of my block home just so I can stop sweating.

Steve: Isn't it all worth it, though? You may be running the risk of getting caught after curfew, but

following are only parts of what I've experienced.

1. Just this last summer, I worked for a fast-food chain. The rules were given to all employees and strictly enforced. Among those set rules were no smoking, stealing is punishable by law, and termination of employment. The employees of the franchise took freely of what they wanted whenever the manager wasn't around; if caught, they would confess their "innocence" and blame another party.

Quite a few lost their jobs. For some, it was the only income they had and their only source of survival. Smoking was to be done on breaks, for employees. However, the rule didn't seem to stick to the employer. Cigarette ashes could be found on burgers that were sold, in the take-out cups, practically in all foods that were served.

On late night shifts, about closing time, the employer would be seen taking the cash boxes into the office. Many witnessed the employer stick cash into his pockets. Everyone just kept hush.

2. I attended an institution this past summer. One rule was that

tobacco was prohibited, and disobeying meant punishment or perhaps expulsion. A hired permanent worker could always be seen smoking and/or with a big wad of "chew" in his mouth. The people that were caught were either punished or sent home. The staff of this institution knew about this person, yet no action was taken against him.

3. In Anchorage, a "white" man murdered a police officer. His violation? Running a red light. His sentence? Seven years in prison. He was completely sane. In a village, a man shot his brother. His sentence? Twelve years in prison. This man was also sane.

4. Reports of high-ranking officials being prosecuted for conspiracy, bribes, and even murder. America the beautiful, eh?

I'm not saying that people are perfect. The nature of a person turning on his word is only human. It happens every day. It happens to everyone in one way or another. There isn't any cure for hypocrisy, but we as a society can at least try and control this part of our nature, and at least better ourselves since being perfect isn't human.

Eric Henelriekson, 17
Anchorage, Alaska

I think those who are in positions of authority who show the most hypocrisy are parents. While they tell us not to lie, cheat, and steal, they turn around and totally betray their supposed "values." They cheat on their income tax and lie about their age and weight.

When it comes time to elect a new leader, they spend maybe five seconds choosing a candidate and then complain profusely. . . .

When asked to do some sort of volunteer service or work, they moan and groan about their health or how they can't make it or how they "gave at the office." But when it comes time for you to do something which you would probably

you're having a hilarious time. I'm not given the opportunity to lie that often. My parents don't give me any cause to lie so it doesn't come up.

Kelly: That makes sense because I don't lie as much as I did in the past. Up until last February, my mother was very restrictive about what I could do and who I could see. She always dictated these things for me. If I wanted to see someone different I'd have to lie to get around it, which was basically foolish. Now, as long as I pay the long-distance bills, I can call whoever I want.

Steve: When I worked at Sambo's, I used to say that I was going to work the graveyard shift. Then I'd go out and party all night, go over to Sambo's and have a cup of coffee, then come home. I'd say, "Boy, what a night's work!" But now I don't have to do that because I can stay out as late as I want to anyway.

Kelly: I was just thinking about you staying out as late as you want. I still have a curfew, but now we argue about whether it was a quarter after twelve when I got in or twelve-thirty. I can lie a little bit now and not get in quite as much trouble.

Maribeth: Some people are afraid to let their parents know what they do, but I'm not. My mom lets me do stuff. She knows that I go to parties, that I drink. I'm sure she minds, but I haven't gotten in trouble. She trusts me. She knows that I'm able to handle myself. If I did go away to college, my parents wouldn't be there to say, "Don't go to that party. Sit home and do your homework." You have to be on your own. You have to do what you think is right.

Mary: The only time I lie to my parents is when I know that I'm going to do something that they won't like. They might not agree with me or they might say no, but I

rather not do, they almost force you to do it. They say it will be some sort of an enriching experience.

When it comes time to do work around the house, you're told how lazy you are and how they had to work all day long or they wouldn't receive any dinner. We all know that they were just as lazy, if not lazier, than we are.

The same thing happens with our grades. When we bring home our report cards with all A's and one B, all they do is complain about how your grades are slipping. The B is usually in some rinky-dink course like advanced knot tying.

When you complain how you hate school, they say that you're lucky to have it and that it's not that bad. I really wish that parents would be a little more consistent.

Greg White, 15
Milford, New Hampshire

I can't stand to listen to people gossip about their so-called "friends." When you hear everyone else gossip, you wonder what your friends say about you.

Kimmy Zielinski, 17
Brookfield, Illinois

Politicians are . . . susceptible to criticism and ridicule for their actions and policies. The public demands that they answer for every decision made or not made during a term in office.

Somehow, though, many politicians, including foreign diplomats to the U.S., feel themselves above the law. This hypocrisy among government officials should not be tolerated. . . . How can these people expect their laws to be followed, when they abuse them and the privilege given to those in a democratic society?

Diplomats especially think themselves free from law, claiming diplomatic immunity when involved in trouble. There have been continuous incidents where diplomats are involved in accidents where permanent damage is done to the victim. Whereas any normal citizen would be sued and forced to compensate the victim, the diplomats are set free with a reprimand and sent back to their countries. Some are even allowed to stay in the United States.

Congressmen also follow the same pattern. Recently a congressman was stopped and booked by Maryland police on drunk driving charges. When police found out the position of the politician, he was allowed to go free.

His trial is not expected to come up for a while, if at all, whereas another citizen would have been held in jail with the trial to come up soon. Drunk driving is a serious offense. What if all people could claim immunity?

These men run our country. They are public figures. . . . The law of the United States is not a case of "do as I say, not as I do," or is it?

Kris Garnett, 17
Fairfax, Virginia

There are certain instances where honesty is not the best policy. . . . I have reached an age where I feel it

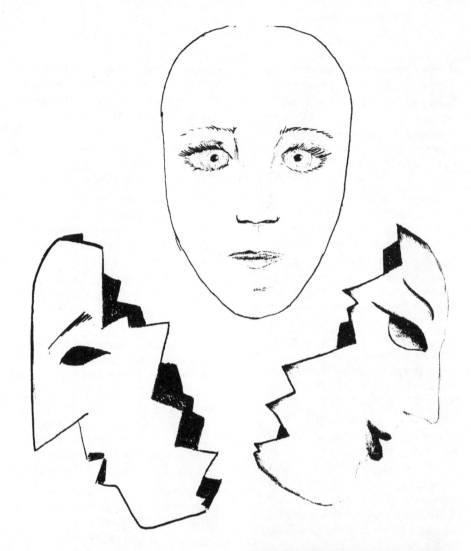

know it's okay so I'll do it. I'll tell them I'm doing something else. And it makes me mad that I have to do that! I'd love to tell them everything I do and have them say, "Okay."

Melanie: I think it's important to tell the truth, but it's also important to make sure that you're in situations that you won't have to lie about. A person's never forced to lie. I wouldn't want to get in a situation where I'd be ashamed to go home and tell my parents where I was or that I'd be afraid I'd get in trouble for it.

John: Okay, suppose your mom says you can't go out tonight or you have to be home by ten. You tell your mom, "I had to help Dave or give Dave a ride home" when you really just ran late. Is that gonna kill anyone?

is not necessary to tell my parents all that I do. I am almost an adult, and it is time for me to decide things for myself. Although they don't inquire about my every move, I do find silence a type of dishonesty.

17-year-old female
South Carolina

Honesty is one of the main things you have to work for in high school. Once I cheated on a test and was caught. I did not get punished, but that teacher thought from then on that I was dishonest. It took two years to show her I was not a dishonest person any more.

Kerri Mustin, 14
Clemmons, North Carolina

Honesty plays an important part in family life. A child who is honest will be trusted with bigger and better privileges. I will always remember all the lectures I received from my father. I will always remember because now I have seen what his lying has done to our family.

I always trusted my father, but now I wouldn't trust my father. I don't know if I even believe what he says anymore. You see, he was living a lie. Now it has wrecked our family, all because he wasn't honest.

17-year-old female
Washington

With adults honesty is important because no matter how good a story you make up and no matter how many times they say that they believe you, they know and you know that they really know what happened. . . .

Some teachers could really care less how much you lie to them. Then there are some that always think you're dishonest.

Angie Spencer, 15
Apache Junction, Arizona

Honesty and dishonesty are two extremes, and a person should not be either one or the other all the time. Being "honest" usually ends up meaning that you're somewhere between the two extremes.

To be "honest," you should be truthful in cases where the truth makes a real difference. In cases where your response is trivial and a truthful response may cause bad feelings or an injured ego, you need not feel that you've been dishonest because of a lie.

Neal M. Greenwald, 17
Joliet, Illinois

Hypocrisy is apparent when a person . . . goes to church and acts like "Mr. Good Christian" but then goes out and curses, drinks, and really acts non-Christian.

Jennifer Fulkerson, 15
Frankfort, Kentucky

Honesty is definitely necessary, but society doesn't think so. The government lies to us so why should we tell the truth? You get further by lying than by being honest. . . .

Michelle: If you're doing something that your parents won't let you do but you feel that it's right for you to do—like if they don't want you to go to Dave's house, but you know there's nothing wrong with going to Dave's house—then just say you're not going there but go there anyway.

Matt: Also, I think it's important to experience some things in life. You've got to lie a little bit about drinking or whatever.

Michelle: I was at my friend's house and on school nights I'm supposed to be home at ten o'clock. I didn't end up getting home until about eleven-thirty. My mom called over there and said, "Is Michelle there?" And they said, "No, she's not." That made me mad because I didn't want to lie to her. It just got me in a trap. I felt really bad, and I felt mad at the same time. I felt guilty. I wanted to tell her the truth, but I didn't want her to think badly of my friend.

Kelly: Something like that happened to me. It was Christmas, and I wanted to go to this small party at my boyfriend's house. My mother said, "No way." His folks were home and all, but she just didn't approve of him. I called a friend, and she knew about the party—she only lived a couple of houses down from him. I arranged that I would go and stay at her house for the evening and that I would come home at ten or something.

My mom dropped me off at her house. Then we walked to his house. Well, she left and my boyfriend wound up driving me home. A block away from my house I was just stricken with terror that my mother was going to know where I had been. I didn't assume my mom would be up, but she was. I was really afraid that she would say something, but she didn't. I went to bed and everything was fine. The weekend came. Sunday I

Yesterday I spotted a kid cheating on a test in one of my classes. Today when we got the test back, he got a higher score than I did. It makes you wonder whether it is best to be honest.

Greg Frick, 17
Seattle, Washington

One of the "forms" of dishonesty that makes me angry is gossip. It is so unfair for a person to talk about other people and start nasty rumors about them. . . . Even some of my friends gossip, and I wonder if they talk about me when I'm not around.

Stacie Halpin, 16
Bellaire, Ohio

I know a lot of students who have cheated on exams, myself included. I have never cheated because of any other reason except that I need a good grade. When grades are so important, as they are in our society today, how can you expect anything else?

If I were to ever have gotten caught cheating, my explanation could only be that it's not only my fault but the teacher's also. He or she is pushing me to get this good grade so, in turn, I want to get it.

Jolynn Marie Freed, 16
Fargo, North Dakota

Children being dishonest with their parents can cause many serious problems. . . . Not too long ago I had a boyfriend that my parents didn't approve of. He asked me out once. He met my parents, but they didn't like him because of what others had told them. I continued to see him after they told me not to.

I really liked him a lot and told a lot of lies so I could see him. My parents finally caught up with me. He was at my house one night while they weren't home. My father found him there, and many terrible things were said.

I was ready to run away because I was so mad at my father. This went on and on until we got caught

Honesty

107

three or four times. It was causing very serious problems with my family. . . . It pays to be honest.

Michelle Eken, 15
Poinciana, Florida

To be honest, you do what you actually think is right. We all have something in us that tells us if we are right or wrong. Dishonesty would be going against this.

Danny Ellis, 17
Lewiston, Idaho

In writing a newspaper, honesty is very important. After working on a high school newspaper for one year, one realizes this. One reporter of the newspaper I worked on made up quotes from teachers.

This incident made the staff realize that the truth must always be published because a paper has the trust of the readers. . . . Dishonesty, especially in the media, is very risky. . . . A newspaper must print the truth or risk losing the trust that readers put into that newspaper or any other paper.

Carol Peay, 17
Rock Hill, South Carolina

I was in a math class taking a test when my teacher accused me of cheating. I tried to ask why, and all my teacher would do is accuse even more. When I went to the guidance department for help, they listened to my story and then to his.

But . . . he said he didn't accuse me. He claimed he said, "Move your paper over so that this girl to the left of you can't see."

When the guidance counselor told me what he said, I just burst out into tears crying because I knew he wasn't being honest. Later on, I saw in his roll book a zero for that test. I just couldn't believe he gave me a zero when he said he knew I wasn't cheating.

I think that if he would have been honest and told the truth that we could have gotten everything worked out. But now he holds a

asked her if I could do something, and she said, "No." It wasn't a real horrible thing that I had asked to do so when she said, "No," I wondered why. She had known all along that I wasn't where I had said I would be. She wasn't going to tell me she knew. She was just going to let me squirm, and I did. Finally, when I realized that she was denying me things that she normally wouldn't, I admitted it. I said, "I feel real horrible, but I lied to you. I've been feeling bad ever since." Before she even dropped me off at my friend's house, she knew what I had been planning.

It really bothered me that she had let me hang myself. I remember feeling really awful. I don't know if it was so much that all of a sudden my mother wasn't going to trust me anymore or if it was because I got caught.

Steve: There are three policies here. One: you should always be honest with yourself. Two: lie as little as possible. Three: when you do lie, make sure it's a calculated lie. Think it out. Make sure it will work. Being honest with yourself is part of that. Always think about how you're going to lie. Make it very calculated.

What are the causes and effects of lying in school?

Karen: Once, just recently, I was cheating on a math quiz. The teacher decided he was going to sit right across from me. I had all the answers in my pen, and I'm sure that he could see that. But he didn't catch me. I still failed the quiz. I didn't learn anything from it.

Jeff: I cheated in biology. I think that's what got us our A. I cheated in English but only on one test. I felt guilty in English. I got along with the teacher more. I liked him more. I didn't respect the other teacher as much.

Steve: But cheating is not necessarily undesirable.

John: It's being dishonest to yourself.

Steve: It's being dishonest to yourself only if you then see an A on your quiz and think, "Hey, I'm pretty good." If you knew exactly what you were doing as you were cheating, it's not being dishonest with yourself.

Kelly: Okay, but it's still dishonest. Other people may have tried their best and remembered what they had to for the test instead of having it written on their desk. You're being dishonest to yourself if you think you did a good job.

Steve: It's only dishonest if you're caught.

Melanie: The grade isn't that important to me that I would have to cheat for it. I would think less of myself if I were to look over at the other guy's paper. I think it's my sense of guilt, my sense of self-worth, and my sense of wanting to make God happy which keeps me from cheating. But there are occasions when I have cheated. That's because of my pride.

Jeff: You've got to lie to people sometimes to get ahead in life.

How do teenagers regard stealing?

Manish: Cheat, lie, do anything. It's perfectly all right until you get caught. I shoplifted. It was just for the thrill. At the time, I felt that was a great accomplishment. I have an uncle who's always testing me. We're good buddies. We were at a restaurant one day. He has little cards with his office hours and so and so. At the restaurant there was this cardholder and he says, "I want that to keep my cards in."

I can't take it. What am I supposed to do? Ask the guy to take it? He says, "I don't care what you do. Ask the guy if you can take it, steal it, anyway you want. I want you to get that cardholder for me." I swiped the cardholder. He said,

"Good job. I was proud of you."
Then, outside—my aunt's there, my mom and dad. "What kind of kid are you?" He starts yelling at me just to embarrass me. He just does it for the fun of it.

Michelle: I used a fake credit card once. When I was a freshman, some lady left her credit card in an ice cream store where my friend worked. We charged about 75 dollars worth of clothes on it.

Jeff: Yeah, I stole ice one time from an ice machine, but it was okay because the guy left it open and wasn't even there so I couldn't pay. I thought, "It's just frozen water." I wanted cold pop.

Steve: I've taken glasses from the restaurant where I work. It's so easy to do. I know that if I had been caught by the manager who was on duty, he probably would have looked in the bag and said, "Well, I don't care." So there was no risk involved. I don't commit crimes just because it doesn't seem worth it. Everything I want, I can have. Second, I don't steal because I don't want people to steal from me.

grudge against me for trying to straighten everything out.

Keller M. Bardin, 16
Beaufort, South Carolina

Sometimes dishonesty can be a good thing. I would never tell someone what someone else said about them because I know it would hurt their feelings. I could never tell someone that the clothes they are wearing are ugly or that I don't like a member of their family. I feel they are better off not knowing.

Parents feel they should never be lied to, but sometimes lies keep them from worrying. Everyone has a right to privacy, and parents shouldn't expect to be told everything about their child's life.

I don't mean you should withhold something really important from them because that kind of dishonesty is not good for a healthy relationship. People should be open with each other and say what they feel, but only to a point. Some things are better left unsaid, or, if need be, covered up.

Jackie Korellis, 16
Munster, Indiana

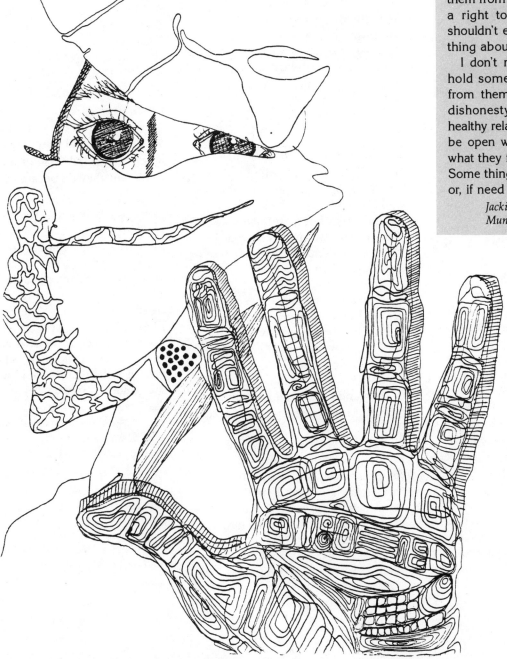

Kelly: I have this unreasonable fear of authority. My cousin and I didn't have any tennis balls. We wanted to play tennis so we were going to go to a store and open a can and take a tennis ball and leave. We were so paranoid. We couldn't even leave. We didn't take it. We were so afraid people were watching us.

How is gossip a form of dishonesty?

Michelle: If I hear something about a person, I'll ignore it. Even if it is true, so what? So what if this girl screwed around with that guy? It's their business. I guess you've got to judge a person by how they are to you. You can't judge them by rumors.

Kelly: There are a lot of people who judge by gossip. There's a popular rumor about a friend that he's less than straight in his relationships with girls and that he's gay and all. It's just not true.

Steve: It always seems like just one big game that some people enjoy playing. I know of girls and guys who lie to each other like crazy. They love it; they enjoy it. It's the same sort of people that are into the soap opera life.

Kelly: It depends on whether they're gossiping the truth or gossiping total lies. You can laugh off a story that someone is telling about you. But if they're saying something that isn't supposed to be common knowledge, then it hurts other people. It's not just a game.

Leslie: I used to come to school and put on a certain act just to please my friends so they wouldn't talk about me. And then I thought, "Hell, I don't need to please anybody but myself. If they are my real friends, they won't talk behind my back. If they're not my friends and they talk behind my back, I don't care. They're not important to me."

Michelle: A lot of people do it for revenge.

Steve: So don't give in to them. They lie because they hope you'll get upset and worried about it. If you don't get upset and worried about it, they don't get their revenge.

Matt: That's the only way they can get back at you.

Michelle: Well, just recently this guy was yelling stuff at me down the hall and there's so many people in the hall, you know? He is one guy I wish would just be wiped off the face of the earth.

Steve: He obviously has a reputation of being that way. Nobody is going to take him seriously, whether he's telling the truth or not. Even if he gets hold of a piece of information that's completely true, you have no cause to worry because no one's going to believe him.

How does it feel to be lied to?

Steve: I had a friend who used to lie a lot about ridiculous things, and it used to irritate me. I knew when he was lying and when he wasn't, but I would never say if I knew. I would just accept what he said because he was an insecure person. You know, I didn't think it was my place to say to him, "You're lying." I don't have the power to make him secure so why should I take away the lies that he used to make himself feel a little more secure? His motivations were understandable. It did irritate me at first, but I was never upset or mad at him.

Kelly: If that's the case, where you know the motivation and you like the person anyway, okay. But if not, then hearing lies really makes you reevaluate what you think of a person. I had a friend for a long time—and I always thought that she was honest, at least to me. Then, when I found out in a

roundabout way that she wasn't, it really made me think differently of her.

How is dishonesty rationalized?

Michelle: I called my boss and told him I couldn't come in because I had a lot of homework. He got mad at me. I told him the truth, and he got mad. Thursday night I took off. I had somewhere to go that night that I didn't want my boss to know about. I didn't think it was any of his business. I just said that I was sick. It was a lie, but I didn't want to tell him the truth.

John: If I call in sick, someone else has to work for me.

Steve: But you won't call in sick because you are a sensible, mature person, and that's exactly why you have that job.

John: What if I really am sick, though?

Steve: If you call in sick, they know you are sick, and they'll deal with it. They won't question it.

John: But they do because I'm a kid.

Matt: If you're a kid, they don't trust you.

John: I've only called in sick twice. Once was about a month ago. I said, "I really can't make it. I've got a high fever." And I work in a freezer, which doesn't help much. They said, "Well, you have to come in. If you don't, Mike will have to work six days this week." I believe in your policy, Steve, but I hate to say, it doesn't work 80 percent of the time.

Compiled by Holly Hager

Honesty

Chapter 9.

Sex

The Youthful Experience

Richard Roe was like most seventh graders with the exception that he was one of the youngest in his class. He often wondered how things might be if he were as old as most of his friends. Richard lived with his father in an apartment close to school. Even though he was an only child, he was not spoiled. However, he did have one habit that threatened to become his future career . . . girls.

In sixth grade Richard was class president, but everything changed in junior high. More classes, more teachers, and more guys who were more popular than he. But most of all, more girls.

Richard didn't mind not being popular anymore because he knew schoolwork came first. As he walked down the hall, he thought of what his father had told him. "Just get good grades now and school will be much easier as you get older. There will be plenty of time for girls in high school." Just then Richard saw a girl, with what he considered to be a nice tush, walk into a classroom. His father's voice puffed into nonexistence.

Richard began to notice that all the good-looking girls were "dating" the "studs" or "jocks." Richard was by no means a stud, but the Puberty Fairy did visit Richard in his sleep at least once a month and stick a few blond hairs on his chest, chin, and armpits. This made him happy, for a while.

Richard also wondered why his friends said they were "going out" with each other. One day during lunch, he had a talk with his best friend Biff.

"Why do you and Susan say you're going out? You know darn well you ain't goin' anywhere. Do you drive? Of course not. So why can't you just say you're going steady or something?" To which Biff replied, "Listen, Dick (most of his classmates called Richard "Rick the Dick" or simply "Dick"), I don't care what anybody calls it. All I know is she's got a great ass. The only thing she ever wants to do is french."

Richard knew what "frenching" was and wondered how people could stand doing it, especially after lunch. Yech! "There's more to girls than just frenching ya' know," Richard said loudly.

"Yeah, I know. but she's also got great lips. Know what I mean?" Biff ribbed Richard with his elbow, snickering softly.

Richard appreciated a good sexual innuendo every now and again, even if it was in bad taste. Then he thought of his long-time friendship with Susan and began to protest. "But why do you . . ."

"Listen Dick. You don't even have a chick. You never have. What's the matter, you a gay-rod or something?"

This hit Richard square in the face. He wondered why he had never asked a girl out. He was afraid of rejection. He often pictured himself in a situation similar to the following: Richard approaches Roxanne, the most popular and perhaps the most beautiful girl in the school. Sweat is running down his back and armpits, which have been collecting hairs for nearly a year now.

"Hi Roxy . . . ah . . . how ya' doin'? Um . . . I was wondering if . . . ah . . . you'd ah . . . ya' know . . . like to . . . ah . . . go out with . . . me?" Laughing inside, Roxy decides to string Richard along. "Sure, where are we going? Ha Ha?" I knew it, Richard thinks to himself. I knew she was gonna say it. Of course he never planned to take her anywhere. He just wanted someone to hold hands with in the hallways and to french with. Not to be humiliated, he quickly improvises a stud tactic. He reaches around and pinches Roxanne's rump, gives her a wink, and begins to wave his tongue while grunting in a low tone.

"You faggot!" Roxanne screams into his face as she raps him upside the head, causing him to bite his drooling tongue.

The answer was simple. He would not ask a girl out until he could literally take her out. "Soon as I get a car," he mumbled. "That's when the action starts." Richard knew this meant waiting a few years until he got his license, but he was willing to sacrifice.

The summer before his sophomore year in high school, still no car, still no girlfriend. Richard fell in love. He had moved into a new housing development in the far western suburbs. The neighborhood was small, and there were only eight other kids his age there. Only two girls. All summer he and his friends would play softball, frisbee, and go bike riding. It was during the softball games that Richard first realized his strong sexual desires. Lori would always wear those tight silk shorts and terri-cloth tube tops that sent Richard into hysteria. He made sure to always have Lori on his team, then made her the pitcher. Like a junkie, Richard would stand on second base and just smile and make funny noises. Something inside told him he had to possess this girl. He didn't want to have sex with her;

he just wanted to hold her in his arms and caress her long, black hair. He never had a girlfriend and he figured he was due, but he wasn't into kinky stuff . . . yet.

The big day finally came—Richard got his license. Lori was going out with some football stud, so Richard asked out a girl in his gym class named Eydie. With spring vacation coming up, he planned some experiments to further his sex education. One day during lunch he revealed his plan to some friends.

"Okay guys. Who wants to lay money down that Eydie and I go all the way this Friday night?" (Richard has learned a lot since junior high.)

"Two bucks!" says Chris, his best friend. "But how you gonna prove it?" Two other friends, each thinking they have easy money on this one, also throw in two dollars.

"I don't have to prove it. You know I'll do it," Richard assures them.

"Yeah, right. I think you owe me two bucks, buddy," Chris demands.

"Hey! I'm taking her to Hi-View, boys. In my truck . . . with a big front seat. I believe this loot is mine, thank you!"

Arguments turn into good-natured fun, and the lunch room fades away.

The fog slowly forms into a clear picture of row upon row of cars all perpendicular to the giant screen looming in front of them. Richard's pick-up truck is parked somewhere six rows from the back fence. Richard and Eydie are cuddling with a blanket around them, munching popcorn. Richard ponders on what his father would do if he found out that Richard was at a drive-in movie trying to get a piece off his pompon girlfriend instead of at the roller-rink. Just then, Eydie begins to tease Richard, and the image of his father beating him to a pulp puffs into non-existence.

One month later.

Ring. . . . Ring. . . . Ri(click) "Hello?"

"Hi Dick, it's me [Eydie]. Guess what? I'm three weeks late for my period. Do you know what that means?"

"You're going to fail English. Ha Ha!"

"No Dick. I might be pregnant. I haven't been with anyone for the past eight months except you, so guess who might be the lucky father? Hello . . . Richard! Are you still there? You can't leave me now Richard! Do you hear me?"

Richard didn't like guessing games. "Oh my God!"

The Male Experience

The setting is a dark bedroom in a borrowed apartment of J.D.'s friend. The scene is two half-clothed teenagers: J.D. and Ann making out.

J.D.: What are you thinking about?

Ann: Oh, I don't know. I'm just relaxing and thinking about us. Why, what are you thinking about?

J.D.: Well, I'm thinking we should take off the rest of our clothes and make love.

Ann: Boy, you sure get right to the point.

J.D.: Well . . .?

Ann: But . . . we're not even going out.

J.D.: Oh, those are just words.

Ann: To you maybe.

J.D.: Look, I've been seeing you for three months now. We went to homecoming together. I've never forced you into anything.

Ann: Well, it's just not the right time.

J.D.: All right, all right, it's no big deal. C'mon, let's go home.

Ann: What do you mean it's no big deal? Do you mean that even if I had let you, it wouldn't have been any big deal to you?

J.D.: I didn't say that. Just relax for chrissake. I'll talk to you tomorrow, okay?

Exit Ann.

J.D.: Boy, what a drag she is. All the time teasing and making come-ons until I get her alone. Then she clams up and freezes. I'm so sick of wasting my time with her. She's not the type of girl you bring home to meet your parents anyway.

Once at home, J.D. wonders what to do about Ann. "Things sure were different when I was going out with Helene. She never left me hanging."

Unable to remember why he broke up with Helene, J.D. retires to his room and locks the door. He turns on the radio quietly so no one will wake up. He pulls a new Penthouse from under his mattress. While thumbing through the pages, he becomes conscious of his now aching hard-on that he has been stuck with for hours. J.D. starts masturbating while thinking about how he could be screwing Helene right now if he hadn't dumped her.

He thinks back to the first time he masturbated, when he was 11 years old. On hot summer days when he was left home alone, he used to sneak into his father's closet and pull out a stack of ratty old girly magazines. Most of the time he just looked at the pictures. "It's only normal I guess. If my dad looks at them, it must be just a normal thing to do."

Once in a while he would look through the articles to see if all the pages between the pictures were serious reading or space fillers. An article about masturbation caught his eye one day. It was a strange word to him so he decided to read the article and find out what it was all about. After he finished, he thought masturbation sounded like the best thing to be invented since hockey. Being curious, he tried it.

Ever since then, he had been masturbating almost every day whenever he got the urge. From then on, he read the articles in all the magazines and learned that all kinds of things were possible. When he read a description of intercourse, he simply couldn't get it through his head that his parents had done it at least three times (once for each brother).

He figured out his father had intended that he find the books to save himself the embarrassment of teaching J.D. all the essentials. J.D. thought back to one time when both his parents had confronted him with the birds and the bees. He had made some stupid immature comment which mortified them so much that they never brought up the subject again.

That was the only education he had received. His teachers and his mother, however, had tried their best to instill the idea that sex before marriage was sinful. J.D.'s magazine told him differently so he decided to believe in his old friends, the girly books, to steer him right. His teachers had also told him that girls always become interested in boys before boys become interested in girls. J.D. could never figure out why he didn't fit in with this theory. As long as he could remember, he had always been the first one to strike up a game of spin-the-bottle or truth-or-dare. He always wondered why everyone else was running from girls while he was always running after them.

J.D. became a teenager. By the time he entered high school, he had a well-developed sex drive, which was normal according to his books. After all his intensive reading, puppy love, and kids' games, he was ready to test his skills. J.D. dated a few girls during his freshman and sophomore years, but they frustrated him. Some wouldn't kiss, no matter what he tried, and some wouldn't stop kissing. Sometimes he would get inside their shirts or in their pants only to be slapped away before reaching his goal, but on occasion he met no resistance and would see what he could find: like where to touch a girl to make her shiver or gasp.

Most disappointing of all was that all through high school hardly any girls would give anything back to him for his pleasure. They usually lay there like mannequins while he did what he could to excite them. He had read that it was better to give pleasure than to ask for it. He kept hoping that someday someone would return the favor.

When J.D. went out with Helene and found that she wanted to go to bed with him, he was thrilled. "This is finally it after all these years of wasting my come in a towel. I'm going to have sex." The first time J.D. was embarrassed. Putting on a rubber in front of a girl wasn't very easy. After he had dated her a few more times, they began to get pretty good at it. J.D.

began thinking of how to ask Helene if she wanted to try some different positions and oral sex.

He gave Helene head one night. She seemed to enjoy it, but she didn't have any mind-shattering orgasm like he thought she was supposed to have. He must have been doing something wrong, but he didn't know what it was. On a different night Helene told J.D. she wanted to try something on him, but that it was very hard for her to do it. She moved down his body and began to give him a blowjob. Apparently she was disgusted because she stopped right away.

After a few more weeks J.D. got bored with Helene. She always liked the same positions. One time J.D. didn't have a rubber, but she said, "Oh, it's okay. We'll just make out. We won't do it." They got heated up and pretty soon they couldn't stop. Afterward, J.D. thought to himself how, if she had gotten pregnant, his whole life would have been over. Luckily she wasn't. He thanked God for sparing him, but he knew that he couldn't take any more chances with her. He decided to break it to her gently.

Coming back to reality, his thought travels back to Ann and the problems he is having with her. "There's nothing I can do till I call her tomorrow. I'll give the bad news to another one—we'll have to break up."

The Female Experience

The setting is a dark bedroom in a borrowed apartment of J.D.'s friend. The scene is two half-clothed teenagers: J.D. and Ann making out.

J.D.: What are you thinking about?

Ann: Oh, I don't know. I'm just relaxing and thinking about us. (To tell you the truth, J.D., relaxing is the last thing I'm capable of doing.) Why, what are you thinking about?

J.D.: Well, I'm thinking we should take off the rest of our clothes and make love.

Ann: Boy, you sure get right to the point. (I knew it! Now what am I going to do? Sex is one thing; making "love" is another.)

J.D.: Well . . .?

Ann: But . . . we're not even going out. (Dumb excuse, Ann, you know that doesn't have anything to do with it.)

J.D.: Oh, those are just words.

Ann: To you maybe.

J.D.: Look, I've been seeing you for three months now. We went to homecoming together. I've never forced you into anything.

Ann: Well, it's just not the right time. (Actually, J.D. buddy, I don't want you. Not when you put it that way. You can't put a time limit on desire. Homecoming? What does that have to do with sex?)

J.D.: All right, all right, it's no big deal. C'mon, let's go home.

Exit two frustrated lovers.

In the car on the way home, Ann and J.D. are silent. Pressed against the door, Ann reflects on the disastrous evening. She realizes she'll most likely lose J.D., but that fear of losing a boyfriend is no reason to have sex.

Besides, Ann knows about J.D.'s reputation for "love 'em and leave 'em." He's a popular jock, but that's never held much importance with her. "Oh well," she thinks to herself, "chalk it up to another learning experience."

Ann considers that everything from her first french kiss to the finer points of sex is a learning experience, as are romantic failures and learning not to give in when she doesn't want to. Sometimes the two go hand in hand.

Though her mom wouldn't let her officially date until she was a sophomore, Ann started learning the finer points of french kissing and "making out" in junior high. She never had a chance to get involved with any of the older guys she kissed because her summer romances ended when school started.

Ann was always afraid of the boys she knew because her mother told her, "they're only

118

after one thing." Though Ann was only 14, she knew what that "thing" was. Also, Ann was still trying to get past the groping stage. Messing around scared Ann. She was never sure whether the guy liked her or only wanted to mess around. The guys she had associated with had been so callous and lewd. When they talked about girls they dated, her boyfriends talked the same way. Ann was always uncertain about their intentions.

When Ann entered high school, she faced more conflicts. First, if you weren't "going out"—dating? out to the movies? steady?—with one guy but dated different people, you were considered a "whore" or a "slut." It didn't matter if you had sex or held hands. The unspoken rule instilled a fear in Ann that caused her to stifle her emotions. Second, there seemed to be an unspoken schedule for how far a girl should "go" with a guy:

1. Hold off until you're "going out"—steady.
2. Once you're "going out," take things real slow. There didn't seem to be a definition of "real slow," but Ann didn't like the sound of it. She believed that when you felt good about holding hands, making out, petting, you should do it. But her feelings didn't conform to the rules.
3. Never have sex. That rule seemed to be written on stone tablets. Even though Ann was a virgin, saving herself until marriage was not one of her life goals. Like most of her friends, Ann believed that when the time was right, she'd go ahead. Sleeping around was wrong, but she didn't think sex was.

In high school, Ann became more open-minded and lost the frightened feeling that went with inexperience. Though she felt more comfortable with guys, Ann always wanted more. She wanted someone special but she never seemed to be attracted to guys her own age and had no way of meeting anyone older.

Sex

When Ann was a sophomore, she had her first "steady" romance. She remembered how it was the first time she openly talked about her period with a guy. That was another taboo. Ann's mom told her that her "friend," as some people called it, was hush-hush as far as guys were concerned. That was, of course, impossible when it was "that time of the month" and your boyfriend was reaching for your jeans. Also, it was a popular excuse among girls when they weren't "in the mood."

Ann's junior year seemed the popular time to lose one's virginity. All of her friends did, and, eventually, so did Ann. For something she had desperately kept sacred for 16 years, it went fast. Luckily, her lover was considerate and actually cared about her.

Ann believed that the majority of teen guys didn't give a damn for the girl but were out only for a "piece of ass." Once they got it, they lost respect for the girl and dumped her. Ann couldn't understand why girls were considered "whores" for having sex but guys were "studs" if they slept around. She couldn't understand why guys had so little respect for themselves, let alone the girls they had sex with.

It was even worse when the guy told the girl, "Oh baby, I love you. If you love me, prove it." She figured if any girl fell for that line, she deserved what she got. Except the girls who got pregnant. A junior girl in her class was pregnant and was dropping out to have the baby. She didn't even know who the father was. Ann realized that if she was in the girl's place, she would get an abortion even though she hated the idea.

"What a waste of two lives when a teen gets pregnant. Sex and responsibility come together. If two people lack responsibility, they shouldn't have sex," Ann thought.

Ann was glad she turned J.D. down. He was just another jock who uses girls. She hoped he'd be different, but he wasn't. The next man would have to be as special as the first.

As a senior, Ann was glad that she and her mom could finally talk openly about sex. She'd never admit she wasn't a virgin, but she now knew her mom understood a lot more than she had given her credit for. Ann knew that whatever happened, good or bad, she'd have a good friend.

"I've got a long way to go," Ann thought, but she realized that she was headed in the right direction. "At least I know what I want," she said aloud, "even if it isn't J.D."

Discussions

My opinion of premarital sex is that no matter what anyone says, it's always going to happen. I really don't think that people should do it. It's a sin. But also teenagers and grownups think that they should have sex with their boyfriends to hold on to them.

If you were going with someone and they get at you for not having sex with them, then I believe you should leave that person and find you somebody else. I have a boyfriend, and I made him wait before we had sex. That may not be such a long time, but he didn't hassle me about having sex with him. I wanted to have sex with him.

Male: *Sex is something special with me. I would not have sex with just any girl. This one friend of mine was once like that. He would find a different girl each weekend and get everything he could. Now he's got a girlfriend that he's been going out with for about a year and a half. He regrets that he ever did that. This girlfriend, I think, kind of holds it against him. She feels like she's sharing his body with somebody else.*

Sex should be a part of love. I like surprising my girlfriend. I tell her I love her. I don't go around saying, "I love you, let's have sex." I like to surprise her. I like to give her presents. When we "make love," when we have sex, we'll usually be sitting there watching TV and we'll be close to each other—we usually lay next to each other watching TV and it comes natural.

I show my love that way, but that's not even half of it—how I show my love. Caring for her when she has a problem. There are times when I've been tired. Like last night I was real tired—didn't want to do anything. But I went over to her house at ten-thirty because she needed help with her homework. I show my love by doing things that are out of the ordinary. You go out of the way for her. Sex is part of it, you know. You learn to say, when she doesn't want to have it, you don't have it.

Her parents and my parents never

120

said, "Have a lot of sex," or anything, but they know things go on. My parents are real strict. They just said, "Don't get her pregnant." They never talk to me about sex. My sister teases me when she sees me and my girlfriend kissing. My parents said, "Just remember how old you are." That's it, though.

A lot of guys have a hard time getting a girlfriend. They have sex with lots of girls, but they don't have a girlfriend. Having a girlfriend is different. Sometimes it's a pain, but it's nice to know somebody's there.

In some ways, I'm conservative about sex. At Great America I saw two girls wearing bikinis—just two little squares of cloth. C'mon. Or the t-shirts with just underwear underneath. If my girlfriend wears a pair of shorts that are too short, I tell her to change them. She bought a bathing suit that was too short. It started creeping up on her. I don't like that. It's disgusting. I don't care if it's another girl or my girlfriend. So I bought her another bathing suit that we both like. Girls are showing too much. Why do you have to see it? Especially if she's walking with her boyfriend and she's showing everyone else what she's got. All the surprise is gone.

Female: When you first meet somebody, holding hands can be fulfilling and satisfying. But as a relationship goes on, the couple becomes more intimate. It just develops. A little

GIRL WATCHERS

DISEASE

bit is okay at first, but it progresses on to more and more.

For a long time, I had my standards that I set with my boyfriend. I always thought I was compromising him because he was so adamant about what he thought was wrong. But sometimes I'm not thinking clearly, and things develop that wouldn't normally. Sometimes I'm thinking very clearly, and I'll say, "All right. This is okay." When I feel like I've gone too far, I get very mad at myself. A lot of times it isn't something that I don't want to do, but just on that day I don't feel it's right. Sometimes I'm just content having him hold me and cuddling with him. But he doesn't seem to understand that. Sometimes we do go too far, and I get very mad at myself. I get very quiet for a long time, and I'm very angry.

Sex has caused tense moments between me and my boyfriend. Not tension between ourselves. He and I have survived, but often we think we're really on the wrong track. Often we have to straighten ourselves out and say, "Wait a minute." Both of us has had to make sure that sex is not what is holding our relationship together. Often we say, "We're getting ahead of ourselves." And then we make arrangements not to be alone together because it makes it too easy to get involved. Sex is not a major part. It's something that we enjoy, but it's not the basis for our relationship.

I guess my feelings have changed radically in the last year or so. I can say that it's easier to be a virgin than to live the life of one. It's not so much that I'm acting. But it's very difficult, once you know what's out there, to deny yourself that. I guess I can say I've blown the standards I've lived by. But I don't feel bad about it, and it's not something that's recurring. I knew what I was doing, but I was disappointed with myself afterward. Everything I've grown up with says intercourse before marriage is wrong. That's real easy to say if you don't have someone specific in mind.

My feelings have changed. I'm to the

But we are planning on getting married sometime in the late part of next year or the early part or middle part of '85. I asked my preacher if it was okay to have sex if you are planning on getting married and he said that it was okay. I think I am doing the right thing.

But as for my mother and other grownups like her, I don't think that what they do is right—having sex and even another child by a man she's going with and they don't have any intentions whatsoever to get married. That's not right. If they love each other, they would get married.

I mean this child wasn't no mistake. This is what she wanted. I would never live with a man, have his child, and not be married. And I don't think that other people should.

17-year-old female
Tennessee

I don't really know if our fathers or their fathers as teenagers had the same problem that my generation is going through.

As a guy speaking, I think that the greatest pressure comes from all your friends. Maybe a year back it was, "Did you touch her boobs?" (I'll make this as clean as possible.) Today it's "Have you ever had intercourse with a girl, not just any girl, but a great looking one with a body to match?"

When the subject comes up between friends, the guys who haven't been with a girl may lie or stay out of the conversation. I think most guys feel the first one is just for the sake of saying, "Yeah, I did it." Afterward you realize it's no big thing.

Another pressure may come from within. A boy may torture himself because he doesn't want to screw up when he's finally with the girl he wants. He knows gals talk to each other about such things.

The big thing is that if you choose to be free about intercourse, take the necessary steps to protect yourself and the gal.

17-year-old male
Michigan

I don't believe it is marriage that makes sex all right but age. If a 25-year-old woman has sex with a man and they aren't married, there is no problem. But if a 17-year-old girl has sex with a member of the opposite sex and they aren't married, it is considered to be dirty, ugly, sinful, disgusting, and immoral. I don't think it is fair to convict someone of something that they did. It was their decision, and they made it. . . .

The choice to have or not to have sex should be made by two people that are willing to accept the responsibility. The choice should be their own, but it will be influenced by your parents and friends.

Pete Geren, 15
San Leandro, California

My opinion on premarital sex is that everybody does it. . . . In school, you overhear this conversation while you're at your locker.

Kelli asks Liz, "What did you and Charlie do Friday night?"

Liz says, "Oh, Charlie made me a really romantic dinner, and then afterwards I showed Charlie how much I appreciate him. And do you know what he did?"

They both walk away laughing. I feel premarital sex is wrong, but kids are always shown sex even when they are younger. They see sex on television.

Susan Alford, 18
Bettendorf, Iowa

When I was younger, such as eighth or ninth grade, the pressures to have sex were very great because we were all blossoming into man or womanhood, and the differences between sexes were becoming more apparent, making me want to explore and find out just exactly what the differences were. Everybody experimented with sex.

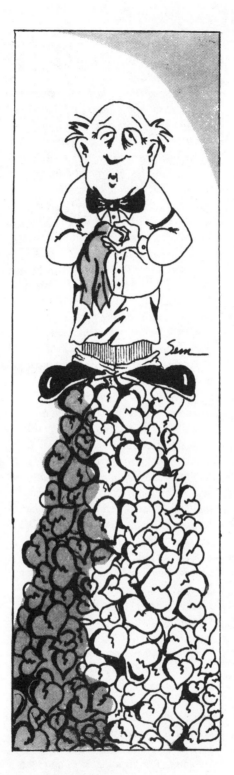

point now where I think if I'm 18, an adult, and I can handle the consequences, it's okay.

Importance of Sex

Kelly: In a relationship, equal love or trust should be able to stand up without sex as something to keep you liking each other. It should not be the main pull or the main attraction.

Jeff: I had the same girlfriend for two years, and I would say sex was pretty important. It became more important as we got to know each other better. But it isn't just something you do when you have the urge. Sex isn't just an escape. It is a mutual feeling.

John: To some people, it's more of a novelty. Well, really, they walk into the locker room and they say how great it was with so and so. I think it shouldn't be an everyday thing. You don't want to say, "Tomorrow night your parents won't be home so I'll be over and we'll watch TV and have some sex."

Manish: It's not something I have planned out. I don't list it in the top priorities for a relationship. It's not some cheap thrill.

Maribeth: If you put sex as very important, that means that's all your relationship is. A relationship should be more than sex—it should be friendship.

Melanie: It's something really special. It's not just an emotional valve to be let off. Some people say it's a medical thing and you have to have it when you're of age. That's not what it's intended for. It's really sad when you pick a partner and say, "Hey, we've been going out for two months so I think we should have sex." Then you have it, and you're missing out on the emotional, physical, and psychological feelings that come with it.

Michelle: There are people who go have sex just to have sex, and there are people that go out because they love somebody. I think it should be because you love somebody.

Steve: What type of love is necessary to have sex?

Diane: An unselfish love.

Michelle: A real love.

Steve: A love like you must marry the person? You must believe that in the future you're going to marry the person?

Michelle: You shouldn't use a person—being with them just to have sex with them.

Steve: But what happens if the other person wants a relationship like that? If both people want a sexual relationship?

Matt: I don't think it's right. I disagree with the one night stand thing. If they're both in love, I think it's okay. Sex is part of love.

Kelly: No, love is part of sex. Sex is not part of love.

Karen: Sex is simply making kids.

Matt: That's not true.

Diane: Sex is physically showing that you love somebody. Sex is not a beautiful thing if you don't love somebody.

Kelly: I don't think there should be sex without love, but there can be love without sex.

Michelle: A lot of people are in love with the idea of sex, too.

Jeff: There's a big difference between having sex and making love. To make love, you have to feel love and be in love.

Mary: I think girls just need someone to love them and care about them.

Steve: It's no big deal. Casual sex, you know. It's not that big a deal.

Michelle: When I was in Florida, I knew a kid who was 12 and had already lost his virginity. At 12 years old you're not old enough to know what sex is for. It's for when you love somebody. They're just out to try it—to see what it's like.

Leslie: Face it, if two people are going out for a long time, it's going to happen.

Maribeth: At first kissing, or maybe a little more, is fine. But as you keep going out things start to happen. It just comes naturally.

Melanie: To me, having sex with someone is like a covenant with them. It's something really special.

Something that you save for marriage.

Premarital Sex

Kelly: I think virginity is extremely important.

Jeff: I don't think that it's important to be a virgin anymore. What if you marry somebody, and you're both virgins and you have these weird hangups? You'd have to live with it. I think sex before marriage is pretty important.

Kelly: A lot of what I stand on or what holds me up is what I've found in the Bible. You're only supposed to have sex after you're married. So you have to be a virgin when you're married. So it's not even okay to have sex with the person you intend to marry because, outside of marriage, intercourse is wrong.

Karen: There are lots of good reasons, of course, not to have sex. One, fear of pregnancy. Two, well, I don't want to get married and already be broken in. That's something for your husband to do. There have been so many times when I could have, and wanted to, but I just wouldn't.

Steve: I think it's of absolutely no importance at all.

Kelly: How about it makes no difference—not that it's unimportant?

Steve: It's not important.

Karen: That's because you're a boy.

Matt: That's not true!

Michelle: Steve, can I ask you a question? Say there are two girls you like. If one is a virgin and one has slept with five guys, does that make a difference?

Steve: No, I really, really, genuinely couldn't care less.

Karen: I think it's pretty important for disease's sake. How would you like to get married to somebody and then find out they have herpes or something? Wouldn't that be horrible? And then, also, I guess

In the locker room, that's all the talk was about. How far did you get last night with her? Did you hear about Suzy Q.? I got a date with so and so tonight. Where you gonna go? Then as I matured and reached the high school level, sex became more of a personal, less-publicized thing. You only told your good friends.

Sex was much more acceptable in tenth grade than it was in ninth grade. I don't see what a big difference three months made. Maybe girls thought, "I'm in high school so it's okay." I'm not sure. Also, in junior high at parties people would neck a lot and maybe there would be a little petting. At high school parties, you go with your girl. There's very little kissing or petting but a whole lot more socializing with your friends. There is a very relaxed atmosphere.

Sex is more of a private affair in high school. I felt very pressured in junior high to have sex. You know a few of the other guys are having sex so you want to be with the "in" group. Maybe you lie and say, "Yeah, I had sex with her last night" when you really didn't, but you wanted to be accepted.

After the first time, which you'll always remember, it's really not that big of a deal. There's really not any pressure in high school. Although I feel a little pressured when I'm with a girl alone, I'm thinking, "What should I do? Should I kiss her? Or more? Does she want to?"

To me, having sex is a very intimate special thing. I wouldn't have sex with just any girl. She's got to mean a great deal to me. If I fell in love with a girl, I would want her to be a virgin—pure, natural. That would make making love that much more beautiful—to know that you mean that much to her and you're the first and only one.

Robert Gillispie, 18
Iowa City, Iowa

Sex

Homosexuality is not something I care to involve myself in. My only viewpoint is that I am glad it is being brought out in the open. It is a relief to know that people do not have to hide from what they are or love.

The changing morals are appealing to me. Parents discussing "sex" with their "adult" children is wonderful. One aspect I find appalling is that the youngsters today know more than I even cared to know at that age.

Kim Winkley, 17
North Vernon, Indiana

There are many ways to look at premarital sex, but the easiest way is to look at the people who have it and the people who don't. . . .

The teenagers who have premarital sex usually get bad reputations from their friends although sex seems acceptable. A friend of mine had sex at 15, got pregnant, and had to have an abortion. A lot of people don't think too highly of her and she will have to live with this forever.

On the other hand, the young people of today who don't have sex aren't much better off. . . . These teenagers often feel out of place or that they're the only ones who haven't had sex yet. Also, these people get a bad reputation because they're virgins and they are not doing what everyone else is doing. . . .

I feel premarital sex is a confusing subject. It doesn't matter what your decision is. According to our society, you're in the wrong.

Patti Stender, 16
San Lorenzo, California

I am 16 years old, and I have a boyfriend. We can talk openly and comfortably about sex, and I feel two people should be able to do that. We have not had sex because I am not ready although I love my boyfriend. I want it to be perfect so I can feel good about it.

Stephanie Miller, 16
Kissimmee, Florida

I'm old-fashioned, but I wouldn't feel right. I'd feel pretty scummy if my husband found out I wasn't a virgin.

Matt: If he loved you, he wouldn't care.

Karen: I would be ashamed of myself if I was some "sleep around girl." I wouldn't have any self-respect.

Kelly: I think a lot of times what's important is not only keeping your virginity but not losing your self-respect. If you figure something is all right—if somebody feels that sleeping with someone is all right, it's not as important whether they lose their virginity or not. It's whether they lose their self-respect.

Steve: You don't lose your self-respect with your virginity. You lose self-respect when you get freaked out about losing your virginity. And the only time you get freaked out about it is if society gets freaked out about it.

Kelly: If it wasn't such a big deal, where would the conflict come from?

Steve: You don't feel different after you've lost your virginity. No way. What do you do—stroll down the street thinking, "Wow, I feel different"? There's no way. You just don't.

Diane: Sex could be the most beautiful act for two people because they are virgins. Because they're willing to wait for the one they really love. You're giving. You're saying to that person, "I love you and I'm giving everything I possibly can to you. Something I waited so long to give someone."

Matt: What if you fall in love with someone, and they're not a virgin?

Steve: Is it any less beautiful?
Michelle: No.
Steve: So what's the difference?

Diane: I think it's more beautiful for two people to wait until they're married.

Melanie: I have a friend who's married. She's older, of course. The way she explains it to me, sex is something a man gives to a woman and a woman gives to a man. It's like a covenant.

BE WITH YOU IN A MINUTE, HONEY

124

Leslie: You shouldn't have sex before marriage because what about that white wedding dress? This may sound silly, but I'd feel horrible wearing a blue one or something, or wearing a white one and feeling guilty.

Contraceptive Concerns

Leslie: Teen pregnancy, I can't believe. They're teaching you about birth control in school now. It is so open. Birth control is so easy to get.

Kelly: There is only one way to be 100 percent sure—that's abstinence.

Michelle: The pill works if you use it the right way.

Leslie: If you're going to do it, you'd better get birth control.

Steve: If the girl is using contraception, then she can't get pregnant. Or, at least, the chances are slim.

Matt: It's the guy's responsibility.

Steve: There is no one individual who is responsible.

Michelle: I think it's both people's responsibility.

Diane: Yeah, it's equal.

Kelly: It should be both. It doesn't mean it is.

Matt: It's usually the girl's.

Kelly: When it gets down to abortion—I may be unreasonable about this—it's the girl's decision, not the guy's. If he's the father of the baby, that was irresponsible enough of him.

Steve: Oh, rubbish.

Kelly: All I can say is what I think for myself and what other people I know say. And I have to say that if I were in that position right now, where I faced giving birth or having an abortion, it's my decision. Not my husband's or my boyfriend's.

Steve: Your decision?

Kelly: My decision.

Steve: Like a couple?

Matt: It should be thought out. You just shouldn't say, "Well, I'm going to have an abortion."

Diane: Yeah. How many times, though, when a girl gets pregnant, does a guy say, "I don't want anything to do with this"?

OF COURSE, BEFORE ENGAGING IN SEX, THE PROPER PRECAUTIONS SHOULD BE TAKEN— DID YOU LOCK THE DOOR?

I think teenagers are careless if they do make the decision to have sex. No one plans to get pregnant, but it happens. This results in unwanted children, adoptions, poor marriages, uncalled-for marriages, and murder through abortions.

I realize that children given up for adoption most often live very happy lives, but my opposition to PMS (premarital sex) comes from the fact that I, as an adopted child, know (after research) that I was the unwanted child of a 16-year-old. I would never want to give that feeling to any other child.

17-year-old female
Ohio

I really think that it's all right to have sex before your marriage, but it's really up to the couple that's involved. If it was me, I would have sex before I would get married.

Bertha Brown, 16
Frogmore, South Carolina

I have a girlfriend who had a baby about a year ago. She decided to keep it, but it seems she has no interest like an older mother would have about her child. It's really sad because that child will probably have a hard life because her mother made a foolish mistake.

Kristie Ender, 17
St. Clair Shores, Michigan

People should not be bound by titles such as "marriage." If two people decide to have sex, it should not matter what they are. The title marriage is just that, a title that makes each person, as well as their families, secure. If people need titles to feel secure, then that is fine. But if people don't feel they need that title, that they are secure in their relationship, then their sexual activity is up to them.

Ted Grossman, 17
Chicago, Illinois

In tenth grade I was dating my good friend's brother. It seemed to me all he wanted was sex. Everytime I was with him and my friend, he would start up about sex. Then my friend would say, "What's wrong? Don't you want to have sex? I know I do." But I know I couldn't find it in myself to have sex. I didn't think I was ready for it.

I know a lot of people who think there is something wrong with you if you don't have sex, but I just didn't feel right about it. Maybe I'm the only one who cannot handle it. At least at this age I know I can't. I don't think I could look at, talk to, or be around the guy I made love to. I guess I'm old-fashioned, but it is something I look forward to after I'm married.

One time I was so close to having sex because I thought the guy would hate me if I didn't. But I told him I had never done this and walked away.

It is so scary because if you do, then the guy might go tell some other guys. Then when another guy asks you out, you don't know if he's asking you out because he likes you or because of what he heard some guy say about you.

Shannon Appel, 17
St. Clair Shores, Michigan

I think premarital sex is part of today's society. Today's American teenager has to deal with premarital sex with friends at school and at home. I remember when I was 11, I was playing catch (baseball) in front of my house with my friend. This girl, who lives next door to me, was about 13 then, and she really had a thing for me. She asked me to come in front of her house to keep her some company.

At first I said no, but she convinced me to come anyway. When I came to the porch, she asked me to kiss her, but I had never kissed a girl before. So I told her no because I feel that when I'm going to have sex, I'm going to do it with good intentions.

Brian Turner, 14
Chicago, Illinois

I used to not believe in having premarital sex, but I do now. It is a

Michelle: A lot. Guys aren't mature enough to handle it.

Matt: Some guys aren't.

Kelly: I wouldn't want a guy to have that control over me. When you're talking about sex, there are two people involved. When you're talking about giving birth, there's only one person involved other than the fetus itself. That's the woman. And it's her decision. I don't approve of abortion, but I think it's a woman's choice. I don't think someone can say, "You can't have an abortion." I think it's totally her choice. If she doesn't have any religious conflicts with it, or moral or ethical, or even if she's not scared, then that's her decision.

Steve: If the father says he feels that you should get an abortion and you say no, should the father provide financial help?

Kelly: No, then it's my responsibility. If I assume responsibility for the child and say, "I'm going to carry it and give birth," then it's my child. It's my responsibility. If he wants to back out and leave, he better leave quickly because he's not going to have a pleasant time. But I don't think it's right for someone to back out after they've fathered a child.

Sexual Experimentation

Kelly: You have to decide how far to go before you get started. I think if it's something you don't feel comfortable with or don't feel comfortable doing—if someone is not ready to give of him or herself—any distance is too far.

Leslie: I talk a lot. I explain my feelings about it. I've been in those situations. Things slip away from you. You're doing one thing, and it moves on more and more. Sometimes I don't know what to do. I don't. I'm so naive. I really am. It depends on the guy. If it's the first date, I'd just let him kiss me. But when you've been going out with a guy for a long time, you get feelings

for him. And you want things to happen, but then you're scared. You don't know what to do, and you don't know how to deal with it.

You've got the whole thing about, "What happens if I get pregnant?" And you don't want your relationship based on sex. So it's really hard for me. I think you should talk a lot about it. If you're going out with a guy for a year or something, you should be able to talk with him about anything. A relationship of mine broke up because I couldn't handle sex. Even though I loved him, I couldn't do it. It was like, "If you love me, you'll give me time. Give me room to breathe."

I think I could handle things better now. I know I could. Before, you're so scared because you don't know anything. Guys are just so horny. I think they're all out for a piece of ass. But for me and my boyfriend, we knew each other very well. And I couldn't handle it. I loved him as a person, and he had never pressured me before. But suddenly he changed, and he wanted everything. I couldn't deal with it, and I avoided the situation. We didn't talk about it then, either.

Now I think I don't have to avoid the situation. I can express my feelings. I can say "no." I can say "yes" if I want to.

Karen: I went out with this one guy. I asked him out. He said yes, and so I picked him up. But the minute he kissed me, he was all over me. I was like, "Get off me!" But he said, "Well, you asked me out. I thought you wanted to have sex." I thought we were going out for a nice evening, and then he was pawing me. Jesus Christ, I mean there's a limit. That stuff about being "technically a virgin"—that's bullshit. The girls are whores in every respect except they haven't gone "all the way." They've done everything except that.

John: How far is too far for me to

I DON'T THINK PREMARITAL SEX SHOULD BE TAKEN LIGHTLY —SO SERIOUSLY, LET'S GO TO BED

go? I don't think there's anything that's too far. My girlfriend and I have been going out for over three years.

Maribeth: Sometimes I don't know how to handle it. It's really weird, but right now there's this 35-year-old man calling me and asking me on dates. At first, I just said, "I have a boyfriend," but he keeps calling me. I tried to think of a way I can get out of this situation. So next time he calls, I'm just going to say, "I'm sorry, I can't see you."

But with guys our age—if I go out with a guy on a first date, I think a kiss, or maybe something a little more than a kiss, is okay. Just

kissing is all right for a while. But when you have a relationship for a long time, I think it just comes naturally. I don't just go out because he has a nice body or to see how much fun I can have with that person. It's something that just happens. But on a date, if a guy tries something I don't want, I just say, "Stop it. Don't do that."

Once one guy was trying something on me so I said, "I have my period" just to avoid it because I was too embarrassed. But that's embarrassing, too, because when you say that, guys reconsider. I know a lot of guys think they can get something off of me, but I say

very useful tool in finding out whether or not a couple is compatible for marriage. If a couple can make love, enjoy it, feel passion, and love, then they probably will have a good marriage. If not, then it wasn't meant to be and they may have saved themselves or their kids from a painful divorce.

One of the worst marriages is that of sexually incompatible people. I should know—my father went through two such marriages and was miserable. They almost constantly fought. All they succeeded in doing was to mentally hurt each other, my sister, and me.

I know from personal experience that sex life can determine a good or bad marriage. My old girlfriend and I thought a lot about getting married. We then had sex, but there was something missing in it. I didn't want to go through what my dad had so I told her I didn't feel ready for marriage. I know I did the right thing. . . .

Premarital sex may be a sin, but used the right way it could prevent many divorces before they become marriages. It should be used when two people are thinking about marriage. It's like a blood test. You have to be compatible.

18-year-old male
Colorado

From a boy's point of view, you've got to use protection or you have to be prepared to take on the responsibility of a child. I believe it is a little harder choice to make for a girl. You have to think about your reputation, protection, if he will stay with you after you're pregnant, and, most of all, your parents.

The way most girls are today it's a wonder the people of the U.S. aren't stepping on each other.
David Cook, 17
Clarksville, Tennessee

Being brought up in a Christian family and school, the girls who have premarital sex are bad girls. But because of the great changes in the thinking of society, I have not followed my mother's and her mother's value of being a virgin when married.

Having sex with a person does not exactly mean you are totally in love with the person anymore. I'm not saying that I believe in having sex with anyone you meet because I do feel you should really know your mate first. The couple should have a solid relationship. I think the legend of being a good little girl and saving yourself for your husband is a silly one.

18-year-old female
Ohio

I strongly oppose premarital sex for a number of reasons. My first reason is that I am a religious man who loves and serves God to the best of my capability. I am a man who believes in the Bible, the Word of God, which strongly opposes premarital sex.

I cannot comprehend what has happened to our country in this age. Twenty years ago, if a couple were involved in premarital sex, they would be taunted, tormented, and punished for their sins. Instead, in this time, premarital sex is not only popular, but it is accepted. One is thought less of if he is not engaged in premarital sex than if he is.

I strongly suggest that our society has to put a stop to this unforgettable and reprehensible occurrence of sin. The training of the minds to this new idea should start with the family in the home.

As well as teaching youngsters to eat their spinach and make beds, mothers and fathers should teach their youngsters strong moral and ethic values. Maybe if the training started in the homes, then America could cut down this enormous and popular sin of premarital sex.

Mike Glick, 17
Rockville, Maryland

I spoke with one girl on the subject of premarital sex. She said, "I'm stuff to guys—I try to be open with them. I say, "Don't expect anything from me. We'll date or whatever, but don't expect anything." If they do, I say, "I'll see ya later. Goodbye right now." They might try something later, and I'll just be the same way. Then they know I'm serious.

Steve: I don't believe that you should ever in any way push a girl into something she doesn't want. As far as I'm concerned, the one night stand or whatever, it's fine as long as both parties are having fun. But I don't think it's right for guys to push girls around.

Karen: How far is too far? Too far is when you know you don't want to go back.

Social Consequences

Kelly: Though psychologically the risk is great for both parties, the girl always has the chance of getting pregnant, which deters a lot of kids from having sex. But if we're not talking about intercourse, I think the responsibilities are the same for both, because you can hurt a person's feelings and affect the way they think about you. In love, there's a basis for sex. Without it, I don't think there is.

Diane: It's different because when a guy has sex he's a man and when a girl has sex she's a whore.

Steve: But why?

Diane: Because guys want to marry somebody pure.

Kelly: Not every man, but some of them would like to have that woman as their possession.

Steve: But that woman is a human being!

Diane: I think men fear that if their wives have had sex before with somebody, they may go out and do it again. I think that's more in the

minds of men than women.

Karen: God, you just kiss guys, and they want to have sex with you.

Michelle: Oh, everybody wants it. But they don't want to admit it because of their reputations.

Karen: Well, there are a couple of times when I wouldn't have minded. But I just wouldn't. Girls want to have sex. Sure, if a guy is gorgeous and he's persuading you, and you're a little bit drunk, you might think, "Why not?" I kind of support the double standard in a way. I don't care if the husband has had sex before marriage. In fact, I'd want him to have sex with other girls just so he knows what he's doing. I don't want to get into bed with some dud who doesn't know what he's doing.

Steve: I do not believe in a double standard whatsoever. There should not be one. Girls who have a healthy sexual appetite and enjoy sex and conduct themselves that way are no less of a girl than anyone else. They can still be good people.

Karen: I don't think so. I'll look at somebody who's slept with all the guys and I'll say, "What a slut." But then you look at the guy on the football team who's slept with all the cheerleaders. And you think, "What a great guy."

Maribeth: Girls have feelings too. They are horny, or they have sexual feelings. Sometimes they don't get enough love at home, and they feel secure when a guy is with them.

Steve: Sometimes people just want to be loved, to have someone love them.

Homosexuality

Kelly: It's their business, not mine. I'm not going to tell people what they prefer in bed. It's not up to me.

Matt: Homosexuality is disgusting. How many people agree and think it's wonderful that

two guys have sex?

Steve: I had a friend who was a homosexual. You wouldn't believe it. This guy was a totally cool person. And I didn't find out he was a homosexual until after his girlfriend did. I was good friends with the girlfriend, too. Finally it started to come out. The relationship started to get to the point where a sexual relationship could develop. The girlfriend wanted to have a sexual relationship, but the guy didn't. Because he was a homosexual, he didn't feel any attraction. But this guy was absolutely, totally, cool. He was a nice guy.

Diane: What about oral sex in a heterosexual relationship?

Matt: Why is it kinky?

Michelle: Why do people make such a big deal out of oral sex?

Diane: I'm not saying you can compare homosexuality to oral sex. How do you define the right way to have sex?

Kelly: Right. You cannot tell somebody in what position or who's on top, nor can you tell somebody who with. I mean it. All I was trying to say or bring up was it doesn't matter in what manner or who with.

not going to have sex with a guy until I've been going with him for two years." I said that was stupid and that if she was going to have premarital sex it shouldn't be the amount of time you've known the guy or been seeing him but how you feel about him.

Robert Patrick, 15
San Leandro, California

I feel that premarital sex is okay. It really all depends on who the people are and what their values are. I mean if you feel that you're going to go to hell if you screw around before the vows, then don't. But don't cut down someone who thinks differently.

My parents are totally against anything before marriage. I've been chewed up one side and down the other that "if you get pregnant. . . ." Personally, it's none of their business what I do, when I do it, or with whom.

Lots of people are into premarital sex. I mean I couldn't name two people that I know that are virgins. I feel, "Don't knock it till you try it. And if you like it, keep it up."

17-year-old female
Colorado

I feel no pressure to have sex. My boyfriend and I have had sex, but we don't feel pressured to do it just to please the other person. My doctor put me on the pill so I feel safe when we do have sex. I just wish my parents would have told me about sex so I would have understood more than "it's just a way to have babies."

I ended up asking my doctor about sexual intercourse. This upset my mom, but she wouldn't tell me so. Teenagers sometimes make wrong decisions, but they learn from them. My mom was so worried that my first "sexual experience" would be a letdown.

It wasn't, though, because I didn't know what to expect. I was pleasantly surprised by the way it turned out.

16-year-old female
Colorado

There are many pressures on teenagers to have sex, but this is true of most age groups also. I'm still a virgin but not totally innocent. When I first started high school last year, I held a very naive view of sex. I hadn't fooled around at all, never even been kissed. I felt undesirable and like a freak. So I decided in my own mind that I was going to change that.

There were many guys over the course of one year that I pleased only because I wanted to be wanted. Emotionally it was tearing me apart. The guilt was tremendous. Now I wasn't Miss Goody Two Shoes but the school slut.

Nobody else sees it this way . . . but the guilt has consumed me so. What I really want is romantic involvement, not just sex. I'm sick of feeling dirty, empty, and hurt.

16-year-old female
Iowa

Premarital sex is definitely out of the question. Sex is something that should be saved until after marriage. I heard somewhere before that sex is God's wedding gift to the two newlyweds—not to be opened too early. If you do wait, I think it would tend to strengthen a marriage because the two are learning together, learning from their mistakes. . . .

I know that there are a lot of people who would rather marry a virgin (both girls and guys). If everyone goes around having sex, there won't be any left to marry.

Barb Logue, 16
Larkspur, Colorado

Premarital sex is not worth the risk of getting pregnant and having a child before you're ready for one. . . . I have a friend who's now pregnant and the father will have nothing to do with her or the baby. If two people really love one another, they will wait till they're married and ready for a baby, not insist on "proving" their love.

Karla Brunig, 16
Kissimmee, Florida

Pressures to have sex, of any type, in high school are very strong. You always hear such comments as "Why not? We're seniors." When someone asks if you're a virgin, they make you feel ashamed to say "Yes."

Guys, I think, have a greater pressure than girls because it's the "only way" to prove they're a man. I feel it takes more of a man to respect the innocence of his girlfriend than to prove to his friends "he's a man."

Cari Goddard-Trumble, 17
Thornton, Colorado

Steve: "The United States government recognizes this as the accepted form of sexual activity . . ."

Diane: Who can define what is "normal sex"?

Steve: Really. What is normal?

Matt: Whatever's okay with you.

Diane: For some people, oral sex in a heterosexual relationship would be abnormal. As abnormal as homosexuality.

Maribeth: There was this TV show about older men seducing younger guys. I was so grossed out I had to flip the channel.

Manish: Maybe we're at a stage where homosexuality is considered to be "Wow!" Maybe in the future it will be a part of life. I personally think it's a little weird. If it's okay with them, it's fine, but I don't want them to force me into their way of life or to recruit me.

Steve: If two guys have a sexual relationship, let them keep it to themselves.

Compiled by Abby Rhamey

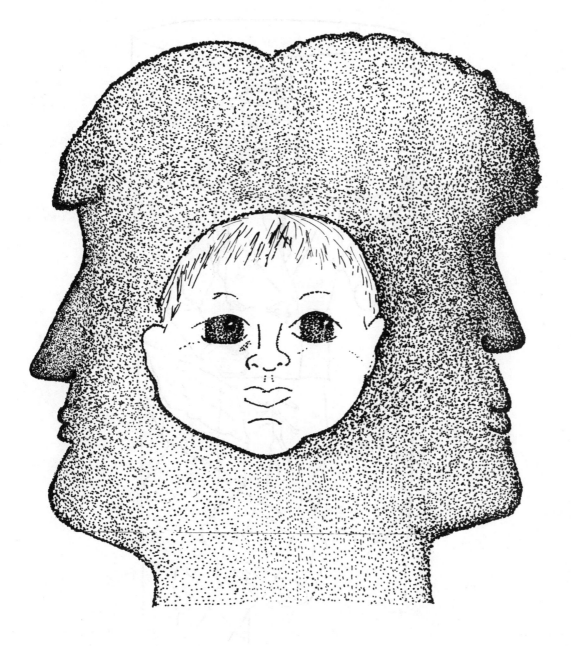

Sex 131

Chapter 10.

Drinking and Drugs

Teenagers. Drugs. Drinking. Teenagers. Drugs. Burnouts. Alcoholics. Teenagers. Drunk driving. Teenagers. Stereotyping.

When it comes to alcohol and drugs, the teenage stereotype is an easy explanation. According to the National Clearinghouse for Alcohol Information, 75 percent of teenagers drink. Almost 15 percent are considered heavy drinkers. But statistics give only a partial picture of teenage drinking and drug use.

At 273 Elm Street, Jane wakes up. Her head feels like it is clamped in a vise. As she walks to the bathroom, she wishes she had left her nauseous stomach at the party last night. After desperately trying to scrape the fur from her tongue with a toothbrush, she pops two aspirin into her mouth. Staring at her image in the mirror, she reflects on her night out. "Getting plowed sure makes getting up in the morning difficult," she thinks.

Janes smiles as memories of last night break through her cloudy mind. She and her friends had gone to a movie, but first they had had a private party at one of the girls' houses. Her parents were not home, and they helped themselves to the huge bar. After getting sufficiently buzzed, they ventured to the movie, a typical gory horror flick which Jane had seen before. This time, the film was better. She was "relaxed."

That's why Jane drinks. Drinking makes ordinary activities more fun. After the show they went to a party. Everyone was "gone" by the time they arrived. Jane blushes as she remembers telling the guy she had a crush on for six months how cute he is. "Why do I say things like that?" she wonders. Then she remembers her drunken pursuer. "Oh, God," she thinks. He was a quiet guy from her English class. She had spoken to him perhaps five times in three years. Last night he was after her—following her around, offering her beer.

Despite the embarrassing evening and her hangover, Jane admits she had fun. After all, what else is there to do at night in her boring town?

Across the street at 276 Elm, John reluctantly drifts into consciousness. It's eight a.m., and he has to get up for church. Punching on his radio and rolling out of bed, he thinks of his evening out. He and his girlfriend had gone out to eat and then to a party.

John doesn't like going to parties, but his girlfriend really wanted to go. Besides, all his friends were there. They were all wasted. That is the main reason John doesn't like parties; he doesn't like to drink. He can't understand why his friends indulge so freely when statistics show how many thousands of teenagers die because of drunk driving. Once he had gotten a ride home from a party with a drunken friend, and it had scared the hell out of him. His friend swore to God he could drive better when drunk, but the near-miss with a telephone pole and the "lawn job" on John's yard disproved that theory.

Downstairs in the kitchen, as John pours some corn flakes for breakfast, his thoughts go to Jane. She was really plowed at the party. John had grown up with her, and he hated to see her like that. Giggling uncontrollably—she just didn't seem like herself. He worried about her when she left with her equally drunken friend. He didn't like being around his friends when they were like that. It made him wonder what kind of people they'd be in 20 years—still getting bombed every weekend at age 40? However they will turn out, he doesn't like it now. Not at all.

Down the block at 297 Elm, Susan is munching on doughnuts while intently watching the Smurfs with her younger sister. She is thinking how incredibly loud the TV seems and how incredibly bland the doughnuts taste. Susan went to her first party last night. Now she has her first hangover. She had not intended to drink, but she finally gave in to temptation. All of her friends were, and she was the only sober person there. She got a strange feeling when her friends began talking to her and saying things they wouldn't normally say. They seemed to be having so much fun. Finally, when a game of quarters (a drinking game involving bouncing quarters into a glass of beer) started, Susan joined in. Since she was not an experienced player, she was sloshed within a half-hour. Soon she was saying funny things and laughing like her friends. Now she can't wait for Monday when she can trade tales of drunken antics at lunch. "What did you do this weekend?" "Me? Oh, I got wasted, you know," she imagines herself saying.

One thing worries Susan this morning—her parents. She wonders if they know. They didn't say anything when she came downstairs this morning. Her mom was reading the paper while her dad was getting ready to mow the lawn. Everything was normal, except Susan felt like she had GUILTY written across her forehead. She knows how disappointed they'd be if they found out. But she didn't get in any trouble, and she was with her friends, so why did this pang of guilt keep gnawing at her? She wonders what her friends say to their parents. Her close friend, Amy, got caught once. She was grounded for a while, but everything was back to normal after a few weeks. Amy didn't seem to worry about it. "Oh, well," Susan thinks, "I suppose I shouldn't worry about it either."

Down past the grocery store, at 314 Elm Street, Dave is cleaning up his room while his mom is preparing the Sunday morning french toast. He had had some friends over because his parents went out. "What a bunch of animals," he thinks. "They left my room a pigsty." His friend had gotten hold of some good weed so they had "partied hard." It had been three weeks since the last party, Dave recalls as he flicks ashes off the carpet.

His girlfriend is always nagging him about getting high. He's not an addict or any-thing—he only smokes pot. She is such a hypocrite; at parties she gets so drunk that she can hardly walk. But when he asks her if she wants to get high, she turns up her moralistic little nose and says, "No way. I'm no burnout. I don't need drugs to have fun."

"Yeah," he thinks, "What does she suppose alcohol is? Getting high might mellow her out a bit." That's what Dave likes about smoking pot—he gets so mellow. For a while he can forget all the pressures: school, work, track, and his girlfriend. That reminds him—he's going to have to quit smoking because track practice starts in a month. His coach has a strict rule about that. Anyone caught smoking anything is kicked off the team for good. Besides, it feels good to clean out his lungs for a while.

As Dave attempts to find the mate to a crumpled gym sock on the floor, he thinks back to his one and only freak-out. He had gotten some pot which was laced with something—he couldn't remember what. He was told it was safe—just a little extra buzz. So he and his friend smoked a bowl or two and drank some beer. Then Dave started to freak out. His body was numb, and he felt as though he could fly. He started seeing weird things and hearing

strange noises. Dave cringes as he remembers. Since then, he's been careful. He only buys pure stuff, and he never mixes it with booze. He isn't terribly anxious to end up in an institution somewhere with the brain-wave patterns of a zucchini.

At 346 Elm, Sunday morning finds Bill in his usual post-party position: worshipping the porcelain god. Leaning over the toilet, Bill attempts to recall the previous evening. "How did I get home? What time? Were mom and dad up?" He hopes they didn't hear or see him come in. He knows their speech by heart:

"Bill, we know what time you came home. We also know what condition you were in. Bill, we've been through this before. We don't understand why you drink so much. We thought a morning like this would teach you, but it didn't, so you're grounded next weekend. We're sorry, but we have to do it."

"They aren't sorry. That's bullshit," Bill thinks. Now, though, he had a way to get around them. He had found his dad's army flask in the attic. He fills it with whiskey to take to school. He doesn't use it that often—just sometimes between classes to calm his nerves because his teachers irritate him. "Bill, you used to do so well. Now your grades are slipping."

Sometimes he wishes he could tell them to go to hell. His parents can go to hell too. Always on his back: they complain about his falling grades, how he's never home, and whatever else they can think of.

Drinking and Drugs   135

Thinking that he's through, he leans up against the bathroom wall. His friend wants him to get help—like AA or something. She said that her father was a member and that he'd dried out now. "She can go to hell too," he mumbles. "That's where the whole world can go—to hell."

As he reaches for the faucet to turn on a cold shower, his head starts to pound, and his uptightness starts all over again. "Geez, I need a drink," he says.

At 345 Elm, Sarah pops open a can of Tab and lights a cigarette. Her mom has already gone to work, but her step-dad is still asleep. She makes sure she's gone before he's up. She hates him. Coming in after her dad left, trying to run her life—who does he think he is?

She's not sure where she'll go today. Everybody's probably meeting at the orchard or 7-11 or something. On school days the parties usually start after school, but on the weekends they continue for two days straight. She'll probably go there and get stoned. No reason for her to stick around home. Her step-dad always tells her that she dresses like a slut. She doesn't see what's wrong with concert t-shirts, faded jeans, and moccasins. That's the problem with her parents—they don't understand her. But her friends do. When she and her friends get high, they don't care how she dresses or what she says. They accept her for herself.

Sarah looks down at her biology lab book on the kitchen table. She has homework, but she probably won't do it. She'll just cut biology on Monday. One more cut won't matter. She hasn't been to gym all semester.

She wonders what her friends will have for her today. Last week they had some cocaine, and a few days ago they had some ludes. Sarah always gets nervous when she tries something new, like the first time she dropped acid. Her best friend Jill once freaked out on acid and was put in a hospital. She was okay for a while, but then she got out and started shooting heroin. Sarah hasn't heard from Jill in a few weeks—maybe she's back in the hospital.

When Sarah hears her step-dad getting up, she puts on her moccasins. "Time to get out of here," she thinks.

Across the street at 357 Elm, Jim and his family pull the 1979 station wagon into the driveway. Getting out of the car, Jim reflects on today's sermon about the evils of drugs and drinking. Jim agreed completely with what the minister said, but something bothered him. His two friends were snickering and making snide remarks about the preacher. "They're not my friends anymore," Jim thinks. They stopped being his friends when they picked up their first can of beer. At first Jim thought they were going through a stage, and he tried to help them spiritually. But they would not see the light.

They said they only drank on weekends, but Jim believed they were drunk all the time. Jim clamps his eyes shut as he thinks, not wanting to remember. The three of them had been inseparable before. Now they disgust Jim when he sees them in church. "They can't be good Christians and serve the Lord when their minds are clouded by the devil's influence," he thinks.

As Jim changes into sweatpants, he feels lucky that he finds the strength to resist such temptation. His friends have tried to let the devil get hold of Jim, but Jim knows his choice is made for life.

Elm Street, U.S.A.—a typical American street which illustrates the prevalent but not-so-easily-stereotyped drinking and drug habits of teenagers.

Discussions

Female 1: *I got high. That was just what I did because that was in our plans for the day. I mean we had the same schedule every day. Every day we'd get off the bus, go to Mister Donut for breakfast, go get high, go to 7-11 to meet more people, go get high, and go back to 7-11 to rip off a bunch of munchies. We had pockets full of candy and all kinds of stuff so we'd go eat that. Then we'd go get high. Then we'd go into Just Pants. Sometimes everything I wore, everything I had on, I'd ripped off. Then we'd go get high some more. Then we'd go to the laundromat, and after that we'd go to the pet store and look at all the pets.*

It was kind of sad, but in a way I'm glad it happened because now I know better. Now I can't stand the smell of pot. It makes me sick.

Female 2: *I see the effects alcohol has on other people, and I hate it. Have you ever seen a person with the shakes try and get off it? I'll demonstrate. [Shakes feet and hands vigorously]. It looks foolish, but it affected me so much. She was sitting there with her drink, and it*

was spilling all over the place. She was trying to set it down. Literally, her foot was shaking, and she couldn't get it off the ground long enough to get it in front of her so she could take a step.

You see a person before they're drunk, and it's like that's the person I know—that's the person I can love and that's the person that loves me. Then, they're drunk, and it's like I don't know that person. I don't even love that person. That person doesn't know me from the guy off the street.

My fear and hate of alcohol drives me to the point where I don't drink at all. Just don't even touch it. Don't even smell it. And I know that is close-minded. I don't like to be that way. I think that my hatred of alcohol is sometimes even more than I know how to handle. Just the hate itself. But this is the way I am. I don't think I want to change because I know that if I hate it any less, I'll drink. And I don't want to drink. When I'm really depressed, I've gotten so far as pouring just a little bit to taste it. About half an inch in a shot glass, thinking, "This is the big time. I'm really going to try this." I'll go up to

Two years ago I wouldn't be caught dead smoking a joint, but now everyone does it. People ranging from the age of 11 to 90 smoke it daily. To my parents, this would be surprising. They still think just the hippies from the '60s smoke it.

I remember one time when I smoked two joints of scence [sensimilla]. I was also drinking peppermint schnapps. I had the funniest feeling. It's the best I've ever felt.

I walked around the block to air out, and I felt as if I was floating down the street. I felt so relaxed I didn't care about anything. . . .

I know if all my friends went straight, I probably would too.

17-year-old female
Arkansas

I don't know why my parents think it is so wrong to drink. They do it all the time.

I remember the day my mom found out my brother drinks. She asked him if the empty beer bottles and rum bottle in his car belonged to him. He said, "Yes."

My mom cried almost all night. I told her that he could take care of himself, and she told me that he was still her baby boy. I can't believe she called my 17-year-old brother a baby. Ever since then, at least once a week, she gives him pamphlets about teenage alcoholism or drinking and driving.

My dad still doesn't know about my brother drinking, and I don't think my mom will ever tell him because he would probably do something drastic like kick my brother out of the house. He has done that before.

I don't see why any responsible teenager can't drink. We're almost adults like mom and dad.

16-year-old female
Michigan

The outside world really affects me with the thought of nuclear war and peer pressure of all kinds. I think kids are always looking for

I ONLY DRINK WHEN LIFE GETS ROUGH — IT JUST SO HAPPENS THAT LIFE IS ALWAYS ROUGH

escapes of some sort, either drugs, music, games, or other things.

In junior high I got into drugs and pills. Around ninth grade I quit. I was really doing bad in school even in my good classes. . . . I thought I was escaping, and it just turned into a bigger problem.

I started because kids didn't like me. After I started, I found out more kids didn't like me. Since I quit, more kids like me. I'm still one of the outsiders, but maybe by twelfth grade I will be accepted.

The way I escape now is a game called Dungeons and Dragons. It's way better than drugs, and I meet new guys.

Paul Erntson, 15
Clarks Grove, Minnesota

If a parent says, "We know you drink—when you're drunk, call us or have someone else drive you home," they are probably doing a wiser thing than forbidding the child who will do so with or without permission.

Kaki Kelly, 15
Kirkwood, Missouri

I used to think it was a big deal to drink. When I turned 18, I realized that drinking was no big thrill. I used to drink before I turned legal age. Then when I did turn of age, i started to drink less. When you are not of age, you tend to drink more because you are getting away with something.

Tom Celone, 19
Brookfield, Connecticut

I started smoking pot because my sisters did it and because it looked like a new thing to do or try. Now I find myself starting to talk my friends into trying it because I tell them, "It's fun."

I'm totally against the idea of drugs and alcohol, but yet I still do them. Sometimes I just sit and think about what I'm doing to myself. Then I wonder why I just don't stop. . . .

I got caught once for drinking in

my room and I'll throw it away. I'll dump it out in the bathroom before I get to my room. No matter how hard I try, I just won't do it.

My fear is that I'll become an alcoholic for some reason. I don't know why I hate it so much. I just don't drink at all.

Female 3: *Our family will go out to dinner, and we'll have a bottle of wine or something between the family. My dad'll ask for four glasses because that's how many there are in my family, but I won't want to drink. He'll say, "Either*

you drink here with me, or you can't go out with your friends and drink." We'll sit around the table, and we'll have three glasses of wine. I'm buzzed then. My mom is too. It's fun.

My dad doesn't like me to drink behind his back, although he knows I do. He knows at parties that that's what goes on. He'll say, "Have one and pretend like you had a lot the whole night. Just have one, and hold it in your hand." But it's okay if I do it at home in front of him.

My mom knows I drink. She gets mad

at me when I drink too much. She always knows, and she always threatens that she's going to tell my dad. But now I think I know I shouldn't abuse my privileges anymore. What's so wrong is that in public my dad says I'm 21, and we'll go to bars. There's one bar in Elmhurst—we'll go to watch SportsVision, and we'll have a couple of beers there. I guess he's there to watch me. But still, if I can handle myself there, then why can't I handle myself at a party?

Drinking Experiences

Michelle: I remember the first time I got drunk. I was in seventh grade, and I was with a friend. She was a year older than me. I was lying in the cemetery on Main Street. I was just throwing up all over the place, all night long in my sleep. I'm lucky I didn't get hurt. I remember she passed out in the middle of the street, and I had to drag her home. And there's her little brother about seven watching us. Her grandma was over there nagging us, and I felt bad because it was a bad example for her brother. You're supposed to be a good little Catholic girl in a Catholic school.

Mary: I don't drink a lot of whiskey anymore, but I used to drink with a lot of guys and see if I could drink more than they could. That's stupid, but it was fun. I got attention that way. I know that's wrong. I don't do it anymore. There's been a lot of times when I don't remember what happened the night before, and it's really scary waking up and having my girlfriend call me and say, "Do you know what you did?" I'll say, "No, I don't know, and I don't want to hear about it." I don't even want to know about it.

Steve: I got drunk one time, and all I remember is I woke up the next morning; my motorcycle was down there and the lock's on. I had my wallet open, and all the money is in neat rows on the desk. I woke up

and saw I had absolutely everything there. It was really weird because I don't know how I got home. I must have cruised the bike from wherever I was.

Parental Reactions

Matt: I tell my parents just about everything I do when I go to a party. In the summer, they always let me drink beer because it's hot out.

Michelle: I admit to my parents that I go to parties. I can come home drunk, and my dad won't say a thing if I can walk and I'm not sick. But if I have to face my mom, she gives me the third degree just for the smell of alcohol. "Where were you? Who were you with? How much did you have to drink? You're grounded!" That's why I go to my dad's house on weekends.

Jeff: My mom usually waits about three months. Then she says, "Jeff, I know you went to a few parties. I know you got drunk. I saw you come home. I have spies on you. I know what you did, and I think I'm handling this very well." My dad comes out, but he doesn't know what's going on. My mom, though, has all these secrets about what I do and springs them on me months afterward.

Mary: My mom is so mean when I'm drunk. She knows I feel awful. Then she says, "Okay, get up!" Then she makes me do all this stuff. She does it to me all the time.

Kelly: I don't drink very much so it's never been a problem. About the only thing my mom said about it was, "If you don't feel you can drive yourself home, call me." And once on my brother's eighteenth birthday, the kids from work took him out. He came home and got sick all over the place. It was his first experience drinking, I'm sure. She set down the rule that if you get sick, you clean it up yourself.

Steve: I guess I drink more than

my house, and my mom grounded me for a month. Actually I was out the next day. Sometimes I wonder whether my mom is strict enough. . . .

I've done a couple of reports on the disadvantages and harmful effects of smoking pot, and I know most everything there is to know about the drug. . . .

There is no possible way to escape the dangers except if you just don't do it. . . . It's not worth it, and you'll regret it in the future. . . . I already do, and I'm only 14!

14-year-old female
New Hampshire

My view on drinking is very much different from my parents'. My parents feel that it is all right to drink. They would not care if I went out and got drunk, but I would. I think that it is very wrong. My parents tell me that I can drink whatever and whenever I want. Many problems arise from drinking, and I do not ever want to have any of those problems.

Danielle Greer, 18
Amity, Oregon

An experience that really was quite unfortunate was the death of one of my brother's good friends.

She was going to the high school prom with her boyfriend, and they had been drinking. She told him to slow down, but he thought it was funny and increased his speed. They struck a telephone pole, and the car rolled over. She was thrown from the car. She died instantly.

Janean Toomer, 18
McMinnville, Oregon

My parents have mildly accepted that I drink occasionally. It's a lot more often than they think, though. They figure that if I drank two beers I'd be really belligerent. That bothers me—that people can be so naive. I drink every day . . . sometimes I wish they would know.

17-year-old male
Oregon

My father is an alcoholic so I think I know what I'm talking about. I think drinking is acceptable once in a while for a teenager, but most of the time it's not.

My friends drink, but I don't because I don't really like the taste. Some of my friends drink way too much, and I don't go out with them too much anymore. They get . . . into trouble, and I don't need that. The sort of funny thing is that they go right to it again.

My best friend drinks a little too much. . . . I told him it could ruin his whole life, and he hit me. He was drunk at the time. I guess a little of what I said sunk in because he doesn't do it as much anymore.

15-year-old male
Wisconsin

I myself have a bottle of lime vodka hidden in my bedroom that I occasionally drink from when I need it. I haven't had any in a month, but it is a comfort to know that it is there if the pressures of life get too hard and I need to escape for a while.

16-year-old female
Minnesota

When I came to the United States I was shocked by the attitude of teenagers toward alcohol. It seemed that having a beer was the most exciting game you would ever play, a challenge that any mature person had to take.

I come from a country where there is no limit of age to buy alcohol. When my host family (I'm an exchange student) asked me about the subject, they were astonished and immediately thought that with so many facilities at least half the country, and especially teenagers, would be alcoholic. We do have people with alcohol problems, but as amazing as it can seem, comparing the countries, I think the situation in the United States is much worse.

I have grown with alcohol as part of my culture. For instance, my country is one of the main pro-

the average person here. I drink every weekend, and I always have a beer when I come home from school. And once in a while a couple of beers for lunch. But I don't think I'm out of control. I really, genuinely don't. I will take a six-pack out to a party. When it's gone, I usually stop drinking. I do that Friday night and Saturday night. Other times I'll just drink one or two here and there.

My dad buys the beer. In Europe everybody drinks so there's a whole different attitude, a whole different outlook to it.

Legal Restrictions

Michelle: I've gotten caught by the police, and I've never ever been arrested. They say, "If I catch you again. . . ." They make you dump your beer. They do that for girls more than guys.

Steve: That's not true. The police are like that to everybody. I've been caught so many times I can't even remember. I was scared the first time, but now it's like, "Aw, now we have to pour it out."

Matt: When I got caught, they didn't make us pour it out. They took it. I was sitting with a couple of friends in Yorktown parking lot. We had a case of beer we were drinking, and all of a sudden he came behind us.

Steve: Was that a regular cop?

Matt: Yeah—and he took the case.

Michelle: He probably took it home and drank it himself.

Matt: They should bust you right away.

Steve: No! What are you talking about?

Leslie: I think they should.

John: It's illegal. If it's illegal, it shouldn't be allowed.

Michelle: It's illegal, but you do it anyway.

Matt: Yeah, but what about the kids who can't handle that beer and go out and drive after they drink?

Leslie: One time I got really drunk. I was driving, but I don't remember driving at all. I woke up the next morning, and I had run over the grass. It really scared me because I heard what happened to some kids from the Catholic high school. They were drinking and hit some ice. A girl went through the windshield. She had stitches in her head. Bad injuries. It scared the heck out of me. So now I won't drive and drink.

Well, I'll drink, but I won't be drunk. It just doesn't mix. Especially after that experience, not knowing what I did, I felt so guilty. My mom lays this big guilt trip on me. I think drunk driving should be prosecuted more.

Michelle: I think they should be strict on drunk driving. But if you find some kid with a six-pack of beer, you don't crack down on him.

Kelly: But that's the reason there's more drunk driving and accidents—because they don't crack down on it. If they're driving while they're drunk, then the police should get them. But why don't they get them before they're drunk and before they have an accident?

John: I'm not saying it's right, but the law says that if he's under 21 he is not capable of handling—

THE PROS
AND CONS
OF HARD DRUGS

GOT ME
A MILLION

HARD
DRUGS

GOT ME
5 to 10

PROS

CONS

Michelle: Yeah, but what about those who are under 21 and can handle it? And what about those who are over 21 and can't handle it?

Mary: What's wrong with going to a park and having a bottle of champagne with your boyfriend?

Jeff: Alcohol is more accepted by society than drugs. You can see advertisements and ads on TV. When you buy a joint, you know it's illegal.

Kelly: A lot of things society takes less strictly. Neither of my parents drink very much, but the fact that your parents can do it makes drinking a little more acceptable. My parents wouldn't do any kinds of drugs. When it's accepted by your parents, it's easier to make it accepted by you.

Reasons for Drinking

Matt: It's fun. It tastes good.

Steve: It relaxes you, loosens you up, makes you more receptive.

Matt: Relieves the pressure from school.

Mary: Makes me more comfortable.

Leslie: Yeah, it's kind of social. When you go to a party, you don't just sit there when everybody else is drinking. You drink to fit in.

Karen: I didn't drink at all till my junior year. And I couldn't stand it. It made me feel sick, embarrassed, really cruddy—like I had degraded myself. But then it became a part of my social life. So when everyone is drinking, and they say, "Have a beer, Karen" I'll have one. And then another one, because the second one is always easier. And

ducers of wine in Europe, and it is an important part in our meals. Maybe because of that, it is no big deal.

I've always been taught that alcohol is something that with moderation isn't bad, but when abused it degrades the person and makes of it an object, a thing.

Elena Cortes, 17
McMinnville, Oregon
(Madrid, Spain)

To drink and take drugs is very important to teenagers. Many teenagers drink to have fun, but some just want to get rid of their depression. I fit into the depression category.

I take drugs whenever I can afford them. Also, I drink to forget about all the damn things that happen that piss me off. I tried to kill myself twice because I'm be-

Drinking and Drugs   141

ginning to hate this earth and my life.

School is one of the things I hate most. Too many kids bother me because of my weight. After listening to comments about your weight, it's hard to listen and study in school. If it weren't for drugs and alcohol, I probably would really try to kill myself.

16-year-old male
Minnesota

To drink or take drugs is very important to all teenagers. Anywhere you turn nowadays, there is always some kind of drug. It is important to the non-users just to keep away from it, but it's hard when your friends turn to it. Once you start taking them, it's hard to quit. That's why it's important to users.

Drugs make you do weird things. I'm a user, and my grades have dropped. My absences have raised. A good friend of mine was sent to the pen.

I don't get along with my father anymore. I would leave the house and go away for a couple of days. Then when there were no more drugs, I'd end up back home. My dad got tired of that and beat me up pretty bad. He kicked me with his cowboy boots until I had to crawl.

If it weren't for the drugs, I wouldn't have had stitches in my head, a broken hand, and bruised ribs, not including all the other bruises.

I've had help, and I don't take speed or any kinds of pills no more. But I do drink a lot of coffee and smoke a lot of cigarettes and pot. At least I don't get out of control anymore.

16-year-old female
Texas

I drink on occasion, but I never drink all the time because my father was an alcoholic. He drank (and got drunk) about three times a day on his days off and every night after work. He finally went

SATURDAY NIGHT AFTERMATH

then comes a game of quarters or something. Well, I never feel good when I do it, but I do it.

Leslie: I don't like to drink every weekend. I mean, God, I'm getting hangovers, and they are affecting me. They make you feel really bad. Plus, now that I'm working, I usually work the weekends. I don't like to go to work not feeling good. And I know my mom doesn't like it when I drink every weekend. She knows when I've been drinking—I tell her. A lot of my friends live for Friday and Saturday nights, and they always go out and get drunk. I don't think it's right to drink every weekend.

Steve: I went through a stage sophomore and freshman years, when I went out, got drunk, and got wasted. I think a lot of people did. You did it once a month—or every two months. You went to a party and thought yee-hah! A party! Now I go to a party every Friday and Saturday night. And you no longer feel it's necessary to get wasted because you no longer think of a party in the same light. The fact that I drink more often makes me drink less when I do.

John: Well, I don't do it anymore. I'm a distance runner, and it kills me for running. You guys say, "Oh, I drink to just get a light buzz, have a good time." I think that if you can't have a good time without alcohol, you should try doing something else.

Kelly: I can count on the fingers of one hand the times I've been to a party where alcohol was served. I guess with most of my friends, at the parties we have, there isn't any alcohol. Alcohol's not the center of attention. It's what you do with your friends for the time you're there.

Melanie: You know what's really weird? People say that social drinking is okay. But more and more the people who say, "I'm a social drinker" are becoming alcoholics. The statistics are going up like you wouldn't believe. Those social drinkers are now alcoholics.

Drug Experiences

Matt: Sometimes just the thought of smoking scares me. My dad smokes four packs of cigarettes a day. I know one of these days he's going to die of cancer. Even if I were to smoke just one or two joints a month, who knows what that stuff would do to my lungs? I'd rather drink and put it in my stomach.

Kelly: My mom always told me I shouldn't use drugs. I'm sure that's a big part of why I don't and never have. Also, it's illegal, and I'm not the criminal type. No, seriously, I don't because I've seen what it does to people's lives who abuse it. You can't help but hear about the bad effects, and I'm not willing to risk it.

Mary: I used to get high a lot freshman year and the end of

142

sophomore year. Now I never get high. I was scared to start high school. I felt so rotten. I would be scared to ask somebody the time it was, or, if my nose was running, I would be scared to go and get a Kleenex.

I used to get paranoid when I was high. "Oh my God, what do I look like?" or "What do these people think of me? Did I say anything wrong?" That's why I don't do it anymore. It was hard not to do it because my friends would say, "Come on, this is really good pot." And I'd say, "No, I don't want to do it. Why do you guys want me to bum out?" That's what I do when I get high. I get really depressed.

But I like to drink. I drink more now than I did before. I don't drink a lot. Now the only time I really drink and get drunk is maybe one night a week or something.

Steve: On weekends, I usually smoke a bowl with a friend. We just sit around and talk. I just relax. I also talk with a friend who works with me. He's pretty cool. We have some very interesting conversations. Smoking a bowl doesn't make you stupid. Sometimes I do it Monday through Friday.

Michelle: When I was a freshman, I was with a couple of guys who live up the street from me. We were smoking pot. And I don't know if it was because I was in the mood to get really high or if there was something in it, but I was so stoned that I couldn't swallow. I felt like my whole body was pulling apart. It was so much pain I was near tears. I found out about a week later that it was laced with coke. We didn't smoke all that much. We had a half of a bowl between two people, and that's not a lot. Ever since then, I can't touch it because the effect on me is so bad.

Mary: Well, I personally like to do coke.

Steve: Yeah. I've done coke before, but it's an expensive buy. It's certainly not worth it.

Mary: I just like it. I only do it on

and dried out, which was the greatest thing.

Whatever the reason teens drink, they must know their limits. Most don't, and that's the major problem. Some learn the hard way; others haven't yet, but I'm sure their time is coming.

Bob Bodnar, 18
San Lorenzo, California

I don't drink myself, but sometimes I wonder if it would be easier if I did. I think teenagers drink because at a certain time in your life, your thinking can really get mixed up. You go through the times of rebellion, emotional growth, and changing roles—and your body's changes don't help matters.

Jeff Neitcke, 16
Winona, Minnesota

The only danger of taking or selling drugs at Bear Creek High School is that the Bar-Bearians don't like it. If they catch you, they'll kick your ass. They're not administrators or police, just a group of five of the biggest students you've ever seen. They go out into the halls with only one thing in mind: "Kill freaks and dealers."

Nobody has ever beaten the Bar-Bearians at their game. Even the big Denver dealers don't stand a chance. The only way to escape the Bar-Bearians is to quit school and leave town.

Mike Dobrowski, 16
Morrison, Colorado

Last month, a child in my neighborhood was hit and killed by a teenager who had been drinking while driving. Until disasters like this happen, teenagers don't realize the danger of alcohol and drugs.

My generation has been given too much. Parents have unfortunately substituted things and money for love and time. Consequently, we have never had to worry about our future or day-to-day existence as our grandparents did. Instead, most teenagers only

Drinking and Drugs

live for a daily good time and are under the impression that drugs and alcohol are just more privileges owed to them. . . .

After the death of the boy in our neighborhood, the phone in the church rectory rang constantly with suddenly-aware parents begging that their children be helped. Both parents and teenagers encouraged friends to attend the movies and seminars about drugs and alcohol that suddenly appeared.

It is unfortunate that it takes disaster to make people aware of what is going on, but it seems to be necessary to shock this generation out of their aimless fog.

Susan Simone, 17
E. Greenwich, Rhode Island

special occasions. If one of my friends has a lot of money, they'll buy it and turn me on. I don't do it every day, like maybe once every four months. To me, coke doesn't seem like a hard drug because it doesn't get you off that much. Drinking beer gets me more wasted.

Use and Abuse

Michelle: My friend just had a baby. She's the same age as me. She partied throughout her whole pregnancy, doing bongs. Real cool, you know. And the baby was born. She said it's perfectly fine. I don't even want to see it. I don't even

I love to party. If it means drinking with some of my best friends (which in my peer group is accepted), rocking to some tunes, or just getting wasted with an easy chick, I'd do it in a minute. Maybe it is unacceptable here in Pennsylvania for a teenager to drink, but that doesn't mean it's wrong.

Getting wasted is great, but my attitude . . . is mixed. When you're so stoned that you can't stand up and so gone that you screw a perfect stranger, it makes you wonder about the practicality of alcohol. When I'm drunk, I test people. I'm the door of perceptions.

Here is my best example of the way I feel about alcohol. My friend "Nick," leader of our band, was missing from our debut at the under-21 VIP party. The manager said, "Where's your singer?" I said, "I don't know, ah, we'll get him right now."

So we went to his house. Nobody was home. We walked in his room, and there he was—blitzed, acid out his eyes. He stumbled to his nightstand, opened the cabinet drawer, and there were 15 vials of liquid, purple acid. Then he opened the other drawer. There was a kilo of grass, a huge brick of grass.

Well, we dragged him to the VIP, and we did five or six songs and "Nick" was okay. He was a little slow but not bad. We then came to the song "The End" by the Doors.

"Nick" started making up words—gross, disgusting words—but the kids loved it. The place was wild, let me tell you. Anyhow, everybody had a good time. Unfortunately, we got busted for it.

16-year-old male
Pennsylvania

I help the vice-principal by reporting any pot smoking or joints that are on the school grounds.

Drugs can harm people's bodies and minds. I will report any person so that maybe they can get it to-

144

gether and possibly straighten their lives out—because I know their families are breaking up because of the problems drugs can cause.

Pat Sharp, 17
Fort Smith, Arkansas

Drinking does not get along with me anymore since the first weekend after football was over. I got the hell beat out of me and woke up the next morning with bruised ribs and a worse hangover. Since then, I will only have a beer or two at a time.

Drugs are also very painful. I have not known what was wrong with me, but my so-called friends were slipping things in on me. Also, they would get me drunk and then give me a so-called cigarette.

On one such occasion, the so-called cigarette had been dipped in cocaine, which was diluted in water which they dipped the pot in, then let it dry and rolled it with hash mixed in, too. I didn't get a fully-clear head until two weeks from that day. Believe me, with friends like that you don't need enemies.

17-year-old male
Texas

The entire population seems to think that drinking and taking drugs classifies you as a bad person. In actual reality, these kids aren't bad but are victims, who have been led astray by the generations before them and the generations before them. These pressures travel from father to son to grandson as well as develop within peer groups.

Heather Swanburg, 17
Milford, New Hampshire

At age 14 I had my first drink at home. Since then, I have changed and grown. I'm now 17 and have been drinking every weekend for the past two years, but I'm not an alcoholic.

I drink beers because (1) my friends do, (2) I enjoy it, and (3) it relaxes me.

want to look at it. The first thing she said was "God, I can't wait till it's old enough to get high." That's not fair to the kid.

Mary: It makes me sad to know what other people who get high are doing to themselves. I mean most of the people now that I know who get high are older. That's sick. They're that much older, but they still do it every day. When I was a freshman, I could see doing it for a year. It wasn't good, but at least I got smart. I had some common sense after a while. But God, those people are sad. Every time they sit down somewhere, it's, "Wanna smoke a bowl, do a bong?"

Manish: I don't do illegal drugs because I see no advantage to it. I do things in life because they're pleasing to me. I do whatever I enjoy. I know everybody's saying, "Aha, you've heard, but how do you know?" Well, for the record, yes, I've taken a hit on a joint. Just one. It wasn't too thrilling.

Steve: How can you get high on one hit?

Manish: No, of course. I understand I won't get high on one hit.

Steve: You won't get high on the first joint you smoke. Even if you smoke an entire joint, you wouldn't get high.

Manish: But, I mean, it didn't stimulate me or anything.

Jeff: Not the first time.

Steve: That's right. You don't.

Manish: I wasn't happy so I just don't do illegal drugs. That's basically my reason.

Jeff: I don't—very often. Why? Because I don't have that much money very often. I find better things to spend it on right away like my car payments—stuff I have to pay. Then there's hardly any money left over, but that's not the only reason. I'm not that interested.

Maribeth: I'll be honest. I've taken speed before, but I didn't think it

As an adult reads this, they would say, "Why does a kid need to relax? He has no problems like we do." Any adult who thinks that is full of crap because kids (1) are growing every day, (2) have social and school problems like what are your grades, you look ugly, your clothes are funny, and (3) life itself.

At 17, what are you going to do—more school or army or work or marriage? Drink helps relieve. Yes, it really does, and God save the goody-goodies who stay home with mom and dad and watch JR on Friday nights.

17-year-old male
Iowa

Drinking in excessive amounts (and even a little) can sometimes lead to disasters, such as injury to oneself or somebody else (including friends) in a careless accident or a fight. I remember my friends and I getting into a wreck one weekend. But we only drank two cans of beer each.

So why did we miss the turn doing 70 mph and fly 33 feet in the air into a flat clearing during the evening? Because even a little amount of alcohol can affect you. . . .

The driver was speeding because he was confident about . . . handling any situation, but the fact was he was under the influence of alcohol. He was incapable to respond fast enough to avoid the accident. He misjudged the turn and couldn't react because it all happened too fast.

We were lucky because we just received some minor bruises and nobody else was hurt, but the next time we may not be so fortunate.

18-year-old male
Kansas

For some teenagers, drinking or drugs is their whole life. I can remember when it was partially my whole life and my sister's. I remember when we would get up in the morning and start drinking and do speed.

We would come to school but wouldn't go to any classes. My sister got into drugs much deeper than I ever did, and today I am thankful that I am off.

My sister was not so lucky. As of right now, she has been in an alcohol and drug rehabilitation hospital for about two months. She is doing better, but I'm glad I didn't end up like that. . . .

My attitude and my parents' differ greatly. My parents feel that alcohol is for adults. They were both very upset every time they found out me or my sister had been drinking. Our whole family fell apart mostly as a result of my sister, but I also did damage.

My sister and I both went through the stage where we hated our parents. We stayed away from them as much as possible, and eventually we both ran away. I did run away once. My sister went on to become a chronic runaway.

My attitude towards drinking is that I don't consider a couple of beers "drinking" as long as a teenager doesn't go overboard.

15-year-old female
Illinois

It seems like drinking and drugs are now a main influence to many teenagers and even to kids younger than that. When I was a freshman, around 14 years old, I thought I was really cool so I started hanging around with the wrong crowd. I never got into heavy drugs, but smoking pot was enough for me to change.

At first, it was great, but then the mood swings started to come in. I would bite everybody's head off. I also started drinking quite heavily. I thought I had the best in life, but I didn't realize how much my grades started to slack off. Even if a person doesn't do drugs very often, it's still very bad for you and so is drinking. A person can really screw up his or her brain cells.

When I was smoking, my parents came up to me and said, "If

was worth it. I had a headache for two days. It kept me awake, that was for sure. I guess that's why I used it—to keep me awake like maybe in school. I guess it didn't affect me so much that I wanted to use it again and again and again. It was stupid, and it didn't help me at all. I thought, "I'll just drink coffee next time." Plus, I consider the risk of it being illegal—and the consequences that you face if you're caught. Plus, who wants to be spaced out all the time? What kind of life do you lead that way? How do you know what's going on if you're always on drugs?

Steve: There's a distinct difference between use and abuse. I'm not about to argue whether I use or abuse. For the most part, drugs for me are recreational. I don't like speed at all. I've tried speed, and I didn't like it. But as a philosophy, it was not a recreational drug. I used it on the gymnastics team. A lot of people on the gymnastics team did, and it wasn't being used for fun. It was being used so that they could do gymnastics better. That was a rather distasteful thought to me.

Drugs are completely recreational, and that's how I ought to keep them. I don't say, "Today I'm not gonna do drugs." I say, "Today I'm gonna do drugs" or "Tonight I'm gonna do drugs" because it's fun. I feel like it. Furthermore, when I say drugs, just for the record, I don't mean I'm a heroin addict. I've tried cocaine once. I do smoke marijuana on a fairly regular basis, but I've probably gone through a quarter of a bag in two months so I'm not a very heavy user. I don't think it's been too detrimental.

I'm sure, if I were to abuse it, and I know people who do, it would be detrimental. I know it's going to have a physical effect in the same way that smoking cigarettes has a physical effect and drinking alcohol has a physical effect. Alcohol does

you don't stop the thing with the drugs, we're going to throw you out of the house." (I didn't know that they knew I did anything.) They had searched my room but found nothing, but they knew I was up to no good. I finally confessed, and I have even quit smoking cigarettes. . . .

My parents love me very much, and they just don't want anything to happen to me. . . . I've been through that hell, and I made it. I'll never do anything so stupid in my life again.

Christopher Allen, 17
Ludlow, Massachusetts

I personally have gotten drunk just to tell a girl how I really felt about her, or I have been drinking with someone just to find out information. There have also been occasions when something bad happens and you need to drink, but it never helps.

I guess by being brought up by parents who trust my decisions, I have a better attitude towards drinking. One night my friend and I went out to dinner with two girls. My friend's parents know of his drinking, but they trust his judgment. We ordered dinner, and the waiter asked if we wanted cocktails.

The two girls immediately said yes (they were under 21). I declined, and my friend had a beer. The girls were shocked that I didn't have anything. They said that I should drink something because I don't get served very often. I then said that I could drink any time and that I didn't feel like drinking now.

The girls were shocked because their parents strictly forbid them from drinking so when they could drink, they did. I, on the other hand, can drink pretty much any time I want and most often decline an invitation to drink.

I can't say that every parent should trust their teenager to control their drinking, but it seems to me that it would help reduce the

146

amount of drinking. I respect my parents greatly for their trust in me, and I think that if parents trusted their children they would create a better bond between the two.

Steve Wolfer, 16
McMinnville, Oregon

I have learned not to get behind the wheel when you've had too much to drink. One summer night a girlfriend and I went out and bought a 12-pack of Millers and indulged in some Everclear punch. I didn't seem that drunk—I was still seeing one.

Well, I managed to take her home with a friend in the car with us. On the way to his house we turned off on a gravel road, and suddenly I felt as if I was Janet Guthrie, woman race car driver. Well, to make a long, horrifying story short, we turned too fast on a curve and rolled the 1980 Buick Regal over about three times over the embankment.

It was like I was just paralyzed. Glass was all over the red interior. The hood was smashed down to where my friend and I were crouched down in the seat. We managed to get out of the window and escape.

I thank the Lord we survived. The insurance person who examined the car said if the seat would have been up any farther, the hood of the car would've smashed us and there would've been no way of surviving.

I've learned. I won't drive when I go out if I know I'll be drinking. I just wish the families and the friends of the teenagers who have died or been killed by abusing drugs and alcohol would be more aware of its danger.

Kristin Curtis, 17
Cedar Rapids, Iowa

In our city, the most vital part of the weekend is getting drunk or high. Every weekend there's a party somewhere that virtually everyone goes to. Mostly there's

kill brain cells. I know that's true. For the most part, the reason people become less intelligent because of marijuana use is because they fail to use their mind.

The mind is just like any other muscle or any other part of your body. It needs exercise. You have to constantly stimulate it, or it's going to get worse. I think people who start smoking large amounts of marijuana get into dead-end jobs which don't stimulate their brain so it's out of practice.

I don't think I would do that, and I really don't think I've had any noticeable detrimental effects so far. I've been using it for about three years. All the books I've read say there are detrimental effects within months, so I don't know what to say.

I don't picture myself smoking marijuana for the rest of my life. I suppose I do consider it a rather juvenile sort of thing. I imagine if it

beer and mixing, people playing quarters or passout, and there are always the ones that do driving.

The drugs aren't nearly as concentrated as the drinking. Here there's pot, but of course other stuff, too.

Our school's basketball season just ended. Our tournaments are in Rochester—about an hour away. Kids were driving over that were so drunk they got lost and never made it to the first game. At the semi-finals, the band members were getting on the bus. A student government leader, National Honor Society members, and almost all of the spring play cast were busted.

The parents are really naive. They think drinking is only isolated cases when a party gets busted. The school tries to keep it all hush-hush because we're a private, Catholic school, and it's bad for the school's image. Most parents

try to deny that booze is that important in their student's life.

It's really too bad all of this goes on. Kids like me who don't drink are . . . often left out because we don't know the private jokes or what exactly happened to so-and-so at that party. . . . Some of the most outstanding kids in the community don't drink. . . .

The option to drink has always been there—you don't have to. I'll tell you, though, it sure helps.

Amy J. Carroll, 16
Winona, Minnesota

gets legalized, I probably would smoke it for the rest of my life, maybe less and less. I'm sure that everybody goes through a stage, probably between the ages of 16 and 24, where they're drinking a lot more than they will ever drink the rest of their lives. I imagine that's also true of marijuana.

Compiled by Denise Gajdos

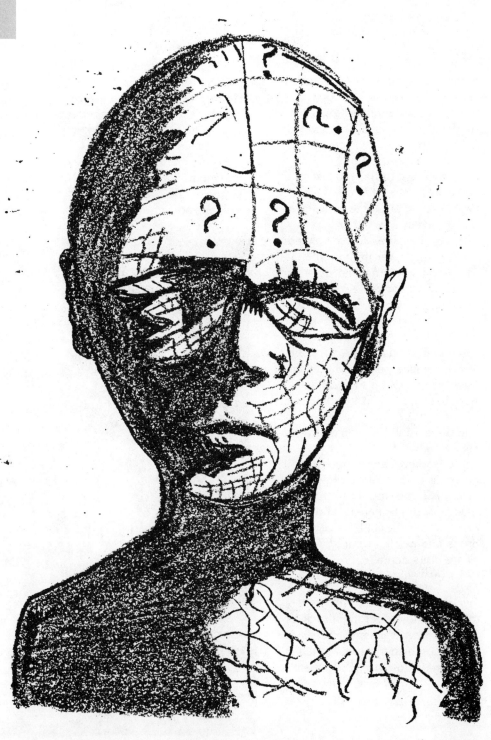

Chapter 11.

Religion

I'm human, God's divine. I'm finite, God's infinite. I'm flesh, God's spirit. Then how am I supposed to relate to God?

Everyone is always full of advice: read the Bible, pray, meditate, find a guru, read your horoscope, commune with nature, don't worry—God doesn't exist. STOP! The more I hear, the more confused I am.

Everyone seems so sure about what they believe—from fundamentalists to atheists. Where do they get their assurance? When I pray, I don't hear any voices telling me how to handle my problems. When I don't pray, I feel alone. I want to know the truth.

I wonder if being religious is a cop out or if it's the other way around. If I'm not religious, I avoid a lot of responsibilities. My time isn't taken up by praying, by reading religious books, or by going to church. I don't have to change my life-style or reevaluate my morals. I don't have to feel guilty for enjoying myself. But enjoyment of my short life will not matter if I'm sent to hell. On the other hand, if I am religious, I avoid a lot of responsibilities, like thinking through decisions. I can make instant judgments based on religious doctrine. I wouldn't have to search for a purpose or for comfort when I'm hurting.

I can't help but feel guilty about not being religious. I'm not sure, though, if it might be better to use religion as a way to be safe rather than sorry. Maybe I should at least go through the motions and have a free passport to heaven. After all, this life means nothing compared with eternity.

Unfortunately, I don't think I will respect myself if I use God only to keep from being punished. That doesn't really seem fair to someone who is a thinking, feeling being. Besides, this life is the only thing that I can be sure means anything. It would be horrible if my only accomplishments were serving and worshiping my imagination.

Where does blind ignorance stop and faith begin? I keep trying to understand faith. . . . The closest I come is that faith is an ability to believe and hope when there's no visible proof. But it is harder to believe the stories as I get older and learn to be more critical.

It's hard to believe that the earth was created in seven days when evolution makes so much sense. I guess neither explanation can be proven, but I have to decide which is easier for me to accept. At least I can see some visible proof of evolution.

I don't think God would give me a mind and not want me to use it. Besides, I'm not being defiant and saying to a God, who I know exists, that I refuse to believe. That would be ridiculous. While I can't prove God exists, I know that sometimes I hope He does and other times I hope He doesn't. But I don't think God would put me in hell just because my mind, which He created, can't comprehend belief without proof.

If the absolute truth is that God condemns us unless we do what He says, I don't have a choice. That's not fair! But if He's God and I'm just a puny human, what I think doesn't matter. If God's like that, I don't want to spend eternity with Him.

I'd like to think that God will always be merciful and forgiving. After all, if He made me, then He knows that I'm going to mess up sometimes. I doubt that He would make humans if He only meant to condemn us. I wonder how people can compare God to a father and in the same breath talk about hell. Good parents, even mediocre parents, would never condemn their child to a prolonged, horrible punishment. Eternal damnation doesn't serve any purpose other than revenge. A so-called perfect being couldn't be that sadistic.

If there's not a God, I guess my chief concern should be my relationships with other people. I should try to strengthen my friendships. I wonder what should happen to those relationships if God is real. . . . I'm not sure I like the idea of shutting myself off from other people in order to please God. I'm definitely not the ascetic type. But some people say that their relationship with God gives them a common ground with other people and more reason to make human relationships work.

Sometimes I wonder if God even wants me to communicate with Him or if He just wants to be left alone.

If communication is necessary, I wonder how to do it. All the different religions are so confusing that sometimes I think it would be ridiculous for God to want me to worship in one particular way. There is no logic in a God who condemns a person because they choose to chant rather than to pray. I think He should be happy that the person is worshiping Him.

I have to decide how much I can believe. I wonder how much of it is just to please people.

I know I can't believe all of it. Or can I? I wonder if anyone can find the truth.

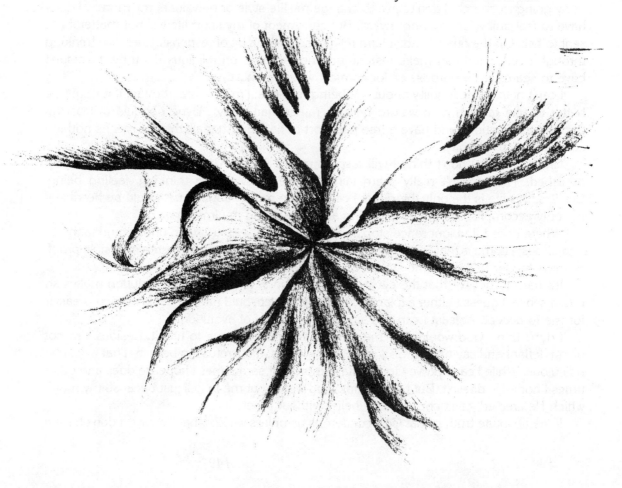

Begetting Prophets Through Pollution

Once upon a time (not just any time—this was two thousand years ago—hip?) there lived a little man named Bartholemew Neil Simon Smith Goldstein. His friends called him Geez. (This, of course, was their reaction when they first heard his name.)

Bart Geez was depressed. He worked in a lumber yard. (Contrary to popular belief, lumber yards, political corruption, and McDonald's restaurants have always existed.) Naturally, Geez was isolated from the rest of the city—and hence his world. No one could convince him that talking to a two-by-four was any fun at all.

So one day, when Geez was walking past a lake, he came upon a sign, and he stopped. And lo, he gazed upon the waters, and there was a fish, lying on its side in the bubbling orange water. The purple fumes wafted around Geez's head, and the fish spoke unto him.

"'ey, what'sa matter wid you? You harda herring?"

Geez stood back astounded. The fish spoke! It revealed new mysteries unto him—the secrets of life, death, the universe, and McDonald's secret sauce! Geez sat beneath the sign by the lake and pondered what the fish had said. And a thought came upon him—a prophet. He would proclaim this new word throughout the lands.

So Geez took himself to prophets' row and took a pedestal between a teacher of witchcraft and a student of science. However, while he prepared to unveil himself unto the world, a man who once worked with him (by the name of Judas) walked up.

"Hey Geez, what the hell do you think you're doing?"

"I'm preaching unto the world a new way," Geez proclaimed.

"Why?"

"For the Halibut."

For many days Geez stood on the pedestal. He gathered his followers; all one of them. Peter Paul Simon was a former linebacker—the man who jumps in the water and pulls the fish off the line and puts them in the boat—one of the most important people in the fishing expedition for a trawler company. When the trawler company was bought out by a fast food franchise, Simon was told only to pretend to catch fish. This, of course, was tremendously boring for one who had actually felt the slippery squirm of a worried fish.

So, besides being bored, now Peter Paul Simon had a mission. At the beckoning of Geez, the only true profit, he went forth with a picket sign and performed the ancient tribal art of lobbying. For there were those who wanted to "clean up" the sacred lake where Geez had his visions. Besides, Polydetremorphane isn't all that terrible.

This attitude created much concern with the great white horse, who wanted oh so much to keep the environment safe to live in. So Lord Geez and his follower Peter Paul Simon were dragged before the grand court.

"This religion of yours . . ." started the Grand Inquisitor.

"'ey!" said Geez. "It's not a religion, tis a club."

"This club . . ."

And so the evening went, and morning came, and evening went again, and pretty much later the trial came to an end.

The Great Profit Geez stood before his people and told of the sacred papers of green that could be obtained by dumping just a little Polydetremorphane into a few little lakes.

"On the large scale, the only ones who would notice are the finnish."

And so the sacred green papers circulated, and the rivers turned orange, and the Lord Geez—the only true Profit—was heralded as a great hero. At least, until everyone realized what they were doing.

Religion to me is the belief and worship in your own God(s) and in your own way.

Most of the time my reaction to religious concerns is extreme anger. By that, I mean when a religious group tried to tell other people what is right and what is wrong, like whether to have an abortion, what kind of music can be played.... I think it's up to the individual to decide for themselves.

As it says in the Bible, we are all sinners. Religious groups such as the Moral Majority are no exception, and I don't think that they have any right to tell anybody what to do.

Dawn Martin, 15
Parkersburg, West Virginia

Religion is a type of outlet for me. "God" ... is someone or something that is always there to listen. There is no guarantee that "He" is listening, but just the idea gives me a sense of hope. Teenagers today have a great deal of pressure placed on them. Usually, they have no one to turn to or sympathize with them except for their peers. However, this is usually not enough.... Religion is my hope.

Colleen Carter, 17
Brookfield Center, Connecticut

Each individual has his own religion, whether it's sports, music, career, or Christ. As far as church-related religious subjects are concerned, I've become disgusted and deeply disappointed at the hypocrisy of the church. Jerry Falwell has depraved the house of God with his greed and commercialism, causing people everywhere to lose faith in Christianity.

Ingrid Foerster, 17
Morris, Illinois

There is a pro-life movement in my church that contradicts itself in my eyes. The pro-life group is working against abortion but closes its eyes to other injustices against human life. They are so wrapped up in the

PLACE YOUR ORDER...

UMM, I'LL HAVE ONE SALVATION TO GO PLEASE —HOLD THE SERMON

Discussions

Who is God?

Steve: I can rationalize God in the sense that He is a creator. We exist; therefore, we must have been created. That does not necessarily mean to me that He is some incredible human being. I think it's more likely that He is some chemical reaction, and I do not intend to worship a chemical reaction.

Mary: I'm not sure exactly what it is. I just know there's somebody up there who loves me.

Diane: God is more like a best friend to me than a superior God.

Does God exist?

Manish: If He can come down and show me on a one-to-one basis without any gimmicks and prove to me that it is like this, I'll say fine, I'm willing to convert.

Melanie: He has come down. The Bible is accurate, accepted history. Jesus did come down to perform miracles. So it's up to individual people, through studying His character, to decide if He is actually Christ.

Michelle: I believe in God and

concern for the unborn that they fail to sympathize with the deaths of people already walking and feeling.

They are ignorant of the many abused children killed, both physically and emotionally, each year for unjust causes. Another major problem is the drunk driver who kills innocent victims, but this is not of concern to the pro-life movement. How can this organization call itself "pro-life" when they have such a narrow aspect of life?

Michele Mueller, 17
Greenfield, Wisconsin

Being raised a Roman Catholic, I believe in only one almighty God. Having put faith in Him, I would put my life in His hands even if I don't really know if He exists.

Franco Coladipietro, 14
West Joliet, Illinois

In our school, the separation of church and state is a hot issue. Our school choir performs in churches before the service, and the Minnesota Civil Liberties Union is trying to prohibit this.

Why can't a choir perform in a church? Nobody tries to sway these people's religious views. If a student doesn't want to participate, they are not coerced. It is a voluntary act. Yet, the MCLU insists that our rights, as students, are being infringed upon.

Anne Boser, 17
Brooklyn Park, Minnesota

Jesus comes first in my life because somehow I feel like I couldn't have made it this far without Him.

When I was nine years old, I accepted Jesus as my personal Savior. Life seemed easy enough in my younger years so I continued to grow. As I became a teenager, I began to struggle with life. My smile started fading, and my moods became obnoxious. I was so lost and confused.

Now I am 17, and I have continued going to church and growing in the Lord. But it has been a long struggle. I learned new things in high school, and actions I knew were wrong I began to do. I thought it would make me a bigger, smarter person.

I got involved with guys and drinking, which I thought was fun until I started to break down and cry to the Lord. When it seems like no one else was there to listen, He was. Sometimes I felt like dying or even wishing I weren't alive. But my parents and friends didn't stop caring, and they didn't give up on me. They began reaching out to me, and I was reaching back.

I plan on making something of myself. I want my parents and even Jesus to be proud of me. Things are better. Whenever they start going downhill, I just say a little prayer. Jesus is always listening. I'm shaping up, and I haven't stopped learning.

I do know that Christians can have fun, too, and I never realized that until now.

Daureen Day, 17
Tucson, Arizona

When I was studying in a Christian school, I was a nobody. I didn't care much for anything, especially the

praising the Lord. I just don't believe in a certain religion.

Steve: I think it's a distinct possibility that this whole thing is a waste of time. That's why I'm a hedonist. I might as well have as much fun as I can while I'm at it.

Melanie: I believe in Christ. Through Him, I can go to the Father and confess my sins. Because of His resurrection, He will accept and forgive me. I can never rationalize Christ because His love and forgiveness are so great that they're beyond my understanding.

Responding to Ceremony

Kelly: I wasn't thrilled about the Lutheran church. There seemed to be too much ceremony, too much regalness as opposed to a simpleness I feel about God.

Michelle: With the Catholic church you've got to go in a little box and tell a priest your sins to be forgiven. Well, if you're sorry for your sins, that's how they're going to be forgiven.

Matt: The Presbyterian church I went to as a child was beautiful, and I think it really influenced me. It seemed like there was a lot of money floating around. That doesn't sound good, I know, but that's what influenced me.

Choosing a Religion

Steve: The main influence was that I should go out and explore all avenues and try to understand all religions, and I did so. Many religions have gone by me, but I think I understand the very common ones. Nobody's ever given me the answers to the questions. I want to know why I'm here. But nobody can tell me. I'm not prepared to accept something on blind faith.

Kelly: I've searched into half a dozen different religions— Methodist, Lutheran, Catholic, Open, Presbyterian—and I've looked and picked one for myself I can believe in.

school work that I needed to do. In other words, I was a perfect loser. The only thing I cared for was having fun. But as I got older, I started to be ashamed of myself and my grades. . . .

Three years ago, I learned our family was moving to California and I realized that I had a second chance. I knew I not only had a new start after I got there, but I also knew if I didn't take this chance, I might never amount to anything. So I developed a strong faith within me, and I also had the faith that God would help and lead me on.

Without faith, I would be the same old lazy self that I used to be. Believe it or not, I changed into a very hard working student, with goals for my life and with an ambition to be a successful person.

Angela Lam, 17
San Lorenzo, California

Religion should be a major part of everyone's lives and should give some fulfillment to them. If the religion is not giving a fulfillment to a person, that person should have the right to convert without disapproval from others.

Scott Freese, 17
Burdett, New York

I am a Methodist and the Methodist religion is a very open religion so I have an open mind about religious concerns. I may not agree with what they are saying, but I would not put them down for their beliefs.

What I dislike is when people think that everyone must believe the same way they do. Every person has the right to believe the way they want to and should not be put down for their beliefs. Just because you believe something doesn't mean that that's the only belief there can be.

A friend, "Betty," is evangelical, and a guy, "Ken," likes her. She won't go out with him because he's Catholic, and her religion doesn't believe that Catholics are Christians.

I think religion is your own private business and shouldn't be a factor in relationships, except marriage. In marriage, the two people can be different religions and still make the marriage work as long as the two religions don't clash.

Colleen Crowley, 18
Brooklyn Park, Minnesota

Church dwells on what is going to happen to you after you die. Youth don't believe that they're going to die so how can we believe in what's going to happen after that? Death is an impossibility to youth. We're free, young, and never-ending.

Michelle Foss, 17
Fargo, North Dakota

I think that since God gave you the privilege to be alive, you should thank Him and live for Him every day. I must admit that being a Christian does try me at times, but I always think of what God's Son went through for me. Who cares what other people, mostly non-Christians, say about you? They're only hurting themselves.

Michelle Thomas, 15
Sapphire, North Carolina

Religion, to me, is a way by which others give up themselves. They create some essence, which they call a superior being, and endow it with qualities of their own, which they refuse to recognize. Then they ask their god to grant them strength and courage while humbling themselves to their own creation. To me, religion demeans the human character. It is the ultimate lie to oneself.

Dave Fischer, 16
Gahanna, Ohio

I don't believe that even one-fourth of the religious affiliations are even honest. They try to make a dollar off of innocent, naive people. That is sick—screwing up people's minds for money.

Debbie Nesbitt, 16
Eugene, Oregon

Jeff: I went to ministers and pastors of different churches to see if they could answer the questions I have. One of the basic ones is, "How could a God let so much suffering go on in the world?" Everyone has his own answer. God got us rolling—now everything just happens. But why the hell should I worship anybody with all the suffering going on like it does?

I can't find time in my schedule to do that, and I don't think it's worthwhile to do that. I'm not saying outright that I resent God because that's not what an agnostic does. One of my favorite sayings is not that God created man in His own image, but that man created God in his own image. There are all these different religions, and these different gods. How am I supposed to say this is better than Buddha? How is one god better than another?

Melanie: There was a time when I was really searching and pretty desperate. I looked at other religions, but I chose Christ because He did live and to this day He is still changing people's lives. He has never been proved a liar or a hypocrite. The reason I believe in the Bible is that it's been around for thousands of years and has never been disproved.

Manish: Nobody should force you into believing. I was force-fed Hinduism, and I was too young to know any better. I realized when I was 12 that this is all bull. My parents, my grandparents, my great-grandparents—my whole clan—they're all very orthodox Hindus. They're pretty strict, and Hinduism is it. My parents pushed it upon me.

You have to know a little bit of background in India. It's a country where religion plays a major part in life. You're living in a different society. It's hard to grasp the idea. Sort of take my word for it, religion is intermingled, intermixed. It's

I feel that my whole life has changed since the day I became a Christian. My whole life was very depressing, and there were a number of times that I found myself thinking of trying suicide or doing something stupid. . . .

But somehow I never could bring myself to try anything. Now I know it was the Lord that helped me through my problems. Ever since the day I became a Christian, my life has been taking a turn for the better.

Gregory Thad Bridges, 15
Rock Hill, South Carolina

I define religion as a way to seek help. I haven't really decided whether there is a "God" or whatever watching us. Many of my views on religion coincide with that of Shinto. For example, I believe that all a person's life is planned for him. This is called Karma. They have a saying something like "leave Karma to Karma." This statement pretty much sums up what I believe pertaining to religion.

I haven't really thought much about heaven or hell or the like because I think when a person is dead that's it. People should enjoy the present while they are able instead of worrying about being good and perfect.

I disagree with any kind of religion that tries to dictate good and bad to its followers. . . . For example, the Catholic church . . . says, in no uncertain terms, that abortion is a sin. I think someone should question how they know if it is.

Chris Gill, 15
Burdett, New York

I define religion as the way a person chooses to worship. My main reaction about religion is the way it has found its way into politics. Another is the misuse of church funds. For example, here in our area we have what is known as the PTL (Praise the Lord). It is a big-money operation and has recently

been indicted for misuse of its funds.

It was rumored that the head of PTL had bought a condo in Florida. None of this has been proven yet, but still the viewers give millions of dollars to this organization, thinking that it is going to some good cause. . . . I just hate to see all these people suckered out of their money.

Jackie Feemster, 17
Rock Hill, South Carolina

A religion is an organization. A set of people with similar attitudes toward life and death make up a religion. They give it a name and write up a book of rules and regulations with explanations and examples, like a math book or Bible.

People live, fight, and die for their religion and for those beliefs their religion represents. Religion there in every part of daily life. To fit in, you want to go along with the crowd. I guess that was basically one of the reasons that I was a Hindu.

I guess I changed about five or six years ago. I started wondering— a shot of brightness or I got smarter, all this intelligence started to flow. I started to wonder, "Who is God?" The Christians say it's Jesus Christ, the son of God. The Hindus say that there are so many gods. The Moslems say Muhammed is the prophet sent by God, who is Allah. Everybody agrees there's a god, and there are seven guys running around saying, "I'm God!" I mean who is God?

Practicing Beliefs

Diane: I'm the type of person who goes to Mass once a week, but I represents a unity of spirit among many people. . . .

If anything, religion is remarkable. Religion has been reported to save souls and move mountains. Religion can motivate people to help the suffering or to kill the people of another religion. Religion demonstrates the power of personal belief.

Alice Mills, 17
Rapid City, South Dakota

In my life, God comes first. I have set my priorities on the fact that God will last forever, and nothing else I know will. He comes before my family, my friends, my school work, and my personal wishes. A personal relationship with God is the most wonderful thing any human being can have, and anyone who believes in the Lord Jesus Christ can have it.

I constantly run into conflicts with my goals and desires. I want to sleep; God wants me to go to church. I want to yell at my brother when he leaves muddy footprints on my jeans; God wants me to be patient and loving.

I want to visit my friends and go to games and dances on Saturday nights; God wants me to spend Saturday with my family. As I do not live at home, it is my only chance to see them.

The list of conflicts is endless, and I know I will always have them. But as I continue to grow in Christ, they will become easier. I know that I must submit my will to His always in order for His plan for my life to work as wonderfully as He plans.

Although I have mentioned several conflicts so far, they have all been superficial ones: the real battles are much deeper. It is when I ponder God vs. Freedom, God vs. Truth, and God vs. Maturity that I run into trouble. The three just mentioned I have already fought.

They were "won" only by reason of evidence that there was no conflict in the first place. God is Freedom, God is Truth, and God is Maturity. God, in fact, is all good things. If ever I discover an actual conflict, I do not know what I would choose.

For example, if given a choice, would I take slavery in heaven or freedom in hell? A joyous, beautiful falsehood or a hellish truth? Childhood in heaven or maturity in hell? I don't know the answer to these yet, but I have a feeling that, given no other choice, I would choose freedom, truth, and maturity, no matter how much joy and happiness I was giving up. If this is the way of the universe, then I pity its inhabitants.

My choice of freedom, truth, and maturity is not in conflict with my statement that God is first. I worship a God of truth and life and freedom and wisdom and

don't sit home and read the Bible. I don't consider myself a very religious person. I believe in God and all that, but I believe more in just trying to be a good person than reading every line of the Bible. I can turn to God when I have troubles or when something really good has happened. Rather than worshiping Him, it's more like sharing with Him when I'm down and when I'm up.

Karen: I'm not really that religious. I believe in most of the Catholic things but I don't like the way the Church is run sometimes—for example, the way they pushed mission donations at my old school. I went to a Catholic high school for a while. In religion class, they really pushed the religion on you. If you weren't Catholic, you were an outcast.

Well, for a while, after I first got to Glenbard East out of Montini, I

thought, my God, I can't stand religion anymore. It's driving me crazy. I'm sick of it. Then I started to think, maybe I'll become a Jew— I'm serious. I was thinking of converting because a lot of my friends are Jewish.

Now, since I've had my history course at College of DuPage—we've been studying all the religions—I guess I like Catholicism best after all. So, I'm back to believing my original beliefs. There's always a period where you're sick of it, the same with school. Then you view it from a different viewpoint—like in history. In history, they don't shove it down your throat. We see all the different religions like Moslem and Protestant, everything. I guess I just like Catholicism the best. I don't know why, probably because I was raised that way by my parents.

Maribeth: I believe in Roman Catholicism because I was raised

that way and was sent to a Catholic school. I believe in God, but I do go against some of the things that the Church does. For example, I don't believe in confession face to face. I don't believe it's wrong, but I believe it makes a person more nervous so he doesn't want to go.

I also don't believe in communion in the hand. Maybe some people like that, but I think it should be from the priest to you. I don't think that you should have to handle it. But I believe in going to Mass and in praying to God. I don't believe you have to be in church to pray. I think I can pray wherever I like to. Also, I have no offense against anyone who's not Catholic. I'm not very religious either. Maybe I'm just sick of it, too, because I had to go through school.

Matt: I went to all the classes on Sundays, but now, since I've been confirmed, I just kind of lost it. I still believe He is the Creator, but after I was confirmed I just lost interest. I do believe it. I just don't practice it as I should.

John: Though I am a Roman Catholic, I haven't gone to a Catholic church in two months. I don't really know much about religion, about the Roman Catholics. I listen, but I don't comprehend. I just sit there and watch. I believe in God. When I'm in a bind, when I need help, I always ask for His help and He answers me.

Michelle: I like to do my own thing. If you go by the Bible and make it a personal relationship instead of a community thing, what you believe is the best way to do it.

Mary: In junior high and a little before that, I was really confused. I used to freak out about heaven and hell. I thought about death all the time, and I was so scared of what would happen to me. Any little thing I did, I was worried about what would happen to me.

It's hard to be a Christian. It's hard to love every single person, to be kind to everybody, accept everybody. But it's harder not to believe anything. I guess I'm a Christian, and I believe the only people who are going to go to heaven are people who believe in Jesus and believe that He died on the cross for you and that He's going to come back.

Michelle: When our whole family sits there on Sunday night, I say grace and I think when I say it. I don't say it because everyone else is saying it.

Steve: Do you thank God for the house and food because you don't want Him to take it away? [Laughter]

Michelle: If I had no house or food, I don't know what I'd do.

Melanie: God is offering you eternal life. He won't take it away from you.

Steve: That's a nice thought, isn't it? [Silence]

strength. If one of the aforementioned conflicts arises, it is because there is no such God. Therefore, my first statement has no meaning.

For now, I am content with my God. The peace, the joy, and the love I receive from Him are more wonderful than anything I have ever known.
Bethany Kenner, 17
McMinnville, Oregon

The thing that comes first in my life above anything else is probably my religion. My parents brought up my sister and I to be Wisconsin Synod Lutherans. I believe, without a doubt, what was taught me over the years, and I can explain to others what I believe and why.

The pastor of my church asked me to go into Evangelism Training. That's where I, along with one other teenager and four adults, are learning to go with the designated committee to people who have shown an interest in the church

you? Why doesn't He perform some miracles?

Kelly: Probably because I don't ask Him to. I don't demand that He prove something to me.

Jeff: No, I'm not saying that. Well, do you pray for other people, starving people?

Kelly: Yes.

Jeff: Well, I don't understand why they are still starving.

Kelly: I don't either, but I can see spending part of my lifetime trying to change that. I'm not waiting for God to change all of the bad things. I'm willing to do some of it myself.

Considering School Prayer

Melanie: I think the whole issue of passing all this prayer legislation is junk. Why not let the people decide what they want individually? I pray in school. Why is it that you have to go through legislation to say that the whole school must pray? Just let the people who don't want to pray not pray. Those who want to pray can pray.

Michelle: You can't force people to pray who don't want to pray.

Kelly: It wouldn't work because there are so many different people. It's stupid for someone to force a religion on them. The Moral Majority is trying to force people to believe everything they do, and it's wrong.

Steve: It's un-American.

Understanding Cults

Mary: I don't know much about them. All I know is that they shave their heads, wear weird robes, and sell flowers.

Steve: Or get people to commit suicide.

Mary: It seems they always try to influence others unwillingly. If I want to get in a cult, I'll do it on my own free will. I don't need anybody to push me like they do.

Steve: How about the evangelists on TV? Would you have them taken off?

and explain more about our beliefs. I wasn't too crazy about the idea at first, especially because the meetings were on Monday nights and I'd miss the first part of M*A*S*H. . . .

It's not going to be easy to talk to others when I can't even talk to my own sister, who wants to change religions when she is 18.

Kim Butenhoff, 15
Greenfield, Wisconsin

Church-going is not necessarily synonymous with religion. A great many people go to church on Sunday—all dressed up—and they don't even understand what the minister is conveying. This is their

Accepting God's Existence

Kelly: What do you mean, "Prove to me it happened?"

Steve: For instance, if somebody could prove to me that God did come down and burn a bush, that would be sufficient, but nobody can.

Kelly: I'm not looking for the physical transformation of something. You could turn milk sour. That's not a miracle. I'm not looking for the physical miracle. I believe that God has come down into life and said, "This is how it is. This is what you believe." This is what I believe.

Jeff: Well, so is that His miracle to

Leslie: It's kind of different with the cults. There you've got programming and deprogramming.

Steve: But it's still propaganda. It's coming into your own home and jamming it down your throat.

Manish: We're talking about brainwashing. There's a guy here who's got a cult going. He says, "I want you," and he does weird things to you. He takes you into a cult. So you're saying he's brainwashed this kid into a cult, right? Would you think your parents are doing the same thing when they say, "Since I'm Catholic, my son must be a Catholic." Aren't they forcing their views on you?

Melanie: But there's a difference between influences and brain-washing.

Manish: Brainwashing is just a strong influence.

Melanie: Whether it's influenced me, I don't know. My parents let me go to church. And that was an influence on me. But it didn't brainwash me. It didn't mess me up.

Kelly: But the difference with cults is that they don't allow you to get out as you would hope your parents would. If your parents saw you had a different belief than theirs, hopefully they'd let you believe what you want to. Whereas a cult seems to be very strict. There are probably many parents who say, "No, I'm sorry. This isn't the way it is." And that could be brainwashing. When you take on and believe it, it doesn't matter what influenced you.

Evaluating Religious Need

Steve: I think there are two reasons for the decline of religion: less need and more ability to research other avenues. People are exposed to a lot more.

Kelly: Your second point is valid about more researching, but I don't think you can say there's less need

for religion today than there was 100 years ago.

Steve: Let me finish. The need was greatest and will always be greatest for the peasants.

Kelly: Are you saying religion is something you lean on?

Steve: Heaven is a reward for suffering. The more you suffer, the more you need a reward.

Michelle: Heaven is a reward for a good life. It's not just for suffering.

Kelly: People can find their happiness in religion.

Steve: Exactly, but they're doing it less and less.

Michelle: People don't need religion; they do it willingly.

Manish: Many years ago the pagans would say, "Oh my God! Thunder! Lightning! The gods are angry." But now we know it can be scientifically proven so people don't need the gods as much.

Steve: I think religion is dissolving. People are capable of dealing with the possibility that there isn't a god and that when they get through this world, they won't be rewarded for what they did. People who need support are more likely to go to religion than people who don't need support.

Religion is dying because more and more people are becoming self-sufficient. They don't need the comfort of religion. They don't need support in their moral decisions. People are starting to realize that right and wrong are relative things. There's no such thing as an absolute, and they're learning to deal with it.

Diane: I agree with Manish. I think the technology we have today tends to contribute to people not being so religious. Today, instead of turning to the gods, we turn to the scientists. People look to technology to solve their problems.

Kelly: That's when a passive faith is based on fear or misunderstanding. You said before that religion

false assurance that they are getting to heaven. Others think that if they never smoke, never drink, never partake of drugs, or never swear, that they are "good" people and this will work them into heaven. No way! It has to be something that you really commit your life to.

As a teenager, I resent ministers who are so busy telling everyone what not to do rather than what to do. They give you the speech that scares the life out of you. "If you don't do this, you are going to burn in the fiery hell!" Wouldn't you think that this would turn more away from religion rather than to it? If God is a God of love, then why do ministers preach such fear and anxiety?

Religion is a personal belief that should be felt and viewed without any form of bribery or fear as a determiner. It's about time some of these spastic ministers relax and preach calmly. It would benefit them a great deal.

Beth Elliott, 18
Front Royal, Virginia

Religion is somewhat of a game. If you win, you get to go to some great reward somewhere. "However!" If you lose, you supposedly are damned to a prison where nothing but suffering and pain rule.

My act toward religion is a strange one. I'm not religious. In fact, I'm somewhat of a great sinner.... I feel that if I were to die right now, I would lose the so-called race. I don't let the thought bother me though because I'm happy with the way I am and nobody can change me but myself.

Donald Holbrook, 18
Smithfield, Pennsylvania

I can remember two years ago when I was signed up for a summer church camp.... The last thing in the world I wanted was to waste my summer in a dumb church camp. Apparently my voice didn't carry a lot of weight in the matter because I went—reluctantly, but I went.

Let me tell you, I had a ball. I thought it would be reading out of the Bible all the time, but we had dances, rode sailboats, waterskied, and that was only the start. I went the next summer and am planning on going the next summer also.

Most people think of religion as strict Bible reading. That's not the case at all. Through my church activities I have had some of the best days of my life.

Paul Johnson, 17
Marshalltown, Iowa

I go to church and I pray and I try to believe in God. I also think about this. What if God is just a big hoax? Five or six guys out of work get together and smoke a little weed. They write about things that can easily be predicted: death, adultery, starvation, and all kinds of hardships. They set everyone up, then offer them an escape, God—the healer, transformer, and executor of all good; the key to eternal peace after death; and the forgiver of all sins.

I still go to church, and I still pray. Anyway, who wants to be wrong and find out God is not a hoax? I can't take religion seriously yet. I need a lot more facts.

Brad Swearingen, 16
Marshalltown, Iowa

I'm Catholic, and I basically believe in what the church tries to tell me, but there are certain ideas within the church that I have a hard time believing. I go to church every Sunday, on holy days of obligation, and I even sing in the church choir, but I just can't accept some of the

was passed down through the family. The family has separated more and is less of a unit. Maybe that's why religious belief is not strong—because there's no input from the parents.

Jeff: Also, it wasn't so long since evolution was introduced in public schools. There's more open-mindedness. I wouldn't say the family isn't a close unit because I have a close-knit family. I just think there's more of a choice.

Kelly: There was a time when divorce was unheard of. Now the marriage that stays together is the unique one.

Jeff: People were afraid then. Things are a lot more open these days.

Melanie: Steve said that maybe the decline is because people are more confident in themselves. I don't agree with you because my primary purpose for believing in Christ isn't for financial or emotional security. It's a need I have for my soul because I know I'm sinful. I need someone to save my soul and to bring me back into communion with God. I can't do that with money, technology, research, or even self-confidence.

Diane: I think what Steve says does apply to a great many people. And I think you are the minority, Melanie. What Steve said is what I said. You look to God to solve your problems, but now we have an alternative, and many people turn to the alternative. I think the majority of the people want religion for security, for problem-solving.

Compiled by Eric Kammerer

readings . . . from the Bible.

I have even considered myself to be somewhat of a hypocrite from time to time because I'll just nod and say, "Yes, I understand" or, "I believe that really happened" when I really don't.

I've talked to many different people, and it sounds like I'm not the only person that feels this way. More and more, people are questioning the old teachings, which has always been considered a bad thing to do in the past. You did not question God's judgments, and you did not question your church.

Now people are becoming a little more open-minded about their faith. They are also realizing that you're not condemned to hell if you don't agree with something that is said. . . . It will also save you from having a church full of hypocrites.

Rick Sampson, 16
Brooklyn Park, Minnesota

Religion 161

162

Chapter 12.

Prejudice

"Who me? I'm not prejudiced. I just don't want them moving into our neighborhood."

This hypocritical statement illustrates how prejudice has rooted itself in today's society. Prejudice has become a disease. In many ways, it is similar to high blood pressure, a silent killer, whose carriers are virtually unaware of its progress. In other ways, it's like AIDS where mere mention of the disease sends chills down society's spine.

The symptoms of prejudice are easy to detect in its early stages. The carrier may exhibit a dislike or distrust for stereotyped groups, shown by racial jokes or by outbursts of crudely-coined names. As the disease takes full control, the carriers judge people on the basis of their sex, skin color, nationality, financial status, politics, and religious affiliation. Prejudice most often compounds itself into discrimination and violence. Unfortunately, the disease is highly contagious.

Prejudice originates in the home. Through misinformation it spreads throughout all facets of life. The disease is usually contracted during a person's early years when one's thoughts are more easily influenced. After a so-called education in the "real world," parents feel they must warn their children about "dangerous" groups of people. It doesn't matter if Junior likes "minority" friends. Parents honestly feel that they are saving Junior from bodily harm. They think a child's ability to see through color barriers is only a sign of naivety.

Children are first exposed to prejudice when they hear a parent say, "Junior, you are never to play down by that family's house." They interpret contact with the house as bad, ranking right up there with sticking one's head in a microwave oven. Another way children are exposed is through "innocent" racial jokes. Unfortunately, the jokes often are racial slurs. They may seem funny to whomever is telling them, but the object of the joke is usually hurt. If a kid went home and asked his dad how many of his dad's friends it takes to screw in a lightbulb, he'd probably get slapped across the face. However, the jokes continue. The sad part is that a six-year-old can't tell the difference between a joke and a slur.

Once children sit in front of a television set, the disease is transmitted again, through a tide of misinformation. They receive a narrow picture of society. The average black man is a seven-foot-tall basketball player or a pimp. The average Hispanic is an illegal alien and wants a citizen's job. The average Oriental cleans people's clothes and is a terrible driver. The average woman is into the equal rights movement and participates in aerobic dancing one hour a day. Last but not least, the average teenager is oversexed, overdrugged, undereducated, and, of course, disrespectful to parents.

If kids haven't been afflicted by prejudice by the time they reach high school, they will get their fill during the next four years. High school is a microcosm of society, a place where constant power struggles exist. Clubs, gangs, ethnic groups, athletic teams all are pitted against each other. The issues are how you dress, how you talk, how you act, who you hang out with, who you like, and who you dislike.

Although the groups are diverse, their attitudes toward one another are similar. They reflect the symptoms of prejudice. The groups are highly critical of others and believe they are superior to the "competition."

Brains: "It's unfortunate to have to inform you that we've rejected your application to the National Honor Society. Your grades were commendable, but your insistence on wearing gaudy blue jeans and raunchy concert t-shirts gave us no other choice but to reject you. You do understand that in the Honor Society, we try to project the proper image. If you wish to join next year, we suggest a more suitable wardrobe. Perhaps a polo shirt (collar turned up) highlighted by a pair of khaki straight-leg Calvins, rounded out by a pair of leather boat shoes."

Burnouts: "Ya, they're a bunch of stuck-up pricks. They'd rather stay home and study their frickin' biology. There's gotta be something wrong with them if they're not getting wasted on Friday nights."

Jocks: "Would you take a look at those losers in their souped up Chevy. They're on a road to nowhere. They'll be lucky to get a job in a gas station. Remember him? He couldn't make the team last year because his lungs were cashed from smoking."

Maybe it's too optimistic to hope that someday people will be judged as individuals. The disease would have to be stopped right at its source, the parents. Chances are, however, they'll find a cure for the common cold before they find a cure for prejudice.

Radiating Drops of Hatred

Carl poked his head up out of the earth. All around him lay the rubble that was once his home. The scent of stale air and urine urged him to move farther out onto the blistered earth. The radiation counters on his suit started to whine, their little needles popping up the scales but still within acceptable limits as long as the suit was on.

From the look of things, the city hadn't fared well. Once proud, tall buildings were reduced to little more than rubble. Out in the distance there was the rumble of a storm.

"Thunder. Oh man . . ."

Carl ran through the ruins in terror, for if it rained there would be a fallout that would most certainly kill him. He ran and ran deeper into the city. Little beads of sweat clung to his ebony skin.

And he saw it.

A building.

A tall building.

One that was still standing.

Carl, trying to outrun the thunder, hopped, skipped, stumbled, and ran towards the edifice.

Panting and wheezing, he found himself at the door. He grabbed the handle and ripped the door off its hinges.

The inside looked like almost any other office building, except that the once creamy ivory walls were now a burnt black.

Glancing at his Geiger counter, Carl unlatched his radio. He heard a voice.

A human voice.

So he sat, stunned for a moment, and waited to hear more. It was better than just human—it was female. Carl whirled—the voice was down the stairwell. Bolting down the stairs, he took three, no four, steps at a time. Rounding the corners on the walls, hurtling down, further and further, he saw the door come closer and closer, until it filled his entire field of vision. Then he didn't bother to look anymore.

When he came to, he was sitting on a bed, in what looked to be a spare room. He picked himself up off the bed, and the ground rushed up to meet his face.

"Ouch."

Climbing up again, he made his way to the door.

"H-Hello," he croaked.

"Hello? Are you up?" responded the voice he had heard.

SLAM. The door burst open, hurling Carl back onto the bed.

"Oh! I'm sorry. Are you all right?" she said. A female—maybe a little pale for some tastes, but she was a person and—most important—alive.

"N-No. It's okay," replied Carl.

"Why don't you take your radiation suit off? It's safe in here."

A quick glance at his counters told Carl that what she said was true so he began to unlatch his helmet and take it off.

And she looked at him.

"What are you looking at?"

"You, you're colored."

"Funny, I thought I was born this way."

"It's not funny," she started. "I was told all about your kind. You probably want to steal my virginity right from under my nose."

"That's a funny place to keep it."

"Stop making fun of me!" Out of the folds of her clothing, she conjured up a tiny, deadly .38.

"Hey, come on lady. Put that away. I'm not going to hurt you. . . ."

"You're going to have to leave."

"Lady, you're nuts. It's gonna rain out there. There's gonna be fallout. . . ."

"I—I don't care. You have to leave. . . ."

Carl looked into her eyes. "Okay, fine. I'm gone, lady."

"Y-You're gonna leave?"

"Yep."

Amy Regutti

Prejudice

Carl grabbed his helmet and snapped it into place.
"Th-Then leave. Go ahead. See if I care."
"That's the thing lady. You don't."
The air smelled crisp, like a fine spring day before the rains.

Discussions

Prejudice in our school is an epidemic because every time we have an assembly program blacks sit on one side and whites sit on the other side of the auditorium. Not only is this seen at school but at games. For instance, whites come to football games. Some blacks attend, but it is few, and blacks attend basketball games.

Another incident is that our proms are not mixed; rather, they are separate. The prejudice in our community has affected the way each school person acts, feels, and talks.

Pamela Mathis, 17
Madison, Georgia

Nearly all of the people in this area are prejudiced. They're Mormons and don't really approve of non-Mormons. They are always telling stories about how awful the Mormons were treated in pioneer days because nobody liked the Mormons and didn't want them around.

Now, in Utah county if you're not an active Mormon, you're not accepted very well at all. I've had friends for two weeks, and then they tell me they can't associate with me anymore because their mother hasn't seen me in church. I really hate that.

I'm not some little "devil worshipper" or anything. I'm just as good as other people, whether they want to face the fact or not that Mormons aren't totally perfect.

People in Utah don't give other people one chance. . . . I guess I shouldn't have ripped the Mor-

Karen (voice rising): Manish just said that he doesn't give a damn about the unemployed. He's got a lot of nerve to say that when he wasn't even born here and he's taking jobs away from someone else who should rightfully have those jobs. That's unfair.
(Minor uproar)
(Slight pause)
Manish (slams table, screaming): What the hell is an American? Who came over here? Who slaughtered the Indians? Who threw them in reservations? You threw them in reservations.
Karen: I didn't do any of that! You just came over here. We've been here. We have been working here.
Manish: What do you mean "we"? What is "we"? Your father may be German, your mother may be Polish, their father may be Italian. What are you? What is "we"?
Karen: Not you.

How is prejudice evident?

Leslie: I know I'm prejudiced against blacks. For example, if I don't know them or if I'm in Chicago. I think, "Stay away from me. I don't need your hassle." Yet, when I know black people, I have no prejudice against them. I don't know people who live in housing projects or who are in gangs. I know I'm prejudiced against them. But when I know people from camps and things like that, I'm not prejudiced against them.
Matt: When they built that new sub-division behind us, Foxworth, a couple of black families moved in.

mons apart so bad because I'm a Mormon, but that's the way I feel.

Kelly Christofferson, 15
Orem, Utah

My parents recently have been very much against mixed couples, probably because I am dating a black person. They feel this way only because it is for the good of those involved. On the other hand, I see nothing against the situation or any other black person. I do not look on the outside of a person; it's what's on the inside that counts.

Liz Quill, 18
Canton, Massachusetts

I feel that prejudice is discriminating against a particular group or its beliefs. Prejudice happens all the time, all around us. In our beautiful state of Hawaii, there is a wide assortment of different racial groups and beliefs. At my school of Kamehameha, students must have Hawaiian blood in order to attend. This was part of the will of the school's founder, a Hawaiian princess.

In the past, many opposed Kamehameha's requirements of claiming Hawaiian ancestry to attend, saying it was racial prejudice. However, Kamehameha was founded solely to benefit children of Hawaiian and part-Hawaiian ancestry.

Racial groups in Hawaii must learn to interact to survive. The Chinese, the Filipinos, the Japanese, the Samoans, the Hawaiians, the Caucasians—although all have the ability to interact, many do not. Business in Hawaii thrives when all groups cooperate with each other to survive. In Hawaii many different groups have learned long ago to do just that. There are many different religions in Hawaii also. Roman Catholics worship next door to Buddhists in some parts of our islands. By interacting to help each other, all are happy.

Amy Soares, 16
Honolulu, Hawaii

An example of prejudiced people is the use of one of our gas stations around the corner from my house. This gas station is owned by a Chinese family so only Chinese men work there. The people that live in my neighborhood would rather drive an extra mile or

It was obvious that they were of a cultured nature. I guess I would say they were not the stereotyped black. The neighbors got very upset, and they put a big fence up.

Karen: That's like the carwash owner who wanted to move into Oakbrook.

Matt: They said his business wasn't good enough for him to live in Oakbrook.

Manish: Considering my skin color, brown, you know, it is a minority here. For me to say I'm prejudiced against another skin color is kind of weird. But when I lived in Chicago, I was mugged and beat up by three young black men. From then on, I've always

two just so they won't have to be served by Chinese gas attendants.

I feel that this is very wrong. A Chinese gas attendant can serve gas just as well as any other nationality gas attendant.

Sandy Scalise, 15
Chicago, Illinois

My teacher will ridicule me in class and actually physically separate me (I am Jewish). He will bring up old prejudices and beliefs that Jews are money-hungry devils. He will also totally ignore me in class. Once, I remember him telling me that I must think I am a better person than him because "you never have to do anything because you just were born into money."

On the contrary, I have a job that is part-time and pays minimum wage. I also do not get an allowance from my parents. I buy my own clothes and will eventually have to buy myself a car.

Dan Rips, 15
Omaha, Nebraska

The only reason that my special friend and I stopped dating each other is because I am a Mexican-American, and her parents are very prejudiced. They demanded her to stop talking to me and never to see me again. Well, as it turned out, we had no other choice. . . . We had to hide to just talk to each other. Whenever I would call her, I would have to use another name so that her parents wouldn't know that it was me.

Well, this went on for one whole year. Finally, we realized that we would have to see each other a different way. As it turns out now, we're the best of friends, just like two loving brothers and sisters.

Her parents don't mind. I think they're finally getting to like me. There might still be hope.

Ricky Mendez, 17
Lubbock, Texas

In my family, there is prejudice everywhere. My dad just doesn't like blacks. Even if they are nice to him, he swears at them and still hates them. When someone murders some blacks, he's happy. I think that is just sick to wish someone dead. . . .

I grew up hating blacks. That's all anyone ever told me—that they were bad people and to hate them always. But as I grew older, I grew smarter. Now I don't judge people by color.

I really wish there was no prejudice in the world. It would be a happier place to live.

14-year-old female
Illinois

Oh, it's not difficult to be accepted. As long as you curse, smoke, wear Calvin Klein, Sasson, and Gloria

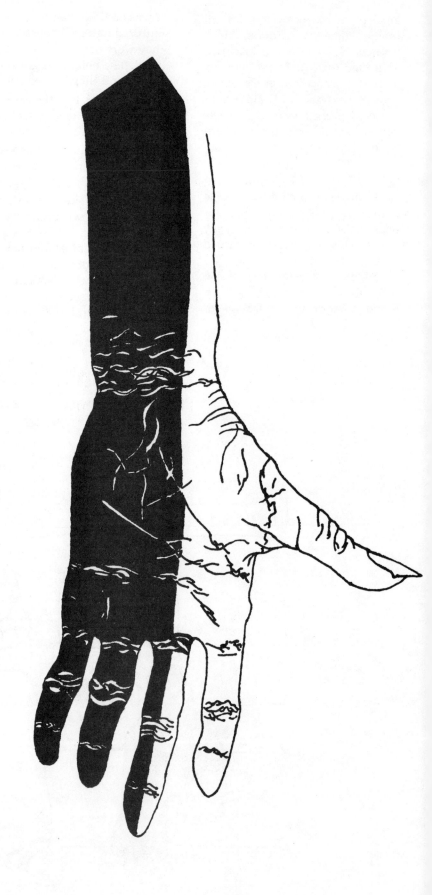

Vanderbilt jeans, and people think you have a lot of money—you're fine. I can't understand why people judge by what's on the outside. What's on the outside doesn't matter. What's inside your heart really matters.

Michelle Thomas, 15
Sapphire, North Carolina

Prejudice is often towards homosexuals, poor people, and low riders. In my community there is a lot of prejudice toward low riders.... It is very difficult to be able to agree with different lifestyles and/or habits. It is sad in a way because so many opportunities or encounters are missed because of someone's prejudice.

Sheri Thornton, 17
Redwood Valley, California

We are not born prejudiced.... We learn to hate. Surely we can unlearn too. The experience of practicing and feeling prejudice shows very clearly that prejudice is a two-way street. It twists the prejudiced person as well as the victim.

In the two years I have been at my high school, I have only experienced one case of prejudice. The case involved a young Korean and myself.... The boy and I started a good friend relationship. Then he wanted more—like to start going out with one another.

I went home and discussed it with my mother. My mother didn't seem to care. Suddenly her attitude changed so rapidly. Then after discussing it some more, we had a family feud. Now the whole family was involved.

I had to decide to talk to the young man and see if we could have the relationship that we had earlier. We got in a fight. So now we don't talk at all that much. And we really don't know what to say to one another.... I really wish the situation could have worked out a lot better.

17-year-old female
California

stereotyped black teenagers as massive guys who come over and beat your head in. I know a few black people, and they are just like anybody else. They're just like any other normal person. But unless I get to know a person for what they are, and they're black, I always think of these people who, you know.

Jeff: Before I met Manish, I think I had a prejudice against East Indian people because I went to Kenya, Africa about three summers ago. Instead of the black people whom you would think ran the shop, especially in the big cities, everywhere you turned there were East Indians running everything. I felt bad for the native people who were pushed out of their jobs by Indians. Then again, when I met Manish, I discovered there were nice East Indians. That helped me overlook my prejudice, but it stemmed from natives over there.

In the case of blacks, it's more of an unknown, a communication gap. We don't take the time to listen to how black people think. They don't take the time to listen to us. We just assume that they are the enemy, almost. If people would just take the time to listen to each other, I'm sure there wouldn't be a lot of prejudice. Usually prejudices are passed on from parents. If they don't like something, you don't. You never get to know anything firsthand. You just believe what they say.

Leslie: Well, I had neighbors who were—I don't know—Indian, East Indian. I didn't know, I was little. There was a family of them. They were always really nice to me, and I was always really open and always saying hi and stuff. I was in grade school then. The father used to play catch with me. I was on a softball team. He taught me how to play cricket, too, or he tried to. My parents were always prejudiced against them. The whole block

It is very difficult to be accepted at our school. Our school has a total of 450 students, coming from four small towns in the area. Most of the students have lived in the community all their lives, as have their parents and grandparents.

I moved to Stillman Valley two and a half years ago. Since most of my classes were with guys, they were about the only people I talked to. The girls in Stillman took this as a "threat" on their territory. So, instead of trying to get to know me, they started rumors about me.

It has taken me two years to live down those rumors and to make people realize they aren't true. I went through this experience alone. There were many days when I just wanted someone to say, "Hey, what's wrong?"

It's been within the past few weeks, but now I've found a friend who really cares. If I had it all to do over again, I would definitely not move to such a small, closed town again.

Krista Rundquist, 17
Stillman Valley, Illinois

Prejudice

It is exceptionally hard to be accepted in my school. I moved in six months ago, and it was like culture shock. . . . The clothes and social gatherings are new to me. I admit it has been an experience I'll always remember.

It's also difficult because the academic structure is different. I'm competing for grades, and I don't like it.

I don't try very hard to please anyone because no one tries for me. I'm a cheerleader, but it didn't help. I was simply the new girl who didn't know the cheers. I still have many close friends in Maryland, and they accept me. But that doesn't help now because I'm here in Missouri.

Vicky Rhodes, 16
St. Louis, Missouri

I don't feel the police in this area like teenagers. . . . They will pick on them for any reason. My girlfriend and I were talking on the swings in a park just after dusk, and a cop came over to see if we were drunk. I don't drink and never will. They also love to give teenagers traffic tickets. I have friends who got tickets for pulling five feet out of a parking lot before turning their lights on. That's picky.

Martin Rigby, 18
Reno, Nevada

Western Springs is predominantly a white community. About six months ago, a white man and his black wife moved into Western Springs. The family is the subject of much ridicule and racial jokes. . . . I admire the family's pride. They are still here today and probably will stay.

I think the children of Western Springs suffer from the all-white community. I had never come in contact with blacks until high school. . . .

The school is still dominantly white, but there are a significant number of blacks. Racial problems are minimal, but so is interaction

was—they didn't want them living there.

Yet here I was playing and talking with them, watching the little kids, until finally one time he just made rude comments because we used to ding-dong ditch and he thought we did it to their house. He thought that we were doing bad things. I don't even want to say what threats he made, but ever since then I didn't like him. Ever since then I've had sort of a block against Pakistanis or whatever.

What is the relationship of conformity to prejudice?

Manish: I think that there definitely is a relationship, like Jeff pointed out earlier. You never get a firsthand experience. Everything's passed on. You are influenced by the community around you, especially your parents. I assume, if you go to the same school every day, meet the same friends, they keep talking about the same thing, like "Oh, those damn niggers." I'm just making a quote—I don't mean anything against anybody. Pretty soon everybody uses the same phrase and one day you do: "Those damn niggers." That's it. Later you think you did mean to say it. You start to change your opinion in that form or manner.

Leslie: I find, for me personally, when I'm with my friends and they are all prejudiced, I'm prejudiced. Yet, when I've had experiences outside of my friends, I find that I'm not really that prejudiced. When I'm out from my family, like when I went to camp, I became really close with this one black girl, and we're still friends. But when I'm with my friends or my father, watching TV or something, there'll be something with black people on and he'll say, "Turn that damn thing off. I don't want to watch them." When I'm with him, I can understand it sometimes. But I'm always open. When I'm away from his influence, I'm free. I do what I

want, and it really doesn't rub off on me that much. I tune him out now. I know I do. I tune out from his views.

What prejudice exists in high school?

Matt: Prejudice against short people.

Steve: Football players.

Karen: Cheerleaders.

Steve: There are general prejudices in this school. Things that affect people every day, such as common prejudices against jocks and burnouts.

Matt: Are you prejudiced against jocks?

Steve: Yeah, in a sense, yeah.

Matt: I'm interested to know why.

Steve: Let me put it this way. I felt that both me and Todd were catching an unbelievable amount of prejudice when we tried out for the variety show. The show was pretty much planned by a small group of friends of which Todd and I weren't a part. We were like an act that just slipped its way in. The adviser pretty much favored that small group of friends.

I felt we were getting totally different treatment. For example, it was the second day of practice. Todd and I did our act for the first time so of course it needed work. Afterward, the adviser came up to us and told us if we didn't get our act together, we wouldn't be in the show. The other acts hadn't practiced much, and they weren't very good either. But he didn't say anything to them.

It seemed people were going out of their way to make life difficult for us while making life easy for everybody else. When we had that cast party, I really tried to be friendly, going around giving people sips of my beer. I was trying to be friendly and was just getting nothing.

Manish: Maybe that's why. Maybe you overdid it, and they were

170

scared of you in a way.

Steve: I can't see that anybody would be afraid of me. I was really not in any way being offensive, and it's not really a matter of what I am. It's what they believe me to be. I don't know. I was guilty in my prejudice, too. But they were prejudiced against Todd and me.

Leslie: That happens both ways. When I was a cheerleader, some teachers used to treat me differently.

Karen: Our science teacher.

Leslie: Oh God, he interrogated me for two years about being a cheerleader. I got teased that I was a rah-rah. Some teachers would just kind of tune me off.

Matt: Why is it so bad to have school spirit? I don't understand what the deal is.

Leslie: It works both ways—it does.

Steve: Either way, teachers and administration, people who are in control and should be trying their absolute hardest to make sure no such prejudice exists are the very same people who continue those prejudices and are the most prejudiced of all. Let's face it, often enough, there are burnouts who ask for it. They're given a fair chance, but they blow it. But often

between the two groups.

The school stays segregated. I don't feel that the school encourages interaction. They don't discourage it, but it's probably not going to happen all by itself.

Ginny Kemper, 17
Western Springs, Illinois

I am irritated when I see signs of reverse prejudice. More often than whites putting down blacks, I see blacks putting down whites.

If a teacher gives a white student an A on a report card and a black student a C, both parties earning their grades, frequently the black student will protest that the teacher is prejudiced. This same student frequently will be the cause of class disturbances and will show apathy towards learning.

I also hate to see that employers have to hire a specified number of each race and sex, often turning away a more qualified job applicant for a less qualified one who fits the racial quota.

I believe that employers should not consider race, national origin, religion, sex, or any personal practices of a job applicant that would hinder him in his work. They should look only for potential and ability, being willing to train those who are willing to (and can) learn.

April Courson, 18
Sumter, South Carolina

Prejudice is extremely evident in the reaction to black Congressman Harold Washington winning the Democratic nomination for mayor of Chicago. Washington's victory is the step forward, in this case. . . .

Going to school on the day following the primary election awakened me to the widespread prejudice felt by many of my classmates in our white, all-girl, parochial high school. Remarks about families wanting to move out of the city flourished.

Students searched for the reasons why this had happened in class discussions. The overall feeling was one of anxiety, fear, and hatred as to what the future would hold for the city and how it would affect the once "secure majority."

Lynn Johnson, 18
Chicago, Illinois

An example of being prejudiced against a black person found inside the high school would be letting a fellow black borrow a personal item such as a comb, hat, or lip balm then later, after it is returned, treating it with disinfectant or even throwing the borrowed item away for fear of catching germs. If one feels this way about blacks causing germs, then maybe they would be better off not lending anything out.

A common example of prejudice against the Trainable Mentally Retarded students would be not eating lunch in the lunch room because the only table left is the one which is for the TMRs. . . .

Not everyone in McMinnville High shows prejudice against others. In fact, some even try to live without it. An example of where it might not exist in McMinnville

enough you get someone who fits in the burnout category, and they get it from the teacher.

Karen: That's my prejudice. [Fake voice] "Hey man, smoke a bowl."

Steve: What's wrong with freaks?

Karen: What's right with them?

Steve: Do they have to be right? Can't they just be not wrong?

Karen: I wouldn't hang around with them.

Steve: Why not?

Karen: Because. They give you a bad reputation. Seriously, they don't know what they're doing. All they're out for is a good time. They don't care about their future.

Matt: There you are, lumping people together again, generalizations.

Karen: Well.

Steve: So, I understand you have this prejudice. Why did you get to a point where you have this prejudice? What led you to this?

Karen: Against burnouts? I don't know—they're there. They make fun of me. So, I don't like them either.

Matt: Why?

Karen: Why? Because I'm not a burnout, and they're always trying to push their drugs on me. I don't like that.

Steve: So, what other prejudices do you have?

Karen: Well, why don't you ask someone else, like Matt?

Matt: Well, I'm prejudiced against some burnouts. I'm prejudiced against them because it seems like some kind of cop-out. They just kind of let everything go and say, "I'll just do drugs."

Karen: Exactly.

Matt: "And I don't care about anything else, just sit around and be lazy. Blow off school, blow off work, whatever. Drugs are my life and acid rock music. Just sit around, be lazy, be a nothing the rest of my life."

Karen: Yeah, then they live off welfare and take money away from people who need it.

Matt: I don't know about that. I guess I can just say I'm prejudiced against people who can make something of their lives and don't.

Steve: In what ways do you express that prejudice?

Matt: You mean an example?

Steve: Yeah, how would you treat a burnout differently from somebody else?

Matt: I don't respect them.

Is prejudice in the world decreasing or increasing?

[Murmurs of "less"]

Matt: I mean there were separate drinking fountains and bathrooms, back of the bus.

Steve: I don't mean to be defensive, but it was America. Then again, there's still South Africa. That nation is ridiculous. I mean they have blacks living in different areas of the city. There are black areas of the city and white areas, and you can't move.

Leslie: That's how we used to be, kind of.

Steve: Yes, in one sense, but it wasn't supported by the government.

Leslie: It wasn't supported by the government directly.

Matt: Let's ask a minority. Manish, do you feel like we are prejudiced?

Manish: No, not really. My friends I hang around with—they make jokes, but I know they are kidding. And they know that I know they

are kidding. [Laughter] They can say like, "Oh, man. I hate these Indians. They are all like so and so," but they are always smiling. They don't mean anything unless inside they are holding a personal grudge against me, which means they're awesome actors and I haven't been able to detect it.

I feel everybody disregards my color and thinks of me as a normal person. I have heard, though, in this neighborhood, some comments behind my back. But that's not very frequently. It's not like every day. It's like once every two years.

Leslie: But everybody gets that too.

Mary: You don't have to get comments about your color. You can get them about anything else.

Karen: Like what you're wearing.

Manish: So, maybe people are very open-minded or discreet about what they say or very cautious. They don't want to be on the bad side of somebody. But I've noticed 99.9 percent of the people—no make that 100 percent—don't treat me differently from anybody else.

Karen: They don't pick on your nationality as much as they pick on something else.

Manish: Like, we can be sitting around and maybe be making fun of black people, and it would be very ironic because I'd join in. If I look back I think, "Hell, I'm not much different." You think, here's a bunch of white guys making fun of another group of people, and I'm not like that—I'm not white. Caucasian, yes, but—

Steve: In the sense, I know a man who tells the best Polack jokes in the world, and he's 100 percent Polish.

Manish: That's what I mean, you know? You sort of go along with it, and nobody is prejudiced against you. But maybe I'm thinking

High would be volunteering to become a peer tutor to let someone "special" know that they are cared for. Another example might be choosing a partner for sports who is unaccepted by society in PE.

Kimberly Ault, 18
McMinnville, Oregon

Minorities often suffer because of white people, who think "white" is the only color that counts. Also, people who are very smart are thought to be "aliens" and are walking computers. I have a 3.6 GPA and am taking advanced classes. Many people do not like me because I get good grades. My real friends know I am a person and can make mistakes too. . . .

God obviously didn't want people to be alike or He would have created them that way. We all need to learn a lesson from that. Everyone is unique in his own way. They shouldn't be criticized or prejudged without a fair chance to prove themselves. . . . Everybody can learn from each other. We should make use of this fact, not destroy it.

Lori Austin, 17
Sterling Heights, Michigan

I think a lot of people are prejudiced even though they think they're not. If you ask a white girl if she is prejudiced against blacks, she will probably say "no," but then she will never go out with a black guy.

Laurel MacLaren, 15
Kirkwood, Missouri

When you are a sophomore, everyone looks down on you and treats you like dirt. Then in your junior year, it's usually a little better. By the time you're a senior, you look forward to treating others the same way you were treated as a sophomore. It's a continuous cycle that is very exhausting.

Now that I'm a senior I regret all my wasted effort of trying to please everyone and put on an act. I now realize that if people can't accept you for who you are, that's fine. But there's no need for you to try to get them to like you. Kids in high school can also be very cruel. If they choose not to accept you, they can make it rough for you.

I would summarize my high school years by describing it as one big "game," always trying to get ahead, be the most popular, have the best looking guy, or be the best dressed. Now that I have outgrown that stage, I am so glad, so glad that I can just be myself and be happy with me.

Karen Hull, 17
Altoona, Pennsylvania

I was completely shocked at a certain party when "The Jeffersons" came on. All of a sudden kids began throwing candy bars, records, and shoes at the screen. They were yelling at the characters because of their color and making negative racial comments.

I could not believe that they were so prejudiced. I immediately began to question why they were doing it, but they could not supply sufficient answers.

Wendy Hulme, 17
Brookfield, Connecticut

I know plenty of people who claim that they aren't prejudiced "because they have a black friend or a Jewish friend." But when they are in downtown Boston, they don't hesitate to yell racial remarks out of their car window at them. It doesn't say much for those people. They must feel so threatened by those different people in order to say things like that.

I think anyone that allows a public showing of prejudice should wake up to today's society. Why anyone ever lets the KKK march is still confusing to me and stirs up an unquenchable anger inside me.

Kathleen McKie, 17
Newton, Massachusetts

Being accepted around here is a little tricky. Your parents want you to get good grades. Say you get all

sometimes when I'm not there, they'll be talking about me. But I seriously doubt that. I've never felt treated differently than anyone else.

Matt: Society has accepted minorities more.

Manish: Take Leslie for example. I don't mean to pick on you, but you said your dad is rather prejudiced against black people.

Leslie: Prejudiced. Yes, okay.

Manish: And you are more open-minded. Right there you see change. You see Leslie's becoming more open-minded. She's accepted minorities more. How do you know her kid won't be totally open-minded? And her kid, his kid, whatever, will be "Hey, everybody is equal." I see a definite change.

Will our nation ever achieve total equality?

Matt: No.

Mary: No.

Jeff: But people never dreamed of there being a black or Indian mayor in politics. Now they are changing so much. Think of the sixties when you had racial riots. They were bad. Right over at Proviso East, there were knives. I mean that was a bad situation. More and more every year, it's getting better.

Manish: It's like saying from here to go to that wall. Let's say I go halfway. Then I go halfway of that. Then I go halfway of that. Will I ever reach the wall? Ideally, no. I'm always going to be cutting in half. I think it's the same thing with this prejudice idea. [Laughter] You guys making fun of me again, huh? [Miscellaneous laughter, chatter] It will always reduce and reduce, but there will always be that certain minority who will always, for some reason or another, hold something against those who are labeled a "minority."

Steve: It might get to the point where skin color doesn't matter. But then it will be some other thing.

Compiled by Chia Chen

A's or close to it—you're pleased, your parents are happy, but the kids your age won't have anything to do with you because you're a "brain." So you don't do good in school and your parents get mad, and all you hear is "Oh my God, I did better than   . I can't believe it!" That really gets on my nerves.

Being a jock is a great way to get accepted. Sports are big around here, so if you like sports, you're all set. If not, you're thought of as a burnout or a brain. I can't wait till I'm finally just me.

Elaine Warner, 15
Athol, Massachusetts

Prejudice

176

Chapter 13.

Violence

Justin Adaise trudged through his front door, tired and hungry after a long day at school. He carried his afternoon snack into the family room, balanced them on the arm of the chair, and switched on the TV for a rerun of "Starsky and Hutch." Justin stifled a yawn while numbly gazing at the usual scene: a long car chase that ended without a crash. Starsky and Hutch had cornered the criminal and were involved in a shootout.

"It's strange that no one ever gets seriously injured or killed during these shows," Justin thought. Sure enough, despite a barrage of gunfire from the villainous crook, neither Starsky nor Hutch was hit. The bullets whizzed by their heads. And when the criminal was captured, he was not shot in his stomach or any other place where a serious wound could be made. He was shot in his thigh—big deal! Starsky and Hutch could have him taken to the hospital and fixed up. The criminal would soon be well and ready for jail.

"Amazing—just amazing!" Justin proclaimed, impressed by the seeming invulnerability of human beings to gunshots. He changed the channel to a Daffy Duck cartoon. The duck was being pelted by shotgun blasts. Justin, however, did not worry for one moment about the possible demise of the wacky waterfowl. He knew that Daffy would survive a mere shotgun blast with no problem. Daffy's beak was turned backward, his skin was singed, and his feathers were blown away. Sure enough, though, Daffy removed his beak, emptied the shotgun pellets, and put it back on correctly. He then gathered up all of his loose feathers and, being a modest duck, stepped behind a tree. Two seconds later, Daffy stepped out and looked as good as new.

"That duck is more resilient than a Sherman tank," Justin thought.

Justin picked at his raisin bran. He had seen violence on TV for so long that it no longer excited him. He yawned, stretched out on the couch, and fell asleep. His subconscious stayed wide awake, however, and his dreams took over. . . .

Justin found himself wandering aimlessly through an unknown land. The colors of the land were so bright and bold that he was dumbfounded. Suddenly Bugs Bunny ran by, yelling, "Look out, Doc! It's Yosemite Sam!"

Justin heard a gun fired, and then he felt a sharp pain in his lower body. "Aaah! I've been shot!" Justin screamed as he fell to the ground. Justin rolled his eyes at Bugs Bunny, who was bending over him. Bugs told him to roll over so he could see how bad the damage was.

"Well, you'll have to patch your pants, Doc. Otherwise, no problems. I'm getting outta here!" Bugs said as he sped off. Justin twisted around to see for himself. There was a hole in his pants that was still smoking, and his bare bottom showed through, but there was no blood, no wound, nothing!

"I don't believe it!" Justin exclaimed. "I was sure there would be bleeding, and surgery, and, and . . . I've never been shot before! I was worried about dying."

Then Justin laughed. He realized how foolish he must have looked. Of course, a gun shot couldn't do any harm. All it could do was sting his rear end a little.

Next Justin met the Three Stooges. Moe brought a sledge hammer crashing down on Justin's head, but of course nothing happened. In his best Curly imitation, Justin taunted Moe by saying, "Nyuk, nyuk, nyuk. Don't try to tickle me Moe! Look—you broke the hammer!"

For this outburst, Justin had his stomach bonked, his nose tweaked, an ice pick inserted into his nostrils, and his eyes poked. But he didn't care. He was having one hell of a good time.

After the Three Stooges faded away, Justin popped into the passenger's seat of a beat up car, in the middle of a high-speed car chase. "Don't worry ace, we'll get him—and you can take that to the bank!" growled the unknown driver. Justin turned and looked with astonishment. It was Tony Baretta!

Justin replied that he agreed and nervously settled back to enjoy the thrill. Suddenly the pursued car turned into an alley. Baretta followed, turning too fast. Justin saw a brick wall looming before them. Shading his eyes, he crouched for the impending crash. "Smash!" the car slid sideways into the wall. It was nearly totaled. Of course, Justin and Baretta were unharmed. Baretta leaped out through the window and, notwithstanding a hail of bullets, finally ended the chase with a clean shot to the crook's shoulder.

Justin sighed, releasing all the built-up excitement. He heard Baretta telling the crook he'd have to pay his dues. "This is fantastic!" yelled Justin. "Violence is fun!"

The car and the alley and the brick walls faded away to reveal an ominous background: a dense forest, a ravaged plain, choking smoke, deafening noise, and charging men in khaki uniforms. Justin soon realized that he was in the midst of battle. Seeing a Panzer tank with a giant red, white, and black Nazi swastika emblazoned on its side, he realized he was in Europe, World War II. "Wow, I can't think of any show with this scenery in it. It must be only on late night reruns," Justin thought.

Justin was sure that this would be as much fun as his previous adventures. When he saw a German soldier advancing toward him, he thought, "This ought to be good for a few laughs." Justin ran into the open, in full view of the Nazi soldier. He yelled, "Hey kraut-face, over here! Hitler's mother wouldn't eat porkchops!"

The German hoisted his rifle and shot at Justin. The bullet hit him in his abdomen. Justin felt the sharp pain and obediently fell over. He began laughing as he waited for the pain to go away, but it didn't. "Jesus, it seems real this time," he thought. He felt a warm trickle down his side, looked down and saw his own blood running like a small river into the grass. The full force of the pain hit him as he conceived the reality of his wound. He screamed a long, pleading, agonizing scream of horror.

He gazed through rapidly blurring eyes at his intestines and other parts of his gut bulging through the bloody, shredded flesh. He prayed and prayed for the pain to end. He saw the Germans circling above him, rifles aimed at his head. He begged them to help, but his breath was quickly failing. The world began to turn black. Justin gasped, "I don't wanna die, no—no! God, please, please, help, help . . ."

The real Justin Adaise awoke with a start, still gasping that he didn't want to die. His pillow was soaked with sweat. He saw his own living room and stared at his abdomen, intact and unharmed. He wiped the cold sweat from his forehead, grabbed a bottle of 7-Up, and gulped heavily.

He glanced at the TV and saw another cops and robbers show. It was the usual climactic shootout scene, with the harmless car crash, the meaningless barrage of bullets, and the criminal being caught after suffering a flesh wound.

The fantasy of television comforted Justin's still distorted mind. He chuckled to himself with a false sense of relief. "Hell, it was only a dream," he reassured himself. Then he settled back to watch the Road Runner drop a boulder on Wile E. Coyote's head.

Ten minutes later, however, the phone rang. It was Justin's friend Pete.

"I've got some bad news, buddy," Pete said.

"What?" replied Justin.

"Mike has been in a car crash. He was driving down Main when a drunk in the other lane swerved and broadsided him. He's at Memorial Hospital with a broken leg and deep cuts in his face, but otherwise he's okay. It was pure luck, though. The police on the scene said that another few inches, and it would have been 'So long, Mike.' He's really upset, and I think we ought to go see him. How about it?"

Justin answered that he'd go, and Pete said he'd be over in a half hour. Justin put down the phone and sat on the couch, badly shaken. The news had brought back the vividness of his dream.

He began to sweat again. He jumped up and shut off the TV. He sat down again. Violence was a real threat, not fun and games. Bullets and car crashes do kill, and often. Justin shivered. He didn't know what to do, but he was sure of one thing: Violence was nothing to enjoy and get excited about.

As the doorbell rang, Justin realized something important. He was living in a violent world that was getting worse every day. For the first time, it scared the hell out of him.

Personally, I'm worried that some day I'll come home and find that half the country has been blown off the map just because one country doesn't agree with the other. Or maybe some day I just won't come home.

Heather Kirkwood, 15
Amherst, New Hampshire

A Minneapolis UHF station says they give their viewers "family programming." They do not show programs with an emphasis on sex, but yet every weekend the station fills the airwaves with westerns and war movies. People are cut down by gunfire like blades of grass under the whirling blades of a lawn mower. Is that family programming?

People quietly eat their potato chips as people are shot, stabbed, beaten, bludgeoned, blown up, run over, crunched, munched, ripped apart, and burned. It should be obvious that some TV shows are turning us into a nation of closet sadists.

The scary part is that it is not just criminals being affected. It is almost everybody. Violence is an accepted part of society. Harmless little comments like "Did any cars crash in the race?" "Was there a fight in the game?" and "Too bad J.R. didn't die" all prove the point that we are violent.

It is ironic in this technological age when things are helping to "better" our lives that we can still act like medieval savages foaming at the mouths for the sight of blood. However, don't worry. It is only a coincidence that we went right back to our dinner after watching the Beirut massacre on the news.

John Berg, 17
Brooklyn Park, Minnesota

I like to think of myself as a fairly intelligent, conservative person, yet recently I have been quite upset with the reaction that many of my peers have had to the possible reinstatement of the draft. . . .

Discussions

Manish: The question is "Are you scared of violence?" I'm one of those people who always says, "It's not going to happen to me. It's going to happen to the next person." It's going to happen to maybe Kelly's friend or Kelly or John or anybody. I think that the chances are so rare that the possibility, the statistics, will make it so that it can't happen to me.

Karen: This weekend a gang took a crowbar and bashed in the window of my friend's car. The glass got in his eyes, and that's about it for him. He was a good friend of mine. They bashed in the window of his car with a crowbar just because he had a jock jacket on. That kind of thing scares me.

Michelle: This girl I know beat me up twice. Once I was lying in bed with a 102° temperature. This girl comes storming into my house, screaming, "You said this and that and this about me." I mean, she started beating on me. I'm laying there with a 102° temperature. What am I gonna do? I was a little kid. I started crying.

The second time it happened I was on the telephone with my friends. It's summer, and I have shorts and a t-shirt on. She starts pulling me around and swinging me around by my hair. I could not get her off me. She hung up on my friends. They called the police. I picked up the dog chain, and I hit her with it. It was the only way I could have gotten her off me. Then the police came in the house.

My mother wanted to press charges because the girl walked into the house and started beating on me. The police talked my mother out of pressing charges. Well, it was my word against the girl's, and there were no witnesses. There are lots of times when crime does happen, and there should be punishment for it. The police, though, act like it's a little petty crime. Let's leave it alone. Let's get the bigger things. Well, the little things are just going to lead up.

Maribeth: My sister was dating this guy. They were going out for two years. She was out with other friends and met this new guy so she decided to see him instead of her old boyfriend. She told the guy, "I don't want to see you anymore." He couldn't handle that. He came over one day. Nobody except my sister was home. He brought a gun to the house and threatened her. He said, "Don't you dare break up with me." Then my brother came home and, you know, freaked out. This guy was hitting my sister. My brother went and got a knife and threatened him. They were fighting. My brother was hitting him and stuff and the gun went off. We had a few bullets in our house—they're out now. He threw my brother against the wall, and he broke a lot of stuff.

I came home, and I freaked out and ran to my neighbor's house. I called my mom, and she called my dad. He came home real fast. By the time he got there, this guy decided he better get the hell out of there, so he just left. We didn't call the police. We called his parents, and we never saw him again.

Daily Frustrations

Diane: I really got mad at my mother one time—probably the only time I ever really got mad at her. She said something to me, and I went upstairs and hit my closet door. My hand felt like mush.

Steve: My brother and I get into fights occasionally, but I've never been in a real life situation where violence achieved anything.

John: When I play football, I let my violence out. There are a few kids on the team I can't stand. So, when I do get my opportunity to tackle them, I really lay into them as much as I can. Sometimes, it is with the intention to hurt them so they won't play again.

180

Only once have we seriously injured somebody. That was when I was in eighth grade. The kid was a real jerk. He'd come to practice every day—he was older than us. He was always picking on me and my friend. So one game he was the kicker. When he was coming down to make the tackle, we just came after him and sliced his leg right in half, broke his leg.

Jeff: When I get hostile and violent, it's usually because my parents say something and I know I'm wrong, but I hate to admit that I'm wrong. So I get very violent and hostile because I know I'm wrong and they're right. I hate that.

Steve: When you don't know what you're doing and you're in a situation where you seem to have lost all control, it seems like you get this feeling that violence will get everything into shape. You'll be able to deal with the situation because reacting violently will help sort everything out.

Media Portrayal

Diane: You know the violence on TV and movies is not real.

Karen: We go to them because it's escapism.

Diane: And because you don't want to go out and commit the violence. Let's say you're frustrated. You don't want to go out and commit a murder, but you watch somebody else kill to get out your frustrations. You know when you're watching the TV set that nobody ever did this. That it's all fake.

Manish: It's not just that—that you want to get out your frustrations. It's not reality; it's something different. You know that in reality you wouldn't accept people who go around hacking each other up.

Kelly: Well, when you're a little kid, you watch Bugs Bunny and the Road Runner. There are cartoons and stuff where you laugh and you think they are funny. Then, when you get older, you are expecting the car chase. How many of you have ever been in an accident in a car? It's not as exciting as it is on TV.

Steve: Yes it is. I thought it was incredible. [Others laugh] I'm serious.

Michelle: It wouldn't be incredible if you broke your wrist and your legs.

Steve: Exactly. If it was serious, it would have immediately lost its appeal.

Many outright refuse to ever have anything to do with the draft, even register.

Having been fortunate enough to travel fairly extensively at a young age, I came into contact with the rest of the world, including the "iron curtain." After witnessing the oppression that a large part of the world is forced to live under, I can think of no other cause worth fighting for than the maintenance of the "American way of life."

Grant Sinson, 17
Elmhurst, Illinois

The draft—otherwise known politely as the Selective Service—is the most useless waste of money and paper. To begin, the draft itself is contrary to the concept of the United States. Our ideal of freedom is shot to hell—as future draftees will be—when our country requires registration of our young men.

How can a country which preaches to its students the greatness of this country, because of its freedom, turn around and then tell its teens that they must register so they can kill?

This, of course, has been taken to the extreme . . . because the requirement does not affect young men immediately. . . . Furthermore, when a guy said to me that he had to go register that day and that he felt girls should, too, I just replied, "I don't think either should." Students should not be so accepting of their elders' beliefs.

I am also tired of the argument about mom and dad or whoever fighting in World War II—and how proud they were to serve our country. Somehow, killing does not strike me as a service. More importantly, we are more aware of what war really is. Didn't our parents sit and watch the Vietnam War in their living rooms?

Do they not see that the people who end up fighting are just people, most without any strong conviction against the "enemy" (that word which dehumanizes the other side to help ease the guilt)? The only concern becomes survival. Men, women, and children are all brought down to an animal level.

Patty Jordens, 18
Gresham, Oregon

I get violent the most when I get frustrated, when the society becomes a blur, and when everyday things start to bug me, like the honking of a car horn or your shoe comes untied.

Doug Johnson, 16
Marshalltown, Iowa

When fights start at school, you'll know it because people start running toward the fight—not to break it up but to watch. I'm from New York, and fights and violence are common, especially gangs.

Some gangs help the New York community. Some gangs are like Robin Hood—steal from the rich and give to the poor. Some gangs are just out for "turf" and violence, like if you walk down the "turf" of

MAYBE I WON'T COMMIT SUICIDE. IF I LOOK HARD ENOUGH, I'M SURE I'LL FIND SOMEONE WHO WOULD LOVE TO KILL ME

Kelly: It goes two ways. Some people see so much violence they don't care about it anymore. It doesn't affect them. They're used to being scared out of their pants so they don't care about it anymore. Everyday things don't bother them. But violence makes other people more sensitive to what's going on.

Steve: I don't think that TV really does a very good job of portraying terribly violent accidents or imagery.

Kelly: Well, it has to be limited. Do you want to see somebody get killed on TV?

Steve: Not exactly, but I suggest to you that if you were to experience it firsthand, it would be very much different from television because TV is civil. It is civilization.

Michelle: You can't hide a problem of society from the people. Violence is a problem you're not going to hide from everyone.

War

Kelly: With Reagan, everybody's always complaining because he's increasing the defense spending. He's already anticipating having a conflict with another power. Why doesn't he increase spending on education so maybe our little kids will grow up smart enough not to have wars?

Michelle: I don't think it'll ever happen.

Steve: At the time when bombs are dropped, we will feel some concern, but at this time there's no point in worrying.

Kelly: Yeah, but we have the opportunity to stop that from happening.

Michelle: It affects our lives. There's so much more we can accomplish. You don't want to die tomorrow.

Kelly: I'd like my children to grow up and have the same things I did. Not exactly the same way, but you don't want to think that maybe the

another gang you better have a good reason or fast legs.

I was in a gang, but we did destructive things, like graffiti with spray paint. Once we almost got caught. We were on the D train going to 125th Street, Amsterdam Avenue. We waited until everyone was off the train. Usually, the cops make their rounds, but they didn't that night. . . .

Then we got the spray paint out and started. We called the painting "Tracks." . . . We threw the cans away. Then we heard something. A gang member spotted a "blue." We were like "chariots of fire" in the wind. We ran up the stairs. There were six of us on the move that night. We made it to White Castle, a food place. We were shipwrecked. We made it back to the home front. But there are also gangs like the famous Guardian Angels which help the people of New York City on subways.

Sean Fox, 16
Rock Hill, South Carolina

Some people, to get away from pressure, kill themselves. A friend of mine had been dating a girl for a long time. She told him that she wanted to break up.

He couldn't handle the pressure, and he blew his head off at the age of 16. . . . These kinds of violent acts are put on the news, which gives other people in their spot the same idea.

Shawn Crouse, 16
Marshalltown, Iowa

I think people act violently because they often have a lot of frustration bottled up inside of them. When they reach a boiling point, they just lash out, releasing all that pressure and anger. Most people feel that when you act violently you are a bad person and should be put away somewhere, but I don't.

I have seen many of my friends and relatives act violently because

182

of some emotional stress. All they need is someone to sit and talk to about whatever is making them react this way. . . .

This violence also has very terrifying effects. I know. When I was in the second grade, I saw my sister die because her husband was in a frustrating stage of his life. He lashed out at her because she was the only person or thing around when he felt he couldn't take it anymore. His violence led to my sister's death and left her family and friends hurt and angry.

Sandra Walker, 18
Catawba, South Carolina

War, of any sort, is a foolish waste of lives and property. It is ridiculous and childish that our country's President is so old-fashioned that he thinks military strength and extreme armament build-up is the best way of maintaining peace.

Our leaders are too clouded by outdated cold war attitudes toward the evils of communism to realize that both superpowers can already destroy each other many, many times over. A freeze would serve to free up much-needed money for things other than defense, such as education.

Eric Wargo, 16
Morrison, Colorado

I go to violent movies because they "turn me on." I don't necessarily like violence, but there is something about seeing thick red stuff squirt out of a stump where an arm has just been axed off. Maybe it's the devil who creates violence. . . .

If we didn't have violence, then heaven wouldn't look so good to us. People killing people: someone's just been shot, stalked, mugged, raped, lynched. Who knows what else someone might think of?

Kerry Erb, 16
Joliet, Illinois

Children aren't affected by watch-

whole community or the whole society could be wiped out within the next year.

Jeff: The next day, actually.

Michelle: Yeah, but think about it. Come on, they're just as human as we are. Are they going to have the guts to do it? I don't think so.

Kelly: I don't think it takes guts. I think it takes stupidity, and they could handle that very well.

John: Well, I mean, look at Hitler. He didn't have his mind. He could always have somebody in charge do it. What if there is a crazy man working for us in the government? Anybody, you know, there's a lot of psychos out there right now. They could easily launch a missile.

Diane: I'm positively sure that sometime, maybe not in our lifetime, but sometime in the future, we'll have a nuclear war. I'm not a historian, but I've looked at other cultures. Each culture started out with low beginnings and reached a peak and then went

ing violent cartoons. They do not analyze them like adults do. Normal adults aren't affected by the violence they read and see. They're just glad it didn't happen to them.

Teenagers do not act violent because daddy says he is "gonna kill you." Children aren't violent because they listen to Black Sabbath and Led Zeppelin. People become violent by their own shortcomings.

They believe that if they are a failure they can always rely on violence to help them. This viewpoint will always be in America, no matter if they stop the presses or turn off all the television. Violence can never be stopped.

Chad Olsen, 16
Joliet, Illinois

I used to hate violent acts . . . but now I feel different about it. . . . After I had punched someone, I felt great. It's a good feeling.

Teenagers are so rowdy these days that everybody learns to like

Violence

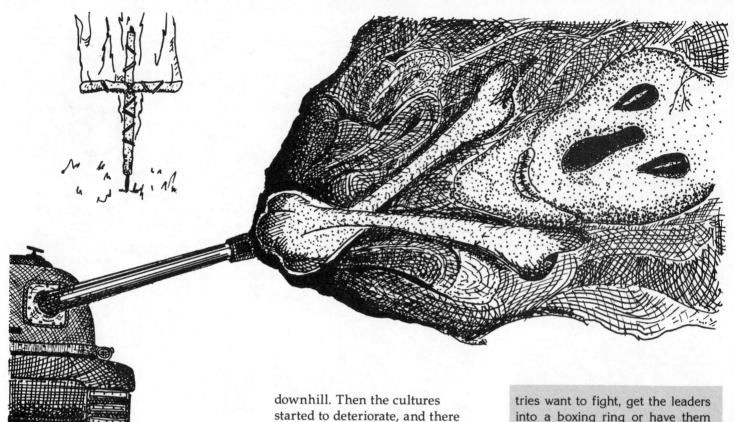

violence. Everyone fights eventually. After the first time it's fun, especially when you win and everyone cheers you on. You're proud so you do it more because you want to feel proud of yourself.

When you watch the movies or TV shows that have violence, you always cheer one guy on. If he wins, you feel smart and proud because you picked that guy.

I used to hate violent movies, but I got used to it. . . . You have to get used to everything in this world or leave it (kill yourself).
Tabitha Nifzger, 14
Fargo, North Dakota

I have a feeling that before I die there'll be a nuclear war. . . .

I am 110 percent for disarmament. I wish everybody would throw down their weapons, bombs, tanks, and all that other stuff and use squirt guns and boxing gloves.

My solution is that if two coun-

downhill. Then the cultures started to deteriorate, and there were two opposing sides. Eventually, even though they tried to check each other, they ended up destroying each other. You've seen it in pre-civilization and all kinds of other sects. I think it comes down to this: one person out there with a finger on the trigger may be greedy and think he can gain something from it. Eventually it's going to happen, no matter how many fail-safes you may have.

Manish: We study history because people say history has a tendency to repeat itself. So, I'm thinking that by this time we are sort of civilized. I would go along with Steve and say yes, we have gained enough intelligence to maybe not let history repeat itself at this moment. Maybe we are sane enough not to go out shooting everybody in sight.

National Defense

Michelle: I don't believe in getting involved in other countries' wars unless a nation needs our help. I can understand if we're fighting to save our country and freedom but not if we get involved in somebody else's war.

tries want to fight, get the leaders into a boxing ring or have them arm wrestle. War is hell on everybody, not just the soldiers.
Scott Hingst, 17
St. Clair Shores, Michigan

I think war is necessary at times. It would be nice to have a peaceful world, but that is not the way it is. . . .

Conventional war measures destroy many homes, buildings, and lives—and it is terrible. But if some country's government subjects them to war, it is not their fault if innocent people get hurt and buildings destroyed. . . .

Conventional war is man against man to see which is the strongest and smartest. Nuclear war is man against machine, in that one button pushed can destroy a whole country. That does not tell which country is better. It tells which one is more inhumane.

This country is worth losing your life for, I feel. We've worked so hard to build it up the way it is—how could we just sit at home and watch it be destroyed? I know I couldn't.

As of March 1, I am a member of the Nebraska National Guard and

184

would be ready to go to war if the President should declare it.

Jody L. Haynes, 18
West Point, Nebraska

CIVIL WAR?

I remember stumbling upon war:
Joey stole my matchbox car
While playing Demolition Derby.
Fat lips and bruises
Became part of the game,
But that was just childhood.

Growing up brought war to me in
    history books,
But war is not history.
Past generations grew up with the
    plane,
Inheriting memories of the Red
    Baron.
The plane was a technological
    advancement
Transporting millions of people
    every day.
The bomb, too, is called an
    advancement,
Yet a bomb never advances;
It destroys and destructs.
No legends or proud memories
Rise from the bomb.

Uncivilized men fight uncivilized
    wars.
And while we may be considered
    civil,
There is no such thing as
Civil War.

Michael Davis, 18
Warwick, Rhode Island

No one can really tell why a person acts violently. Something in their past might be bothering them, or maybe they are scared of the world. Others have no one to care for them so they believe that society will succumb to them if they hurt them. They . . . take out their frustrations on the unsuspecting victims. . . .

I grew up in a tough neighborhood. I know how bad it can get. I was always on my guard and never let anyone push me around. I was never really a bad kid. For a time,

John: What if they're our allies? You can't just ignore them because we need other countries. If we need help, we're going to always ask them to help us.

Diane: We gave a bond to other countries to help them. If they should need our help, whether it be military or economic, we should help.

Steve: But you can't say, "This is the way the government stands. Therefore, I also stand that way. This is what the government says I should do. The government told me to kill. Therefore, it is not my responsibility or my fault or my problem. I'm just doing what I'm told to do." If I was told to go somewhere and kill in order to protect the United States, whether I did it or not, it would be totally my responsibility—not "I killed because I was asked to."

Kelly: Also, because you elected the government. The government is not some being standing up there saying, "This is what we are going to do." Hopefully the government reflects your ideas.

Steve: All right, but you can't, even if it doesn't actually reflect your ideas, abdicate responsibility for your actions. I think that's what lots of people do. "Well, the government told me to go and kill. Therefore, I killed—that makes it okay."

Diane: Well, that's how many people survive. A lot of people who went to Vietnam said, "What the hell are we doing here?" They said—for their own sanity, for their literal sanity—they said, "I was told to come over here. I gotta do it."

Kelly: They don't want to confront how they feel about it.

Steve: Oh, no joke.

Manish: What you said was, "It's not your fault that you kill,"—right? It's the government's.

Steve: No, I'm saying the exact

rivalry was the only reason my friends and I ever got into fights. Later, my grandmother died when I was nine. I was more on the defensive. I was scared of losing someone else. . . .

A grown-up who I know was outside her home one night and was attacked on her doorstep. That incident really made me want to go find him and do something to him. My grandfather was almost killed by some maniac.

I wish that they would keep people like that off the streets or out of the country. I hated those people for what they did to me and my family, but I was not going to lower myself to their level.

Elizabeth I. Culbertson, 16
Rock Hill, South Carolina

I think that war is not necessary but is often brought about by pride. Always, it is over something physical, in the way of land or goods appropriated by another nation.

I think a lot of war could be avoided if people weren't so worried about saving face. The war of the Falkland Islands is an example. Britain doesn't really want them, but she had to save face.

Nathan Oliva, 14
Albuquerque, New Mexico

As I sit outside watching these three brothers drink alcohol, one of the brothers pulls out a gun and kills the other two brothers. I ran into the house to call the police, and the police arrested him. Teenagers like watching violence anywhere because they like to see people get hurt or killed. I think violence is nothing but bull.

Alverez Hemphill, 15
Rock Hill, South Carolina

Violence is a way for people to gain the attention of others. It is a way for people to pay attention to you.

I think that violence makes you stand high on a pedestal for the simple reason that people are afraid of you if you are violent. If

there is a fight at school, people always reward the winners. Maybe they don't reward them for actually winning, but they want to get on their good side.

Carmen Backhaus, 17
Marshalltown, Iowa

I know that once I graduate from high school, I want to continue my education, have a career, and eventually get married, and have a family. However, if the United States and other world powers can't be at peace with each other, how will I ever live my life to its full potential?

I read a book in my junior year of high school titled *Alas Babylon*. The book dealt with the struggle of the human race after the nuclear bombs had been dropped. That book frightened me, and it brought to my attention that the possibility of a nuclear war was real.

opposite. If you kill, it's your fault that the person died.

Manish: You're justifying your involvement.

Steve: I'm not justifying anything. I'm not saying whether I would go kill or under what circumstances I would kill. I'm only saying if I kill, it's my responsibility. I did kill, and I am responsible for that person's death.

The Draft

Manish: It's pretty selfish, but I'm for the draft as long as it doesn't involve me going out there fighting.

Michelle: Yeah, but if there's a draft it's going to involve you.

Manish: Definitely right.

Michelle: You know, he doesn't want to go so exclude him.

Manish: I hope they do that, but I doubt it.

Jeff: I don't think I'm in favor of the draft. I guess I don't trust our

As each day passes by, I thank God that I'm still alive. I will always pray for peace in the world.

Cheryl Lepine, 16
Milford, New Hampshire

I know defense buildup is extremely necessary, but everything is going much too fast. I don't think the draft should ever be reinstated. It's hard when someone has planned their whole life, and they get one letter in the mail changing everything they've planned.

That's a real blow to your system. I think maybe I'm biased about this because I'm young and would probably be a candidate.

Kim Leaor, 15
Milford, New Hampshire

I would rather go one-on-one with any Russian than just push a button and blow the shit out of a mountain of them. Obviously, we should disarm our nuclear weapons, but we should keep our conventional arms greased and on the ready. . . .

I may be called a war monger or whatever, but it wouldn't bother me at all if, say, everyone had to serve six months, just to learn the basics—nothing hardcore. And that goes for women too.

Erik Miller, 17
Iowa City, Iowa

Teenagers act violently for two reasons: (1) they had an unhappy childhood and (2) they are trying to hide their true emotions.

Teenagers who are afraid to show their true emotions are almost always hostile. They just can't show their true feelings so they turn to fighting. . . . As the years go by, they could easily turn to rape and even murder. . . . Instead of looking at the good side, they look at the bad. That's when they start hitting out at the world.

Sheila Geery, 18
Rock Hill, South Carolina

That has to be the worst feeling— seeing people fight people over money, land, or power. Men have to go through life without an arm or leg because the government could not deal with their problems. . . .

The family next door had a son who was at war, and he made it home. My brother never did come home. At first, I was very upset and jealous of the couple next door. But now I almost feel my brother is better off that way.

Heather Quinn, 15
Milford, New Hampshire

congressmen enough. I don't want to leave it in their hands to decide when I'm going to fight. That's directing my morals, and I'm in charge of that. I'd go fight, but it would depend on the situation, on the war. Face it, if we're going to have a war with the Russians, we're not going to need the manpower anymore because it's going to be all nuclear.

Steve: War should be treated as a regrettable necessity. If there was a serious attack on the United States, then we would definitely have to defend ourselves. We may have to defend ourselves on the ground with men. In order to preserve this society, and I certainly believe it's worth preserving, it has to be done. If I was drafted because there was an actual attack on the United States, I think I might go. It might not be particularly admirable, but I would do it anyway. If there was a war like Vietnam or El Salvador, you better believe I'd be on the first plane to Britain. I'd tear up my draft card, and I wouldn't feel bad about it.

Kelly: If they drafted women, there would be a super big baby boom. No one would want to go. I'm serious.

Maribeth: I don't think women should be drafted. I think if they want to go, they'll go. If they do

start drafting women, 90 percent of the women are just going to get pregnant so they don't have to go. They'll do something drastic like that.

Jeff: I think this time we should have an all women war, though. If they want to get pregnant, then it's just a bunch of pregnant women fighting.

Steve: I don't believe they should send women to the front lines because of the potential for rape, but 80 percent of army jobs, even during a war, have nothing to do with the front lines. Why not have the girls typing as opposed to guys who could be fighting?

Compiled by Eric Kammerer

Violence

187

Chapter 14.

Death

Dear Diary, I know it sounds cruel, but in a way I hope she dies soon so she won't have to go through this much longer. No one should have to spend the last few weeks of her life like this—lying in a hospital, not really living; simply existing, waiting for death to come.

I went to the hospital to see Amy again today. She's getting so thin. I hate seeing her like that. She's all bony, and her skin's already turned a yellowy-gray color. She gets shots every few hours, and she's so doped up she sleeps a lot of the time. But you can tell she's in pain.

I had to walk out of the room today. I hope she didn't see me crying—my eyes started watering when the nurse came in and gave her another shot. Now Amy's got a big bruise on her hip, where she's had so many shots, and some bruises on her arm, where her IV's used to be.

I hate to think that Amy's last recollections of life will be of such pain and suffering. I never understood it before, but now I know why a person might want to die at home. Why should you spend the last days of your existence in a place that has nothing to do with your life, in a bed that will be filled again two or three days after you're gone?

The nurses in the hospital are nice to her, but they don't really know her. They don't know what she's done in her life or what she likes or what she laughs at.

It's easy to forget that when a person's dying, an individual's life is ending. Like, there is an old lady down the hall from Amy who's always moaning. She always seemed like an annoying old lady, but then I realized that she's just like Amy. She has a family who loves her. And I'm sure she could probably tell some interesting stories about her life, too. She's a person, not just another patient.

It hurts so much when I think of Amy and what she'll never do. I keep asking myself, "Why her?" What hurts the most is remembering all the times she told me what she was going to do with her life and all the dreams she had for the future. It's not fair.

Sometimes I think if I were in her position, I'd rather kill myself first instead of lie there, suffering day after day, merely waiting.

I shouldn't say that. Who's to say who has the right to end a life? I guess God must have a reason for making her suffer.

I think about her a lot and pray for her too.

Dear Diary, Amy died. The wake was Wednesday, and the funeral was Thursday.

Aunt Gail called our house Tuesday morning. Mom answered. I knew when the phone rang that something had happened. Amy died in her sleep during the night.

We cried at first. Then Mom went up to her bedroom. My sister and I sat there quietly for a while. Then the two of us went out to buy dresses since neither of us had the right kind to wear to the wake and the funeral.

189

The next day it was like getting ready for a social event you really didn't want to go to. I was even trying on different earrings to see which looked better. Amy's death really hadn't hit me yet.

After we finished getting dressed up, we went to the funeral home. I walked in and saw her. She was lying in the casket. She didn't look like herself. You could tell she'd been sick a long time. As I was walking up to the casket, I started to cry. Amy was dead.

I still feel dead inside, as if somebody tore out my insides, leaving me emotionally bruised and numb. I don't feel anything. I just kind of go through the motions of living. At least during the wake and funeral I was kept busy. I had no time to think.

I can't believe that she's gone, that I'll never see her again. Even at the funeral parlor she was still there.

I like to think she's in heaven, finally happy and peaceful.

Dear Diary, Marie, Sue, and I went to Amy's grave today. It's Amy's birthday. She would have been 22 today. Marie talked to the grave and told Amy how things are at home. I know some people talk to graves like the dead person is actually there, but I'm always afraid some stranger is going to overhear her one day and think we're all crazy.

I can't understand why anybody talks to graves. If the dead person can really hear, you could talk to her anyplace, not only at her grave. Besides, the body you're talking to is probably being eaten by worms as you talk. How gross! And if there's such a thing as a soul, I don't think it'd be stuck in the ground.

In a way, I'd like to think that Amy is somehow watching over me and knows what's happening in all of our lives. I'd like to think of her as still being alive in some way—like her soul living in heaven or somewhere.

But then when I think of my own death, I don't know if I'd want an afterlife or if I'd prefer to simply die and stop existing. Sometimes at night when I can't get to sleep, I imagine what death might be like. I don't know how I feel about the idea of not having an afterlife. It's hard to think about dying as the end. Life would stop so abruptly—my mind would shut off, and I'd never be aware of the world or people again. That's scary.

Besides, if there is no afterlife, then what is life for?

But it's also scary to think about living forever. What could a person do forever? When I see movies like *Topper* and *Heaven Can Wait,* death seems like fun. I could come back to Earth to watch my family and friends in their daily crises. Also, in the movies heaven seems like such a cheery, peaceful place in the clouds. I could float around in a white gown and distribute halos to newcomers.

But then I think about the question: "If there is a heaven, what could a soul do in heaven forever?" Forever isn't just millions and millions of years, but it's billions of years. Never ending.

The scariest part is that the Earth won't even be here forever. One day it will blow up, but I'd still be floating around somewhere in the universe maybe.

And, where is heaven? It has to take up space somewhere, doesn't it? But where? I guess Amy knows.

It doesn't help to worry about death. One day each person will find out what actually happens. I don't fear death because one day it'll just happen and I can't do anything about it. If there's an afterlife, I'll experience it. If there isn't, then I won't know the difference anyway.

I better go now. Tom, Karen, and Bridget are going to be here any minute. We're going to a basketball game at West. Maybe our team'll score a few points this time.

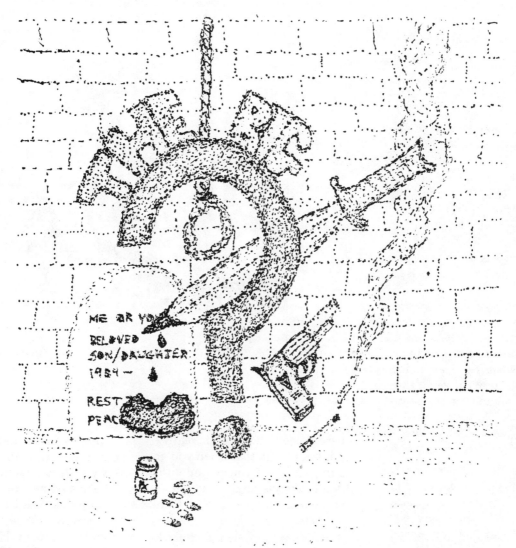

Discussions

Maribeth: I remember when my dad died. We got a call at four in the morning. He was still alive, but the nurse said, "You'd better come. He's not doing too good." So we got a ride to the hospital. I remember they said that he couldn't move, but he saw me like he knew I was there. He knew what I was saying.

So, there was a priest there and a nurse, but there was no doctor. You could see the screen where his heartbeat goes, and I saw that it wasn't going straight but going down. I started saying, "Get a doctor." But the nurse said, "Well, we can't. They won't do anything." I said, "Just get somebody, do something!" But they said, "We can't. There's nothing left we can do."

And so I was holding my dad's hand, and he was looking at me, like he was saying, "I'm so sorry, I'm sorry for dying." And I just remember saying, "Get a doctor, get a doctor." But the nurse said, "There's nothing we can do." I ran down the hall, and I was screaming. The nurses were telling me to be quiet because there were people sleeping, but right then I felt so bad that I wanted everyone else to feel bad, too. I wanted to wake everyone up. I wanted them to know.

I've never been to his grave yet because I know, I know that if I go there I'll accept his death and that's what I don't want to do. I want him to be here. I want his memories to be here so I probably won't go

Death scares me. I don't want to die. I would like to know if there is "life after death" or if you just stay in the dark or if you really do go to heaven. I believe you would go to heaven, but is it really the way people have drawn it in pictures or in the movies?

My father died not too long ago—when I was in the sixth grade. At first, I didn't want to believe that he died, but people constantly talked about him. I never really cried too hard after my dad died, but now I realize that he really is gone.

Since the death of my dad, I have changed, but only to my family, not my friends. I have become less active and grouchier. I don't really know why. Now instead of crying, I am constantly talking about him—mostly I talk only of the "good" parts about him.

Julianna Martinez, 13
Window Rock, Arizona

Death doesn't bother me. Dying scares me because of all the people that worry and suffer. Sometimes I wish people would fall asleep and not have to put up with the pain of dying. No one close to me has ever died. My next door neighbor was really old, and he died. My mom was upset because I didn't go to the funeral because I had a meeting.

I wonder why we have funerals. They cost too much money when the person isn't even there to see it. I think we should have a party for the person while he is alive. Too many people mourn over death while they should enjoy being alive.

Terri Ducker, 17
Englewood, Colorado

Bad attitudes toward death really disturb me. My father was killed in a train-truck accident. Ever since then, I realized that not everybody lasts forever and that you should make the best of life.

When people say "I wish I was dead," that just really irks me. Nothing could be so bad that you wish you were dead. . . . I have grown up pretty fast from my experience and have learned to look forward to life and everything that comes my way.

Lisa Bachman, 16
Eureka, Illinois

Death, of course, is inevitable. Therefore, there should be no attitudes towards death, only acceptance. Death seems to be an outlet for all negative feelings that would otherwise have to be hidden.

My mother died when I was ten years old, and I have yet to "forgive" anyone for it. This is where the idea of acceptance must be applied. I have since felt extremely

there. I know that sounds really bad, but I think that when you go to the grave and you go and visit, then you're visiting a dead person. But I don't think he's dead. I think he's here.

Melanie: My grandpa died maybe a week and a half ago, and we weren't expecting him to die. They said he was in fair condition and he would be home Sunday. That Friday my grandma was there with him, and she said, "Well, I'll see you tomorrow." He goes, "Okay, take it easy." She left, and 20 minutes later he was dead. He just had heart failure, and it was a shock.

I've just been kind of sitting around in a daze. My parents are dealing with his death, and I think I'm dealing with it. But I don't know. I don't know where he is—in heaven or what.

Kelly: When my third cousin—his name was Hal—died, I was really upset. I spent a couple of summers at their home with my grandparents so I'd gotten to know

him a lot. He was physically disabled. He couldn't walk very well. He just sat in a chair. He had been a painter, but now his hands were crippled. He couldn't do anything, but he still told stories and sang songs. He was a nice guy to be around and I really got to love him. Then, one morning before I went to school [long pause, sobs], I really want to tell you—this happens every time I think about him. My mom told me that he died a couple of days after he did so I couldn't go to the funeral.

After finding that out, I remember being in gym class when we were working in the weight room. It was a conditioning course, and a lot of kids were sitting around and trying to find ways to get out of doing what the teacher said we should be doing. It made me really mad to see all these kids who had perfect health, but they wouldn't use it. It made me mad because Hal would have liked to have been able to lift weights instead of sitting around talking about how you can get out of doing the work for the course.

I wasn't so much mad because Hal died. I knew he was going to. He'd been sick, and I did miss him because he had been a friend. But it made me mad to see everybody else who was still living not doing anything. I'm like everyone else. You want to do as much as you can because you're living and while you're living. Be back in a minute [leaves room in tears].

Diane: My mom didn't die, but she came as close as you can come without dying. It was in late fall. Believe it or not, I was delivering a litter of puppies at the time, and my mom had gone to a dog show. My dad had just gotten home from work, and we were delivering the last puppy. There was a knock at the door. My dad answered it, and he came back in. I recognized the woman my mom had left with earlier that day.

My dad said to me, "Your mother's had a heart attack. She's out in the car." I can remember I was in such a bind. Here's this litter of puppies, and here's this life coming out. There was my mom in the car. I can remember going outside. It was freezing out, and I

had shorts on and no shoes. I went outside and I couldn't say a word [long pause, sobs], not one word to her. I tried, but nothing came out.

I looked at her, and she looked just as healthy as when she left. She was just sitting there, and I took her hand. She said to me, "Don't cry." She said, "I'm not gonna die. I had the heart attack, and I know I'm not gonna die." But at that moment I couldn't believe it.

I said to myself, "Why me?" like, "Why is this happening to me? It could happen to anyone else. Why should it happen to me? I've got my own problems." My dad called the paramedics, and I could remember it was so terrible because my dad said, "Go back in the house. You've got to finish delivering the puppies."

Here's my mom dying outside, and I'm running back inside to deliver a puppy. The whole neighborhood was outside, and the paramedics were there. I couldn't figure out why it was taking them so long to get her to the hospital. I was forced not to be with her at the time I thought she might die and that made me mad.

When my parents took off, I was by myself for a while. Then I had to

empty as if I were a horrendous void concealed in flesh, but my acceptance of her death is all-important.

They say to grieve is to be selfish, for what of the Creator's promise of a better life after death? One would think death should then be a glorious occasion. We have become so hung up on material things that we forget there is anything else.

Melanie Duffy, 18
Riverside, New Jersey

The death of my mother made me turn very bitter. . . . I resented all my friends and my family. I was jealous because they had mothers and I didn't.

I tried to shut out people that were close to me. . . . I thought my father's fiancé was taking my mother's place so I was very mean to her. This almost ruined our friendship.

All of these things made me hate death. I still think it's unfair. I couldn't and don't understand it.

Missy Townsend, 16
Portland, Oregon

When I lost a close friend to leukemia, after a long fight for her life, I was exhausted. I knew she was dying and thought I was ready for it. But no matter how much preparation I had, the death still shocked me.

A year has passed, yet the pain is still just as real and sharp as it was the day she died. The death has made me more aware of what I have, so I appreciate it more.

Debbi Jaeger, 18
Sand Springs, Oklahoma

It is hard to cope with the death of a friend or relative because it's hard to say goodbye. . . .

My cousin committed suicide. This was hard for me to handle at 12 years old. I had this gruesome stereotype of people who committed suicide. I thought they were crazy people who were just taken

Death 193

into oblivion by life. My cousin was not in this category.

I don't agree with him because I don't believe in quitting. I guess when you have to come face to face with death you should ask yourself one question: Are they better off? I know one day I will be gone, but I want to show my worth before I go.

Brian Buchanan, 17
Independence, Missouri

Death is somewhat of a hard thing to accept. The hardest thing is knowing that someone is going to die soon. For instance, I babysit for a small boy and girl. I just found out the boy has cancer in his leg. It has spread to his lungs and maybe even to his brain.

Nobody knows how to act in a situation like this because everyone is uncomfortable. This boy could be given treatments, but the chemicals might kill him. He could be left alone, but we know he will die.

He is being treated now. I go up to talk to him, but I don't know how to act. I can't just pretend he's okay because everyone knows he isn't. So I just talk to him, thinking that he's sick and let him know I care.

If this boy dies, I will be very sad. But I will feel much more sorry for his little sister. She has grown accustomed to his presence. She plays with him, talks with him, and fights with him. How will she adjust to him just disappearing out of her life?

Beth Mullen, 15
Bellevue, Washington

When I think about death, I am terrified . . . not of what is going to happen after death, just of death itself.

In December, 1982, about two weeks before Christmas—on a Friday night—my family and I went to bed early because we all had things to do on Saturday. Around 1:45 a.m. the doorbell rang. My mom . . . went to the kitchen win-

call my brother and tell him what happened. I got a grip on myself, and I thought that it was bad for me to say, "Why me?"

I asked God not to let her die but not for me. I thought if I asked God to save her for me that would be wrong. And she might die. But sometimes I think it might be better if she did because every day after her heart attack, I didn't think she was going to make it.

She was so weak. I mean, she was in the hospital for a month and then she went through surgery and all that. And now, every day I'm just waiting for the phone call that says, "Your mother's had another heart attack." And I'm like living on the edge of her death every day. [Leaves room in tears, returns quickly.]

I think the biggest problem I have dealing with the situation is that I made a pact with my mother that if she ever got to the point where she was a vegetable, where they kept her body living but her brain was dead, I would pull the plug or do whatever.

That's what scares me a lot—even though her mind's dead and they're keeping her body alive, will I really be killing her? I wonder if I could bring myself to do it. But I promised her that I would. She said, "You do this. I want you to do this." She begged me or she said, "Put the bottle of pills there. If I can reach 'em, I'll take 'em."

Will I be able to stick with that pact? And what would it do to me if I really went through with it? Would it destroy me as a person? Or would I really not have killed her if her mind's dead? I hope I never have to do it because that's what really scares me the most.

Mary: I was going out with this guy two years ago. He went down to California for a couple of months. His next door neighbor called up one day and said he was mugged and killed. I just couldn't

believe it, that someone could kill a 17-year-old like us.

It wasn't just the fact that they killed him. It was that he was into drugs a lot. He had a lot of problems, and I was just scared that maybe he didn't go to heaven. He could have had the whole rest of his life to get to know God, and he didn't get the chance.

Kelly: It's always a surprise when someone dies, especially if it's violently. My brother's roommate, after a couple of weeks at school, was driving home with a bunch of kids on a break. There was a car crash, and he died. My brother had never known anybody who had died so it was really a big shock. It was a big shock to me, too. I didn't know who he was. I just knew he was my brother's roommate. You think, "Well, that's unfair. Why should a kid just starting college die?"

Melanie: A couple years ago there was a neighbor, a couple doors down on our street. He had just gone to college. He was a young freshman, 17 or 18, and he was stabbed 31 times.

As I look back, that was just so much harder to take than my grandfather dying of heart failure. You think of what the people have gone through. How did this person feel when someone came up to him and started hitting him around and stealing his money? You think about the first time he was stabbed. Maybe he was thinking, "Oh, it's just only one, I'll still live." And then after the second, the fourth, and the twenty-fifth, and the thirty-first time. You've got to wonder.

It's a shock when you find out he's dead. It's like, why did it take so long? Why was it so many times? Why couldn't it just have been he died of shock? I wish that he had. I think it was also not only hard on me—I was his neighbor—but his father. Four months later, he died of a heart attack. I'm sure he thought about a lot of the same things—stab wound after stab wound after stab wound and his son going through that.

Capital Punishment

Mary: Capital punishment is stupid because you're not supposed to kill anybody for anything no matter what.

Manish: [Refers to quote from Gandhi] An eye for an eye leaves the whole world blind. Two negatives never make a positive. And one killing never solved another.

Matt: Number one, we're paying taxes for those prisons and those murderers who are kept in there, feeding them every day and keeping them alive. I don't think it's fair that they should live after what they've done. I think the treatment they receive is too nice after the killings they've done to others.

Diane: That guy, Gacy, deserves to die. He killed somebody else. He should be able to receive the same punishment himself.

Kelly: I don't think anyone else has the right to determine when Gacy dies. My first thought is that he's horrible, but capital punishment is as bad as the original crime. They put it under the guise of jurisdiction and law.

Karen: Say it was your father who was killed.

dow. Out behind the house was a huge ball of fire on the road. The girls who rang the doorbell were in the driveway so mom asked what had happened. They said a car rolled over and hit a tree. . . .

I had never seen an accident before, and I didn't think at all about who could have been in the car. I went to bed about 2:45 because nothing was happening. . . .

The most terrifying scream in my life was when my sister came running down the hall saying it was . . . two friends of mine that I grew up with since I was four years old who were possibly dead. . . . They both lived on my street, and they were only about 500 yards away from home. I never cried so hard.

If they hadn't been going so fast, they would be here today—that is the only thing that keeps going through my head. I will never understand death, and I will always be afraid of it.

Deb Hourihan, 17
Baldwinsville, New York

My father died seven years ago after a three-year fight with cancer. That was a most trying time of my life and of my family's life. My family made countless trips to Seattle while he was in the hospital. It seemed he was always recuperating from another operation.

The cancer would come in waves almost. At times it seemed he might get better. The doctors thought they had won. Then the cancer would appear in another part of his body—in a lung or in his liver or kidneys. He always seemed to be getting a new treatment or therapy which made him sick or something.

Whenever my mom, my brother, and I went to see him, no matter how he felt, he acted as if there was nothing wrong. It was upsetting to see him with tubes and things stuck in him. Well, one Sunday morning, two days since my brother and I last saw him, he died.

Our family, of course, was all very upset but in a way glad it was finally over—glad for my dad because he was free at long last, free. Since that time, my family has become very close—helping each other out. It caused me to grow up faster than I would have imagined.

I have dyslexia (reading difficulty), and all the time I have fought to overcome it and learn as much as possible. At times when I don't see any gain or feel it's all for a lost cause, I look back at my dad. Three years he fought that disease. When he died, his liver was close to 30 pounds over what it would weigh normally.

I'm not planning to let him down. I'm planning to make something of myself.

Greg "Zack" Zatkovich, 15
Bellevue, Washington

Death is a cold, unfriendly thing, but I don't believe death is bad. I believe, out of respect for the person, you should put flowers on the grave of the beloved and visit their grave once in a while.

Apparently my great-grandmother believes different. Because of it, we haven't talked for almost two years. My great-grandfather died. She said she wasn't going to put flowers on his grave because it was a waste of time and money. . . . I got so mad I wouldn't talk to her the rest of the time we were down at her house.

It has been just about two years, and now she is on her deathbed. She isn't terribly old yet; she just turned 75. Even though I still am mad for her saying what she said, I will have to go visit her because I couldn't live knowing I hadn't said good-bye to the only great-grandmother I'd known.

Tammy Huddleston, 16
Independence, Missouri

When my father died, I was in the eighth grade. I really did not know how to act afterwards. I was the only boy that was at home, and I

Kelly: I don't think you should deal out a punishment when you are angry or upset. I don't think you can look at it objectively, when it's that close to you.

Melanie: The murderer of the neighbor of mine didn't die for what he did. This isn't his first offense either. The paper said that he had raped several girls and he had murdered another person by beating him with a pipe. Then he did this, and the guy was put in jail for 30 years. I thought that was a very light punishment.

Jeff: It's a horrible thing to think about, but if one of you women were to get raped, think of what you would feel afterwards. You can think as rationally as you want but you're going to want this guy dead for what he did to you. You're not going to want him to do it to somebody else.

Matt: If you put him in jail, he's going to get out. And you'll be wondering if he's looking for you or not.

Jeff: Rapists just get a slap on the wrists these days. Then they're out doing the same thing again. I saw a survey that seven out of ten go out and do it again.

Matt: Wasn't there a country where if you steal, they cut off your hand? So rapists—

Kelly: I think it would be an effective deterrent to rape.

Abortion

Karen: I think they should abstain from sex if they can't support the baby.

Kelly: But if it was incest or rape, I think they should be able to get an abortion.

Jeff: I'd like to speak from a different angle. I'm pretty glad my 15- and 16-year-old parents didn't have me aborted. They were 15 and 16 when they had me, and they waited to put me up for adoption so I'm pretty glad about that. But I'm still pro-abortion now.

Manish: I'm anti-abortion in any case. Suppose it was a case of incest or rape. I sympathize with you greatly. It's wrong, and I understand, but you have to remember, it's not your life you're taking. It's someone else's which you have no control over. There's no way for you to communicate with that person and ask him, "Would you still want to grow up?"

I agree it's very hard for a mother-to-be with this child if she was raped or brutally abused. She's going to look at that kid as a symbol of what happened in the past and how it came about. But I think she doesn't have any right at all because it's not her life.

Melanie: If they can't handle the child because of rape or incest or an accident, then put it up for adoption.

Diane: I'd like to set up a situation. Let's say a 14-year-old girl has an incestuous relationship with her father and even carrying the baby is a definite threat to her life. They say to her, "Now you can have an abortion. That would be your safest bet. If you keep it, there's a 90 percent chance that you will die." A lot of times when the mother is very young, there is a good chance she'll die. In that situation I see no other alternative than to have an abortion. Giving birth threatens the life of the mother in that situation, and the most important thing is the life that is already there.

Manish: You're saying that you would be willing to have an abortion so you can make it through safely, right? And you wouldn't mind killing the life inside you?

Diane: People have different opinions about where life starts, and that's the biggest part. An egg is three months in the making. I'm 17 years in the making. I have an identity. It's my responsibility, and I make decisions for it because it's part of me. You realize if I die, the fetus dies too. I'm not willing to sacrifice my life or take a 10 percent chance that I'll live. The chance for the fetus is less than that. I can't see that this egg, three months in the making, is life.

Suicide

Kelly: I think it's the wrong way to go. The chicken way out. Nothing is that bad—that you have to take your own life.

Melanie: I don't think a suicidal person is able to judge by himself whether he should live or not.

Steve: If you truly want to commit suicide, then nobody can stop you.

Mary: I think that most of the people who committed suicide just didn't know any better. If they knew what was out there for them they wouldn't have done it.

Matt: When I found out that my friend had committed suicide, I was shocked because I had talked to him the day before he did it. He had just bought a new car, and he was behind in the payments. Apparently, it just built up so he went home and slashed his wrists. That didn't work fast enough so he shot himself in the head. I wasn't that close to him, but the day before I had talked to him for an hour. I'm sure it was something deeper than car payments. But that's what I was told. There was no

felt like it was my own personal responsibility to try and be the man of the house.

I was really scared because I didn't know anything about that. My friends were just so much nicer after that, but that was the one thing that I didn't want. I wanted them to treat me as they had always done before. Of course, my father had died, but I hadn't.

Len Ramsey, 17
Rock Hill, South Carolina

Death is a natural part of life. It is hard to accept sometimes, but I have learned to accept death. I experienced the death of a boyfriend in 1981. I really took it hard.

He was really too young, only 16. It made me a stronger person though. When someone close to you dies, it always takes a part of you. But the best thing to do is always remember the good times you shared with them.

Cheryl Browder, 17
Winston-Salem, North Carolina

I don't understand death, but I know it affects people when they are involved indirectly or directly. I wrote a poem to a friend of mine that was killed in a car accident. His name was Raschelle. I went to the wake and to the funeral. It was so weird seeing him lie in the coffin up at the front of the room.

I felt like all I had to do was close my eyes and he'd be alive again. I sometimes still go back to a classroom, where I had him in class, hoping he'll be sitting there, laughing and telling jokes.

Over this last Christmas vacation, I knew Raschelle was dead, but I said to myself, aloud, "I'm going to call Raschelle and wish him a very merry Christmas." I only said that to myself, knowing he was dead, because he was a friend I'll never forget. I wanted him to have a very merry Christmas, wherever he was.

Christi Pennel, 17
Independence, Missouri

A young girl of my community was murdered. She was murdered six months ago. The police are having a difficult time figuring out the killer. The feeling that is in the air at school, in town, and even in my own home is unreal. It is a creepy feeling.

Sometimes I wonder if the killer is sitting next to me in class or if he is passing me on the streets. The girl died in a way that I hope no one ever has to again. I hope and pray for her and her family. I know that I cannot bring her back, but maybe my prayers will help others.

Jeri Parvin, 17
Mannford, Oklahoma

I remember the day "Phil" died. November 11, 1980 was a cold and windy day. I felt the coldness running through my blood as I began to realize that he was gone forever.

"'Phil' shot himself last night," I said to one of my friends, only half believing and half hearing the words I said. "He's gone." With those words as my stepping stone, I knew I would make it through, for that was the first time I had admitted what had happened to my best friend several hours earlier.

For weeks my thoughts wandered. I felt as though I was walking through each memory in my mind, seldom being able to return to reality. . . .

"Phil" has been gone for two years now. I still miss him very much. There are times I want him to come back so badly to help me through, but I know he is gone.

Many other people take death in such a way that it is hard for them to ever carry on. Life, of course, will be different without them, but a person never really dies if their memories live on in your heart.

Michelle Skinner, 17
Lincoln, Nebraska

note or anything.

Mary: It's sad. What else can suicide be? I knew this girl who was really impulsive. She'd say, "I wanna do this" and just do it. She was in a hospital, a psychiatric hospital. She said, "Well, I think I'm gonna kill myself." So she went. She had a belt, and she tied it to the door. When they found her, she had her hand by her neck. She really didn't want to die. She was only 14. She didn't want to die. She just wanted help. She wanted somebody to notice her.

I think it can be any of us who feel like shit, and I think everyone has the responsibility to everybody to love each other. If somebody is bummed out, just to let somebody know that you are there. Just anything because the people who commit suicide—they're just so lonely. You have to do that.

It's like a final act to show people you had nothing else to do. You don't know what to do, and other people should give the person a reason to live. You don't just find it by yourself. You need other people around you. You need help, I guess.

Life After Death

Mary: It scares me. I know I want to go to heaven, but it's scary. You think about what will happen to your body.

Steve: I think about death quite a lot. When I think about it, it scares me but not because I think I'm going to heaven. I don't know what's going to happen. I suspect probably nothing, and I'll just kind of no longer exist. That's kind of scary, something I can't deal with but the idea makes me want to get some pleasure out of living. That's about it. Really there doesn't seem to be any other reason for going on.

Mary: I think the purpose of living

is so that when we die we can go to heaven.

Melanie: When I die physically, I'll be with Christ. I'll be forever alive, and I won't go to Christ and say I spent my time on earth not caring about anyone except myself. I don't worry about death because I know what will happen to me because I have accepted Christ as my Savior. It really bothers me, though, when someone dies and I'm not sure about their relationship with Christ.

Kelly: Because Steve doesn't feel he knows what's going to happen to him, he's a little afraid of it and he wants to do everything now. When some of us feel confident, we know what's going on. We're not afraid so much of our dying as of other people's dying.

Diane: I try not to think of my body decaying. I think of what I can accomplish in my lifetime before I die and how I can affect other people in the best way I can.

Maribeth: I believe that I'll go to heaven. I think everyone will. I don't think God would say, "You're bad, you go to hell." Even if you're a murderer, there are always some people up there praying for you. But, I always think, will you know what's going on because you've stopped?

Kelly: Yeah, I don't know just what my role will be after I die.

Jeff: I'm kind of agnostic towards religion, and I guess toward life after death. I don't disbelieve exactly, but I can't bring myself to believe in any of that so I just try to make the best out of my life when I'm here.

Steve: Sometimes it's difficult to find motivation for life if there's nothing in death.

Compiled by Tracy Wykert

For the average high school student, death is not a reality because most of us have not experienced it. As for myself, my first experience with death was just a few months ago.

A man I had been particularly close to had been struggling to fight cancer for almost two years. At the time of his death, I had no idea he had been in the hospital again. A mutual friend called (I had met him through her) and told me.

At first, I was in shock. Then I thought it would be best to remain calm for her sake. Another girlfriend, also very close to this man, had to be told so I went up to her house. We sat there and cried.

Both of us found and still find it very hard to believe he is dead. The next day was the funeral. I forced myself to go to school. This was very difficult because all day all I heard was "It will be okay," "Things will get better," and "It can't be that bad."

None of these people knew what was wrong so everything they said was very kind, but I still felt anger and resentment towards them because I knew that it was over for this man. All I could think of was "Things aren't all right, someone is dead, and he will never be back."

I think death brings anger into most people. This is the people's way of accepting the death. I think one must mourn for the death of someone or else they can go on not accepting death. I used to be afraid of death. I never thought it could happen to anyone I knew. When it does, the reality is very hard to handle.

Karin Wahlstrom, 16
Bellevue, Washington

Death

PART THREE
THE WORLD

To teenagers, the world is anything from their high school to their solar system. They regard themselves—who they are and what they may become—as the most important aspect of the world. They may have punk haircuts and earrings in their noses; they may love calculus and struggle through home economics; they may drive a Ferrari or ride a tricycle. Teenagers may be engaged to marry the girl in consumer management or they may try to date everyone they pass in the hall. Teenagers may relate to their nine-year-old brother or they may relate to God. The world is a gigantic video game to teenagers. They choose their targets and zap away, disintegrating each one until the game is over or the goal is abandoned. Goals encourage teenagers to shoulder responsibility: from weeding the garden to studying Shakespeare.

The teenage world is like a set of mirrors, infinitely reflecting different images yet always springing from the same source: the individual. The mirrors will hopefully reflect a future of peace and prosperity instead of a future of polluted waters and nuclear missiles. Teenagers will have a lot to say about which reflection the next generation will see. They do not merely live in the world. They are the world.

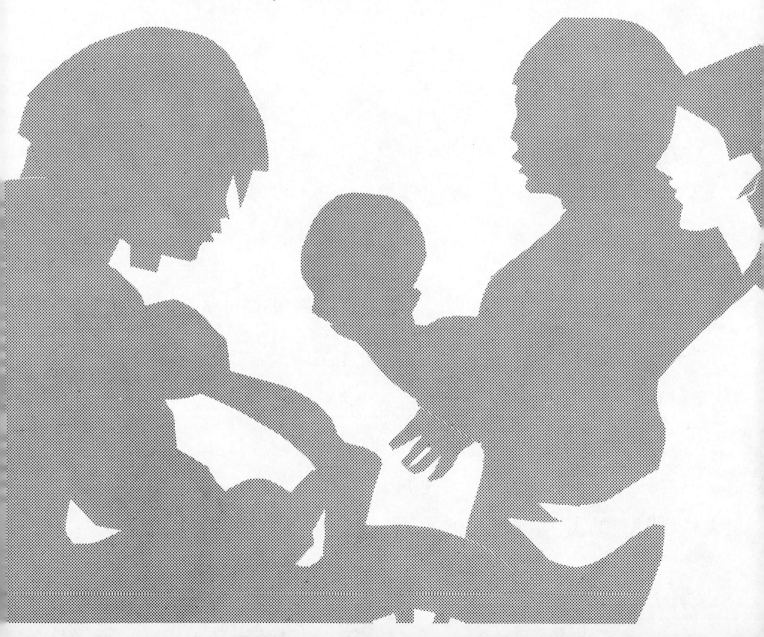

Chapter 15.

Individualism

Wrists flick, and another patty flips onto the bun. Wearing a cheerful, businesslike grin, the burger builder adds special sauce, lettuce, and tomato. The tab clicks and another styrofoam package slides down the chute into the slots. The burger builder goes around front to help the latest horde of diners.

"Can I help you, sir?" he beams.

"Get me a cheeseburger, no ketchup, a coke, and move it. I'm in a hurry."

"Yes sir," the builder says, effectively drowning out a voice deep inside that says, "Screw you, sir. Hurry my ass." The inside voice is throttled into a subdued belch, undetectable to the barbarian customer.

Later, after putting plastic caps on a few shakes, the builder changes out of his uniform and leaves. Reaching up above his hairline, he yanks a tab. The zipper uncoils, splitting his forehead, nose, and work clothes. Stepping out of the combination suit and mask, he puts on the family suit. The jeans, t-shirt, and indifferent face settle into place as he drives home.

"Hi mom," he says, closing the back door. "I don't want to listen to you complain," the inside voice mumbles as he clears his throat. He hears plenty of detailed complaints as he gulps a glass of water. Yes, he agrees, the economy is bad, the President is all wrong, the commies stink on ice. The chair scrapes so mom can't hear the inner voice say, "Quit forcing your opinions on me."

The inner voice is too exhausted to reply as the kid listens to dad say he will ground him if his grades don't shape up. Dad pets Bruiser while he lectures. The shaggy, gray and white sheepdog growls smugly. The kid does not like the dog—it bit him once when he had tried to play with it. Dad, though, loves Bruiser. He tells the kid to get off his dead butt and walk the dog. Bruiser ignores him outside, woofing happily as he bounds from tree to tree, chewing on sticks and barking at squirrels.

The buzzer goes off at six-thirty as it does every morning. Slowly he pulls on the student suit: jeans, polo shirt, and mask featuring a tense expression battling spacy, withdrawn eyes.

Chemistry, English, and lunch, where the eyes focus for a while as the kids at the table throw butter pats at the ceiling. Typing, gym, and political science, usually a dead yawn. Poor old Mr. Billings, stuck forever in the 1950s. Something different today, though—Billings is interesting. The student sits fascinated for a few minutes, the inner voice getting ready to make an interesting observation aloud.

"Mr. Billings."

The bell rings. His eyes withdraw as he picks up his book and heads for his locker.

"I probably should have stayed behind and talked with Billings," the student thinks. It has been a hard week, though. He decides the inner voice would have receded and the student suit would have gotten in the way of anything intelligent he had to say.

It isn't like that with his cousin, valedictorian of this year's senior class. She doesn't have to wear suits. Popular and smart, she really knows how to get along with people. Too bad it isn't in all the family blood, the inner voice remarks once in a while.

It is Friday, and excitement causes the student mask to bend slightly as the bus rumbles home. "Party, party!" the inner voice yells. The girl across the aisle stares at the student. He keeps his mouth clamped shut.

"At least this kind of change only happens on weekends," he rationalizes as he reflects on his junior high friend Pete. During his sophomore year Pete began to live in his partier suit, not even taking it off for school. It began to unravel at the edges, and one day Pete disappeared. Six months later he was back. Pete looked hung over, washed out. It wasn't a suit either. Pete told him they took all of the suits away at the clinic. Pete's scorched-out inner voice was all that was left.

After arriving home, the student suit falls in a heap to the floor. The inner voice flops into bed until seven. Without donning a mask, just some clothes, the voice takes off with his friends for the evening.

Six hours later, the inner voice drags itself toward its room. "What have I done?" Drank, yelled, drank, screamed rude things at girls, drank, threw up on my driveway. "Why?" A drunken snore is an adequate reply.

The voice awakes unclothed in the morning, mutely listening as mother, father, and even little brother chew him out before leaving for shopping. "Rice Krispies, want some Rice Krispies," it pleads.

After satisfying the craving, the inner voice goes back to the room to start work on a new suit. He chuckles quietly as the world and its pressure flashes in front of him:

You really messed up kid. When I was your age. . . .

Young man, you pay attention—school is serious business.

It's a hard world, son, a struggle to survive.

You have such a big future in front of you. You don't want to mess it up.

"Big future, big future," the inner voice snorts. There isn't any suit now to muffle it. The new suit taking shape isn't like the rest. No, the voice has selected this one personally. He knows now what he wants to be when he grows up. The inner voice isn't putting on a face or stitching up clothes. The new suit just has gray and white fur, kind of shaggy.

"It's a dog-eat-dog world" is his counselor's favorite saying.

Some say I'm a mystery. Some say I'm very open. I frankly can't figure myself out.

I surprise myself by how dumb I can be. I really do stupid things, but I can also be clever and creative. I wish I was a stronger person, mentally more than physically.

At one time I was told that I was a joke. This hurt because at the time I was going through many changes. So I guess I'm not always my true person I should be and I

Discussions

Melanie: Individualism is being allowed to have your own thoughts and opinions—not having them dictated to you by parents or a religion or peer groups. I know that my religion, for example, will often dictate the way I make my decisions—like the Bible says, "Don't have sex before you're married." Well, then I won't. Then I'll think that way. But that's the way I've decided to be. My decision

wasn't influenced by the Church because I decided to follow Christ on my own.

Manish: I don't think anybody can be individualistic. I don't even think hermits and introverts and people who just go out there to the mountains or whatever to pray and lead the rest of their lives with God can be individualistic. Because they are praying and thinking of this other guy—a god or

204

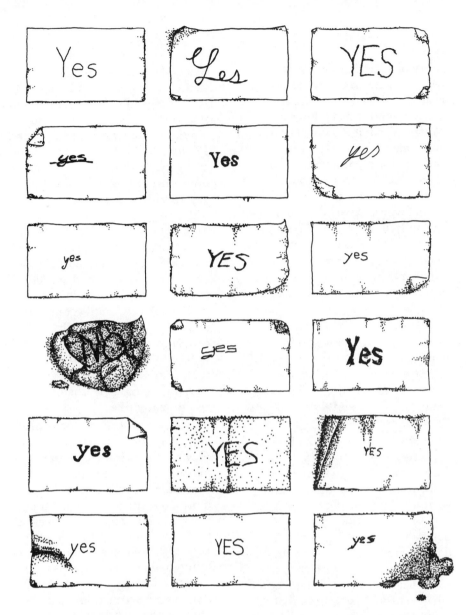

whatever—so that makes a couple. There are two. They're not alone.

Maribeth: An individualistic person can just go out and get what they want—a person who doesn't have to worry what people say about them, a person who's carefree.

Matt: But if you were individualistic, why would you want to be with a lot of people?

Steve: I don't think that being individualistic means that you want to be alone. To be individualistic, you rely on yourself to guide you. You're confident in your own thoughts and feelings. An individualistic person is somebody who does what he feels

is right, not what everyone else feels is right. That does not necessarily mean that you don't go along with the crowd all of the time or that you are constantly bucking the system and being different.

How easy is it to be an individual?

Maribeth: I try to be individualistic. I don't think I am 100 percent, but I try to be as much as I can. Of course, I depend on my mother, and I plan on depending on her until I get married or can live on my own. But I don't want to live on my own because the thought of living alone scares me.

Steve: Often I don't realize I'm conforming until later. I've been

want to be, but I'm not perfect, just me.

Sometimes I feel so small against all of life's trials, but at other times I can be ten feet tall, able to conquer anything that tries to stand in my way. I try to hide behind my friends, but soon friends will be gone. I'll have to take care of myself.

Lorrie Mullins, 15
Sand Springs, Oklahoma

How well do I know myself? I know myself real good, but not as good as I would like to because I am mostly in disguise. I disguise myself as a macho guy, one who only thinks about myself and shows off so that no one will pick on me.

But on the inside, I care about people and I like to play with little kids because they need help to survive in this run-down world. I always hide myself because I am scared of being left out in activities.

Alex Ashenfelter, 16
White Mountain, Alaska

Sometimes I get depressed for no reason, but I think it comes from hiding myself from others.

Andy Sinkleris, 13
Riverside, New Jersey

The group of girls turned around abruptly and began looking at us as if we were freaks in a side show. What we were doing seemed to bother them for some reason, the reason being uncertain to any of the three of us.

"Lenny" and "Joe" and I were simply singing "Shaboom, Shaboom," a song we commonly sing together. In spite of the girls, we kept singing. Eventually they turned back around, I suppose accepting our "harmonious" melody....

This, in some respects, is individualism, I suppose. But, in other respects, it is not. For instance, I wouldn't dare sing alone or probably not even with just "Joe" or "Lenny." Basically, I'm just a fairly shy person until I get to know somebody better. Even after I get to know somebody pretty well, unless they are a really good friend, I don't act silly very often around them. I guess the only time I get brave is when I sing that old song with my two friends.

Eddie White, 16
Independence, Missouri

My sense of individualism is evident by the way I dress. I feel I don't have to dress to please others. I dress to please myself. I am into new wave. When I wear "weird" clothes to fit my style, people give me weird looks. I feel if they don't like what I'm wearing, they don't have to look at me.

One month in school I had my hair one-half blonde and one-half brunette. People looked at me as if I was crazy. I heard weird comments behind my back, but I don't care.

Now I have my hair normal (brunette), and people I don't even know come up and talk to me like we're good friends. They always ask why I did something like that to my hair. I said because I wanted to be different, not like all the plain people in this boring school.

Michelle Shultz, 16
Fargo, North Dakota

The real me sometimes goes away and something else bad comes out. When the real me goes away and something comes out, it is the way my attitude is and the way I act. Those times I wish I was not around because I sometimes give people hard times. I always try to let the real me stay in me because that is when I'm happy with everything.

Raymond R. Andrews, 18
Aleknagik, Alaska

My individualism is evident through my deep faith in Christ or at least I hope it is.... He led a righteous life as an example for us to live by. In this day and time, "righteousness" is much in con-

guilty of sometimes bucking the system for the sake of bucking the system and then realizing that that was foolish. If I'd sat down and thought about it, I would have conformed because conformity under those circumstances was in my best self-interest. It would have been the logical thing.

That would have been being a true individual. I would have decided what was right, and I would have done it regardless of whether other people were doing it or not. Just because other people were doing it didn't make it bad.

Jeff: I try to be unusual in everything I do. I guess I'm kind of hyperactive. Sometimes in gym class or something I try to be as hyper as possible to make people think I'm hyper and then that gets them going.

Manish: I don't think you have to say, "Hey, look at me! I'm individualistic," and go out and walk around on your hands and wear a ski cap during the summer. Consider the actions you take—you don't always go along, and you don't conform to society, your friends, your parents. If they tell you what to do and you refuse to do whatever they say, I think that's being individualistic.

Jeff: I used to be—no, I still am a very shy person. I know that sounds strange, but I am. It's a mask. This craziness and stuff is a mask that I put on. I don't want to be a meek Mr. Mouse guy. I don't know, I didn't like being shy at all because people used to pick on me.

Manish: I'm shy so I do that, too. I try, like Jeff said, maybe not to the extreme he does. But I try to put on a face. I think I have a dual personality. It's almost like that. When I'm with friends or other people my age, maybe to impress them or maybe to give them this type of character that they would appreciate, I put on an act during school.

Michelle: I'm me, and I'm not gonna change for anybody. I've held things in before, and that's just not worth it. My old boyfriend would go out with somebody, and I'd get mad. But I'd figure, "I'm not going out with him. I can't say anything." I held it all in. I didn't say anything. And when I finally did, this guy just totally lost his temper.

I wasn't really being an individual because I didn't let myself go. I'd lie in bed at night, and I'd think, "God, what am I gonna do? Why did I get myself into this?" It got me really confused. I wanted to get out of this situation. Once you've gone that far, you've got all this inside of you. You've got to let them see what you're really like.

Steve: All right. How about this? We are all individuals. Some of us, however, are afraid to express our individualism. We're all individuals, but being individualistic in the sense that you have the confidence to express your individualism is an opening of yourself. To express your individualism is to express your true personality. If you're afraid that people aren't going to like your true personality, then you have a tendency not to express it.

A true individual is a confident person. You have to have confidence in your own ideas and thoughts and attitudes and actions. Some people don't, and that's why they're not individualistic. It's a matter of expression of what we are—not that some people are any less individuals. Some people are better at expressing themselves than others.

Matt: I'm kind of confused. Jeff said, "I'm really a shy person, but I put on a mask and goof around." Well, then that's really how you are. You're not really shy then.

Jeff: I really am.

Matt: That doesn't make sense to me.

206

Steve: Well, I don't know—because bouncing around gym class is meaningless. Nothing can be interpreted from it. Or very little can be interpreted from it. To open up in an area in which people can really get insight into a personality is very scary.

Matt: Oh, I see.

Steve: To mask your shyness, or to express that shyness, you put on a mask of meaningless action, which is very easy to do in gym class. To express meaningful action is a lot harder and probably a lot less common.

Manish: Everyone wants to be accepted by society, and there are two ways to go out and do that. The first is that you conform to all the ideas of society. You go along with the crowd, and they say, "Hey, this guy's cool. He agrees with us. All right, we'll let him in." The second way is to go to the very other extreme as Jeff pointed out. Do something that people would never expect others to do.

Jeff: When I put on a mask because I was shy, I think it helped me. I wasn't confident about myself. But putting the mask on when I had to made me more confident so now I feel better about myself. As Steve was saying, you have to like yourself. And I hated myself. I couldn't do anything right. I thought I was a real idiot. So when I started doing that, I started gaining a little confidence. Now I have to use the mask less and less. I'm feeling better about myself.

Do you know yourself?

Melanie: I don't know myself very well right now. I don't have any confidence, even with things that I'm normally confident about. It's just something that I'm going through. It doesn't have to be analyzed and broken down into pieces and steps and whys and reasons and put into a little box so that I can understand it.

Steve: I think it's very difficult to understand something that is constantly changing. I mean we're very complex creatures. I think I have a very basic understanding of myself, but, in the same context, I am changing rapidly, all the time. The way I feel about things is also changing. My ideas are building and changing so it's very difficult to say you know yourself when your self is changing so rapidly.

Maribeth: I know what I'm always thinking and I know what I want. Sometimes I'm confused about that, but I know that I have to sit and think—myself. I can't sit there and ask other people, "You know

trast with what's going on.

I think my individualism is best shown when I turn down invitations to wild parties or junky movies, or just when I have a seldom heard compliment for someone else.

Heather Nuchols, 15
Oak Ridge, Tennessee

You might find yourself walking down the street with hair down to your feet, wearing a beaten up old pair of jeans, a ratty-looking cowboy hat and a t-shirt. The neighbors turn their noses up at you and the kids laugh, but you feel comfortable.

On the other hand, you might

find yourself wearing a navy blue Izod shirt, a slick pair of slacks, and your hair cleanly cut. The neighbors smile, the kids accept you, but you feel like a mannequin in the window of Saks Fifth Avenue.

Thom Tryon, 17
Schenectady, New York

Yes, I know myself, but I don't like myself. I'm afraid that others won't like me either. That's a big fear in my life. I'm afraid that if people really knew the way I was, they would hate me.

For example, about three years ago I met a guy named "Barry." He and I became very close. He understood me like no one else ever could. We depended on each other. He was my crutch, and I was his.

As the years went by, "Barry" got to know the real me. I felt our friendship start to slip at that time. It hurt me very deeply. I did everything in my power to try to save what we had, but "Barry" gave up. I felt so rejected and confused that I didn't know what to do.

me, what should I do?" I have to say to myself, "Maribeth, what should I do about this situation?" I have to think about it. I have to decide what I want, what's right for me. I can't say, "Mom, what should I do about this?" A lot of times she even tells me, "Maribeth, I can't make your decisions. You have to make them by yourself."

Diane: I know myself because I know what I want. I want to go to college, and I'm doing that. I want to work in a certain field. I know what I like and what I dislike, and I hope that I can have what I like and do away with what I dislike. I don't put on a mask too often. When I'm shy, I'm shy. I suppose just knowing yourself means knowing what you want, not necessarily how to get it, but knowing what you want and what you will and will not do to get what you want. I won't go out and kill somebody to get what I want. I know as a person I won't do that. So I know my limitations both physically and mentally. I know I

can't lift a two-ton car or something.

Steve: I think it's time to stop and think about your emotions. People are constantly doing things without thinking about what they're doing. If somebody was to go away for a month to find themself and then come back and say, "Yep. I found myself," I'd be very much the skeptic because I think that finding yourself is a constant process that must go on throughout life. It's a matter of taking things and trying to make sense out of them. Often it's impossible to understand why you're doing things.

Manish: Maybe that's where I'm individualistic. I don't conform. But there is nothing to find! There are certain things that you just say, "Hey, it's there—it's there. Leave it alone." I think maybe that everyone's trying to decide what I'm like. My friend Joe thinks this is me while Tom thinks I'm so and Dick thinks I'm so and Harry thinks I'm so. Then maybe I

wonder, "What am I to myself?" What everybody's trying to find out is, "What do I mean to myself?" Not what the character I represent to others is.

I think everybody makes out a different Manish in this room because they all know a different aspect of me. They might know more than one aspect—yes, that's true—but you combine those aspects in different ways and get everybody with a slightly different Manish. I am the mixture of all the different aspects that everybody represents of me in this room.

Steve: I think in a certain sense I must disagree. We have a self-image and then we have what we are. Everybody else is a mirror, and they're not always great mirrors. They can be warped and sometimes very weird mirrors, but we see ourselves in the mirror of other people. For instance, I might see my personality as reflected by a certain individual. Now, the closer the reflection coming from that individual to my own self-image, the more confident and the more self-reliant and happy I will feel. Also, the more stable and, possibly, the better adjusted I will be.

I think it is important to analyze what you think you are. It is important to understand your own self-image. It is important to look at those mirrors and say, "Wow, okay. I recognize that these mirrors are sort of warped and they're not always perfect, but this mirror over here is so far different from what I think I am. That's really strange. I ought to think about it. Maybe my self-image isn't right."

And, Manish, you say that you look in the mirrors, but you don't look at them in relation to your own self-image. And I say looking at them in relation to your own self-image is of key importance.

Manish: I think you place a great deal of importance on that. I think

it's no necessity. Eat, drink, and be merry.

Maribeth: You've got to plan your life and decide what you want to do so that you can be happy. I don't sit around every day and say, "Okay, Maribeth, what's going on?" But, at least, once in a while I do.

Kelly: I think it's necessary, and I think it's better that you do it than if other people do it and then tell you about it. You have to figure out for yourself what direction you're going in order to understand yourself. And if you understand yourself, you have a key to understanding the rest of the world.

John: I started knowing myself at the beginning of my junior year. I had no free time. I kept thinking, "This is horrible." I've had to think, "It's not that bad. I've got some money. I've got a girlfriend. I'm getting good grades." It was the first time I really got a job, and people would push me around at work. So I had to learn who I was. I had to realize how I treated people.

What is the individual's place in society?

Steve: I don't think that there's a slot that you're intended to fit into. You can choose your place in the world, or you can change your place in the world anytime you please.

Jeff: Why does there have to be a reason for anything?

Manish: Why must one have a place in the world?

Jeff: I think your only purpose can be self-fulfillment in life. And to reach self-fulfillment, you've got to make yourself happy. This is your place: making yourself happy.

Steve: The only reason that you would ever need a place is if you were to assume that the area that you're living in or the system that you're living in is unexpandable. Therefore, it is necessary to fit into

About a week later "Barry" left town. He didn't even say good-bye. I have no idea where he could be now. It's been over a year since "Barry" left, and I still think about him. Every time I do, the pain starts all over again.

Now I disguise myself in fear that I might be hurt again. I appear as a punk rocker. People seem to accept that more than the real me.

I found that I am the only punk rocker in school. People really look up to me. They admire my originality and courage. I like the feeling of being loved and admired.

I really don't think I'll ever show the real me again. Deep in my heart, I know if I had disguised myself for "Barry" that he would still be part of my life.

17-year-old female
Oregon

I am different from any other person in the civilized world. I do what I want and don't care what people think. However, that doesn't mean I make a fool out of myself. I like wearing off-the-wall clothes, such as bowling shirts, Bermuda shorts, and dyed shoes. But I haven't had a chance to wear my "clad" because of this punishing winter.

My self-expression, though, is most evident in my newspaper column. This column's title is "Up-chuck" and sometimes includes very controversial lines which divide the staff. . . .

I write about things that students like since it is a student newspaper. Such topics include teenage drinking, cutting to the beach, and popping zits. The students seem to like it, but parents don't. But it's not their paper.

The adviser doesn't like the column too much and lets one know it. My second column, titled "Don't tell anyone I blew," had two high school students at a party—one drunk and the other not. The adviser made me take out a couple of lines because they "promoted child-molestation" and "could be conceived in the wrong manner."

Besides my garb and column, my music which I listen to makes me unique. I don't listen to commercial stuff. It makes me sick. I have to find my melodies on the college stations. I've been known to freak out at parties if they play horrendous stuff.

Charlie Henderson, 17
Sunnyvale, California

Most people believe that self-expression is important to all people. I also believe that most of the ways people show their individualism are the same. Having observed these things, I am convinced that my form of individualism is different than most other people of my age.

I don't like activities other people my age do, but I do these things and more. For example, I have been dancing Ukrainian character for seven years and have been dancing ballet for three. It is rare to see a boy in his teens to be dancing.

However, like many people my age, I enjoy playing fantasy war games and other strategy-related games. Many times, however, I must give this up and go to a Ukrainian scouts meeting.

Also, the fact that I speak two languages fluently and speak them at home and with my friends distinguishes me from many people my age as well as many people much older than I. I also spend my summers at Ukrainian resorts as well as Ukrainian camps.

On the other hand, I learn about American heritage as well as Ukrainian because I feel that by knowing another language as well as another culture, I will have a better understanding of today's world. . . .

I also feel that being from another culture, I have much to contribute to the American mosaic of

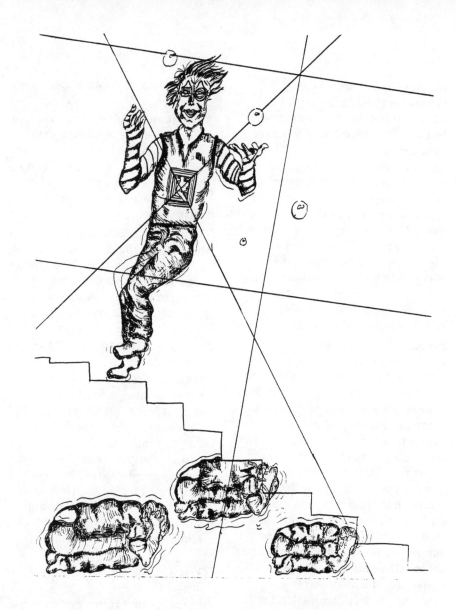

a space—a given, allotted space. I don't think that's true. I think that the universe and that mankind and that we as individuals are expandable. Therefore, there is no need to fit into any given space.

Matt: Well, I think there's a reason why we're here. I don't think that whoever made us or whatever chemical reaction did occur was an accident. I don't sit at home and dwell on the subject and lose sleep, but I think about it.

Steve: Matt's thinking about it, but he is thinking about it within a very narrow band. You, Manish, aren't even thinking about it.

Jeff: What's wrong with that?

Steve: I doubt I'll ever come to any conclusions, but I will not stop

thinking about it because to stop thinking about it is to say it is meaningless.

Jeff: But I think thinking about the things around you—things that are going to affect you directly is a lot more important. You certainly can't think about everything. I mean it's physically impossible.

Diane: I think most people, including myself, do not sit down and spend hours thinking about these great questions of life. My time is limited. There are 24 hours in a day, and I have to worry about my test or something like that. So I spend most of my time worrying about things that directly affect me. The time I spend thinking about this stuff is when I'm in this group. We talk about these high ideals—or when I'm in my humanities class. Once in a while, I'll go home and I'll think about that for a little bit, but then I realize, "Oh, I've got a test tomorrow." So I whip out my book, and I start studying my analytic geometry.

Steve: I can't do that. I cannot stop thinking.

Diane: But I think you're an exception, Steve. I think most people do think about this but not often and not at great lengths. They're just too busy with other things.

How can our generation develop a simpler society?

Jeff: I think we've made life more complicated than it should be these days. How many people really do want to go out there and work for the rest of their lives? In the caveman days everyone had their own little place. They didn't have to go to the supermarket. Wouldn't that be great if all the food in the supermarket were free?

Manish: Society's too complex— let's revert back to simple living.

Steve: I don't think that life's too complex. I think that we gain from our complexity. There are also disadvantages, but there are many great advantages that I think you underestimate. I would certainly hate to be a caveman. I couldn't stand it.

Jeff: The cavemen knew what was going on just as much as—I'd say more than—we do now, probably. Because there was a lot less to know about what was going on. Their world was a lot closer.

Manish: This is my cave and my hunting ground. You stay away, and that's it.

Jeff: It was that simple. When they died, they died the king of their society. We work for our whole lives, and we support a kid or something.

Steve: And you don't think going out and shoving spears at buffalo is work?

Jeff: And then we die.

Steve: That's exactly what they did, though. They worked and they died.

Jeff: They worked and they died, but they were the rulers of their own society. Life was simpler. We're too small a part of the world today.

Diane: This society is complex, but if I'm smart enough I can offer more to this society.

Jeff: And make it more complex, right?

Diane: Not necessarily. I can offer more of what I have to give to this society than I would in a cave society.

Michelle: How can you be important in the world unless you're somebody like the President? He's important in the world, but people around here— nobody's going to be that important.

John: I think I can contribute a lot. All I want to do is what I can do. I don't know if I feel like I'm two people, 200 people, or one person in four billion. That doesn't matter to me. I feel like I'm important.

Jeff: What do you have to give to us that we're going to want here? I'm not trying to degrade you or anything, but I'm just asking what the heck are you going to give us that's going to make us a better society?

Diane: Maybe I can come up with a way to do away with air pollution or something like that.

Jeff: We wouldn't have air pollution if we didn't go nutso with technology. But see we wouldn't have to go to work if we were back in those times.

Steve: Oh, yes you would. I think you work a lot less in today's society than you would if you were a caveman.

many cultures. I try to be both a good American and Ukrainian even if my lifestyle differs from most people my age.

Mark Jakubowycz, 15
Schenectady, New York

I used to be an average student in grade school and junior high. When I got into high school, mostly everything went crazy.

I was hardly ever in school. I cut classes a lot, forged excuses, was tardy, wouldn't do the homework, and wouldn't study for the tests. Also, I was suspended a lot too. I almost was kicked out of school permanently.

Now that I'm a junior, I seem to be putting things in better perspective. During my free time, I talk to the high school psychologist. I talk to him whenever I'm confused, depressed, or in trouble (schoolwise). I find him to be a very close friend to me.

At least with him, I don't have to hide what I'm feeling, thinking, or what I am. When it comes to my friends or teachers, I put on an act, especially with my friends.

They're not used to my moods I have, especially the serious side of me. Most of it is my fault because I don't let them inside my emotions. . . . No one seems like they want to know the real me, just the rowdy, outgoing, always clowning around side.

Whenever I'm in a depressed mood, I give them the expression to leave me alone, the don't-bother-me look, and they do.

But deep inside, I'm crying out for them to ask me what's wrong. . . . Certain teachers, they find me to be unreliable, irresponsible—but how can I blame them? Others . . . know I can do the work—it frustrates them when I don't do it.

If only they knew how much I frustrate myself and how angry I am with myself, that I'm throwing away everything—intelligence, skills, and talents. I want to be a singer so bad. . . .

I guess when I get turned down too many times, you know, not giving me a chance to show what I'm capable of doing, I lose self-confidence in myself, in subjects in school, or in any other activity. But like I said earlier, I never let people know what I'm feeling.

My way of expressing my feelings is by writing them in a lyric form and then putting the music to them. I've been thinking about sending them away to different recording studios, hoping that one of them will like my songs.

Right now, I'm waiting for a big break into a new life for me. I find my life now to be boring. . . . It's kind of hard to change your lifestyle, to turn things around and start over. I figure if you want something so bad, you'll do anything for it.

17-year-old female
New York

I often appear outwardly to be too cynical, paranoid, and vocal for my own good, which is probably quite truthful. My attitudes may be rather "high brow" in regard to others, but on the whole I am capable of relating to almost any sort of person. Sometimes I tend to act the part of supervisor or coordinator even if I have no such authority.

Kevin Freeman, 17
Reno, Nevada

My individualism and self-expression is very evident in my clothing and hair styles. I'm not afraid to wear things that most people wouldn't wear—like my black leather pants and jacket, mini-skirts, unmatched earrings, and pink hair. It's a good feeling to know that people will accept me for who I am as a person, not for how I dress.

Julie Dunlap, 15
Athol, Massachusetts

Recently I went through a very traumatic psychological experience in which I was shaken down to my mental roots. It was a long nightmare which I will never forget

Jeff: But are you happy about it? I think—my idea is that cavemen were happy kinds of guys.
Steve: I think that's a misconception. Being happy is an inner thing. If you are unhappy with this society, the chances are you'd be equally unhappy with the caveman society because you're looking for happiness in the outside, material sense. The only way to get true happiness is to find confidence and happiness within.
Jeff: Who do you think would really be better? A caveman in our society or us in a caveman's society? Honestly. I just want to know that.
Diane: Us in a caveman society.
Manish: We would do better in their society.
Jeff: Yes.
Diane: They wouldn't be able to deal with the complexity of our society.
Steve: And we wouldn't be able to deal with the simplicity of theirs!

How can our generation benefit from nonconformity?

Steve: I think that individuals probably make better social beings than people who just conform because they've, of course, learned to interact. They have come to their conclusions through real thought.
Kelly: I would think that it would be better for everyone involved because instead of having a bunch of people who could follow a corrupt leader, you would have more people putting input into society and giving ideas and having competition for the best idea or the best leader or the best way to do something. You'd have all these individuals contributing all their different ideas to society.
Diane: You can't just have a bunch of individuals, though. That doesn't make up a society. They have to have a basis for living together. I think the democratic society is probably one of the best examples of that. We have the basis of our government, but yet within that you can voice your opinions.

Compiled by Holly Hager

and that has changed my life. During this time I hated everything I did and doubted my own confidence. I didn't even know who I was.

The problem was caused when I wanted to be someone else, someone totally different. I tried imitating that person, but that was when the problems started. Some of the things this person did, my values would not permit me to do.

This conflict tore me to pieces. I became like a ghost. I was neither myself nor that person. I was like between and lost. I spent about five long, dark, and confusing months trying to find myself and regain my personal confidence. It was a terrible struggle, for I still wanted to be that person.

I didn't find out who I was until I became involved with certain clubs and activities that helped me find myself. One activity was the school newspaper. I identified with the people on the paper: their problems, faults, victories, and happiness. . . . I "grew up" once more and found out who I really am.

I know myself very well now. I know who I am and what my good and bad sides and features are. I now don't want to be that person anymore. I am more than satisfied with myself.

Rodney Hess, 17
Hanover Park, Illinois

The major thing that makes me different from the other teenagers in my community is the fact that I ski competitively. Out of a city of 150,000 or more, I am one of the two high school girls in Reno that compete in Far West. This level is pretty high and very serious.

In order for me to ski as much as I do (sometimes even five times a week), I must make a lot of sacrifices, such as staying home on the weekends during competition instead of going out with my friends. But even though I have made many sacrifices, mostly social, I do not regret the fact that I have committed myself to a sport.

Adrian Fletcher, 17
Reno, Nevada

I know myself pretty well, but there are always things I do that may even surprise me. I do not try to be fake or hide my feelings, but I sometimes have a hard time expressing my feelings. It is difficult to just let myself go and tell how I feel if I really don't know a person.

All I can say is that I try to be myself at all times and around everyone. I have my faults, but I will never give up.

Debbie Fann, 16
Sand Springs, Oklahoma

I have a terrible time trying to express how I feel by using words. My self-expression really doesn't exist except in actions and a few other things. "The utmost in the expression of an individual soul through his sport" applies to me as well as to whom this was said, the late Bruce Lee. When I want to say something really special, I can't because "the words get in the way."

Just recently, I asked a girl out, but it took three weeks prior to that time for me to figure out how to ask her.

My best way to express myself is through my martial arts. Truly, it's the only way I can show myself, for it's a way for me to get out all the anger I have inside.

One incident happened between my brother and me. He was trying to show off for his friend so he started beating on me. Well, I gave him a warning and went about my business, but he kept on.

Finally, I punched him. Being older than me, he forced me outside so I could finish what he started. He threw stuff at me and punched me a little. Then I broke loose and let fly a hard, fast, stiff kick. My heel hit the end of his middle finger and jammed the bones clear back into his hand.

I guess then I really expressed how mad I could get.

Mike Beal, 15
Walnut Hill, Illinois

LTHS
MICHAEL PALMER '85

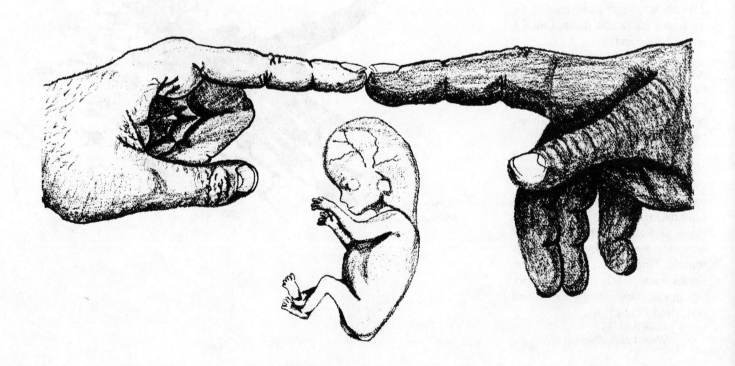

Chapter 16.

Relationships

When Baby is born, she is a dependent child in a cold world. She finds that people provide the warmth she had in her dark, peaceful cocoon.

Mommy is Baby's first friend, and Baby has no choice about that. Baby's trust in Mommy is blind. She trusts Mommy because Mommy provides her with food, shelter, and love. Because she is always tender, Baby believes Mommy is infallible. Baby loves Mommy because Mommy loves her.

As she begins to explore the world around her, Baby discovers other friends. Daddy is always close by. She likes it when he tosses her in the air and catches her. She does not worry when Daddy throws her. Daddy is a friend, and friends are good. Baby cannot understand the trust she has for Daddy, but she feels love. She learns to trust other people.

Baby loves Older Brother because he takes her for wagon rides. Although they screech around the corners too fast, Baby does not worry. Older Brother is a good friend. So Baby does not think about the sharp stones at the end of the driveway and the wagon wheels that spin too fast.

As Baby grows older, she learns about "friends." Mommy tells her that the other toddlers in the sandbox are her friends. Here Baby first encounters lack of trust. She tries to be nice to a little girl, but the girl throws sand at Baby. Baby is surprised. Mommy says that the girl is a friend. But friends do not do things like that. Then Baby feels the sting of the sand again. She decides not to trust this "friend." So Baby throws sand back at her.

As Baby meets more friends, she learns to trust some and not others. When she enters kindergarten, Baby is amazed by the children around her. She can no longer be called Baby; she is Child. She learns to pick her friends carefully. She hates the taunting and teasing of boys. She hates the worms they throw in her face. Child hates to play with boys.

Girls, however, are different. Child trusts her friends with her possessions and her secrets—to a point. She trusts her girlfriends with her older toys but never with the brand new Barbie doll from Mommy. She trusts them with schoolyard gossip but never with her true feelings. Child likes to play with girls but is not sure how much she can trust them.

While Child makes new friends in her classes, she realizes how important adults are. Child respects her first teacher who is smart as well as kind. Child relies on Mommy and Daddy to fill the void that friends and Teacher cannot. She trusts her parents with her fears and questions. She tells them her problems. Child trusts them with her love.

Child can give more to her parents now, but she also expects more from them. Child used to be happy with food, shelter, and love, but now she needs a Barbie townhouse, white go-go boots, a new bike, and pierced ears. She trusts Mommy and Daddy to provide for her. Child thinks adults will never disappoint her.

215

Unlike her parents, Older Brother often disappoints Child. He used to be her protector and guide, but now he is her tormentor. Child becomes the butt of his jokes. They fight constantly over stupid things, like who will eat the last popsicle, who will wash the dishes, and who will select the TV show. Child doesn't trust him with her confidences or her possessions.

When Child enters seventh grade, her relationship with Older Brother changes. Now Young Teen, she expects to be treated as his equal. Because she cannot relate to his high school problems, their relationship is not close. But their constant fighting has ended. Young Teen and Older Brother declare an uneasy truce. She avoids him as much as possible and speaks to him only to ask him to drive her somewhere.

While Young Teen reaches a truce with Older Brother, she wages a war with Mom and Dad. She screams at them when they won't let her go out. She sulks when Mom asks her to clean her room. She resents Dad's concern about her grades. She feels that she is an adult, but she can't trust her parents to treat her like one. She lashes out like a child.

Young Teen despises her teachers because of the demands they make on her time. She questions their right to assign homework or to require that she ask permission to sharpen her pencil. Young Teen can decide for herself what is right and what is wrong. But she keeps a smile on her face to hide the dislike she feels for her teachers.

Her relationships with her friends are superficial. She hangs around with her friends, not because she likes them but because they are the "in" clique. She remembers when Susan was absent one day. All of her "friends" laughed while imitating Susan's lisp. Young Teen knows better than to trust them. Although Young Teen really does not like them, she stays with them because she wants to have fun.

Young Teen's boyfriend is cute, athletic, and popular. She likes him, but she does not know him. They see each other in class, pass notes, and communicate through friends. Although they never go anywhere, Young Teen enjoys the feeling of "going out." Since her friends all have boyfriends, she becomes part of the crowd. But her friends often rotate boyfriends so she doesn't trust her boyfriend and never opens up to him.

Young Teen starts high school and becomes Teen. Teen still has boyfriends, but she is much closer to them. She wants a relationship that will last more than a week. Teen enjoys the security of a date every Friday night as well as good times and laughter. Although spending time with her boyfriends is what Teen enjoys the most, she feels special when her boyfriends spend money on her.

She enjoys talking to her boyfriends, but although she hates to admit it, sex is the main reason she pays attention to them. She enjoys being close to them and being touched. However, Teen has to preserve a good reputation so she is "careful."

Teen saves confidences like these for her close friends. They share fears, hopes, and dreams. They talk on the phone for hours and share their problems. Teen begins to trust others.

They still have fun, but their fun has changed. They enjoy going to parties and getting drunk. They laugh when they remember all the embarrassing things they did at parties, like singing, "I Can't Get No . . . Satisfaction" at the tops of their lungs.

Understanding has changed Teen's relationship with Older Brother. Since she started high school, Teen finds that asking Older Brother for advice has become routine. Instead of talking to her parents about forbidden subjects, Teen asks him about dating, alcohol, and drugs. She hopes to avoid making the same mistakes. Teen is glad that she and Older Brother can finally talk about real issues. She trusts him to keep her secrets safe. Teen loves Older Brother and is happy that they are friends.

Teen's relationships with her teachers also improve. Although she still hates busy work like doing ten centripetal acceleration problems, she realizes that most of her teachers want her to learn. She still resents teachers that scream at their classes, but she begins to appreciate those who stress concepts. She even begins to confide in some of them. They are interested in her, and Teen is happy to occasionally receive advice from someone who's mature.

While Teen enjoys talking to her teachers, she finds that she can't talk to her parents at all. They never listen to her; however, they do yell at her. They do not like her clothes, music, or friends. Teen stays out of the living room as much as possible to avoid confrontations with Mom and Dad.

Teen wishes she could talk to them about the parties she goes to, but she knows they wouldn't understand. They would flip out if she told them she drinks and fools around with guys. Although Mom and Dad don't trust her much anymore, telling them the truth about herself would destroy the last bit of trust they have in her. Teen would be locked in the house until she graduates.

Teen leaves the house whenever possible to escape the oppressive atmosphere. She babysits Neighbor's son three nights a week. Teen and Neighbor become confidantes. Neighbor's respect gives Teen the self-confidence she needs to enter the adult world.

Teen will be off to college soon. She will need to form new relationships. Since Teen realizes her most successful relationships were based on trust, she decides to be open and honest as she builds new friendships. She knows trusting everyone hurt her in the past, but now, as Adult, she is more discerning.

My sister and I are very close. Once I tried to kill myself, and she was there to pick me up to tell me where I went wrong. She tried to kill herself with the medicine she used to take for leukemia. We talked about it.

15-year-old female
Minnesota

I think relationships with your family become more strained during the teenage years whereas relationships with people your own age become better. Both these changes are supposed to be normal, but the one within the family is the most difficult.

I know my parents love me. That seems to make them the best target for my anger and frustrations (even when it has nothing to do with them) because I know they will always love me, no matter how rotten I am.

Denise Fuchs, 17
St. Charles, Illinois

I don't really have a role model or so called "idol," but one of my favorite people is my best friend, "Beth." I guess I do look up to her in a way because a lot of people

Discussions

Melanie: For me, it seems like friends are people I can be real with. I like to be around people who take me for who I am. If I'm in a mood where I'm about ready to cry, I don't want to be somebody I'm not.

If you're in a bad mood, they may say "What's wrong with you?" or "Hey, Miss Joe Christian, you think that you're always supposed to be happy." Well, that's not what being a Christian is to me. I know I'm not always supposed to be happy, and I'm not.

Michelle: I have this one friend, and she's always there for me when I need somebody to talk to. A lot of my friends are good friends. I've hung around with them for a long time. Sometimes you'll be really upset about something, and you'll start to talk about it. But they'll say, "Well, I don't want to hear it." And you'll be sitting there depressed all night. It feels a lot better if you have that friend there to talk to.

Kelly: One of the biggest attractions of a particular friend is that they understand you, which is

often very hard. Scott definitely became my best friend—the person I chose to spend my time with and the one I confided in, especially about my boyfriend.

When things weren't going peachy with my boyfriend, I told Scott. I tell him things that are important to me. Sometimes I'm more embarrassed than if I were talking to a girl because I know most of my girlfriends have the same feelings I do, especially about boyfriends.

Scott and I have shared everything. The advantage of having a guy as my best friend is that he and I don't compete for the attention of somebody else. I'm not real worried about competition from him, but we do have competition for my boyfriend's time.

Diane: I think in a true friendship both people are able to recognize and accept a person's good qualities and bad qualities.

Steve: And even learn to enjoy the bad qualities to a certain extent. Learn to find them in a way humorous. I have a friend named

Todd. He's always late so I've learned to adjust. It doesn't frustrate me in the slightest. I even find it entertaining that he's never on time.

Diane: In grade school there were classmates who I'd known for eight years and considered my good friends. In two years of high school, I became friends with someone who by far surpassed the friends I thought I had in grade school.

Jeff: I had some really good friends in junior high. I thought I'd never lose these friendships. We'd been friends for a long time—lived on the same block all our lives. Then, when your needs change, you grow out of friendships. And there's nothing wrong with not being good friends anymore. Just because you're friends for a long time doesn't mean you have to be friends always.

Melanie: It's not only needs. Where you are, what classes you have, your environment—all these affect a friendship.

Jeff: In junior high, some of my friends started really getting into drugs, and I just kind of turned away. At that age I didn't want to get involved with that kind of stuff. And that's when I put an end to that friendship.

Steve: I sort of had the same experience as Jeff. On the other hand, I wouldn't say I'm heavily into drug use, but I got a job and started going out with some older people. We'd go out drinking and stuff. I started partying.

I had some old friends who I'd stop by and see once in a while. I don't think our friendship has been broken, but certainly there was a veering away. I went my own direction.

It's not easy if you don't want to drink, and there's a group of people who are drinking. I have friends who I'll try to get to come along and join in. But they just don't want to. I don't believe I ever asked anyone to drink, and I never tried to push anybody into drug use. But I tried to introduce them to other friends I had met. They were turned off by drug use, however. Although there was really no pressure on them to use drugs, I could understand them feeling uncomfortable.

Jealousy

Kelly: I don't expect it to be just Scott and me. Even though I don't date him, I get really protective of him when he starts dating somebody. I get jealous because we have something special, and three people disrupts. There are certain groups of people both he and I have friends with. I don't get jealous of those people.

Steve: If your friend wants you to be friends with his new friend, I don't think jealousy comes into it. If you feel isolated because he's gone off to be friends with this other person and has no intention of introducing you, then you can get somewhat jealous.

Manish: Usually if your friend has another friend, I assume you'll become friends with the third party.

Melanie: One time a third party became friends with my best friend Kris and me. I wasn't jealous of her, and it wasn't like "Oh, I'm gonna lose my best friend." The only time I became wary and I got angry was when this person had the attitude, "Oh, I better get rid of Mel so I can have Kris be my best friend." But I thought, "That's great. Now me and Kris and this other girl can go out." I appreciated the third person because we had more things to talk about. Then she just wanted Kris for herself, and I was like, "No, you can't have her."

Kelly: I think Scott and my boyfriend feel they are competing for my time. Sometimes they think

like her, and she's always fun to be around.

The two of us are pretty much known as one. You don't see Donna without "Beth," and you don't see "Beth" without Donna. I kind of like it that way because it gives me a sense of security. . . .

If I need her to talk to, she's a real good listener. When it comes to advice, she's a regular "Dear Abby." She's always laughing or at least smiling.

Donna Jean Johnson, 16
Richmond, Vermont

When I was 12 and 13, I lived with my father and step-mother. I hated my step-mother. Everything she said or did irritated me. She even drove me to trying suicide.

Then I moved out. (I'm now living with my mom.) Now, when I visit my father and step-mother, I can talk to her and, in most cases, I value her opinions although I may disagree. I also understand her better, and I think she understands me too.

16-year-old female
Idaho

I like to have close friends that I can share things with. When I have a problem, I would like to discuss, I can talk to a close friend and get his response. I can't talk to my dad because he has the "Catholic" answer to everything. I don't need to know how the church wants me to do it. I want to know how he would respond.

I don't like to get real serious with girls. I have a girlfriend, but I don't and can't really talk about problems I have. I like to be with her, but I don't like it when she wants me to jump into anything.

Ross Felsheim, 16
Winona, Minnesota

I have two sets of parents: a father and step-mother and a mother and step-father. If I have a problem, I have four people I can go to. And with a unique relationship as I have

Dear Joanna,
France is beautiful this time of year. I miss you a lot.
Love Always,
your friend
Tina
P.S. I'll call you I miss you!!!!!

with each one, I can get four different views.

A teenager, though, really can't divulge all her or his secrets to parents. Most of the parents would be shocked to find out really what their children think. Even with my relationships, my step-mother and real mother know almost everything about me—but not quite. I need the advice of friends.

Donna Grace, 16
Fort Smith, Arkansas

Boy, I remember when I turned 13. What a terror I was—wanting to go out with older guys, 19 and 20 years old, because I felt that I had to be a grown-up "woman" now that I was a big time teenager.

I should make a choice about who I want to spend my time with. But I'm not going to give up the friendship I have with either of them for the other. They often forget that they're friends with each other and think they're just each having a side of me.

Steve: These two guys and I, sort of a threesome, were living in the same apartment building for a while. It is strange when there's a threesome and the first of the threesome gets a girlfriend. Suddenly he devotes his whole life to this girlfriend, and you're like, "You don't do anything with us anymore." Then somebody else in the threesome would get a girlfriend. After a while you get used to it. All of a sudden somebody gets a girlfriend, and you don't see him for three weeks.

Relationships for Romance

Matt: It seems like I knew I was in love right away. I don't know how to explain it. It just seemed right. I'd been going out with Lisa for seven months. As of now I've just kind of broken it off with her. I'd like to date other people. It's come to the point where she's really tying me down, and I'm not able to go out with other friends. It's not that she's saying, "You can't go out." I don't want to say she's making me feel guilty, but she is. She'll make plans and assume I'll want to do that. If I say, "I can't—I'm going out with my other friends," she'll get kind of upset and say, "Oh, okay."

It got to be a routine—pick her up at the train, take her home. It was the same thing every day. I think what really hurt us was seeing her every day, talking to her every day. Now I don't do that anymore, and I'm starting to miss her more. I think that's important—to miss someone you love.

John: I guess I'm still in love. I've been going out with the same girl for three years in October. What makes me think that I'm in love is that first of all, we get along. I can go without combing my hair since morning and be dressed like a slob and I don't have to worry about her saying, "Hey, you look like a slob. Get out of here." I show her that I love her by being nice to her. I go out of my way for her.

Matt: With Lisa, when we first started going out, I brought her flowers every time we went out. It's kind of fun at first bringing your girlfriend flowers or getting her a card.

Michelle: Like Matt was saying, taking somebody for granted is bad. I lost a good, close friendship. It was like a loving friendship. This guy was always there when I needed him, but he couldn't understand that I had to be with my friends, too. I kind of took it for granted that he'd always be there, and I blew him off a couple of times. By the time I realized how much he meant to me, it was just too late. This happened a couple months ago, and I'm still hurting a lot as a result.

I've tried so hard to do something about it. I told him that I realized I took his friendship for granted—and that I was sorry about what had happened. He's going, "It's too late. You don't need me." And I go, "I need your support. I loved having your support there when I needed it."

Matt: I think that right now what has happened with Lisa and me is probably the best thing that could have happened. I know I have spring fever, and I want to see somebody else, but I don't know who. Also, I think if our love is strong enough, it's not going to make a difference.

Steve: But it's not easy to walk away. I had a relationship with a girl that was completely sexual. She broke it off because she thought I was becoming too attached to her. She didn't want a relationship that was any more than sex, and I was getting to the point where I wanted to spend a little more time without sex involved. She didn't want a relationship like that so she broke it off. I was a little upset, but life goes on.

Michelle: It's good to do that. It's good to date different people, to see different types of people. You don't have to go out and find what kind of person you like.

Diane: If you fall in love with the first guy you go out with, and you never go out with anyone else after that, then you really don't know. You're always going to be wondering, "Is there somebody else out there?"

John: The first guy my mom ever dated was my dad. I doubt if she

All my friends were older. They weren't that big of a deal. They weren't that nice or interesting. All they wanted to do was to go out and get blasted. I got over that stage real fast.

My mother wouldn't let me go with the older crowd so, of course, I had to let her think I was going skating. Being the dumb teenager I was, I left when I got to the skating rink. I was a real scared little girl. I was to meet six people there.

One was . . . a nice guy, who at the age of 18 . . . had a crush on this little girl. I must have done everything a teenage kid isn't supposed to do until she is 18 just in that one night. It was a nightmare.

Now my parents weren't the greatest parents in the world. They told me who or who not to hang around with. I just decided to pick my own friends. If my parents didn't like them, they were my best friends. If they did like them, they were my worst enemy.

My boyfriend, now 22 years old, and I get along like a couple is supposed to. We are one. Well, parents (at least mine) don't want their little girl going out with someone five years older. That is bull.

17-year-old female
Arizona

My relationships with others have changed so much during my teenage years. I used to party all the time. On weekends I'd go out and drink and spend all my money. If school got boring, I'd ditch classes. The only thing I liked to do was be with all my friends and have a good time.

I now have a job which I like, and I have many responsibilities that need to be taken care of. Going away to school next year is the most important concern right now for me. I now try to watch over my friends and help them.

I don't party as much as I used to, and I never ditch school. Instead of my friends watching over me, I have matured and try to guide them with their morals and ideals.

Going away to school next year has left me with many confused emotions. I feel as though I am still a child being forced out into the world. I also feel as though I must decide now what I will be doing for . . . my life.

It's confusing and depressing. Money, leaving family and friends, where to go and what to do have been a few things that keep flying in circles in my head. All of these things contribute to the attitudes that I have towards my friends.

All the confusion and depression that I'm feeling makes me want to stay away from my family and friends. I find myself wanting to be alone more often. I like to relax and think about what my future may hold for me.

These pressures make me want to cry. . . . All these pressures seem to be sitting on my shoulders all at one time. I find myself just wanting to stop and give me a while to make up my mind.

Nancy Casella, 17
Oak Park, Illinois

Relationships during the teenage years are very disappointing. Family ties are diminished by rebellion. Teens search for affection that they don't receive from parents and from peers of the opposite sex. Usually they end up hurt and lonely. Some end up in trouble.

The family should work together to make those ties of blood stronger. A closer family may prevent a lot of hurt. Teens need their parents to turn to in a time of confusion and need, but sometimes the parents just don't care to listen. Or they say our fears are silly. This does not build the confidence and maturity of a teen.

Jenny Kopas, 16
Munster, Indiana

Relationships invariably change during the teenage years as they spent many nights thinking, "Oh, was there some cute guy I passed up?" There may be somebody better, but that doesn't make my mom love my dad any less.

Steve: Maybe I don't know love. I once thought I was in love, but I seriously doubt it now. I really don't believe in this concept of one true love—one person out there you're gonna meet. C'mon. Why can't you be in love with several different people?

It's not like I have a certain amount of love, and I'll give you 25 percent and you 25 percent. If you love four people, then you love four people. And they'll love you. I don't believe in the institution of marriage, and I don't see why just because you love somebody, you have to stick with them. You might find a couple other people you love.

John: It's not that one love for one person is better than love for any other person. I love my mom, and I love my girlfriend. I'm not gonna refuse to marry my girlfriend because I love my mom.

Kelly: I know that now I am in love because I can look back and see at a juvenile stage when it was just an infatuation. I can see the great differences even though it was the same person, because we've changed. There was a time when we broke up, and we didn't like each other at all. That was infatuation.

There was no way I could say I loved him. But a lot of that has been changed. Now, through hindsight and through past experiences, I can say I'm in love. But other than that, it's the way the person affects you. It's also how much time you're willing to commit. I think you can be infatuated with any number of people. But in the romantic sense and the marriage sense, I think there's only one person.

Steve: Is it true love that holds you must because people change. Some relationships may become weaker; others, stronger. As a person grows, his perspective grows too. I myself have found that as I grow older, my parents seem more and more like friends and advisers than the slave drivers and jail wardens they were. I can see things more on their level now.

Also, my friendships with people have become more meaningful. My best friend is just that—not because I like to play with her neat Barbie dolls but because we share the same views on politics and morals and principles.

Nancy Oliver, 18
Glendale, Missouri

I remember particularly one day in my first year journalism class, I was sitting quietly, as I always do, listening to a lecture. For some reason the instructor was distracted.

The class started talking . . . and I heard one girl sitting next to me turn around and say to the person behind her how beautiful I was. She went on to say something about my eyes, and I thought to myself how strange that she had noticed when she never looked me in the eyes.

Another day as I was walking to class, she passed me going the other way. I've never been an overtly friendly person, but as I glanced up to see her watching me I smiled. She turned away.

To this day, I wonder why she didn't respond to me. . . . She commented to her friend, saying that I was beautiful, yet I wasn't good enough to be her friend.

Shanley Mason, 17
Reno, Nevada

Relationships with family are important, but you can't be so dependent upon parents that you can't exist without them during your childhood. Your priorities have to change from family to friends because some day you're going to see more of your friends

222

and less of your family.

Often it seems that relationships with relatives have to be faked in order not to hurt feelings. Often you don't see distant relatives for years. But if the relationship between your parent and their brother or sister is very close, then you may have to fake liking your aunt, uncle, or even cousins in order not to aggravate your parent.

Unfortunately, you may not be able to put on a good act, and it hurts like hell when you realize that someone does not want you around but is tolerating you to please their relative that you get along with.

That brings me to what I feel is the worst type of relationship, tolerance. Having to tolerate someone you dislike simply because you are thrust into their lives is the worst feeling. I am the kind of person who will avoid fights as much as possible, prompting some people to say I'm "too nice." But when someone who constantly starts trouble—and there are a lot of them out there—starts with you . . . it eats at you from the inside.

The frustration is incredible. Eventually you blow up, and a fight erupts. Fighting is not fun. No one looks for a fight, but unfortunately it may be the only answer.

Howard Wien, 15
Long Beach, New York

When I was 14, I used to "hang out" with a 17-year-old. I thought she was everything. I wanted to act like her and go everywhere she did. I didn't even want to date. . . . All I could think of was "me, a freshman with a senior—wow."

Now I don't know whether I want to play with dolls or go out with guys. When you "hang out" with someone older, you begin to think you are older a lot of the time. But when you "hang out" with someone younger, you feel older and more mature. . . .

When I was "hanging out" with together, or is it the fact that you've grown together?

Relationships with Adults

John: My girlfriend's parents treat me like I'm just another one of the people around them. Whenever they go someplace, they ask me if I want to go. And when I go, they don't say, "Well, John, you want to go here?" They treat me like an adult, not like some little kid.

Manish: I'm Indian, and in Indian culture you're supposed to respect your elders to the max. You're really supposed to look up to them. I guess that's the way it's always been with me and some of my family members.

But my uncle is cool. He lets me be one of the guys. We can go out and drink or do whatever we want. He respects my opinion. We can talk dirty—talk about sex. You name it, we can do it. With him it's fine. Ever since I was 12, he used to let me drive the car. He didn't mind. I mean he just treated me

this senior, she was into drugs and booze so I was around it a lot. I skipped school once to go to a house where booze and drugs were everywhere.

I was so unhappy. I really didn't want to live because I didn't know how to get away from it. I got stuck with a bad reputation and nowhere to run. I certainly couldn't explain anything to my family.

The senior graduated, and the next year I found more friends my age and older. . . . We're just friends . . . helping each other when we need it.

My dad is having a heart attack. He doesn't want me to grow up. My mother had to just about sit on him to let me and my sister date.

The relationship with my family is great. We can talk about any problems, and they understand and help. I never thought it possible, but parents do understand our problems.

Michelle Favre, 15
Lubbock, Texas

WE WERE THE BEST OF FRIENDS. WE DID EVERYTHING TOGETHER. NOTHING COULD HAVE SEPARATED US, BUT THINGS HAVE CHANGED. OUR RELATIONSHIP IS STAGNANT. I FEEL STIFLED. DON'T YOU UNDERSTAND? —I NEED ROOM TO GROW!

I am very quiet and backward at school. I get along better with the people that I work with because, being married, I can relate better with adult problems and situations than with teenage ones.

Cathy Grubham, 17
Auburn, Washington

When I first moved to Mt. Vernon 11 years ago, I met a girl, "Marcia." She was the same age, and we liked the same things.... To eighth grade, we were the best of friends. But once we hit high school, everything was changing. "Marcia" and I weren't doing things together anymore—we didn't like any of the same things, especially when it came to people. I was really hurt by all of the changes, and I blamed them on different people—never "Marcia" or I.

After about two years of just saying, "Hi, how are you?" in the halls, I realized that everything is changing. But the "things" that changed the most were "Marcia" and I. We're still the same people, just with different interests.

Now "Marcia" and I are both seniors, and we have a couple of classes together. We look back on our friendship and laugh at all our fights and jokes, but what we both realize is we grew up together and nothing can change that.

Rhonda Gray, 18
Mt. Vernon, Washington

It's hard to remember back to the days when everyday life seemed so simple, when you always had a mother to run to or a father to talk to—not that I don't talk to my parents anymore. I do but not about the stuff I really need to talk to someone about.

It seems I'm being pushed toward the brink of my adult life, and I'm not sure I can make it on my own. My friends, which before were just kids down the street I played football with, have become the ones I confide in more and more rather than my parents.

like one of his buddies, and I appreciated that. I think that kind of relationship is better—more advantageous for both of us. Not just me.

Steve: I think the most common or obvious adult-teenage relationship is with parents. I went through a stage where I was pushing for more freedom, but my parents were reluctant to give me as much as I asked for. I think most parent-teenage relationships are going through a changing period. It's a matter of adjustment for both the teenager and the parents. Suddenly the teenager has a lot of freedom and has to learn not to abuse it for his own good—not just because they don't want to get the parents upset. I can stay out till whenever, and I won't upset my parents. But if I have to get up at eight in the

They are going through the same things I am, experiencing the same things I am. I'm able to understand them better, and they understand me better.

It's the fear of the unknown, not knowing what your life will become, not wanting to break the last few strings that keep us with our parents, not knowing whether or not we will find a good paying job or not, just the fear of not knowing that pushes some kids to alcohol or drugs or something even more drastic.

How a person handles this time in his/her life will affect their whole outlook on life. A person sets his standards and his goals now. If he doesn't handle it right, he'll end up messing up his whole life.

Tim Seitz, 16
St. Charles, Illinois

Relationships go through some rather big changes during the teenage years. The biggest change, at least it has been for me, is my relationship with my family. My mother has become much more important to me over the past year. She's like my best friend. I tell her my secrets, and we go to movies and go shopping together. We have a lot of fun together.

Other changes are in our relationships with boy- and girlfriends. I think the pressure is off for having a boyfriend. Boys can be friends, and just friends. Then there are boys you want to have a more serious relationship with. Before this year, it seemed that you couldn't be friends with a boy, without him being your "boyfriend."

Now, in my life especially, my girlfriends are very important to me. For me, it's important to have at least one very close friend you can share your deep-dark secrets and problems with. Then you have other friends to run around with and go to games and parties with.

Denise Possehl, 16
Marion, Iowa

Although I have become much more independent than I have ever been, I feel my relationship with my family is extremely important right now. I can see now why my parents have done things the way they have. Most importantly, I can respect them as individuals.

Granted, I often get really annoyed when I get "unasked-for" opinions on recent boyfriends or on new clothes. But I've come to find that even though it irritates me, a large percentage of the time their "annoying opinions" proved to be true facts.

A couple of boyfriends have not lived up to my mother's standards. Not being one to keep it to herself, she has made the fact well known. At the time all I did was roll my eyes, cross my arms, and say, "For sure, mom, for sure." I'm glad

morning, it's going to be me who will feel it if I don't wake up.

Leslie: I have a real close relationship with both of my sisters. One is ten years older than me, and one's five years older than me. I enjoy going out with them—sometimes more than when I go out with my friends. When we go out drinking or out to dinner, they treat me like a person—like one of their friends. We go out and we have a riot together. They talk to me about anything, too.

Steve: I hardly ever see my relatives, but when I do see my relatives, I get this "Oh, you've grown," and everything. I think it's great. It's what I want to hear. I like my grandma to stroll in, all happy, and give me a cookie and a "How are you doing in school?" I think, "Oh, this is great." I like it.

Leslie: I'm really close to my uncle. Right before I went to France, he and my aunt stopped by to talk for an hour. Later my aunt called my mom and said, "Leslie has matured so much. It was so nice to talk with her"—like she thought I was a baby before. It really bugged me. I guess I really never talked to her that much. I usually goofed off with my uncle. Her comment really shocked me. I thought, "Oh, God, what do my other relatives think of me?"

Relationships with People in Charge

Leslie: At work they treat me like a little girl. They ask, "Do you understand? Do you know what you have to do?" They always come up and check on me. I don't know what the deal is.

Diane: I had to train a lot of older people—older than I am. The last person that I trained was in her fifties. She did not like the idea at all that a teenager was training her—that somebody a lot younger than her was training her. She didn't really smart off, but she was really sarcastic.

John: When I'm around my co-

she's not one to say, "I told you so!"

When all my other relationships end, the one with my parents continues.

Kimberly Long, 18
Cedar Rapids, Iowa

It's not very hard to be accepted at school. You just need to be cool—don't be a smart ass to no one, and you'll get along with most people.

Jay Chavis, 18
Auburn, Washington

When you go to your best friend, she feels about the same way as you do. Y'all have about the same morals and personalities. Your friend is going through almost the same situations you are.

I know if I have a problem that has been bugging me, I'll go to my best friend and tell her about it. Everything goes a lot better. It's like a load of bricks have been taken off your shoulders.

I know a couple of years ago I really didn't have a very best friend. Sure, I had lots of friends but no special person. I would sit and cry about it. I prayed about that situation every day.

Now I have about four super great best friends. I know my life has lightened up now. If I have nothing to do, I'll just call someone up and go do something or talk. We all are close, and our relationship is very, very special to me.

We all feel the same way about guys, religion, and our moral standards. Of course, there are variations in them, but overall it is the same. Every day you practically learn something new about each person, and I learn to grow closer to them.

I love each one very special. Of course, like for anything, I like doing some things better with a certain person than I do the others. We all pitch in together to keep the smiles on our faces and also the smiles in our hearts.

We praise each other for the good things. We don't put each

other down for the actions one may disagree with. I know if ever I need someone to talk to, my best friends will be there.

I would do anything for them. A true friend would die for their friends, and I would die for mine. I care and respect them in every way. If they confide in me, that is where the information is kept—in me. . . .

We keep each other on the right track, and we have a certain "bond" among us. Friendship is very important and a great need for a person.

Brenda Jackson, 16
Lubbock, Texas

From a personal experience, I know what it is like to have a great relationship with someone and suddenly see it vanish. This relationship was with my best friend in my junior year in high school.

We had known each other for six years. I thought that we were best friends until one day she decided to stop speaking to me. I went crazy wondering why this happened. I would try and talk to her, but she would just turn away and ignore me. I was so hurt. I didn't know what to do. I asked my other friends if they knew what was wrong, and they said no.

It was hard on them also because they were caught up in the middle, being friends with both of us. I felt like the world had collapsed around me. . . .

I believe that what happened was due to my jealousy of her and another girlfriend. They would do things over the weekends together. When I saw them Monday mornings, they would talk about it. I felt left out, and they knew it, too. Afterwards they would laugh behind my back.

Up to this day, I am still uncomfortable when around her. My friends tell me that if she can treat me like that, it is not worth having her as a friend. I still hope that in the years to come, she will realize

workers, they say, "Hey, you've got a lot of responsibility. We really need this guy." But then when it comes down to it, they pretty much treat me like trash.

If somebody calls in sick, they call me and say, "You have to come in." However, if you don't come in, they've already told everybody at the store, "John couldn't come into work because he had to see his girlfriend." A few of them treat me like I'm one of the guys. They will be real nice to me on the surface, especially when other employees are around.

Melanie: I don't know if it's because of my own self-image or what, but I find that people can treat you just like trash—just like what John said. I think of teachers here at school. If they want to get a grade out of you, they'll do anything they can to get it out of you, whether that's your ability or not. It gets me down on myself. The teacher said, "Oh, you're just a spiffy teenager—you're too busy fantasizing about your sex life."

"Well, I guess I imagine having a boyfriend."

"See you admit it. You're just too busy fantasizing, and you're not sitting down and concentrating on your music."

I walk out of there feeling like I'm some kind of sex-crazed animal. It's just like somehow she's manipulated me into admitting in her mind that—yes, that's how I spend all of my time.

Now another teacher is fine. He's great—I mean we're getting along fine, but in the beginning I missed quite a bit of school. When I got back, he goes, "Well I don't know what you can do to pass." Then he sat me down and showed me his grade book. He opened it up and said, "Look at all those absences." Well, I was sick. He went on and on so I said, "Should I apologize for my grandpa's death?" He kind of slowed down, and he apologized.

that we had a good relationship and will want to renew it.

All these pressures of teenage life soon disappear and we grow up, but then adulthood pressures arise.

Beth Fuseler, 17
Charleston, South Carolina

Your family relations can get very tense because your parents don't think you are old enough and/or capable of handling certain responsibilities, such as dating, staying out late, and using the car. When someone first hits the teen years, they usually tend to drift from, or become shy around, their parent of the opposite sex. . . .

When I was just entering the teen years, my dad and I became distant. . . . I was growing up, and I was embarrassed. He didn't know how to act to me, or how to treat me. Now, however, we are really close. I guess we passed that awkward beginning stage.

As for siblings, you are supposed to become closer, or at least civil, to one another because you are maturing. My brother, who is a year older, and I used to fight nonstop. Now we are older and more mature, and we are really very close. My sisters, both younger, are a different story. They always try to pick fights with me, but I suppose once they mature we will all be close. . . .

"Interests" is perhaps the main reason for who your friends are. What you like or dislike and what your friends like or dislike should pretty much be the same. I'm not saying that you should be exact copies of your friends, but you need to have a lot in common.

My best friend and I are very close. We both think alike, have the same interests, and get along great, but we aren't like clones. She's a pompon girl, and I'm uninterested in sports.

We talk about anything and everything, and we trust each other

Now I think he's one of my better teachers because he respects me and I respect him.

Relationships with Police

Steve: I genuinely think that cops feel threatened by teenagers. Because they have such fragile egos, cops feel a need to lash back.

Mary: At Blackwell (a forest preserve) the other day, this one cop was just threatening us so much.

Matt: Did you have booze?

Mary: Yeah, but he's saying he's going to charge us 50 dollars a beer and all this stuff. But anyway, we opened the cooler and his eyes opened wide. He goes, "Oh good—cold?" I bet he was thinking, "Yeah, well I know what I'm going to be doing tonight." He took all of our beer. He didn't pour it out or anything—just took it so he could drink it that night. It's like, what kind of example is he trying to show us—he takes our beer and charges us 50 bucks.

Steve: Well that was stupid to pay him 50 dollars cash. I would have told him to go through the legal procedures. I would never ever give a cop cash—no way.

Mary: Why?

Steve: Because he's going to stick it in his back pocket, and you're never going to see the money again.

Leslie: He gave her a ticket. How can—

Steve: You say, "Thank you" for the piece of paper, and you stroll down to the local police station at any time of your convenience within ten days and pay your ticket. You make sure you get a receipt for the money that you gave him. Never give cash to a cop. It's like giving him a reward for hassling you—no way.

Mary: Well, he said he was going to throw my boyfriend in jail, and he said all this other stuff.

Steve: Just stand there perfectly silent. If he's going to take the beer, there's not much you can do—he's going to pour it out. But stand there perfectly silent—with absolutely no expression on your face. Wait till he's finished. And if he asks you for 50 dollars, in cash, just say, "I don't have 50 dollars in cash." Get the ticket, wait till he's gone, and leave.

Mary: Well, he made it sound to me like he was letting us off easy.

Steve: They think they can scare us into denying our legal rights.

Diane: My brother went through the same thing. My brother and his friend were in separate cars going to a restaurant. The guy in the other car needed directions so he asked my brother, "Where do we turn off?" After Mike told him, he pulled back behind. A cop pulled him over and said, "You're drag racing." They were even within the speed limit. He gave my brother all of the bull you could imagine.

My brother did exactly what Steve said. He didn't say a word—nothing. Later, he took the cop to court, and the cop couldn't even remember what happened. It just shows you that if you do end up going to court, chances are that you're going to get off.

Steve: You can't allow cops to bully you because you're going to end up on the low end of it. As long as you stand there completely unaffected by everything, the worst they can do to you is punish you for a crime you've committed.

Compiled by Tracy Wykert and Cathy Zubek

Chapter 17.

Responsibility

Slam . . . the door closes behind J.D. as his mother fumes, screaming curses at his back. He screeches out of the driveway in his dad's car. He didn't bother to ask permission to use the car. He doesn't care what his parents will say when he comes home. He's just glad to be away from their nagging for a while.

"I can't believe it. I get up in the morning, make my own lunch, take out the trash, go to school all day, go to track practice, and when I get home, my freeloading mother tells me she's too tired to cook dinner. Dear old dad calls me a lazy punk for not cleaning up the dishes from last night. I don't understand how I can be so dead tired and still be a lazy punk."

He races down the street to vent his frustrations. J.D. has heard all the same stories so many times he has memorized them. He knows he is right so he has to fight his parents' lies. He also knows he is doing much more than most guys his age. "So why do they bitch all the time?"

He recalls his mother's favorite line: "Your family should always come first. If you're too tired to help out around here after football and track practice, then you should quit sports." J.D. always thought his sports were helping his parents. "Shit, I got a free ride to college. They'll be on easy street when I leave."

Even so, she has no right to be such a hypocrite, J.D. reasons. "When it was freezing outside, she would never drive me to school. I used to spend the first hour sitting on the radiator to thaw out my toes after walking. Now that she works once in a while, she makes me drive her home from the train station three blocks away. I don't dare ask for a ride home from school after a tough practice because it isn't worth listening to dad complaining."

"She tells me the family should come first while I'm busy washing my own clothes because she is too tired. She's been too tired to wash my clothes for six years."

As J.D. drives, he thinks about how every parent, teacher, and coach—and during vacation, his boss—is constantly bitching at him because he is a lazy, irresponsible teenager. "Why is it that they all put so much emphasis on their concerns? My math teacher thinks homework for her class is all I have to do. My English teacher assigns 50 extra pages of reading, and my science teacher crams an entire chapter into one week. Each one is unconcerned about the other responsibilities of students."

As the week goes on, J.D. is overwhelmed by doctor, dentist, and God knows what else. He tells his coach that he has scheduled a necessary eye exam during a practice because of his full schedule. "Coach, the doctor has been so busy. I had to take any appointment I could get. I'm sorry, but I'll have to miss practice today," he explains.

"What? Goddammit. I don't understand you kids. If you wanted to join, why don't you go

229

to practice? I can't see what could be more important to you than track. You got a chance to qualify for state if you come to practice," his coach complains.

Now that he is miles from home, J.D. starts to realize how dumb he must have been to have taken on so many responsibilities. What could his reasons possibly have been? He had joined the newspaper at school because it would look good on his transcripts, but also because he wanted to accomplish something with his brains for a change.

He signed up for the class under his counselor's advice. Little did he know that class requirements included staying after school several days every week and working until midnight every deadline. He decided that the whole deal was set up for people with absolutely nothing else to do. The instructor told J.D. that he had to attend a meeting after school as a class requirement. Unfortunately, J.D. would miss track practice if he attended the meeting.

"C'mon Mrs. Magnola! All my other classes meet for one hour a day. How can I be required to stay after school every other day for this class? It just isn't right."

"You have a responsibility to the paper. You have to be here. You'll just have to miss practice," Mrs. Mag said.

J.D.'s frustrations were at a peak. "How come no one can see that I have other responsibilities that come first? Where did I go wrong? I can't make anybody happy."

Finally, arriving at his girlfriend's house, J.D. says, "To hell with everybody else. I'm going to do what I have to do when I have time to do it. If nobody likes it, that's tough." His girlfriend opens the door with tear-filled eyes. "What's the matter, Julie?" "I got in a big fight with my ex-boyfriend, and I have been trying to call you for hours. You were supposed to call me. Where the hell have you been, you jerk? Thanks a lot."

J.D. knows for certain that everyone is after him for being irresponsible. He isn't paranoid, and he isn't dreaming. Suddenly he bursts into hysterical laughter as he remembers the ageless joke that everyone tells him: "Enjoy being a teenager while you can. Pretty soon you'll have to be in the real world with responsibilities every day. Stay young as long as you can. It's the best time of your life."

Discussions

When I was first allowed to use our car, I was excited and determined not to do anything to cause my parents to distrust my driving and judgment. I was so paranoid that I was going to do something wrong ... that my first experience with the car didn't have much of a chance from the beginning.

While driving home from marching band, it had just started raining. I started up a winding road that had maple trees on both sides. The road is narrow, and it was fall so there were leaves on the road.

Before I really knew it, the car was in the ditch. It was dark, and I got very nervous. Soon two guys

Michelle: I gotta pay for my own clothes. I gotta pay for my own makeup and everything. My parents don't give me money so whatever I eat comes out of my pocket. If I want to go to a show, it comes out of my pocket. If I want gas money, it comes out of my pocket. If I want to go to a ball game, it comes out of my pocket. Everything I do with money comes right out of my pocket.

I spent almost 700 dollars in the last month or so, including my trip to Florida. That's a lot of money for someone who's 17 years old. And with the money I lost from work, from taking two weeks off, that

drove up, and they pulled the car out. I drove home very slowly, shaking. When I got home, I walked into the house and got a flashlight and my dad. We went outside together to look at the front of the car that was all smashed in.

He didn't say anything but put his arm on my shoulder. His face didn't show it, but I knew he was smiling. I suddenly felt at ease with him and my new responsibility.
Allison Kerns, 17
Kent, Washington

When my mother started working nights, I had to watch my little sister, who is now one year old. There is always pressure on me, knowing

230

that I have to go home right after school. I have always enjoyed after-school activities, but now I have had to give them up.

Responsibility is a good thing if it's not suddenly thrust at you and you have to accept it or else. Watching my sister has taught me to keep a level head and think rationally in a tight situation, but it has totally turned me off the thought of ever having kids of my own.

Kim Stratton, 16
Watkins Glen, New York

I love responsibilities. Even though I may get bogged down with them, I still like to have them. First of all, I like knowing that somebody trusts me enough to give me responsibilities. Second, I grow from them. I mature. I really don't know why. I also learn from them.

Sometimes they're scary—like driving a car. Sometimes it hits me like a brick. If I do something wrong, like run a light, somebody could get hurt or even killed. That's why I try to be as careful as possible.

Karma Metzler, 16
Boise, Idaho

I'm not affected by responsibility.... At home my only responsibility is to keep the grass cut and the snow shoveled.... I have no pressures put on me. If I don't do something I should have, I don't let it get me down. Nothing bothers me.

Scott Olson, 16
Maple Grove, Minnesota

I have been having a lot of problems at home ever since my mother and father got a divorce. My mother depends on me too much. She works all day from the time my brother goes to school until late in the evening. It doesn't leave any time for me because I have to clean the house, make dinner, and babysit my brother.

My brother is only nine years old, and it causes a tremendous problem. He knows that he can get

uses up any money I saved pretty fast.

Karen: I don't hang up my clothes. I'm not expected to keep my room clean. My dad pays for gas, insurance for the car, and my clothes. I get an allowance. My dad pays for everything. I don't really have to do anything—wash dishes, take out the garbage. So my only responsibility is getting good grades. Even then I have this tendency to blow off my classes if they're too easy.

___

Determining Responsibilities

Diane: My job's a big responsibility because it's my dad's business. If something happens and it's my fault, I really feel bad because it affects my dad. It is more responsibility than working someplace else. I feel responsible to get things done right and not screw up.

Melanie: My health is a big responsibility to me—almost too

whatever he wants from my mother. She "babies" him so much and never has any time for me.

She expects that by the time she gets home from work the house will be cleaned, dinner will be made, and my homework will be completed. If everything isn't finished, I end up getting yelled at and/or grounded.

16-year-old female
Michigan

I want to be treated like an adult, but I don't like the responsibilities that go with it . . . washing dishes and cleaning my room. . . . Sometimes my dad will clean my room and the kitchen and tell me, "Sean, see how nice the kitchen looks. Everything is in its place. Now it's your job to do this. Okay?"

Then I usually feel guilty and clean the whole house. I really like how nice it looks . . . and my parents tell me the house looks nice.

Sean Smith, 14
Joliet, Illinois

Responsibility

LET ME TELL YOU SOMETHIN' KID! YOU'RE GONNA FINISH HIGH SCHOOL. YOU'RE GONNA GO TO COLLEGE. YOU'RE GONNA HAVE A GOOD PAYING JOB, AND YOU'RE GONNA HAVE A GOOD WIFE, BUT MOST IMPORTANTLY —YOU'RE GONNA BE YOUR OWN MAN

I was married the August before my senior year. I have many responsibilities to my husband, my parents, and also to myself. My husband depends on me for cooking his dinner, washing his clothes, taking care of the house, and being there when he needs me. . . .

For myself, I have a part-time secretarial job. I have many duties I have to perform. Also, I am determined to finish high school. . . .

The best benefit is knowing that I am needed and that I can be there to help and know that I am important to somebody.
Tammy Sue Rinker, 17
Strasburg, Virginia

I have found more responsibility on my shoulders makes me a better person and student. Since I got a job and have been babysitting more, my grades have gone up. I would usually wait until the last minute to get my homework done. Now I know I have to work at night so I get it done right away. . . .

I needed to become better organized. I use a calendar constantly, and I plan a schedule for the coming events.
Heidi Kurtti, 16
Fargo, North Dakota

When I was 11, my mother and I decided that I should control my own budget and be more responsible for the use of my money. Earlier this year I began doing my own grocery shopping and meal planning on a limited budget.

Both of these have made me more aware of all the aspects of being independent, including inflation, tax legislation, and the difficulties involved in making good financial decisions.

I was amazed how fast money can go in just trying to eat well. Now when I hear about cuts in Social Security or unemployment benefits, it makes me wonder where our country's priorities are. It seems wrong to take money from people who already have a

big to handle. I've got to really start being responsible. I get in cycles like this—when I've got to write down what I've got to do today and what I'm gonna eat and how many calories and all that stuff and it's like sometimes I just say forget it—blow it all off. But I think that's a real big responsibility that I've got to keep.

I also have a responsibility in school, just getting all the work done and coming to school and getting halfway decent grades. I feel responsible to my parents. They expect me to do well. They're giving me a loving home and everything so the least I can do is return to them—I want to make them happy with me.

Steve: I have a responsibility to keep my parents informed about where I am, which is something I sometimes forget. Sometimes I'm working, or I just don't come home. I have a responsibility to call my

hard time providing food and shelter for their families.

When I first started doing my own budget, I made a lot of mistakes. I went through the usual cycle of buying something frivolous and regretting it later. Now after seven years of experience, I feel a lot more confident about the thought of soon being totally responsible for my life.
Koni Olson, 18
Seattle, Washington

I always try to willingly accept any responsibility that is given to me. . . . In school, I am the secretary of the Student Government Association, president of the Spanish club, co-editor-in-chief of the newspaper, and am involved in other clubs.

I am also active in the church I attend. . . . Many people hesitate to accept more than "their share" of responsibilities because they can't function under pressure. I am just the opposite. I thrive under pressure. I think everyone needs to have some responsibility in order to mature mentally.
Dawn Lockhart, 17
Bentonville, Virginia

As a youth of today, I feel my two most important responsibilities are to God and society. I have the responsibility to be honest with God and myself in order to find real peace and happiness in life. Since God has given me His best, I feel it is my obligation to give Him my best in return.

In society, my responsibility is to contribute what I have in order to benefit from what it has to offer. I have the responsibility to be honest with other humans and to make the best of myself through education, religion, and experiences.
Debbie Catt, 17
Clarksville, Tennessee

I see a lot of hypocrisy among those in authority.

Many adults say that we should act like adults and yet they treat us like children. . . . Parents want us to be children when it's something we want to do so they can say no if they want to. When it's something they want us to do we should "act like adults" and "take the responsibility to get it done."

I find teachers and administration doing the same thing. We have to have a note from our parents if we miss a day. They won't take our word for it because "you're just children." But in a few months, we will be adults, and a few months aren't going to change us very much.

They then turn around and say that we're adults and will be going out into the world soon—and if we don't shape up, we will never make it.

Cindi Confer, 17
McMinnville, Oregon

My two most important responsibilities are my family and my rock band "Swamphox." My family requires me to . . . help out around the house. . . . My next responsibility is my rock band Swamphox.

It consists of my brother and me and two friends. . . . It needs a lot of time and effort and big money. It takes us all many hours of work and dedication and the ability to work with one another.

I practice my guitar every night to improve my skills. I want to play only the best. . . . Our band is going to go professional and going to be the most famous band since Van Halen.

Jeff Mortka, 16
Kissimmee, Florida

My two most important responsibilities are with the school and with the Castle Rock Fire Department. One of these responsibilities I always handle like an adult, and one I handle like an immature kid. In school, I mess around and have fun, which is okay, but I need to put more time into studying and trying to graduate instead of watching TV and going out.

parents up and tell them I'm not coming home.

Leslie: I have the same responsibility. They like to know where I'm going, just to inform them that I'm all right. Also, they kind of like to know who I'm with. I have a responsibility to school. They want me to get good grades, and I tend to do it for them more than for myself. They pay me for my grades—I get rewarded for A's. I also have a responsibility to my job. I don't do it for myself really. At work they think I'm such a good girl. I think I have a responsibility to keep up the image that I always do well—that I'm not a screw-off—so I keep to myself pretty much at work. I just make my bosses happy, and I have a responsibility to take care of my car. Now I realize how big a responsibility that is.

When I do my work on the fire department, I'm serious. I study all manuals and equipment every day. Maybe I do well in fire department activities and emergency calls because it's not just my life I'm putting on the line. The man behind me is also there expecting me to know what to do, how to do it, and also what not to do. Both our lives could ride on his or my actions. One mistake is all it takes.

Loy Osburn, 18
Castle Rock, Colorado

My main responsibility is to help my parents and family as much as I can, especially my mom who needs my help most of the time. To me, I feel that since I'm the oldest sister I have a responsibility to my little brother and sister. . . . They look up to me for guidance all the time. . . .

Responsibility   233

I feel pressures all of the time at home, and ... most of the pressures come from my parents pushing me and proving to me that I can be a better person. They do this out of love, and it does work. It shows me that I am capable of doing more when I go that extra distance.

Star Taylor, 17
Watkins Glen, New York

I am responsible to keep my grades at a respectable level. . . . I have a lot of pressure to put up with, so much that I almost can't sleep at night. It takes me two hours to get to sleep. I have no time to relax on week nights.

Brant Lancione, 15
Bellaire, Ohio

To be fair to myself and my family, I try to do the best possible job I can at everything I do. For example, when I do my school work, I put everything I have into it. I disappoint my family and especially myself if I get a B when I know I could have gotten an A.

I have a responsibility to help others as much as I can. . . . I work with the YMCA in a big brother program for boys with no fathers. I feel I owe it to these kids to give them some of the opportunities I was given as a child.

Jeff Mathews, 18
Edmonds, Washington

I am affected by responsibility because I have a baby and have to take care of her and go to school. There are a lot of other challenges that go along with it.

There are also benefits. I never get bored, and she's there to give me a smile when other people aren't. She means a lot to me. . . .

Jean McClaire, 17
Front Royal, Virginia

At this point in my life the most important thing in it is my baby. Although it is not born yet, I have a special bond with it that I do not feel for anyone else. I worry about it all the time. Even when I am doing other things, it is always on

Kelly: The biggest responsibility I have is really for the future. I have to make sure I can pay for college since I'm not getting any financial support from my parents. I'm working a lot recently.

Manish: I assume some responsibilities, but none come to mind. I have no job, for example. Some parents say you have to take out the garbage every day, or you have to wash the dishes. Mine are not so strict about small chores around the house. I don't feel I have a responsibility except, like to my friends. Sometimes we cheat a lot so I'm responsible for some part of the homework. That's about it. You must remember—I'm the guy who doesn't care. I never plan ahead for tomorrow. I'm pretty irresponsible, I guess. Maybe I'm just not mature.

Achieving Independence

Steve: Responsibility becomes independence and freedom, and independence and freedom are very enjoyable.

Matt: Yeah, I'd like to have a job because I don't want my parents to pay for all my college bills. I have a job in the summer, but I want to work right now. I'm getting bored. My parents pay for everything, even my insurance. It's kind of a drag.

Steve: The responsibility of a job kind of gives you a certain power or self-respect. When you don't have to rely on your parents 100 percent, you're in a much stronger position. I'm perfectly convinced that if my

parents ever kicked me out, I could survive. I feel a certain amount of independence. I have a job, take on certain responsibilities, and deserve a certain amount of respect and freedom.

Kelly: It's hard for your parents to tell you what to do with your money when you've earned it.

Steve: That's right. For instance, I went to Florida. My money, my motorcycle, my vacation—I'm doing things on my own. I'm not relying on my parents for a lot of stuff. It makes you capable of achieving.

Jeff: Everything I need, my parents pay for. When I go to college, they'll pay for everything. But I don't want that. I don't want them looking back and saying, "Aha— we've done everything for you."

Karen: Once I get out of school, it's going to be a big shock. Nobody's going to pay for my stuff anymore. What am I going to do?

Responding to Parents

Steve: My parents' responsibility is to guide and let go. It's the parents' responsibility to equip us for the outside world, and a big part of that is learning to let go. It's mostly guidance. There is no point in getting upset over minor things anymore—we're past that.

Kelly: Legally my mom has to provide me with a home until I'm 18. Morally she has to raise me right. Beyond that, it is not her responsibility.

Jeff: Your parents should kind of be a coach. They should be there if you need advice. But I want to do things on my own. I'll have more self-respect, and I'm sure they'll have more respect for me.

Kelly: Since I've been working, my mom will sometimes go out and get a really nice outfit for me because she knows I've been paying for everything on my own. It's nice when she does it because she doesn't normally pay for things.

Steve: The gifts mean more when they do come. It's much more appreciated because you know how much work it takes to make that kind of money.

Diane: My parents are supporting my college, but I think they should. My dad's got the bucks. In fact, they forbid me to have a job in college. My mom wants me to concentrate on grades. I feel it's part of their responsibility. If they've got the money, they should dish it out.

Kelly: My two older brothers and I are paying for college. If my mom were able to, she wouldn't. It's something I have to do myself. It is my career. I have to pursue it myself. So I'm responsible, not her.

Manish: How far do your parents' responsibilities to you go? Through grade school? High school? Through college? Till the time they die? Till you're 18?

Steve: Overall, parents should equip the child to make it in the world. The object is to create somebody who is capable of going out there, surviving in the world, and hopefully finding what that individual can find as far as contentment and satisfaction.

Leslie: I think sometimes parents put too much responsibility on their kids. Having to pay for college, getting good grades—it's hard. I don't understand it. I don't know why parents won't pay for their kids' college. It's just not fair.

Kelly: I'm going to a private college. I've set a goal beyond college. College is something I'll have to get through to reach my career goal. I think my mom is an ogre, but really she's done a good thing because I'm responsible.

Leslie: I'm responsible too, but I think they're responsible for that. My dad had to work his way through college, and I just don't think he wants me to go through that hell. He has it made, and he wants me to do good too. There's

my mind. When I am sick, I do not worry as much about myself as I do the chance of hurting my baby.

The biggest conflict is that I am not married. I am not proud of this fact, but I am not necessarily ashamed of it either. I made a mistake, and now I have to deal with it the best way possible.

Having a baby was not in my plans, but now I would not give it up for anything. I am happy with my life and am going to do my best to make my baby's life a happy one.
Colleen Moore, 17
McMinnville, Oregon

My two most important responsibilities are keeping my grades up and keeping my room clean. Keeping my room clean is easy, but keeping my grades up is tough. There's so much pressure to do well in high school, especially if you're planning on going to college.

It's really hard at first . . . to get all your assignments turned in and study. But it's easier now that I'm getting used to it.
Lisa Puyear, 16
Castle Rock, Colorado

Responsibility   235

My real responsibility is to myself, but I never think of it that way. I feel responsible for taking care of my two sisters and their safety. I worry most about my mom and not letting my dad or anyone else hurt her too much. She has been bruised too many times to admit, and I want her to be happy.

My father has had an affair which is supposedly over, but I have written reason to believe it is still going strong. I need to protect my mom from such emotional torture by supplementing it with mine and my sisters' care.

Through all this, I am responsible for myself in growing maturity, objective thinking, safety, and growing up.

15-year-old female
Minnesota

I think that responsibility means there is going to be a lot of pressure because people are counting on you to do something. Say you were responsible for bringing pop to a slumber party. You forgot to bring it, but you came anyway.

Everyone was getting thirsty, but no matter how many times you apologized it seemed to do no good at all. You would know why if you've ever eaten potato chips and drank water. . . .

Say you needed only two big bottles of pop and you brought three just in case someone was a little thirsty. Then there would be no pressure, and you would more than likely benefit from this. Your friend would ask you to another party.

Rodney Sayre, 17
Uniontown, Pennsylvania

At 18 I was kicked out of my parents' house for loving a girl that they did not like. I had to find a place to stay so these two old people let me stay with them. I had to help a man because he was not able to get up out of bed himself plus go to school and work.

I had a girlfriend so one night

no definite restrictions. I guess maybe I'm lucky.

Managing the Workload

Steve: It seems to me to be perfectly logical that if you have two conflicting responsibilities, you're going to be incapable of fulfilling one responsibility. So why try, if you're incapable of fulfilling it? Drop it, go on. It's the only sensible thing to do.

Kelly: Why can't you strive to make sure you do achieve the responsibilities? All I'm talking about is simple responsibilities. I have two jobs so when I'm home, I either sleep or do homework.

Steve: If you're capable of achieving both, then they're not conflicting responsibilities.

Kelly: Not the jobs! The home! When I get home, I have no ambition at all to fold my clothes and put them away or to do laundry or anything like that. What you have to do is set aside the time and you have to make sure. You have to become responsible for everything that you're in charge of. You can't just drop one and say, "Well, I'm never going to achieve it so I'm not going to try."

John: I'm getting straight B's now. I've got to come here, like today, and then when I get out of here at four I'm going to have to make up my track and then be to work at five and get out of work around eleven-thirty. And then comes homework.

Mary: I know that at work if I don't do my job right and I don't get the slips I need, I'll get fired. You don't get fired out of your house or fired from school. If you fail a class, you can try over again.

Kelly: Well, when I'm at work I

me and my landlord had an argument. I had to find some place else to live so my girlfriend's mother let me stay at her shop. Then I had to work, go to school, cook, and wash my clothes the old time way. Sometimes my mother would call, and it would make my girlfriend mad because she did not like my family.

Ronald Mahoney, 19
Front Royal, Virginia

My parents travel, and I live with my grandmother during the week along with my brother. During the weekends my parents are home, but during the week I have almost no restraints. . . . The possibilities are unlimited, and I know it. My parents also know. I live in a small community, but I still haven't taken advantage of the situation.

My own car (indirectly) and some spending money for doing minimal work . . . are two of the many advantages that I receive for living up to the trust of my parents and my relatives. My mother was disabled when I was very young, and I, according to my parents, have matured quite quickly. I feel that by living up to my parents' expectations, I can make them proud of me. That is important to me.

Michael Martin, 16
Hillsdale, Michigan

think I'm a relatively responsible person. Because I'm still in high school doesn't mean I can be late to work or take my homework to my job, which I've tried. When I go home, I may be a crab or I may be irresponsible. But at work I'm in the adult world so I'm a responsible person.

Steve: High school doesn't even respect you. It doesn't make you feel like a responsible person. It's almost like they expect you to be irresponsible so you are. It's very easy to be irresponsible because it's all worked out. At work you have a responsibility. If you do not meet that responsibility, you're out of work. The system is set up so you have a responsibility to try again. So you get a B or C. Or a D, if it's physics, but you can always try again.

Compiled by Chia Chen

237

Chapter 18.

Goals

Justin Adaise came home from school tired and hungry, as usual. His last class, however, had been an interesting one. Well, maybe not interesting, but it did cause him to think.

The class was sociology, and they had been discussing "The Great American Dream" and how it had developed. "Everything seemed so simple back in the 1950s," Justin thought. "A house, a car, a boy and a girl, and, of course, a successful business career."

The teacher had communicated the basic idea that the sixties generation had attempted to smash the 1950s cliché and somehow change the world.

Next, Justin played a rerun of the 1970s in his mind. The American dream now supposedly involved more independence, individuality, and creativity. Women were allowed to have their own American dreams. And, of course, the dream was nearly always obtained through higher education.

Justin began to reflect on what he had learned. As he popped a quick snack of zucchini and brown sugar into the microwave, he realized a common denominator between the cliché of the fifties and the modern, individualistic dreaming of 1984. "They're really just the same," he thought. "Money and success." The revelation frightened him. Reaching for a baked prune whip from the refrigerator, he shivered at the thought of building a life around such an unfeeling god as money.

He felt a strange sorrow for the banker who spends 12 hours a day trying to increase both the capital of Chase-Manhattan Bank and his personal account, then goes home, eats a warmed-up dinner, and kisses his plaster-of-paris wife good night; for the factory worker who puts in eight hours a day plus overtime to help General Motors overtake the Japanese but, more importantly, to pay off the mortgage on his suburban ranch house where his wife spends the days coffee-klatching and trying to keep at least minimal control of the four kids (aged 6 to 16) and the German Shepherd; for the high school teacher who has worked her way through four years of college and two years of graduate school in order to educate today's youth and thus better tomorrow's society, but, having watched that ideal fade over the past 20 years, now works to invest in a condominium in Florida, to buy a new sports car, and to save for a comfortable retirement.

Justin thought: "These are dreams? Life achievements? I'd hate to see the great American nightmare if money is the great American dream." Justin was confused. How could the one single solitary life that each human possesses be aimed at paying off a mortgage on a ranch house in Roselle? Justin saw how it could—by the frequent tendency of humanity to be blinded from ideals by immediate, tempting, materialistic gains.

As he pondered the remains of his prune whip, Justin realized that he didn't know what he wanted to do. His dad told him that being an engineer was the only way to go—all the money's in engineering. His mother wanted him to go to business school and get his MBA—business always has been the most profitable career. His teachers stressed futures in the humanities or the fine arts. Sure, there wasn't as much money, but if you were talented enough you could carve out a prosperous future. Finally there was his aunt. She gave him a choice—computer programming and software design or astrophysics. The "waves of the future."

Justin had no idea which career to choose. He often pondered the advice of his family and teachers, but it only confused him more. He knew well that the choice he made would determine what he would be doing every day of his life for about 40 years. He was comforted, however, by admitting something that his dad had been telling him for years. Despite possessing the knowledge gained from 13 years of school and the cumulative experience of 18 years of life, he admitted, "I'm really just a kid." It wasn't time yet to choose a career. He would go to college for a couple of years and develop his views on life before he worried about that.

His great American dream, therefore, had boiled down to one vague yet important goal: he wanted to be happy. Exactly what would bring happiness he didn't know, but Justin would search for it, he was sure. If he made a career decision and discovered that he was bored, he would not be afraid to change it. His mother had drilled into his head that there is nothing worse than being committed to something you don't like.

Justin also wanted to get married eventually. That, he felt, was the all-important key to a life of happiness. Having someone to share life and love with. Sharing—that's what life's all about. Kids were a part of this dream also. Justin wanted one day to experience the incomparable thrill of bringing new life into the world and the responsibility of raising children to contribute something to the world. It was an exciting dream.

Scooby Doo ended, and the lilting Looney Tunes theme of Bugs Bunny snapped Justin Adaise out of his daydream. He had no concrete American dream. He had only the vague personal dream of happiness and the complexities of life from which to shape his dream. But that was more than enough to satisfy him at age 18.

The world looked bright. Justin felt certain that he would find his dream somewhere, someday, somehow. As he went out to mow the lawn, he was smiling to himself for reasons that went beyond the Bugs Bunny cartoon.

My parents are very moral people, like me and their parents too. They were raised in lower middle class families, who had only the wish for them to carry on their family's businesses. My parents had higher goals. My mother went on to college and became a teacher while my father went to college and is presently a successful business-man.

They have always had high goals and usually achieved them. . . . I have always set high goals for myself, one of which is to

Discussions

What is the American dream?

Kelly: It's all based on materialistic needs and wants. But I think a lot of it has now gotten to the point where everybody wants to be able to do whatever they choose. People just want to do something that they can be happy with—instead of getting stuck in a nine to five job where they don't want to work.

Melanie: I guess traditionally what the American dream is supposed to be is to go to America and get rich.

be successful in having a family and career, in my future.

I believe parents try to instill some of their goals which they have achieved, but more importantly they instill in their children some of the goals which they have not achieved.

Erik Buzzard, 16
Corona del Mar, California

My goals are to be as happy and content as possible. Enlightenment, in Buddhist terms (as defined in the *Diamond Sutra*), is my highest goal. To be a famous avant garde artist is right below that. Also, to be able to play drums, bass, and bongo, falls real close behind.

Juliet Demeter, 16
Phoenix, Arizona

I have always loved the outdoors and would like to earn a living working there. I do a lot of hunting and fishing, and I have done it for a good while. I've been thinking about a job with the Game and Fresh Water Fish Commission. I would like to be a game warden or a forest ranger. . . .

I'm concerned about our forest lands and the animals that live there. I am also concerned about our lakes and their inhabitants. There is too much pollution being dumped into our waterways. . . . Crews are cutting and building roads where I hunt. They are also cutting trees out. They are destroying the places where turkeys roosted. I think something must be done, and I think maybe I can help.

Jay Smith, 15
Kissimmee, Florida

I have never heard of an American dream.

Julie Flokowitsch, 16
Nashville, Indiana

Peaceful production of ideas and materials that will improve the human condition is the most important part of the American dream. It has always been the achieving of the perfect, free society.

Caroline De Watt, 16
Medina, Ohio

In my eyes, the American dream is to see America beautiful again. I'd like to solve all of our nature's problems, such as sink holes. Maybe it's only a dream, but our wildlife is decreasing enormously every year. It hurts me to see polluted lakes and burnt down forests.

Beth Clemitus, 18
Bettendorf, Iowa

There's no American dream for me because nowadays it's kind of hard to see an American dream with

Manish: And that everyone has an equal chance to succeed, regardless of race, color, religion, sex, or anything. This is rather important to me because I'm a minority. But the extensive freedom allowed in America is what I consider to be the American dream. Anybody can make it.

Steve: To satisfy every single member of this society—to satisfy their own individual dream—must be the American dream.

Kelly: Yeah. Everybody does not have the same dream. But the American dream is to be able to build every dream you have. Not the dreams of those around you.

Steve: The utopia! I'd like a utopian world, I really would. It seems to me a utopia is a little world in which everybody is satisfied with the social structure. Now a utopia would be a society in which all the members were satisfied.

Jeff: But the needs and wants of people are so diversified.

unhappy people and no food, homes, or jobs. So my American dream will just have to wait for a few more years.

Joe Martin, 16
Bettendorf, Iowa

My goals are to own a 1957 Corvette, a convertible Mustang, a yacht, a six-level house, own a soccer team, travel around the world, and get rich quick. But I would also like to solve the hunger crisis over in Thailand and Africa, to save the needy, and steal from the rich. Then maybe I'll become well-known.

I figure that I won't get rich but will end up marrying some poor plumber and having about ten kids so that I fit in with the rest of the world (ha-ha). My goals changed considerably because now I am realizing that things just don't come as easy as you think that they do. Right now I'm just happy to get the things that I do get and will be happier if my dreams do come true.

Colleen Dale, 17
Huson, Montana

My personal goal is to some day be the person who announces the Superbowl over live television. It wouldn't have to necessarily be the Superbowl, just any major sport championship. I plan to achieve this goal by going to college, getting my masters degree in sports journalism and a bachelors degree in radio-television communications. Then I will work my way up that long ladder all the way to the top.

Michael Fay, 17
Polson, Montana

So often the American dream is stereotyped, and so often people lose track of why they are here. The American dream is useless. Perhaps the bums on the streets with no place to live have a dream. Perhaps they would like 2.5 children. . . . Why does society insist that we must have an idealized, stereotyped dream?

We are forgetting what life is really about—love, caring for other people. Who cares how many rooms a person has in their house? Who cares if they even have a house? Why is everything based on materialistic things? People are people. We are all on earth together. We all want to survive.

The American dream shouldn't be what a person has or can get or wants. The American dream should be uniting as one and loving your neighbor. And, of course, dreams are never achieved. The Communists tried, but it will never work because people will always want a dog named Spot and a five bedroom house when what they need is to love and be loved.

Erika Humes, 17
Seattle, Washington

My most important pursuit is learning to live. By this, I mean living in high style. It's not only the everyday generalities I want to acquaint myself with, but the champagne and diamonds of life. As in all my activities, this, the most important, is sheerly aesthetic. I can't yet enjoy all of the aspects of the high society I seek. I'm too young, and I haven't the money it requires. In the meantime, I'm taking steps to prepare myself for the life I want. . . .

Perhaps the words Cartier, Cap D'Antiber, and Dom Perignon aren't meaningful to others, but in my ears they all sound heavenly. By giving myself a head start, I hope to realize my dream of a successful life sparkling with panache.

Lisa Burton, 15
San Lorenzo, California

Exaggerated images of Hollywood stars and friendly Presidents typify the American dream today. Americans not only worship these quasi-gods but try to achieve their status themselves. The fact that the Protestant work ethic essentially founded this country and success and the current drive for success

Steve: But that does not necessarily mean that we should not strive for utopia. In fact, striving for a utopia might lead us to situations that are better than the situation we are in now.

Jeff: It seems like in a utopian society there's a mass of individuals just floating around in a liquid plasma cell. That's the first thing that comes to my mind because to be a utopia, you'd have to be isolated from people who don't understand you or who you don't get along with.

Steve: So you have to teach new things. Hopefully human beings will one day be capable of a utopia because they will be different than they are now.

Jeff: But some people don't want to do that. Every Saturday my grandma wants to go to the supermarket and pick up ten-cent unlabeled cans. She'll never want to change. People like that don't want to come around and change.

Steve: It's not going to be a quick process. I'm not trying to argue that utopia is possible, but I do, to a certain extent, dream of a time when we should have utopia. If we were all striving towards it, we'd have a better chance of reaching it.

Kelly: I have a similar dream, but I never applied the word utopia to it. I think the world could be a whole lot better and a whole lot closer in this utopia if everyone had the same religious beliefs in Christ.

Steve: But what you're suggesting is even less practical than my utopia and not necessarily desirable. You're talking not of utopia but mind control.

Kelly: I'm not saying I'd force these people to believe this way. I'm saying I wish everybody did. If everybody was compatible, everybody had tolerance, and nobody was trying to interfere with other people, wouldn't that be utopia?

proves this. Americans dream to be something they're not. . . .

But though the American dream might exist in the suburbs, I viewed the American dream at a farm in Oskaloosa, Iowa. . . . I was at a family reunion. This is America I said. I went outside through the misty farmland, past a field of cows and a small stream. Inside the farmhouse were people I never knew but who were related to me and who built this country. . . .

America is a 21-year-old boy sitting at a soda fountain in Vermont hoping someday, even though he dropped out of Georgetown his junior year, that he will be an executive at a Sixth Avenue ad agency in ten years.

Matt Schuerman, 14
Chicago, Illinois

One goal is to attend college and become either a reporter or a journalism teacher. I am quite undecided in between the two because of my hearing loss. . . .

Another goal is to be able to go out in the world on my own and communicate effectively with other people. I want to be able to do so because I know it is important. It would be like a victory to me if I accomplish this goal because of my deafness.

At the present, I am capable of talking with other people, but I have had setbacks because I couldn't understand a person or vice versa. It has been frustrating for me to try to live in a world designed for hearing people.

Brian Sluder, 17
Clatskanie, Oregon

The capitalistic idea behind the American idea must survive. It is a common belief that man is a greedy being, no matter how strongly he wishes that he was not greedy. The only way for a government to satisfy that greed is to allow the entire population the chance to grow more wealthy. . . .

The socialistic ideas brought

about by Democrats are endangering the American dream. Their programs finance the people who with their education belong in Panama making hats while the people who deserve the chance to become wealthy are taxed to the brink. Americans want their chance to own a Porsche and wear Izods and monogrammed sweaters so that they can flaunt them to their friends.

Without the American dream and that chance, they would all turn into mesmerized robots, as demonstrated by the Communists.

David Arvidson, 16
Castle Rock, Colorado

When I was young, I told people I wanted to be a neurosurgeon because coming from a five-year-old, that was a very impressive goal. Then, in fourth grade, my best friend and I wanted to be paramedics. However, we lost interest in that when we lost interest in the TV show "Emergency."

Then somewhere around sixth grade I resolved to become either a CIA agent or an attorney. The older I became, the more plausible the latter goal seemed. I was constantly told by people that I would make a good lawyer as I was a very argumentative and quite persuasive person. Law also intrigued me—and the idea of influencing people's opinions and decisions.

So now I'm going to go to Columbia University for four years and then possibly Harvard or Boalt Law School (Berkeley's law school) and finally set up shop in San Francisco among the thousands of other lawyers in California.

Heidi Kriz, 17
El Dorado Hills, California

To me, the American dream is no longer a dream, but an individual struggle to stay above water in a competitive society. Americans no longer work for the things they want their children to have. They

Steve: Yes, but they don't necessarily have to believe the same thing in order for that to be utopia.

Kelly: I'm just saying if everybody had the same things that were important to them.

Jeff: That's why your utopia seems kind of out of the question. Right away you could see that you two would be incompatible in a utopian society. She will not accept your viewpoint, and you will not accept hers.

Steve: But as far as society is concerned, we could create a society in which both of us could argue and walk away satisfied with the fact that we're different and

instead turn to welfare and financial aid for such things as college. "Keeping up with the Joneses" has become first priority to the majority of middle-class Americans. How sad.

Jacci Kyle, 18
Apache Junction, Arizona

To me, the American dream can be summed up in one word: success. However, this success does not necessarily mean succeeding at something you desire. It often means obtaining something which society demands you strive for.

If one took a random survey of Americans, they would probably say that success would in one way or another involve power—a power

Goals   243

over others—either by obtaining a high-ranking position or by obtaining money. Ironically, those who appear successful to the public probably are not actually happy. . . .

Those who obtain true success—by actually being happy and satisfied with what they achieved—are probably never recognized by the public as successes.

Dave Fischer, 18
Gahanna, Ohio

The American dream has always been perfection. Being just the best won't do. We're given an irrational ideal to follow. We must be successful in everything. Failure just doesn't exist. Be beautiful, be charming (no personality quirks)!

We all know we'll never match the standard. We just take sport in trying. A dangerous sport, true—but when what you really desire is freedom without responsibility, the world on a silver platter, and godhood, reality takes a back seat.

Karla Jackson, 16
Seattle, Washington

I see the American dream as being able to survive in this world without going crazy. There are so many stupid things going on that it's really very hard to dream of something good. It's even worse for us kids going to school. I mean, you go to school for eight hours out of the day and on top of that you have two hours of homework. . . . The whole day is screwed up.

that we disagree. I think that a society which is based upon a one-religion sense or believing in the same thing would not work because then I would feel that my opinions were pressed. I'm not saying there is no place for arguing in utopia. I actually enjoy arguing.

How are women's goals changing?

Kelly: The American dream used to be the husband supporting his wife and family. Now I think each person can do that for themselves. Just because you're a woman, you don't have to marry a rich husband so you don't have any financial worries.

Diane: I think the dream for men hasn't changed much, but definitely it has changed for women. We have options now that we never had before.

Steve: And women are much better now because of it. I'd much rather have a relationship with a woman who is confident in herself and intelligent rather than with some meek and weak nothing who wants me to make all her decisions.

Manish: I really don't care if my wife stays home and is barefoot,

My great American dream is growing up without getting in any more trouble, going into the air force, and getting a job as a jet engineer mechanic.

Randy Hedin, 15
Kissimmee, Florida

I want to be wealthy enough, crazy enough, and mad enough to wear bright green pants with dolphins scattered about on them.

Diana Walch, 17
Blooming Prairie, Minnesota

The American dream: the biggest farce in existence. Realistically, the so-called "land of opportunity" is only that for those who are in a position to take advantage of it.

Since my youth, I have been told by the establishment that I can be whatever I desire. They are right. I am one of the lucky ones, though. To most people, the "American dream" is exactly that, a dream.

The majority of the citizens of this country will never be more than their parents were. They hear about the "American dream," about the opportunity in this great country of ours, that anyone can be anything in this country, but

OLD AMERICAN DREAM

MODERN AMERICAN DREAM

very few people actually have that opportunity.

Johnny, who comes from a middle-class family in the suburbs, wastes his youth playing video games or smoking reefers and not going to school or doing his homework, but he has the chance. Honestly, does an impoverished inner-city youth have the same opportunity to be president (an oft used cliché) as Johnny? No, he does not. Do inner city public school systems match those in the suburbs? No, they do not.

An inner-city child may have to scrounge or steal to get three meals a day. Try to tell him about the "American dream" and the "land of opportunity." If he doesn't spit in your face, he should.

Talk to a farmer in Appalachia. His children work in the fields so they can eat—survival before education, understandably. Do they have the same opportunity as Johnny? To them, the "American dream" is probably indoor plumbing.

The "American dream" gives every middle-class American something to look forward to. However, there is no "American dream" for so many people who are just fighting to survive. Naturally, a few people rise from the lower classes, but they are the exception rather than the rule....

pregnant, and in the kitchen or if she's a career woman and works daily. However, I wouldn't want us each to work ten hours a day so we would only see each other at breakfast. That's not the sort of family situation I have in mind. But she does not necessarily have to remain at home all the time.

Matt: If I marry someone who is a career woman, that's no problem. But I think it's important that you have children and that the woman stays at home. My dad works, but my mom doesn't work. She was always home when I came home from school. I just hope I can make enough so my wife doesn't have to work.

What do teenagers want from life?

Matt: A dream to me is so unrealistic—so far out of reach—that the only thing you can do is dream about it. To be a billionaire at 22—that would be a great dream. I set goals for myself, but I really don't dream. I think it's kind of a waste of time.

Melanie: One of my dreams is to have a career. But I think my main dream is to have a happy family. That's very vague, but it seems nowadays it's so hard to just have a faithful spouse and a family where you get along.

Jeff: I want to have a condominium on the north side of the lakefront. I

In our current society, the "American dream" is a propaganda device used to portray the United States as a place where anyone can be as successful as they wish; I cannot describe it. The "American dream" is an absurdity!

Mark K. Lewis, 17
Rockville, Maryland

In my life, I hope to accomplish many important things. I want to finish high school, go to college, hopefully an Ivy League school like Princeton, and become a business major. I would also like to get my law degree and become a divorce lawyer with a well-known firm in Chicago.

I want to start a foundation in my name to help people who have never had many of the things that I have enjoyed. My foundation would help little children with diseases or people who live in the streets and eat their meals out of the garbage.

Other goals I would like to achieve are marrying someone from a prominent family in New Jersey and name a foundation after her. This foundation would be for the arts, like music, paintings, theater, and authors. I think it is important for people to have culture.

I also want to have many children and provide them with a lifestyle that I am accustomed to. I

JENNIFER KOLINSKI

Goals

I want to become a truck driver, don't matter what get in my way. Right now truckers are having a tough and rough time to pay for there rigs. Also, those stinking politicians in Washington thinking

also hope to control a major corporation and become a business tycoon like Andrew Carnegie or become a real estate magnate like Arthur Rubloff.
Mike Kelly, 15
Elmhurst, Illinois

Today the American dream has changed. People today don't dream of building a nation. They dream of building condominiums and the money they will make. To a teenager, success is being retired by 40 and having nothing better to do than lie around a pool or speed along in a Porsche.

Perhaps we need a cause to give us back the dream of our forefathers. If we forget the American

want to have a lot of modern furniture in it, a lot of blue and a lot of chrome. One of those couches that can be a bed or a couch. And a huge stereo in a chrome and glass case and a lot of lights that you can adjust. I'd live there by myself for a while until I got really settled in my career. I want to be a geologist,

they can do any damn thing they would to do. I known one thing—they better stay the hell out of my way.

I known they (truckers) want to stay on the right side of the law. But if I'm going to becomes a truck driver, especially because I'm a young Lady, I going to do it any way I can even if I have to break the damn law to do it. In the first place the Law ain't no good in some places, cause there are no good polices out there think they can do anything they please to stop trucker.

If they get in my way, I mean what I say "they better keep the hell out of my path."

16-year-old female
South Carolina

I'm not sure what the actual American dream is so I can only tell my personal goals. I'm in a transition stage. I'm beginning to break away from my parents and their impositions.

It has been their dream that I will become a professional musician since I've played the flute for nine years. However, I have come to my senses. The profession of a musician calls for dedication, love, and a lot of talent. I don't think I have these qualities when it comes to the flute.

My short term goal is to go to college. I think college is necessary in today's society because of the competition in the job market. I also want to go to college so I can have intelligent conversation with other people.

After college I want to get married. My fiancé, a 23-year-old college graduate, lives in California. I'd like to make my life there with him. My long term goal is to live in California with him and our children. I know we can be happy.

Jennifer Griffin, 17
Littleton, Colorado

America should be a land where poverty is long forgotten, where the air is clear and the streets are clean, where justice strides forth swiftly yet quietly. Where there was once violence, let there be peace. Though we would be silent, let us be strong. Such words as disease, sorrow, and pain would be erased. Our once most despised enemy would be our most trusted com-

probably one who travels a lot and makes a lot of money. I want to have good health, and I want to drive a small, expensive foreign sports car.

Diane: My dream is just to have a nice condo, a nice car, and a nice guy for the car. I'm out for myself. I'm a me person. I want what's going to make me happy, not what's going to make the whole society happy.

I suppose material wealth is really what I want. I want to have friends too—I don't want to do it all by myself. I don't necessarily want to get married, but I want to have friends I can enjoy it with. And I want to have a job that I can be happy with. I won't keep a job just because it pays well.

Jeff: Another dream I have is to have no pollution. The current administration is allowing more and more industrial pollution to be produced, and it's killing a lot of wildlife.

It's only going to affect us in the long run. It just doesn't go away after it's put in the air. It takes a long time to break down into its natural form. Right now pollution is being built up. And when we have too much of a buildup it's going to affect us.

When factories pollute the lakes, they kill and disease thousands of fish. Eventually people are going to get this disease because they are part of the food chain. So it's really going to affect our future.

Melanie: My goal is to study music therapy in college. By using music, you can help disturbed children to learn and to cope with their emotions.

Manish: It seems like people want a set life for the future. I'm like, who cares? Whatever happens, happens. I don't really plan things. But I'm always hoping that I'll be a drug smuggler, bringing heroin into the country, or maybe an FBI agent. Maybe I'll be another

panion. Russia would be united with us, and together our technology would overcome the troubles we face today. Nuclear warfare would be a thing of the past. Extremely complicated space crafts would venture deep into the unknown of space producing knowledge incapable to grasp at our present date.

David Cullison, 15
Apache Junction, Arizona

The American dream is different in each part of the country. When I lived in Oklahoma, everybody wanted to get married and have a family. Florida is a lot different. The people here want to live a good life.

Steven Deese, 17
Kissimmee, Florida

My most important goal is to be a business success in architectural/environmental design and to own a conglomerate and to be a free-wheeling capitalist. Art and design are very important and have been as long as I can remember. . . . I have always known what I have wanted to do with my life.

Though my goals changed, or should I say evolved, they have always been design/art oriented....

If I look in a store window and see some terrific clothes, my mind starts spinning and is full of ideas just from having seen something. Then another time—maybe a few minutes, hours, or even weeks later—I might see a building or house and the ideas start flowing again, but this time my head is filled with idealistically-designed towns, villages, or whole cities, based on a total design concept.

I realize I must work in a large metropolitan area but have lived my life in western Montana. Getting accustomed to a large city is very difficult for me, but I know I must make a choice.

Kurt Cyr, 18
Frenchtown, Montana

I wish to become the best Olympic miler ever. In the year 1988, I wish to make the United States Olympic team, winning the gold medal in the mile and breaking the world record. Also in 1992, again I wish to make the Olympic team and to win the gold medal again. This is probably the dream of most runners. To make this dream come true, you ... have to want it and I want it.

Jeff Croteau, 15
Castle Rock, Colorado

Gandhi, you never know. I'm hoping it will be something unusual, but nothing I could put my finger on and say, "It will be this or that." But it's going to be something new and exciting.

Michelle: I plan to get out of the house as soon as I can. I'm trying to save up money now. But I think my goal is just to be happy—and find someone I can be happy with.

Kelly: My goal is to have financial security by doing something I want to do. I want to have my own veterinary medicine practice out in

the country somewhere. Living out in the country would be more enjoyable.

Steve: I would like to have financial security, but my main concern is to have a group of friends who like me and respect me and consider me an equal. If I have that and at least an adequate financial security so I don't have to worry where my next beer is going to come from, that's all I need.

How important is family life?

Matt: Well, right now my future goals are to graduate from college. And then to go on in life, get married, have two kids and a dog. Having a family is really important, but I want to be able to support a family. Since I don't know what career I'm striving for now, it's kind of scary. What would happen if I screw up and don't make it? Especially if I already have a family?

Diane: If I get married, I would still want to be a career person and hope my husband would be a career person too. We wouldn't just come home at five and not be able to talk about things. Maybe our jobs will be related in some way.

Manish: When I was younger, I always dreamed of myself being the permanent bachelor, living it up. But as I get older, I'm sort of going toward the stereotype family— having a wife, a dog, a white picket fence, and two kids.

What is success?

Manish: I will be successful when my parents think I'm successful— when they view me as somebody worthwhile or somebody who has done something. I think I'm trying to basically please my parents at this point.

Of course, I also want to do it for myself because I see how successful people live and I see how pleasurable their lives can be as opposed to somebody who is

less successful. I do have a little of my own personal incentive, but most of it does come from my parents' wanting me to be successful.

Michelle: Success is finding out what you want to do, getting there, and being happy with it. My mom wanted to be a nurse at a children's hospital. Every year now she goes to school for something different. My mom's going to be 40 years old soon. It doesn't seem like she's very happy about what she's doing. I mean she's not really upset about it, but I think she'd like to be doing something else.

Diane: When I was a freshman, I felt that my parents were pressuring me to go to college and do well and become an engineer or something. But then, in my junior and senior years, I found that my parents weren't putting that pressure on me. As soon as I realized that, the pressure went away.

Jeff: There's bound to be some pressure, and pressure's good for you. It gets your heart stimulated a little faster. It makes you think.

Steve: You should apply pressure to yourself. It's called self-discipline.

Kelly: I know what you mean by pressure because I used to feel a lot of pressure from my mom. She wanted me to lead my life differently from her so she drew a straight line.

Diane: My parents are pressuring me to have fun when I start college. Right now I can't stay up past 11. Then they say to me, "Diane, when you go to college, go out, stay out all night, have fun, go to parties if you want." Every time I turn around my parents say, "Don't let the work get you down, have fun." And that's all I hear now. I used to feel so much pressure to do my homework.

Michelle: The only pressure my

parents put on me is to keep my grades C or better and to quit spending my money as much as I spend it.

Kelly: Well, I feel pressure to make money because that's something I have to do for college. But I don't feel it from my mother.

Steve: So for each goal you have, you're going to have to apply pressure to yourself.

Compiled by Tracy Wykert

Chapter 19.

The Future

The future. It's what everyone tells me to plan for. How can I plan for something I don't know anything about? What will my future be? I may not even have one, considering the clown princes of society, the politicians, who guide our world. In my future, I hope the leaders will be qualified—for a change. Since the best a two-party system can offer is a choice of suffering, unemployment, and war or suffering, unemployment, and war, then maybe we need a change.

Italy has dozens of parties that splinter the government so much that nothing is ever decided except to form a new government every year. The Soviet Union has only one party, which makes insensitive and often incorrect decisions. An oligarchy would be nice, but it could be difficult to pick the perfect oligarchs. Dictatorship? No. Germany ran that idea into the ground. Let's just increase the number of parties slightly—maybe five parties instead of two. Then there would be good, healthy political diversity, but not too much. After all, voters would still be able to keep track of the parties by using the fingers on one hand.

Of course, there's always the threat of Communism. Those damn Russkies, always trying to shove their religion down other people's throats. Even worse, though—what if Communism and Reaganomics are combined? Ronmunism? Oh no! I think I'm going to vote Libertarian.

My vote, however, is going to mean less and less. The world population keeps exploding. Whatever happened to birth control? I guess it's easy to forget about it, however, if you're living in a country where you can fall asleep to the pitter-patter of acid rain on the roof and can wake to the soft "clip-clip" of a rifle outside your door.

Those reasons notwithstanding, the ever-multiplying world population is a problem. Sometimes it makes me feel useless, as if I'm just one four-billionth of the world and there's three billion nine hundred ninety-nine million nine hundred ninety-nine thousand nine hundred ninety-nine other lives out there. Rather than look at statistics, though, I prefer to look in the mirror. I see an intelligent, concerned, college-bound teenager. I have an important future. Who needs self-pity?

World hunger, though, does arouse pity—and is on my mind. I must admit that the prospect of not pursuing my favorite pastime, eating, is a bit frightening. We denizens of the United States will most likely have plenty of Fritos and Oscar Meyer wieners for decades to come. The real problems are in India, Bangladesh, Kenya, Chad, Nicaragua, Ecuador, and other countries where malnutrition is more popular than aerobic dancing.

Scientists are experimenting with hydroponic gardening and with harvesting kelp from the deep seas. How far in the future is that solution? The world needs solutions that are viable soon. Perhaps sloths, capybaras, and other heretofore overlooked South American jungle animals could supplement the world's food supply.

Even better, we could replace a useless tradition, the flower garden, with gardens that contribute something to the future of our world. Instead of roses, begonias, violets, and peonies, everyone should plant wheat, oats, barley, or rice. By the year 2000, our loved ones will be tired of getting flowers anyway. On Mother's Day just tell mom you love her and give her a kiss. Then send a sheaf of wheat to Bangladesh. FTD Teleflorist could become Telenutrition. You'll have that special feeling inside; mom won't have a bunch of wilting flowers in her hands; and a few more kids in India will live to see another day.

On to a population explosion of a different sort—nuclear war. We've already got enough warheads to roast humanity. I may have been a C student in algebra, but I don't see how increasing nuclear weapons is decreasing the threat of nuclear war. In my future, perhaps the politicians may remove the masks of ignorance they proudly wear. Or *are* they just masks?

Our lakes, rivers, and air are now dirtier than my sweat socks after a ten-mile run. Industry is a million-armed octopus embracing every vein of our ecosystem and slowly squeezing the life out of it. It is invulnerable to organizations that can make no more than a pinprick in industry's hide without the heavy artillery of Congress behind them.

However, I can see the Congressional point of view. Despite the reality of our lakes and trees and air turning brown and gray, everything gets greener and greener in the Congressmen's pockets. If pollution cannot be stopped, then I've got a swell idea. Use a special chemical to pollute the world that will color the trees, lakes, and rivers red, white, and blue as they die. As least we would never cease being patriotic.

Patriotism will probably become a statistic in the computers of the future. They are becoming so intelligent that soon they'll know whether the avid fan actually sang the National Anthem at the baseball game or just put the dutiful hand over the heart. The government will have computerized data on everything. They'll know Jim Palmer's underwear size and how many gold fillings Dolly Parton has in her teeth.

Outer space will become increasingly important. Earthlings will begin to colonize the planets. Mercury could be the Jamaica of the future, the new hot spot to get a tan. Pluto could be a place to escape humanity and get away from it all. And, of course, Jupiter and Saturn could be the most popular, the Hawaii and Europe of the future.

Hopefully, medicine will also take giant strides. Science will somehow enable people to live forever. Would anyone really want to live forever, though? I would only want to if I could be 27 years old forever.

A better idea would be artificial limbs and organs that would extend the lifespan of human beings and make them stronger. That would be great. The Chicago Cubs could be refitted with bionic arms and legs and finally win the pennant. But, no, it could never happen. The Dodgers, Cardinals, and Phillies would simply buy stronger bionic limbs and keep winning. Oh well, the future can't be perfect.

Wait a minute. I've got six years of school and 45,000 dollars in costs ahead of me. After that, I have to begin the eternal task of "making a living." What a future. I think I'll use the computer technology to erase my name from the income tax files and to transfer a few million dollars of the nuclear weaponry budget to my wallet. Then I'll hop the interplanetary transport to one of the moons of Neptune with a few other intelligent, sensitive geniuses like myself and begin a new society. It's worth a try. And I promise—no politicians!

One of my fears . . . is World War III. The world conditions for the future will involve the state of a push-button era. Today two men can push a button and destroy two continents, probably culminating in the total extinction of mankind.

Leo Mendez, 18
Lubbock, Texas

So much money is being invested in weapons that it's interfering with budgets for education and job programs. . . . I just wish more dedication and money would start going towards preserving peace and educating the nation's young to do the same. . . . We already have the necessary defense to react if attempts at peace fail.

Traci Wright, 17
Albuquerque, New Mexico

The only fear I have is that computers will take over. I'm afraid that humans won't have a chance to use their imagination any more because computers will become their brain. Besides, I know I'll have a challenging enough time competing with other people for a job. I

Discussions

Steve: Running out of beer hops is a major ecological concern.

Diane: Pollution, too.

Steve: And the ozone layer.

Diane: There's going to be a certain point where we run out of natural fuels.

Steve: We won't run out of natural fuels. We'll run out of the fuels we're geared up to use. As far as pollution, I think they should increase the amount of money they file into the space program so that they can get rid of nuclear waste by sending it into space.

Diane: I think it's a horrible notion—that mankind has caused the extinction of so many.

Steve: Rubbish. I don't think we should go out of our way to make species extinct. But humankind is not the only species that has caused other species to become extinct. It's survival of the fittest. I think that many species died out because they couldn't deal with the world as it is and that other races will continue.

hope computers won't become another obstacle. They have already taken jobs away from people nowadays, and I'm afraid that when I get older computers will take up more jobs.

Jamika Catherine, 15
Kirkwood, Missouri

One of my fears for the future has to do with the wasting of our precious natural resources. What is going to happen when we run out of water? Technology may develop ways to provide us with energy, food, and other new innovations, but are scientists going to be able to develop artificial fresh water?

Rick Sampson, 16
Brooklyn Park, Minnesota

I'm afraid of college, trying to start a family, and keeping a family together. The way divorce rates are now, everytime I hear of someone getting married I immediately think, "It won't last more than a few years." I feel bad about this feeling, but it is a very real thing to me.

Crystal Dombroski, 17
Hillsdale, Michigan

We have started to care about our country more. We are dealing with crime and vandalism in our own neighborhoods by sponsoring neighborhood watch programs. America is becoming a better place to live. I am proud to be a part of this society, and I am looking forward to the future.

Laura Burke, 18
Fairfax, Virginia

My fears of the future are many. My biggest fear is money. Our government lends so much money to other countries that we ourselves could use. We could use money to help our poverty, to research disease, and to develop our technology. Instead, we give money to other countries. Then our taxes are raised because we won't have enough money to keep up with ourselves. I fear that we ourselves

How would teenagers like to improve the world?

Steve: Certainly I would help. I would not put my time into the Peace Corps even though I admire what they do. However, if I was a trained engineer and the government said they were building a plant in a certain area— it's going to be a rough job—we want to hire area people and educate them. I would say certainly. I'd go over there and do my best. I'd be rather honored. It would be a very worthwhile job, and I'd get a lot more out of it than if I was doing it in the United States. As far as giving out medicine and dishing out rice to the natives, no, I wouldn't do that.

Kelly: I have a lot of interest in the agricultural development of this

will become a poverty-stricken nation.

My hope for the future is that we could become allies with Russia. It would be such a relief if this really happened. We would be able to trade equally instead of seeing who can outdo the other.

Lisa Bachman, 17
Eureka, Illinois

My one fear concerning the future is nuclear war. I can work around all my other fears, such as an unsatisfactory job or bad marriage, but I have no control over this fear. I am not in constant fear . . . but it is always in the back of my mind, sitting, waiting to be remembered.

Steve Bresnahan, 16
Newton, Massachusetts

My biggest hope is of the eternal salvation that Christ promised me when I accepted Him as Lord of my life. No matter what happens in my life, I can deal with it because I have that hope for a beautiful eternal life with God.

Heather Nuchols, 15
Oak Ridge, Tennessee

My greatest fear . . . is of marriage. It looks and sounds so easy and wonderful in books and on TV, but when I see the marriages around me, it seems so confusing. I don't know if I can commit myself to someone. I don't know if I can put my full trust in somebody for a lifetime.

My marriage would have to last forever. I couldn't get a divorce. I've seen firsthand what a divorce does to a person. I couldn't do that to anyone.

Having my own children also scares me. I think it would be great to have kids, to guide and mold them, but one wrong move and a child could have some sort of problem for the rest of their life.

Karma Metzler, 16
Boise, Idaho

My hopes for the future are great ones, for the youth of today are a group of ambitious individuals with great creativity and intelligence. Top-quality educations are being offered more frequently due to greater financial aid. This knowledge will only bring success from the strengths of the students today, who are building the future of tomorrow.

Wendy Hulme, 18
Brookfield, Connecticut

My greatest fear is the possibility of living in an apathetic and stagnant world, without new ideas or contributions which might change our way of life for the better.

Scott Shadrick, 19
San Lorenzo, California

I believe there are three major problems of the future facing us. No. 1 is our country sticking its nose where it doesn't belong. Right now problems in El Salvador are cropping up so what does Presi-

country and others. I could see, having learned something in that field, going out in the Peace Corps and helping people develop ways to raise their own food.

Manish: Steve, would you still continue with your offer of building the plant, even with having no incentive of getting paid?

Steve: Certainly not, I would definitely want to be paid. I think we as a society have to approach this problem. We have to direct certain energies. Now if somebody said, "We're going to raise your taxes to help out the economy of Brazil," I'd say go for it, and that's what counts.

Manish: I would be willing to help in the financial matter to a certain extent. But when it comes to my time or me having to suffer, physically, one on one, I would be reluctant to because I'm selfish. I think if we do it wisely we're not going to have to sacrifice that much in order to help build the economies of these other countries.

Diane: I would not mind going into a country to help build a plant as long as I get paid as much as I would here or more. But if I was going to take a cut in salary to go over there, I wouldn't. I guess I'm selfish, too.

Manish: We'll go to a certain extent as long as there's a limit.

Diane: I don't know if I'm pessimistic. All the stuff you've said is admirable, Steve and Kelly, but I think both of you are a bit impractical. It seems like we're placing everything on the U.S. We cannot help the whole world or even half the world.

Steve: We, as a leading country, a prospering country, benefit if any other country is prospering. It's good for us.

What should be our nation's role?

Steve: It seems to me the United States does not concern itself in the right areas as far as dealing with

dent Reagan do? He sends troops and ships to keep peace. It's not going to work. Look how the Vietnam war started! I also believe that giving money to hurting countries has to be stopped. . . .

No. 2 is Social Security vs. welfare. How long is a person going to have to work before it's safe to retire with enough money coming from Social Security to live on. I know people that make just as much or even more money on welfare than people that have jobs. Cut welfare! Give people that think they can make it through life on welfare a shovel and a job, and let them dig ditches and earn their money!

No. 3 is capital punishment needs to be reinstated. Eye for an eye, life for a life! Instead of wasting our hard-earned tax money and food for prisoners, invest our money in electricity, rope, gas and bullets. It would solve prison overpopulation!

Scott Olson, 17
Osseo, Minnesota

One of my biggest fears is that I'll never find myself. . . . I know who I am from the outside, but I'm confused about what I really believe or feel about things. I hope that I'll find a job that will make me happy and satisfied with myself. . . .

I know that many kids worry about the U.S. and Russia going to war. Well, that's something that I can't do anything about so I don't worry about it. If that's God's will, what can we do?

Debbie Dowdall, 17
Independence, Missouri

My hopes for the future are mainly concerning my child. . . . I want her to be able to grow up in a society that is peaceful and always improving. I want her to be able to have a family that can live in the same world she did.

My fears of the future are that people are not going to have enough money to survive. We're careless people. We don't think about the generation that will be following us and how we want them to live.

Shelley Rudnik, 17
Winona, Minnesota

My hopes for the future are for me and my family to be happy. Now I have a baby to take care of, and I want to make things as easy for her as I can. . . . When I look at the future, there are many fears. I wonder if things will actually work out the way I want them to. Many times I wonder if I'll be able to raise my baby right. When I see teenagers who have messed up their lives with drugs and stuff, I just pray that my baby doesn't make those mistakes when she grows up.

Colleen Moore, 18
McMinnville, Oregon

I am afraid that a lot of problems may occur in the future, especially overpopulation. By the year 2000, I doubt that very many people will have lawns left to mow. With all the new housing additions being built, soon there will no longer be any farmlands left. As a result, more and more of our vegetables will be hot-house grown. . . . I would certainly hate to think that I have to eat hot-house grown vegetables for the rest of my life.

Julie Flokowitsch, 16
Nashville, Indiana

certain world socioeconomic problems. Once a country gets to the point where its people are literally starving to death by the thousands and thousands, those people are going to get so desperate, they're going to say, "Well, we're either going to die of starvation or we're going to start getting some of the action," and they are literally going to start marching north.

The United States is going to have a very large problem on its hands. When the Latin American countries get to such an extreme point, where they have absolutely nothing to lose because they are doomed to die anyway, they will risk death in a vague hope that if they were to go to the United States they would find something. The United States will have a very serious problem because you can't just shoot people who are starving. You can't scare that kind of person.

If the United States and other rich countries don't face up to the fact that they have to be concerned about the well-being of others and that it is to their advantage for other people to be well off, they're going to be in serious trouble. It bothers me when I meet people who think the United States will be richer if other nations are poorer. It's the reverse. We have to have a realistic concern and not take the attitude

that we'll just throw them money and pretend that they don't exist.

I seriously believe that most of the aid money goes to waste. You're feeding that kid for today. Then tomorrow you have to find another buck.

Kelly: If he's dead, you can't educate him to run his country.

Steve: But what we should be concerned with is putting the money into education. Don't waste the money on food. If a couple of kids die now, big deal. Put the money directly into education because more lives are going to be saved in that way than if you just postpone initiating a plan.

Kelly: Who are you going to educate? These people are dying because you won't feed them. I also think it's very important to have self-sufficient countries, but you have to have healthy people to teach.

Steve: We're not dealing with a romantic wonderworld. We are an economic power, but we're not gods. We cannot save them all. We cannot actually save them. We can only teach them to save themselves.

Kelly: You're right in that respect, but I think it's very cruel of you to say, "Let these few die so others can grow up."

Steve: Cruel but practical and realistic. That's what it takes.

Kelly: You have the attitude that this is what needs to be done and that this is how far I'm going to help, but it's not my problem.

Steve: Oh, it is my problem. I seriously consider it my problem.

Kelly: But when they asked you who are you going to feed and not feed, you said, "Oh, I don't have to decide."

Steve: I don't.

Kelly: Sure, but where does your responsibility begin and end?

Steve: Why don't you talk to your God about that? I don't know. I

DIG THAT BEAT
LOVE THAT MUSIC JF

don't know why this situation is
around in the first place. We have
to deal with it in realistic terms.

Diane: I think the people
themselves are going to decide. It's
going to come down to survival of
the fittest. Some people will be
able to hack it in the educational
system and others won't. Then it
will become survival of the fittest,
and I mean in both the physical and
the mental aspects.

How will computers change the world?

Leslie: I think computers are
making us boring because we kind
of don't have a choice. Computers
are taking over manual jobs. But
then they're also taking over other
jobs. You put your stuff in a
computer, and you have it done.
You don't have to think about it.
You just put the damn stuff in the
damn computers—it makes me
mad.

Steve: The computer's not doing
any thinking—

Matt: You become a boring person
who sits there and punches
buttons.

Diane: Somebody had to think.

Leslie: I think it's dumb.
Computers are taking over too
much. They're taking away from
people.

Diane: I think the video games
may help. I mean, I think our
society is going more and more to

computers. If a kid is raised with
video games, they might end up
helping teenagers when they
become adults because chances are
they may be going into some
computer field. If they were raised
on Barbie and Ken, they may have
no interest in it at all. If they were
raised on video games—

The nation is improving very little because the government is using the money more for defense (military). That's important, but I think they should use it for society more.

Joe Martin, 16
Bettendorf, Iowa

My hopes for the future is a secure and good marriage with my fiancé. I want us to have a home and provide for our family, but I do not want riches. Money is the root of all evil. As long as I have a happy family, I will not hope for more.

Cheryl Denise Browder, 18
Winston-Salem, North Carolina

Our world is constantly changing, both internally and externally. No one really knows what the future has in store for us, but everyone has his/her own opinion about it. Three fears that I have concerning the future are the possibility of world war, the possibility of major industrial poisoning, and the possibility of our world being run by machines.

My first fear is world war. The world today is full of many conflicts. I am afraid that all the tension that has built up will spark off in a war. A war would probably end all life as we know it because we have developed extremely powerful weapons which can destroy our environment. My fears are for the millions of children of the future. If we were to have a war, they would not have the chance to live.

My second fear is major industrial poisoning. Industrial contamination exists today. I am afraid that in the future, as corporations grow, they will be careless with their industrial wastes. So far the contaminants that have come out of factories have caused illness, birth defects, acid rain, etc. These contaminants, I'm afraid, will become more volatile in the future. I am worried about the many lives that may be harmed.

My third fear is the possibility of the world being run by machinery.

In the past few years we have developed machines to do almost anything. I'm afraid that we may become too dependent on machines in the future. Some day we may not have to go outside our homes to go to school or to go shopping. I'm afraid that this will end the "mixing" of people. I believe that people need others to be around them to stay sane.

Linda Tanaka, 15
Sunnyvale, California

Matt: That's not gonna help you much in the future world.

Diane: They pick up strategy. When you go into your data processing course and they say, "Okay, we're going to make a logic chart," the kid says, "I understand this. It's just like the strategy behind a video game." I know a lot of kids in my data processing course who are into video games. A lot of the stuff comes very easy to them.

Steve: Say you have a trigonometry problem. If you don't have a computer, you will go home and spend three hours doing it. Now you can go home, use your computer and spend 30 minutes doing it. Then you crack open a beer and go talk to your dad about morals. [Everybody laughs]

Leslie: They do have some advantages, but they take away things, too.

Diane: I think they do have disadvantages, but we're being forced into a society where we have to learn about computers. We started it up, and it started going. We depend upon it more and more.

What concerns face this generation?

Manish: I've thought of all these past empires. There's been a Byzantine empire, a Roman empire; then the sun never set on the British empire. And now in America, there's no way any other country's lifestyle is better than America. All the past empires have fallen, gone downhill. I'm worried. Is that going to happen to America? And if it is, will it happen in my generation? Will I have to worry about it? I hope America will be better as long as I'm living.

Steve (smiling): I'm going to fiddle while New York burns.

Manish: I'm just hoping that everything will happen after I die.

Jeff: I think our economy is pretty sad. We have to give the Japanese a humungous tariff.

Manish: Are you like the people who say "America, love it or leave it"?

Jeff: No, not at all. Are we gonna sit on our butts and let them ruin our economy?

Steve: I think redistribution of wealth is probably the greatest concern that man has. I'm not necessarily a socialist, but I believe there has to be a redistribution of wealth in order for the world to run in a harmonious way. You get fewer rich people and more middle class, and society gets better. The United States' major concerns should be education of the people of the world and the redistribution of wealth. I think our goal should be the uniting of the world.

Melanie: People say we have to study the past in order to prevent problems in the future. For example, if we were to study computer crime and how it has been used, in the future maybe computer crime wouldn't be possible. It may sound idealistic, but it's just an example.

Matt (jokingly): I think the major problem facing our generation is drugs. We can solve it by killing all the burnouts. How can people waste away like that? To be honest, I don't think the world will be that much different. The only thing I think will really change is computers getting bigger. Robotics is going to move in. People are going to lose a lot of jobs.

What is the role of today's teenager in tomorrow's society?

Manish: I'd like to sum up my feelings. Then you can all yell at me if you like. Yes, I am Mr. Nonchalant. I do not want to get involved. I don't give a damn. But if it comes to my backyard, if they come knocking on my back door, then I have no choice but to get involved. But till that extreme, I will do nothing. At least I think I'll do nothing until I'm forced into the corner.

Kelly: In that respect, in what you just said, do you see yourself as an apathetic person?

Manish: What do you think?

Kelly: Yes. The apathetic person is the one who does not influence the future. Maybe nobody's going to come pressure you. That's where apathy affects the future.

Steve: It's in your best interest, even if you don't realize it, to use the democratic system in the way it was set up to be used. You should do it.

Kelly: Jeff says because there are so many things to be worried about you don't have time to worry about them. They can't concern you because there's so many of them. But then you guys have to figure if you're not worried about it, who is?

Jeff: But society is changing every minute anyway.

Kelly: But if you don't like something, you're the one who has to change it. And you have to know about it before you can change it. You have to care about it before you can change it.

Jeff: Do you know what kind of job is going to be on your shoulders? You're gonna just break down.

Kelly: No, because I can try and do my bit.

Steve: I'd like to make two points. The first is that your attitude is denying reality.

Jeff: Thank you.

Steve: Are you suggesting making enough money in order to survive or dealing with situations necessary to survive is too complex and we must give up?

Jeff: I'm saying that's what society is doing.

Steve: The other point I'd like to make is that a stitch in time saves nine. If we wait until stuff is being dumped in our backyards, all this nuclear stuff, that's a little bit too late to become non-apathetic. We've got to do something about it before it gets dumped in our backyards. We cannot afford to wait until we're stimulated by this negative thing. We should do something right now.

Jeff: But the point is we're not gonna—

Steve: That's not true. As the world goes on, as education becomes better, as the population becomes more intelligent, more capable, we will deal with more and more.

Jeff: The point is the population is not becoming more intelligent or less intelligent.

Steve: Then you and I and all the people sitting around here should change the situation.

Compiled by Eric Kammerer

The Future

Chapter 20.

The Next Generation

Roll opening credits.   Fade in.

At first, nothing is seen. Sound only. A voice from the past calls out, "Hello Central? Give me Elm-six-oh-four. . . ." This voice dies out and the click-clack of a rotary dial phone cuts in. The click-clacks die out as the beeps of a Touchtone phone emerge. Fade in on Television monitor. Cursor blinks at the top left of screen. Woman's voice calls out, "Ring my brother, please." The words appear on the screen as the woman speaks. Another voice answers, "Acknowledged." Two beat pause. "Ringing." Woman calls out again. "Put me on the living room camera. And put his image on the living room screen."

Once again the other voice acknowledges.

CUT TO: Shot of living room wall. Wallpaper patterns fade and are replaced by a head and shoulders shot of a man who looks to be middle-aged and in good health. He is the woman's brother.

Brother: Hello. Is that you, sis?

Sis: Yes, of course it is. Now will you back up or something? I don't want to see every one of your pores magnified ten times on my wall screen.

Brother: Oh, sorry. I keep on forgetting that you have a wall screen.

Camera pulls back. Brother lounges on a form-fitted recliner that hovers two feet off the ground.

Brother: Hey, are you still smoking? Don't you know that the Surgeon General just said that THC is hazardous to your health?

Sis: Sorry, I don't spend money to get lectures—remember?

CUT TO: Shot of Sis sitting on a barstool. Continue to cut back and forth between Brother and Sis as they speak.

Brother: So how have things been going?

Sis: Fine. How are the kids?

Brother: Is it my imagination, or are teens mutating into a new life-form? Sometimes my kids don't even seem human. They wear clothes that would make the punk rockers of our day look conservative. I only let them wear what they want because I always hated being restricted. Remember Dad's dress code?

Sis: Do I ever! It didn't really affect you because guys could wear anything as long as they didn't look like fags. I tried to follow the styles, but they always violated the dress code.

Slow dissolve into Flashback No. 1:

Open with exterior shot of two-story suburban home.
CUT TO: Interior shot—kitchen of two-story. Dad shovels in eggs while reading news-paper. A teenage version of the Brother munches Coco Puffs.
CUT TO: Kitchen doorway. A teenage version of the Sis runs by.

> **Sis:** Bye! I'm late for the bus. Gotta go!

Sound of door opening. Dad looks up.

> **Dad:** You've got ten minutes till the bus comes. What's the rush? Come over here and have some breakfast.
>
> **Sis:** [Not seen] Uh, no, that's fine, Dad. I'll grab a doughnut at school. Well, bye again.
>
> **Dad:** Hold it. Sit down, and get some nutritious food into you.

Brother tries to hide his grin in the Coco Puffs.
Sound of heels on tile. Sis appears dressed in a tube top and short shorts. Confronts Dad.

> **Sis:** Well, what's for breakfast, Dad?
>
> **Dad:** My God. You've certainly . . . matured. However, you obviously did not grow up to be a lady. Please change into something less comfortable and less . . . revealing.
>
> **Sis:** Come on, Dad. It's summer, all the girls wear this kind of stuff.
>
> **Dad:** Only if they're going into vocational school to learn the world's oldest profes-sion. Now go change. I'll drive you to school if you're late.
>
> **Sis:** But Dad!
>
> **Dad:** If you do not go and change right now, you will be grounded.

Sis leaves and stomps upstairs.
Slow dissolve into regular storyline.

> **Sis:** Eventually, Dad gave up and just pretended not to see me when I wore outfits that exposed too much skin. I didn't like the restrictions.
>
> **Brother:** Yeah, I know. Sometimes Mom and Dad made decisions or rules that I knew were wrong. I'd promise myself that I would correct those wrongs if I ever had kids. But, you know, sometimes I find myself making the same mistakes. It's hard to avoid parental instincts in favor of reason.
>
> **Sis:** Well, I should know soon. I'm pregnant.

Brother almost falls out of his floating recliner.

> **Brother:** Hey, that's great! When are you expecting the little guy?
>
> **Sis:** In about nine months, of course. I just found out today. I don't know how my husband will take the surprise.
>
> **Brother:** Well, how does he like his new job? He always did enjoy cheating the government.
>
> **Sis:** He's doing fine, thank you. Really, just because he has a higher salary. . . . You don't have to be bitter.
>
> **Brother:** Hey, at least I work for my money. You just married rich.
>
> **Sis:** You know damned well that I can get a job any time I want to.
>
> **Brother:** I know, I know, your engineering degree from that obscure college. But you

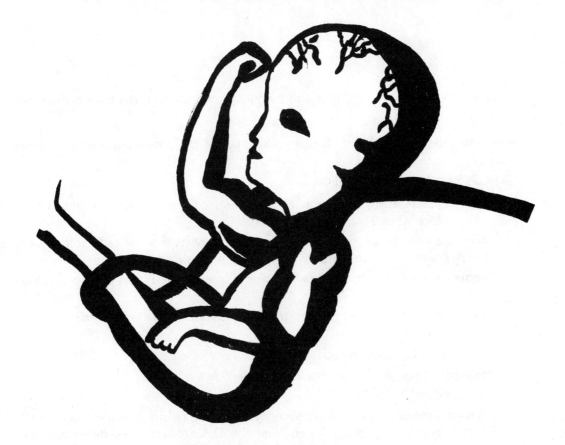

never had motivation. Why, Mom and Dad practically had to kick you to get you to find a job when we were kids.

Sis: Yes, my straight little brother. You were the perfect teen worker. You took bullshit from anybody. Except that one time. . . .

Slow dissolve into Flashback No. 2:

Open with close-up of frying hamburger patty on grill. A spatula appears and slides under the patty to lift it up and place it on the bottom half of an open bun. Pull back so that the cook, who is Brother, is seen. Brother turns around as the boss approaches and stands beside him.

Brother: Yessir?

Boss: Time to clean the grease traps.

Brother: I just cleaned them yesterday. It's not my turn.

Boss: I don't give a damn about whose turn it is. I want those grease traps cleaned out, now.

Rest of the staff has stopped working to watch the confrontation.

Brother: I'm sorry, but I won't clean the traps.

Boss: Why, you're risking outright dismissal, boy. Get your butt back there and clean those traps—now!

Brother turns and takes the half-finished hamburger and screws it into the Boss's chest. Brother then takes off his apron.

Brother: Respectfully, I must now submit to you my resignation. Due to personal reasons, I find that I can no longer work at this establishment. My apologies for not giving you two weeks notice, but I'm sure that you can find another suitable peon to hire for minimum wage.

The Next Generation 263

Brother walks toward the counter and then leaps over it. He turns toward the Boss.

Brother: Oh, hot water gets out grease stains.

Half-stifled giggles are heard. Brother walks out of the restaurant and gets smaller and smaller.

Slow dissolve to regular storyline.

Brother: It was worth it, though. I'll never forget the expression on the manager's face when I took off, just like that.

Sis: For a while there I thought that you still might have some redeeming qualities. But, alas, you turned out to be a straight-arrow after all.

Brother: Maybe I still have a few surprises. I just resigned from my job with the law firm.

Sis: What? Don't tell me. You resigned for personal conviction, right?

Brother: Yeah.

Sis: Well, let me hear the dirt.

Brother: Do you remember my stint at the D.A.'s office?

Sis: Yeah. . . .

Brother: I received a high-level security clearance rating with the Social Security computer system. When I left the D.A.'s office, they didn't rescind my clearance. . . .

Sis: Have you ever pulled my file for a quick look?

Brother (smiles): No, but I was tempted to pull files on everybody.

Sis: Oh, this is so refreshing! My brother, the potential white-collar criminal! Do go on.

Brother: Well, somehow the top brass at the law firm found out about my clearance,

and they wanted me to "dig the dirt" on a Very Important Person whose case we were handling. Of course, I refused.

Sis (shakes her head disconsolately): I should have known.

Brother: They threatened to fire me, but I threatened to disclose the amorality of the prominent law firm. They were scared silly. Then I resigned.

Sis (smacks her forehead): You dumb bastard! You could have bargained for more pay, higher position. . . .

Brother (frowns, shakes head): No. That's not the way to do it. I may be a bit poorer, but I've gained one hell of a lot of self-respect. Come on, Sis. I'm sure you agree that I did the right thing.

Sis: I respect your courage, little brother, but I worry about how you're going to eat and support the kids.

Brother: Relax. I've already got another job. It's with a less prominent law firm, but I have a higher position and almost as much pay. I'll get by.

Suddenly there is nothing but static on the screen. It lasts for just a moment. Then the image of Sis comes back.

Sis: Godammit. I don't care what they say. This kind of communication is definitely not reaching out and touching someone. When are you going to step up to space travel? You have to come up to see me.

Brother: I told you I have no intention of going up to your prefabricated domicile. I've always hated suburbs, and where you live is the ultimate suburb. All your houses are made out of the same material, and they are the same shape. There's no individualism out there.

Sis: Don't give me your rehashed Thoreau. You're just afraid that you'll like it up here. That would positively shatter your golden ideals.

Brother: If you're so damned open-minded, why not come down here?

Sis: Don't be silly. I would simply suffocate in the smog down there. Not to mention the criminals. . . .

Brother: Don't be stupid. The air here is as clear as that piece of ice you're wearing on your ring finger. They cleaned it 15 years ago. As for the criminals, there aren't many of those left. Ever since they outlawed industrial robots, people are too busy working. So why don't you come down?

Sis: Well, it would be rather quaint. But if I visit you, you must come and visit me. I'll even pay the shuttle fare—anything for the satisfaction of personal contact. I never thought I'd get bored of doing whatever I wanted, but I am. I think a little familial visitation might cure my blues.

Brother: What's ailing you? Admittedly, it would be fun to watch no-gravity ballet and football.

Sis: Oh, it is—for the first few times. But then everything becomes mundane.

Brother (slaps his knee): I knew it, I knew it. Everything is too static up there. There is no change. When I go on my solitary nature trips, I see something different every time I go—chirping wrens, swaying sea grass, sparkling quartz. Nothing ever stays the same in nature. But artificiality. . . .

Sis: Please, Mr. Self-righteous. All I want to know is: Are you coming up here?

The Next Generation 265

Brother: Well . . . I get space sick! I'm not accustomed to no gravity. . . .

Sis (laughs): Don't worry, you'll get used to it.

Brother (also laughing): I remember that's what you said to me the first time I took a drink.

Slow dissolve into Flashback No. 3:

Open with CUT TO: Exterior shot. Car pulls up on curb and stops. Headlights are doused, and doors open to reveal teenage Brother and Sis getting out of car. She carries two bottles of vodka. Brother stares in amazement.

Brother: Where the hell did you get that?

Sis: Never mind. Now let's go inside.

CUT TO: Montage of drinking scenes. In the first few, Brother has to be forced to drink. Later he guzzles drinks like the most experienced. He is more and more intoxicated as the scenes progress.

CUT TO: Pan of living room. Messy aftermath of drinking party. The pan stops at the supine figure of Brother. He is sloppily laid out on a couch, dozing away. Sis shakes him.

Sis: Come on, oh corrupted brother of mine. Time to go smell the coffee—as well as drink it.

Brother grunts and turns away.

Sis (gestures to person off-screen): Would you give me a hand with him? Thanks.

Another person helps drag him to the door.

CUT TO: Exterior shot—front of hostess's house. Brother is dragged through the doorway. He makes a gurgling noise, and Sis turns his head toward the bushes. He pukes. He finishes. He gasps.

Brother: Are we there yet, mommy?

Slow dissolve to regular story line.

Brother: It was probably also the first time you've ever seen me being bawled out by Mom and Dad. I thought I was going to be grounded for three years.

Brother looks at his watch.

Brother: Listen, sis, it's been great talking to you. But I've got to go to work now. I'll be expecting you down here. Bring Wayne if he wants to come. I'll be talking to you next week. Good-bye!

He waves.

CUT TO: Sis on barstool. She waves.

CUT TO: Shot of living room wall. Screen fades. Wallpaper comes back.

CUT TO: Shot of sister. She gets off stool. Walks over to window. Camera looks over her shoulder and Earth is seen.

Fade to black.

Roll credits.

THE END

I feel that society is improving because people are starting to care more about the way they live. People are trying harder to achieve a better education to get a chance at a higher job position. They want to learn more about the computer industry, which is what technology is bringing us to. Therefore, there will be more capable people able to run large business corporations with ease.

But that's not the only part of an improving society. Another important part of society today is acceptance. People are expanding their minds and changing their attitudes. Society today is accepting not only new technological advances but other people as themselves. . . . Acceptance helps a great deal . . . because it allows people to get along with others and also to learn from their ways.

Elizabeth Quill, 18
Canton, Massachusetts

Society is getting worse. People don't care about anything or anybody. They don't want to take part in anything, and most people are willing to sit down and watch somebody else work or sweat over something.

My fears of the future is with the way people are acting. Adults of today are terribly greedy. They are using things up that we need for our future. I believe that we deserve the same chances that they had. My hope for the future is that all nations will come to live in peace and harmony together.

Kim Novak, 16
Denham Springs, Louisiana

Although people in some areas would say society is improving, they are blind to the under-developed areas in our world. They are so involved in their fortunes and glamorous living that they fail to realize the hardships most countries are going through.

Lorrie Mullins, 16
Sand Springs, Oklahoma

Teens today are so wrapped up in themselves, planning their future, finding the right person to marry and have two or three kids with, putting the down payments of some large material possession or another—that we forget it's up to us to better the world. I hope it's us—that we can be the generation that ends the wars, stops the senseless weapon-building, revitalizes education and industry, and sends people to the stars. But, to use a football cliche, you have to want it. And in the eyes of our generation, I do not see the hippie's dreams and desires, or the power and determination of other generations needed to make the world a better place.

Natalie John, 16
Monterey Park, California

Because the teenagers of the '80s are used to bigger, better, and exciting things, as adults, I feel we aren't going to want things to change. We are going to be challenged to keep the flow coming to improve on what we have now and expand the horizons for newer ideas to benefit not only us but the next teenage generations.

Thomas Tryon, 18
Schenectady, New York

I often wonder how we are to grow as a nation, when all we have to offer are drug-addicts and drop-outs. . . . It's a shame that they have to rot their brains on chemicals when they could use them to help cure diseases or invent useful machines for the benefit of mankind. Maybe the ones that exercise their minds and are willing to be themselves could somehow solve the world's problems of drugs and crime.

David Cullison, 15
Apache Junction, Arizona

Today's teens seem to grow up fast. They aren't the long-haired radicals of the '60s, but they are concerned. I think that today's teens have the awareness and edu-

cation to contribute anything that they set their minds to.

Hopefully, when these teens are adults, they won't make the same mistakes that they have seen around them. But there will be different mistakes. No society is perfect. I think that these teens will contribute everything that they can to make it easier for the upcoming teens.

Nancy C. Wallace, 17
Oak Ridge, Tennessee

Society is on a downhill slope. I feel that the cause . . . is that the people are no longer paying attention to God. People are no longer believing the Bible as the Word of God. Society is getting worse. It is very obvious, seeing that rape is on the rise and divorce is moving into almost every home, causing many families to just totally fall away and break up.

Brad Williams, 15
Lubbock, Texas

When you try to define improving or getting worse in terms of society, you have to look at the improvements closer than you do the defeats. They, the defeats, will always outnumber the successes. But they are also worth less, which makes us feel slightly better. . . . The problems we face are greater, but so are the answers.

We are now close to finding a cure for cancer. More people can afford the "luxuries" of life. These are just two improvements.

Melissa Misner, 17
Inglis, Florida

I think society is getting worse. If people would study our recent history, they would see that a lot of our social problems started when a lot of the very popular movements of today began. Some of the examples of these movements are ERA, legalized abortion, the freedom to murder, and the banishment of God from public schools. Were these things made to make the "one nation under God" country better? Because of my religious

beliefs and convictions, I cannot help but feel that God is punishing our society for turning its backs on Him.

Jennifer Swanson, 16
Arlington Heights, Illinois

For me personally, I would like to help the handicapped and disabled child. I would like to see that they get more rights and have a say in the laws that would affect them.

Jean Eckert, 18
Oak Park, Illinois

From the construction workers to the doctors, we will all contribute to our world. . . .

I plan to contribute to the world by passing on the knowledge I have to young children. I'm going to become an elementary school teacher. This may be a small contribution, but I think what I have to teach, as teachers in the past have proven, will make a difference in the next generation.

Julie Christy, 15
Macon, Georgia

Society is getting worse for the world and the people of the world but better for the Christians who are faithful.

Christopher E. Barber, 19
Winston-Salem, North Carolina

More of the old ways are being forgotten, and people are starting to say, "Live and let live." If you ask me, that is what we need, a truly free society. People could just let it all hang out, and then we'd be free of a lot of emotionally disturbed people. Why can't a black guy be out in public with a white lady and feel just normal. But shit, how could they? Everybody looks and whispers.

I know. I have a nephew whose mother, my sister, is white, and his father is black. Everywhere they take "Larry," people just can't cope, but that's mostly assholes who think they are important with a $25,000 a year salary. Well, my stepfather, whose salary was almost triple that as an electrical engineer (he passed away January 13, 1983, at 12:33 p.m.) thought "Larry" was just a thrill. And my mother's friends all know, and they think nothing of it.

Carl C. Ochs, 18
Cedar Rapids, Iowa

Society . . . is improving in the sense that the overall intelligence has increased. People are so much more aware of problems, struggles, and situations. . . . Society has formed an opinionated population.

The problem with this is that people seem to think that they can have everything. There is no longer incentive to work because the government allows some to take advantage.

Our moral standards have also gone down. There used to be a time when abortion was out of the question. Now it's used as birth control in some places. The law has also swayed toward protecting the criminal instead of persecuting him. I would hope that things would improve in this area, but I think they'll only get worse.

Susie Vincent, 18
Filer, Idaho

Today's teens are more imaginative and probably will think up many more devices to make things easier in life to come.

April Garrett, 16
Southfield, Michigan

The world is slowly progressing toward a future of less and less religion. More cults and actual non-believers are becoming evident. As this happens, the world situation is slowly getting worse.

Unemployment is at an all-time high. Even highly skilled engineers are struggling at home with only their degrees to keep them happy. Our natural resources are dwindling, and unless our generation takes an active interest in finding more resources, the small supply we have might run out.

Denise Walsh, 16
Liberty, Mississippi

How can we be expected to be sensitive and caring to friends and neighbors when we don't even know how to relate to our parents or brothers and sisters? If we could only develop a higher level of respect towards these vital relationships, possibly we would be more optimistic. With divorce much more socially acceptable, it is so easy for people to give up and cop out on marriages rather than try to improve the marriage. Hopefully our generation can become aware of how destructive this has become and learn to become stronger.

Dawn Gropel, 17
Brooklyn Park, Minnesota

When I was 10 years old, I played

with dolls and watched the "Brady Bunch." Now, ten-year-olds play with computers and watch the "A-Team." That's an amazing contrast.

It seems like they are growing up so fast that they don't even have the chance to be carefree and ornery. Ten-year-old girls already have boyfriends; I didn't even know boys existed when I was that age.

Times are moving so fast that I sometimes wonder if childhood exists anymore. The thought of no childhood is absolutely devastating. I try to be open-minded and liberal when I look around me. I just can't find any of the childhood magic.

Judy Hoyte, 17
Las Cruces, New Mexico

Afterword

Teenagers today find a sense of worth and security in the middle class. Their experience has assured them that education opens up prestige jobs. The words "well paid" surface frequently, "satisfying" rarely, in this businesslike, success-oriented generation. Women rarely talk of their futures in terms of "a husband, two kids, and a radar range." Today they speak of "a career, a husband, and maybe kids."

Despite its affluence, suburbia is a limiting place, where people of similar backgrounds lead similar lifestyles. Teenagers often seem to have a narrow perspective: like everyone else, they fear what they don't know about. Many speak as if they never read newspapers, or watch the news.

The "we're going-to-change-the-world" attitude that has characterized youth in the past seems to have vanished, replaced by "I-want-to-be-happy-now." Perhaps this attitude exists because teenagers are uncertain about where they, and their generation, are going. Perhaps teenagers don't want to label themselves a "we" or a "me" generation. Perhaps teenagers simply don't see that much purpose in their lives.

Society's complexity forces this generation to rethink its values. Teenagers respond to the pressure in wildly disparate ways, ranging from hedonism to religion. Slowing—or at least learning to deal with—change is an unspoken goal of all.

Fear is what deactivates today's teenagers. The media, teachers, and parents filter down information about wars, pollution, politics, usually all bad. The problem isn't a lack of controversial issues. It is an overabundance of them. Nuclear issues aren't going to unite this generation in protest. Teenagers have opinions about nuclear power and arms, but they think consciousness-raising marches to Washington are historical events. The same is true of politics and national defense: "Doesn't affect me . . . yet" or "Our generation has to do something about this . . . are there any parties this weekend?" No fuse is being lit; teenagers are waiting for teachers to tell them what to do about it all. Then, if they get paid for it, they'll help out.

But this generation does care, in a different way. Instead of worrying about the starving people in Upper Volta, they worry about their best friends' problems. Helping a little brother through a rough time takes priority over helping free MIAs in Asia.

Teenagers need people to be close to. The family is usually mentioned first. This basic human need for affection and approval is plainly evident. Yet, increasingly, because of divorce and other problems, family support isn't always available today. So, teenagers stay together—with boyfriends, girlfriends, and siblings—to find happiness through togetherness. This generation may want love more than any other.

Searching for a slot to fit into seems to be what many of today's teenagers are doing. Sometimes they feel like all the slots are filled, and there is no place for them. Other times they feel as though they can make a worthwhile contribution to the world. A lot of ambition is expressed during discussions, along with a lot of fear about the future. Teenagers admit that their insecurities about the world often stifle their dreams.

Their opinions about their place in the world are neither optimistic nor pessimistic. Realistic, actually. Ambitions of being a future president or Martin Luther King are rarely voiced. Teenagers in the 1980s think that their importance is to their family, to their friends, and to people around them. They matter—not to the world perhaps, but to someone.

Compiled by Eric Kammerer and Abby Rhamey